Daily Learning Drills

Grade 4

Thinking Kids®
An imprint of Carson-Dellosa Publishing LLC
Greensboro, North Carolina

Thinking Kids®
An imprint of Carson-Dellosa Publishing LLC
P.O. Box 35665
Greensboro, NC 27425 USA

ISBN 978-1-4838-0087-5

14-085187784

Table of Contents

Name _Tamanna_

The National Pastime

Print the names of the National League Baseball Teams in ABC order on the lines below. Then write the letters in the circles on the lines at the bottom of the page to decode the message.

1. (A) S T R O S
2. B R (A) V E S
3. C A R D I (N) A L S
4. C (U) B S
5. D (O) D G E R S
6. (E) X P O S
7. (G) I A N T S
8. M A R (L) I (N) S
9. M E T S
10. P (A) D R E S
11. P H I L (L) I E S
12. P I R A (T) E S
13. R (E) D S
14. R O C K (I) E S

Teams

- Marlins
- Padres
- Phillies
- Giants
- Rockies
- Cardinals
- Reds
- Dodgers
- Braves
- Mets
- Astros
- Expos
- Pirates
- Cubs

These teams belong to the:

$$\frac{N}{8^2} \frac{A}{10} \frac{T}{12} \frac{I}{14} \frac{O}{5} \frac{N}{3} \frac{A}{1} \frac{L}{8^1} \qquad \frac{L}{11} \frac{E}{13} \frac{A}{2} \frac{G}{7} \frac{U}{4} \frac{E}{6}$$

8^1 = 1st circled letter 8^2 = 2nd circled letter

Name *Tamanna*

Are You Alphabetically Inclined?

Below are several groups of words. If the group is in the correct alphabetical order, draw a star around it. If it is incorrect, write it correctly in the blanks provided at the bottom of the page.

slithering	dialect	tomahawk	mingle
Seminole	doleful	thatch	metallic
sorrowful	deafen	tourniquet	mythical
salvage	defiance	turban	muslin

platform ☆	abrupt	strewn ☆	capable ☆
pompadour	askew	superintendent	college
prominent	accordion	suspend	comprehend
protrude	arthritis	swamp	cymbal

gig	hammock ☆	awaken	bloodhound
garfish	hoist	astonishment	bellow
gawk	horde	adz	bespeak
glum	inaudible	atmospheric	bewilder

Salvage	dialect	thatch	metallic
Seminole	deafen	tomahawk	mingle
sorrowful	defiance	tourniquet	muslin
Salvage	doleful	turban	mythical

abrupt	garfish	adz	bellow
accordion	gawk	astonishment	bespeak
arthritis	gig	atmospheric	bewilder
askew	glum	awaken	bloodhound

Name _____

Compound Checkup

Write the compound word from the Word Box that matches each definition.

1. physical examination – _____checkup_____

2. a giant Pacific coast evergreen – _____redwood_____

3. difficult thing to bear – _____hardship_____

4. an outdoor advertising sign – _____billboard_____

5. small metal pot for cooking – _____saucepan_____

6. on a lower floor – _____downstairs_____

7. a glass container used for measuring time – _____hourglass_____

8. a movable ramp to a ship – _____gangplank_____

9. to betray – _____doublecross_____

10. a person with a quick temper – _____hothead_____

11. to intimidate – _____browbeat_____

12. delighted – _____overjoyed_____

13. a logger – _____lumberjack_____

14. lower half of a chicken leg – _____drumstick_____

15. a very clever person – _____mastermind_____

16. a robbery – _____hold up_____

17. a limited-access highway – _____freeway_____

18. an insect with brightly-colored wings – _____butterfly_____

19. a large area for dancing – _____ballroom_____

20. a path in the street marked for pedestrians – _____crosswalk_____

Word Box

ballroom	billboard	browbeat	butterfly	checkup
crosswalk	double-cross	downstairs	drumstick	freeway
gangplank	hardship	holdup	hothead	hourglass
lumberjack	mastermind	overjoyed	redwood	saucepan

Name _____

Compound It!

Help Rufus find as many compound words as you can by using the grid. First give the location and then write the word. Use the back of this sheet if you run out of room.

	R	U	F	U	S
1	light	foot	class	house	some
2	birth	her	tooth	snow	base
3	thing	man	side	him	day
4	room	one	work	out	bare
5	boat	roar	every	in	ball
6	self	time	no	mail	paste
7	stairs	to	shop	mate	up

	location	word
Example:	F-2, S-6	toothpaste

	location	word			location	word
1.	R-2, S-3	birthday		10.		
2.	F-1, U-7	classmate		11.		
3.	F-4, U-4	workout		12.		
4.	R-4, U-7	roommate		13.		
5.	U-6, U-3	mailman		14.		
6.	U-2, S-3	snow day		15.		
7.				16.		
8.				17.		
9.				18.		

Bonus

How many of your words can you draw rebus clues for? Trade your drawings with friends and ask them to guess the words.

Example: basketball +

Name _____

Words That Break

Divide each word into two words with a slash (/). Then choose one of the two words and combine it with a word from the Word Bank to form a different word.

Example: side/walk→boardwalk

1. afternoon _____
2. junkyard _____
3. handkerchief _____
4. football _____
5. downstairs _____
6. eggshell _____
7. understand _____
8. heartbreak _____

9. outgrow _____
10. without _____
11. everybody _____
12. inside _____
13. overripe _____
14. teapot _____
15. lighthouse _____
16. cowboy _____

Word Bank

back	day	in	town
base	heat	off	wear
bell	flash	sea	where
board	thought	spoon	some

Take two unrelated words to create a whole new compound word. Then tell what it means and use it in a sentence.

Example: junktea – a blend of tea made from garbage. We bought our junktea at a
reduced price.

1. _____
_____
2. _____
_____
3. _____
_____
4. _____
_____

Name _____

Comma Quandary

Look at the underlined parts in each sentence. If each is a complete thought, place a comma in the box. If it is not a complete thought, place an X in the box.

Oh, now I get it!

1. <u>Squanto crawled up a sand hill</u> ☐ and <u>looked over the top.</u>

2. <u>He was not afraid</u> ☐ but <u>he remembered what his mother had said.</u>

3. <u>It was good to see the sky again</u> ☐ and <u>to breathe the fresh air.</u>

4. <u>They sailed along the shore</u> ☐ and <u>into the port of Málaga.</u>

5. <u>The Brothers took Squanto to their home</u> ☐ and <u>soon he was well enough to work in the gardens.</u>

6. <u>The captain said that Squanto could sail with him</u> ☐ but <u>the ship was going to London, not America.</u>

7. <u>The Indian was hungry</u> ☐ but <u>he had no money to buy food.</u>

8. <u>That night Squanto ate</u> ☐ and <u>slept in the home of John Slanie.</u>

Copy these sentences adding capitals and punctuation as needed.

9. squanto liked living in london at mistress robbins' house but he still wanted to go back to america to see his family

   _____

   _____

   _____

10. squanto wanted to help the people from england but some of them were not very kind to him

   _____

   _____

   _____

Name _____

The Prisoner's Sentence Is Imperative!

SHHHHH!

Match each sentence with the correct type by drawing a line.

"I don't want a slave in my room!"   interrogative

"Are you a freedman?"   declarative

"Go to the cellar and get some food."   exclamatory

The fall sunshine felt nice.   imperative

Use vocabulary words in the Word Bank to help you write each type of sentence.

Word Bank			
apologize	doubtfully	confided	maddening
rudeness	impatiently	enthusiastically	sprawled
cantered	scornfully	dumbfounded	defiantly
convince	lurking	denser	good-humored
collided	exhausted		

Imperative _____

_____

Declarative _____

_____

Exclamatory _____

_____

Interrogative _____

_____

Name _____

Makin' Room

An apostrophe is used in contractions to represent missing letters and in possessive forms of singular and plural nouns to show ownership. Add an apostrophe where it is needed in each sentence.

1. The doctors decision was helpful to Sadako.

2. Sadakos classmates sent her a Kokeshi doll.

3. Sadako wasnt very hungry when her mother brought the food.

4. The golden cranes wings blew in the wind.

5. Eijis paper donation smelled of candy.

6. Sadakos good luck cranes became a symbol for peace and hope.

7. "Ill get better," said Sadako over and over.

8. There wasnt enough room on the table for all of the paper cranes so Masahiro hung Sadakos cranes from the ceiling.

9. Chizuko really didnt believe in superstitions like Sadako did.

10. Sadako couldnt sleep very well after she was told she could go home for a visit.

11. Mrs. Sasakis slippers slapped softly on the floor.

12. "Heres your first crane," said Chizuko.

Name _____

Keep It Simple

Underline the simple subject in each sentence. Then on the line write a synonym for the simple subject using the thesaurus or dictionary if necessary.

1. The voyage took many long, hot days to achieve. _____

2. Lanterns were used to guide the spirits home. _____

3. The ballast of the ship was the passengers themselves. _____

4. Many refugees were very lonely in Hong Kong and after awhile wanted to go home. _____

5. The kerosene was used to fuel a lamp so Mai could study when it became dark. _____

6. The ceremonial altar was an important part of Mai's household.

_____

7. The huge temple was empty because the government had removed the Buddhist priests. _____

8. The seasonal monsoon would be over the area soon. _____

9. Great pyramids seemed to rise into the sky as they neared the city.

_____

10. Chrysanthemums made a lovely border on the plate. _____

Name _____

That's Mine!

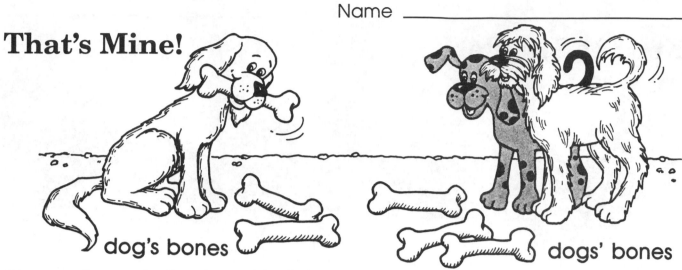

dog's bones   dogs' bones

Change the underlined word to show possession by adding an apostrophe or apostrophe and **s**. Write the possessive form on the line.

	Possessive

1. Mother took me to <u>Tony</u> house. _____

2. The <u>chickens</u> eggs were large. _____

3. <u>Jonathan</u> bicycle needs new brakes. _____

4. Follow the <u>team</u> rules. _____

5. The <u>shoes</u> soles need repair. _____

6. Mrs. <u>Thomas</u> car was in the driveway. _____

7. My <u>brother</u> story won first prize. _____

8. Our <u>neighbors</u> lawns need cutting. _____

9. <u>Ellen</u> paintings were on display. _____

10. The truck <u>drivers</u> routes were long. _____

11. The <u>babies</u> toys are put away. _____

12. The <u>principal</u> office is small. _____

13. The <u>bird</u> nest is completed. _____

14. The <u>doctors</u> hours were long. _____

15. The <u>painter</u> brushes were clean. _____

16. The <u>skunk</u> scent was not pleasant. _____

17. The <u>aliens</u> spaceship had landed. _____

Name _____

Know Your Nouns

Find and circle the proper nouns in each sentence. Then write them correctly.

1. Miss brophy grew up in lake champlain, new york.

_____

2. The children really enjoyed the stories mr. fency told them when he visited.

_____

3. Addie had to visit the settlement of ree heights to see tilla.

_____

4. Addie carried her doll ruby lillian everywhere she went.

_____

5. Addie and her family were living in hutchinson county.

_____

6. The mills had moved from sabula to oak hollow.

_____

7. Malcolm and daniel connolly were very mischievous boys.

_____

8. Addie wrote a poem titled "the wild prairie rose."

_____

9. Miss brophy often recited poetry written by henry wadsworth longfellow.

_____

10. Tilla, katya, addie, and nellie all went on a picnic down by the creek.

_____

Name _____

A View of the Past?

In each sentence below, change the underlined verb to the past tense.

1. Martin <u>will escape</u> to the North to find freedom. _____

2. Laura and Martin <u>will run</u> through the woods at great speed. _____

3. Bert <u>was hiding</u> Martin while the sheriff searched the house. _____

4. People <u>were watching</u> the Eastman home for runaway slaves. _____

5. Laura <u>was looking</u> out the window at the dark, still night. _____

6. Laura <u>will sew</u> a ruffle at the bottom of her green cotton dress. _____

7. Joel <u>will catch</u> Laura helping Martin escape. _____

8. The horse <u>will dash</u> through the street pulling the carriage. _____

Now rewrite the sentences using a present tense verb.

1. _____
2. _____
3. _____
4. _____
5. _____
6. _____
7. _____
8. _____

Name _____

Are You in the Past or Present?

Underline the verb in each sentence. On the line after each sentence write if the verb is past or present tense.

1. Sadako ran home from school every day. _____

2. The wind almost blew the light out of the ceremonial lantern on

   Peace Day. _____

3. Sadako dreamed of good health. _____

4. The wind caught the paper cranes. _____

5. Sadako's gums were swollen. _____

6. Sadako read all of the letters. _____

7. The sun shines brightly on the balcony of the hospital. _____

8. Sadako slept very soundly after the shot of medication. _____

9. Sadako runs faster than almost anyone. _____

10. Kenji knew about leukemia. _____

Name _____

Three Playful Kittens

Rule   An **adjective** is a word that describes a noun or a pronoun. It tells **what kind**, **how many**, or **which one**.

Example   *All of these adjectives can be used to describe kittens : black, several, these, playful, furry, three, many, young.*

Exercise   Place an **X** in the blanks in front of the adjectives. Then complete the sentence with those adjectives.

---

1. ____ striped
   ____ one
   ____ carefully
   ____ soon

   _____
   zebra ran through the jungle.

2. ____ powerful
   ____ ahead
   ____ two
   ____ cautiously

   _____
   elephants trudged along the path.

3. ____ yesterday
   ____ quickly
   ____ scaly
   ____ spotted

   A _____ , _____
   snake darted through the grass.

4. ____ colorful
   ____ graceful
   ____ happily
   ____ however

   The _____ , _____
   birds soared through the air.

• Underline the nouns in the sentences below. Circle the adjectives.

1. The huge, gray elephant lumbered through the hot jungle.
2. Three swift lions raced through the long, green grass.
3. The playful monkeys swung from the high tree branches.
4. The lazy, green turtle slept under the hot tropical sun.
5. The large, horned rhinoceros slipped into the muddy river.
6. The scaly, old crocodile blinked its large, dark eyes.

Name _____

The Fragrant Flowers

Rule **Adjectives** answer these specific questions about the nouns they modify.

| **Which one?** | **What kind?** | **How many?** |

Example

| *these, those,* | *tall, colorful,* | *three, many,* |
| *that, this* | *red, majestic* | *several, few, one* |

Exercise Underline the nouns in the sentences below. Circle the adjectives that modify these nouns. Then write the adjectives you circled in the correct column.

1. Those fragrant pink carnations have five ruffled blossoms.
2. These vibrant white roses have a sweet fragrance.
3. Each flower has several dainty petals.
4. The refreshing aroma of the sweet-scented lavender filled the air.
5. That large, colorful canna is a tall, ornamental plant.
6. It has many large leaves and bright red flowers.

Which one?	**What kind?**	**How many?**
1. _____	_____	_____
2. _____	_____	_____
3. _____	_____	_____
4. _____	_____	_____
5. _____	_____	_____
6. _____	_____	_____

Daily Learning Drills Grade 4

Name _____

Adverbs Answer

Adverbs modify verbs or adjectives and tell **how**, **when**, or **where**.

> **How**—I read **slowly**.
> **Where**—I read **inside**.
> **When**—I was reading **today**.

Write either **how**, **when**, or **where** after each adverb.

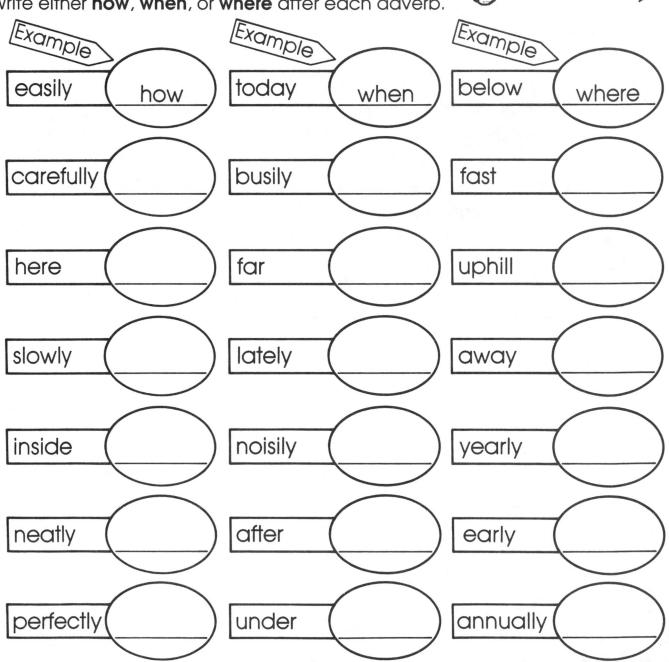

Example		Example		Example	
easily	how	today	when	below	where
carefully		busily		fast	
here		far		uphill	
slowly		lately		away	
inside		noisily		yearly	
neatly		after		early	
perfectly		under		annually	

Name _____

That's How It's Done!

Adverbs answer the questions **when**, **where**, and **how**. The adverbs in the sentences below answer **how**. Underline the adverb(s) in each sentence. Then circle the verb it describes. The first one is done for you.

1. The two boys <u>solemnly</u> (shook) hands.

2. Chip looked down incredulously at the fallen shingle which landed softly at his feet.

3. "I don't salvage," remarked Rudy calmly when his counselor glared at him.

4. "Rudy," whispered Mike warningly. Chip was glaring in their direction.

5. The door opened and Mr. Warden emerged, smartly dressed in a white tennis outfit.

6. "Harold, you have no soul," explained Rudy pleasantly.

7. "Why do you immediately assume that I'm guilty?" asked Rudy in a hurt tone.

8. "I'd rather go back to arts and crafts," nodded Mike sheepishly.

9. "Tomorrow," Rudy said thoughtfully as they carefully daubed pale blue paint onto their creation, "we'll go earlier."

10. Arms flailing wildly, Chip rushed anxiously toward his cabin.

11. "Let's just walk directly away from the lake," decided Rudy.

Write four sentences of your own containing adverbs. Underline the adverbs and circle the verbs that are described.

1. _____

_____

2. _____

_____

3. _____

_____

4. _____

_____

Name _____

They're Coming!

Circle the 24 pronouns in the following story.

 A Scary Dream

"They are coming after us," Rhonda said to her brother, Scott. Believe me, Scott, I saw them with their funny-looking faces. The two of them had long, orange hair, and they had gigantic feet. I thought they could be from Mars because they spoke a funny language.

One of them glared at me with his strange-looking face. The other one looked like she had on her clothes from outer space.

Scott, you can't imagine my thoughts as I saw them coming after me with their weird looks and their weird clothes.

Finish this story. Use at least six different pronouns. Circle the pronouns you use.

_____

_____

_____

_____

_____

_____

_____

_____

Name _____

Listen to the Music

In the sentences below, label each of the following.

N—noun   **Adj**—adjective
P—pronoun   **Adv**—adverb
V—verb

Example:

Adj Adj N V   Adv
The little girl ran outside.

1. We feed the birds regularly.

2. Derek planted a maple tree yesterday.

3. Charles wrote them a letter.

4. They have two small dogs.

5. Rosie will be dancing tomorrow.

6. The toys were everywhere.

7. The three children are going swimming today.

8. You can eat now.

9. They washed the car carefully.

10. Several thirsty children drank cold lemonade.

11. We run three miles often.

12. The chorus has been singing beautifully.

13. He gave Chuck five dollars.

14. Pam washed the dishes slowly.

15. That tiny baby was sleeping soundly.

Name _____

Break It Up!

For each word given below, give the base word and the prefix and/or suffix. Remember, some base words' spellings have been changed before adding suffixes. Not all words will have a prefix and a suffix.

Word	Prefix	Base Word	Suffix
resourceful			
accomplishment			
numbness			
convincing			
merciless			
sturdiest			
disobeying			
unmistakable			
disinfecting			
disclaimed			
reopening			
inventive			
restless			
precaution			
imitating			

Name _____

Fore and Aft

Fill in the blanks with the appropriate affixes. Some will be used more than once.

Prefixes: dis- im- mis- re- un-   Suffixes: -ful -ish -ist -less -ly -ness -ward

Meaning	Root Word + Affix	New Word
1. having no fear	fear ___ ___ ___ ___	_____
2. to vanish	___ ___ ___ appear	_____
3. toward a lower level	down ___ ___ ___ ___	_____
4. having no friends	friend ___ ___ ___ ___	_____
5. an error in action	___ ___ ___ take	_____
6. to enter again	___ ___ enter	_____
7. too many to count	count ___ ___ ___ ___	_____
8. not happy	___ ___ happy	_____
9. perfection seeker	perfection ___ ___ ___	_____
10. quality of being dark	dark ___ ___ ___ ___	_____
11. not possible	___ ___ possible	_____
12. having doubts	doubt ___ ___ ___	_____
13. without a care	care ___ ___ ___ ___	_____
14. sad from being alone	lone ___ ___	_____
15. not thinking	___ ___ thinking	_____
16. without shoes	shoe ___ ___ ___ ___	_____
17. in a mysterious way	mysterious ___ ___	_____
18. appear again	___ ___ appear	_____
19. in a quiet manner	quiet ___ ___	_____
20. call by wrong name	___ ___ ___ call	_____
21. somewhat yellow	yellow ___ ___ ___	_____
22. cautious	care ___ ___ ___	_____
23. to release	___ ___ ___ engage	_____

Name _____

Don't Miss This!

The prefix **mis** – means wrong or *wrongly, bad* or *badly, no* or *not*. Underline the base words in the following list. Then circle the base words in the wordsearch.
Words may go → ← ↑ ↓ ↘ ↗ ↙.

misadventure
misapply
misbehave
miscall
miscast
mischance
misconduct
miscount
misdeal
misdeed
misdirect
misfile
misfire

misfit
misfortune
misgovern
misguide
mishandle
mishear
mislay
mislead
misname
misplay
misread
misrule

S	F	A	P	P	L	Y	G	F	R	E
A	I	O	D	E	A	L	I	N	E	L
T	L	E	C	V	O	R	E	M	A	U
L	E	V	A	H	E	B	A	Y	D	R
D	E	P	L	A	Y	N	S	T	I	F
I	L	A	L	C	A	S	T	C	R	M
R	D	S	D	L	E	D	I	U	G	T
E	N	U	T	R	O	F	S	D	R	H
C	A	O	H	M	C	H	A	N	C	E
T	H	B	L	K	T	N	U	O	C	A
G	O	V	E	R	N	T	N	C	O	R

Choose a word from the list above to correctly complete each sentence.

1. Jeremy is _____ in the play – he should have been the villain.

2. Did I _____ the car keys?

3. It was my _____ to be the first to be called on in class.

4. I think I saw you _____ the cards.

5. Did the cannon _____ ?

6. Our vacation turned out to be one _____ after another.

7. Don't _____ that crystal vase or you might break it.

8. I think I _____ that paragraph – I didn't understand it at all.

9. Robbing a bank is a _____ .

10. The drawings of the beautiful vacation resort _____ us – it wasn't even half finished.

Similar in Some Way

 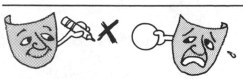

Name _____

Put an **X** in the circle by the phrase to correctly complete each analogy.

1. conductor is to orchestra as . . .	◯ scene is to actor ◯ director is to play
2. absent is to present as . . .	◯ adult is to child ◯ levy is to tax
3. button is to blouse as . . .	◯ coat is to hat ◯ zipper is to skirt
4. pork is to hog as . . .	◯ bacon is to eggs ◯ beef is to cattle
5. allow is to permit as . . .	◯ alter is to change ◯ refute is to confirm
6. mirror is to reflect as . . .	◯ scissors is to cut ◯ read is to book
7. aide is to assistant as . . .	◯ brash is to cautious ◯ convince is to persuade
8. autumn is to season as . . .	◯ winter is to summer ◯ Halloween is to holiday
9. shirt is to collar as . . .	◯ sock is to shoes ◯ trousers is to cuffs
10. ice cream is to dessert as . . .	◯ cereal is to breakfast ◯ supper is to dinner
11. graph is to chart as . . .	◯ present is to past ◯ explore is to investigate

Name _____

Analyzing Analogies

Put an **X** in the circle by the phrase that correctly completes each analogy.

1. hobo is to tramp as . . .	◯ vagabond is to vagrant ◯ knight is to serf
2. hopeless is to desperate as . . .	◯ pessimistic is to optimistic ◯ certain is to confident
3. sow is to reap as . . .	◯ gather is to pick ◯ plant is to harvest
4. miserly is to generous as . . .	◯ stingy is to extravagant ◯ mean is to cheap
5. vapid is to taste as . . .	◯ cool is to touch ◯ odorless is to smell
6. ignite is to kindle as . . .	◯ prattle is to babble ◯ gradual is to sudden
7. cloth is to weaver as . . .	◯ money is to banker ◯ book is to printer
8. mechanic is to automobile as . . .	◯ pipe is to plumber ◯ electrician is to wiring
9. throw is to football as . . .	◯ baseball is to toss ◯ fling is to Frisbee
10. quiver is to vibrate as . . .	◯ shiver is to cold ◯ wiggle is to squirm

Name _____

Let's Change Laura's Disposition

Antonyms are words that mean almost the opposite. Replace the underlined word in each sentence with an antonym from the Word Bank.

1. Laura stood by the door with a <u>mournful</u> look on her face. _____

2. Laura <u>retreated</u> at the sound of voices outside the springhouse.
   _____

3. Laura <u>scornfully</u> accepted the fact that they would be hiding a runaway slave. _____

4. When Joel asked Laura to read a book of his, she was very <u>resentful</u> .
   _____

5. Bert asked Laura to look in the wardrobe for Martin. She was very <u>impatient</u> in her search. _____

6. Laura <u>swiftly</u> went to her room and firmly closed the door. _____

7. Martin quickly <u>descended</u> the stairs when they heard a wagon out front.
   _____

8. Laura was very <u>indignant</u> about the idea of having Martin hiding in her room. _____

Word Bank			
respectfully	tolerant	cheerful	gratified
sluggishly	happy	climbed	advanced

Choose three of the vocabulary words underlined above and use each one in a sentence.

1. _____

2. _____

3. _____

Name _____

Antonym Action

Using the words from the Word Box, write a word that means the opposite of each numbered word. Then circle each word from the Word Box in the wordsearch. Words may go → ← ↑ ↓ ↘ ↖ ↙.

Word Box				
hero	deny	clean	bright	ancient
exit	stale	rebel	compel	divulge
raze	solid	greedy	corrupt	educated

1. approve – _____

2. coax – _____

3. conform – _____

4. construct – _____

5. coward – _____

6. dreary – _____

7. enter – _____

8. fresh – _____

9. generous – _____

10. hide – _____

11. honest – _____

12. ignorant – _____

13. liquid – _____

14. modern – _____

15. soiled – _____

```
T E D U C A T E D
H S O L I D A E I
G O T I X E N E V
I R S A N Y C Z U
R E B E L A I A L
B H O Y D E E R G
L E P M O C N L E
C O R R U P T O C
```

Name _____

Code Names

Use the code to write a synonym for each word.

a	c	e	g	h	o	p	r	t	y
1	2	3	4	5	6	7	8	9	10

1. enclose – __ __ __ __
         2 1 4 3

2. inexpensive – __ __ __ __ __
         2 5 3 1 7

3. right – __ __ __ __ __ __ __
         2 6 8 8 3 2 9

4. transport – __ __ __ __ __
         2 1 8 8 10

5. center – __ __ __ __
         2 6 8 3

6. duplicate – __ __ __ __
         2 6 7 10

7. pen – __ __ __ __
         2 6 6 7

8. table – __ __ __ __ __
         2 5 1 8 9

9. conversation – __ __ __ __
         2 5 1 9

10. applaud – __ __ __ __ __
         2 5 3 3 8

11. harvest – __ __ __ __
         2 8 6 7

12. crawl – __ __ __ __ __
         2 8 3 3 7

13. concern – __ __ __ __
         2 1 8 3

14. capture – __ __ __ __ __
         2 1 9 2 5

15. class – __ __ __ __ __ __ __ __
         2 1 9 3 4 6 8 10

16. price – __ __ __ __ __ __
         2 5 1 8 4 3

17. stick – __ __ __ __ __ __
         2 6 5 3 8 3

18. force – __ __ __ __ __ __
         2 6 3 8 2 3

19. task – __ __ __ __ __
         2 5 6 8 3

20. swindle – __ __ __ __ __
         2 5 3 1 9

Write ten new words. Then use the code to write the numbers to spell synonyms for each word. Trade your paper with a classmate to see if he or she can decipher your code.

Example: deed – __ __ __
         1 2 9

1. _____
2. _____
3. _____
4. _____
5. _____

6. _____
7. _____
8. _____
9. _____
10. _____

The Synonymous Sleuth

Write the synonym for the backwards word in each sentence. Decode and use the backwards synonyms at the bottom.

1. Miss Whitehead's feet look regral this year. _____

2. I kniht Miss Elson is one of those people you don't bother to think about twice. _____

3. It's just what Ole Golly says, hcir people are boring. _____

4. When I look at him, I could tae 1,000 tomato sandwiches. _____

5. He looks yppah except I wouldn't like all those cats. _____

6. Is he a tnereffid person when he's with someone else? _____

7. She snworf when she looks at things close. _____

8. I just feel ynnuf all over. _____

9. Spies should not get thguac. _____

10. It was just too suoregnad to go there. _____

11. Every time I have a dab dream, I feel like leaving town. _____

12. Sometimes Sport is like a little old namow. _____

13. I have deman him the boy with the purple socks. _____

14. Maybe they think I'm a gnilkaew, but I'm trained for this kind of fight.

_____

15. There is no rest for the yraew. _____

16. This cook certainly makes a lot of esion. _____

17. Ole Golly is thgir, sometimes you have to lie. _____

18. They're trying to lortnoc me and make me give up. _____

19. I will never give up this notebook, but it is raelc that they are going to be as mean as they can. _____

20. I will be the tseb spy there ever was and I will know everything. _____

Clues						
egnarts	ydal	reggib	slwocs	delebal	derit	tekcar
yksir	ruoved	eveileb	yhtlaew	pmiw	elur	tcerroc
tnetnoc	tcnitsid	derutpac	nialp	tsetaerg	elbirret	

Name _____

Super Synonyms

Read each sentence below. Write a synonym for each underlined word. You may want to use a thesaurus.

1. Mattie and Toni find a <u>beautiful</u> pin for Mattie's mother. _____

2. Matt is <u>thrilled</u> to be on the basketball team. _____

3. Mrs. Benson works very hard to keep everything <u>done</u> around the apartment building. _____

4. Mrs. Stamps is a <u>friendly</u> person to visit. _____

5. Mr. Ashby tries to be a <u>fair</u> teacher. _____

6. Angel is <u>wicked</u> toward everyone around her. _____

7. The Bacon family really <u>enjoyed</u> Mattie's babysitting service. _____

8. Charlene took the bracelet from Angel because she was <u>envious</u> of Angel. _____

9. Mr. Phillips was <u>amazed</u> by Mattie's story. _____

10. Mattie had been very <u>helpful</u> to her mother. _____

Now use the thesaurus to find an antonym for each synonym you wrote above.

1. _____   6. _____

2. _____   7. _____

3. _____   8. _____

4. _____   9. _____

5. _____   10. _____

Name _____

You Can Count on the Count

Homographs are words that are spelled the same but have different meanings. Write the correct homograph for the underlined word(s) in each sentence.

Word Bank		
bank	spruce	pupil
flag	hide	stake
brush	arms	bay

1. She hid the gold by the <u>evergreen</u> tree. _____

2. The soldiers carried <u>weapons</u>. _____

3. I have a <u>dark center in my eye</u>. _____

4. The children had a lot at <u>risk</u> if they were caught with the gold. _____

5. The kids could <u>signal</u> for help if needed. _____

6. The <u>skin</u> on the alligator was thick and dark. _____

7. The ship docked in the <u>inlet</u>. _____

8. The <u>tentacles</u> on the octopus moved constantly. _____

9. The dog suddenly began to <u>howl</u>. _____

10. The children could <u>conceal</u> the gold in the snow. _____

11. Uncle Victor had a <u>banner</u> hanging in his ship. _____

12. Someone was hiding in the <u>bushes</u> by the Snake River. _____

13. The <u>land along the river</u> was covered with brush. _____

14. She had a close <u>encounter</u> with danger. _____

15. The snow <u>pile</u> was as tall as a tree. _____

16. She was a quiet <u>student</u>. _____

17. I will help you <u>fix</u> up things around here. _____

18. They drove a <u>post</u> in the ground to mark the spot. _____

Name _____

Help with Homophones

Circle the correct homophones in each sentence.

1. I'd like to (halve, have) a piece when you (halve, have) that apple.
2. Please give me the (real, reel) fishing rod (real, reel).
3. Our (guessed, guest) (guessed, guest) the correct answer.
4. I heard (him, hymn) sing the (him, hymn).
5. The robber was (scene, seen) at the (scene, seen) of the crime.
6. The (band, banned) could not play the (band, banned) song.
7. I heard Alex (moan, mown) when he was reminded he had not yet (moan, mown) the grass.
8. The weather forecaster said the (missed, mist) had (missed, mist) our area.
9. When the knight hurled his (soared, sword), it (soared, sword) into the air.
10. It's so (chili, chilly) today, let's have (chili, chilly) for supper.

On the lines below, write a sentence for each pair of homophones.

ate, eight _____

_____

dear, deer _____

_____

we'd, weed _____

_____

hoarse, horse _____

_____

scent, sent _____

_____

Name _____

Homophone Hype

For each word given below find and circle the homophone(s) in the wordsearch. List the homophones in the spaces provided. Then write a sentence using the given word and at least one homophone.

```
W R I T E L D U E R C
G N I R A B L Y N I B
R M E T O D S Y R A E
O A L N R I S E M H A
T I H E C F B A O G R
H E I S L E R A D I I
G R D E W A G E O E N
I A Y E H W O T Y A G
R H K P O O T L G W L
G N I R E B R O U T E
```

1. **Main** _____ _____

   Sentence: _____

2. **Liar** _____

   Sentence: _____

3. **Farrow** _____ _____

   Sentence: _____

4. **Bridle** _____

   Sentence: _____

5. **I'll** _____ _____

   Sentence: _____

6. **Graze** (Hint: plural form of a color) _____

   Sentence: _____

7. **Here** _____

   Sentence: _____

8. **Way** _____ _____

   Sentence: _____

9. **Do** _____ _____

   Sentence: _____

10. **Sent** _____ _____

    Sentence: _____

Name _____

Indefatigable Idioms

Use the code to find idioms for each phrase.

Code	
A	N
B	O
C	P
D	Q
E	R
F	S
G	T
H	U
I	V
J	W
K	X
L	Y
M	Z

1. wasting time

___ ___ ___ ___ ___ ___ ___   ___ ___ ___ ___
X V Y Y V A T   G V Z R

2. start to think

___ ___ ___ ___ ___ ___   ___ ___ ___ ___ ___
J U R R Y F   O R T V A

___ ___   ___ ___ ___ ___
G B   G H E A

3. become weak and weary

___ ___ ___   ___ ___ ___ ___
E H A   Q B J A

4. self-evident

___ ___   ___ ___ ___ ___   ___ ___ ___ ___ ___ ___ ___
V G   T B R F   J V G U B H G

___ ___ ___ ___ ___ ___
F N L V A T

5. take back what he said

___ ___ ___   ___ ___ ___   ___ ___ ___ ___ ___
R N G   U V F   J B E Q F

6. what a person deserves

___ ___ ___ ___   ___ ___ ___ ___ ___ ___ ___ ___
W H F G   Q R F F R E G F

7. she attempts to do too much

___ ___ ___ ___ ___   ___ ___ ___   ___ ___ ___ ___   ___ ___ ___ ___
O V G R F   B S S   Z B E R   G U N A

___ ___ ___   ___ ___ ___   ___ ___ ___ ___
F U R   P N A   P U R J

8. poorly planned

___ ___ ___ ___ — ___ ___ ___ ___ ___
U N Y S — O N X R Q

Challenge: Write a story using as many idioms as possible. You might want to include: play it by ear, child's play, eyes peeled, double cross, ham it up, see red, over a barrel, wound up, down in the dumps, time flies, make ends meet, on the tip of my tongue.

Name _____

Watch for Grandpa's Watch

Each "watch" in the title of this worksheet has a different meaning. One means "to look for," and the other means "time piece." Write two meanings for the words below.

	Meaning 1	Meaning 2
1. spring	_____	_____
2. run	_____	_____
3. ruler	_____	_____
4. duck	_____	_____
5. suit	_____	_____
6. cold	_____	_____
7. fall	_____	_____
8. tire	_____	_____
9. rose	_____	_____
10. face	_____	_____
11. train	_____	_____
12. play	_____	_____
13. foot	_____	_____
14. pen	_____	_____
15. box	_____	_____
16. dice	_____	_____
17. fly	_____	_____
18. seal	_____	_____
19. bowl	_____	_____
20. ride	_____	_____
21. line	_____	_____

Challenge: Choose some of the above words and illustrate their two meanings on another piece of paper.

Name _____

Double Trouble

Fill in the blanks with the correct definition number for each underlined word.

Example: __3__ I was covered with <u>pitch</u> after climbing the pine tree.

winding	1. having bends or curves
	2. the act of turning something around a central core
wolf	1. to gulp down
	2. a large carnivorous member of the dog family
pitch	1. to sell or persuade
	2. to throw a ball from the mound to the batter
	3. a resin that comes from the sap of pine trees

____ 1. Do girl scouts <u>pitch</u> cookies?

____ 2. We are <u>winding</u> the top's string tightly.

____ 3. The adult <u>wolf</u> returned to her lair.

____ 4. Red didn't <u>pitch</u> after the fourth inning.

____ 5. The Mather family had a <u>winding</u> driveway.

____ 6. The young ball player <u>wolfed</u> down his lunch.

choke	1. to strangle
	2. to bring the hands up on the bat
hitch	1. obstacle
	2. to fasten or tie temporarily
wind-up	1. the swing of the pitcher's arm just before the pitch
	2. to close or conclude

____ 1. We <u>hitched</u> the mule to the cart.

____ 2. Tip would not <u>choke</u> up on his bat.

____ 3. Paul wished to play, but there was just one <u>hitch</u>.

____ 4. We wish to <u>wind-up</u> our program with more music.

____ 5. Mom was afraid the dog would <u>choke</u> itself on its leash.

____ 6. He has a great <u>wind-up</u> and curve ball.

Name _____

Words We Can Hear . . . Onomatopoeia

Words that imitate the sounds that they are associated with are onomatopoeic. Use words from the Word Bank to write a poem or short story.

Word Bank					
whack	buzz	hiss	creak	squeal	honk
twang	cuckoo	grind	clink	ping	crack
thump	crash	bow wow	chug	moo	blip
flip flop	squish	beep	smack	chug	chirp
ding dong	rustle	clomp			

_____

_____

_____

_____

_____

_____

_____

_____

_____

_____

_____

_____

_____

_____

_____

_____

_____

Name _____

Describe It Please!

Decide in which category each word from the Word Bank belongs.

LANGUAGE ARTS

Word Bank				
robust	slimy	sour	energetic	forgiving
aggravated	devoted	enormous	outraged	prickly
affectionate	delighted	tart	spiteful	silky
enraged	happy	gooey	well	depressed
miserable	adorable	fit	ecstatic	
gloomy	gigantic			

Anger

_____

_____

_____

_____

Sadness

_____

_____

_____

Joy

_____

_____

_____

Love

_____

_____

_____

_____

Feel (Touch)

_____

_____

_____

_____

Taste

_____

_____

Size

_____

_____

Name _____

As Sharp As a Tack

Similes use **like** or **as** to compare two unlike things that share a characteristic. Draw a red line under the two things being compared in each sentence.

1. The snow reached high into the sky like a mountain peak.

2. The barn door felt like a lost friend.

3. The Connolly brothers are as mean as skunks.

4. The huge hill climbed into the sky like a giant's belly as he lay on his back.

5. The wood stovepipe was as red as a fire engine.

6. Tilla's eyes were as blue as a cornflower.

7. The barn was dark like a cave.

8. The warm cow was like a comfortable blanket.

9. George looked like a coyote peering into a henhouse.

10. Tilla's brother was as strong as an ox.

Draw lines to make similes from the following sets of words.

1. Blowing snow is . . .   like contented cows.

2. Miss Brophy is . . .   as friendly as a lost puppy.

3. The boys moved their jaws . . .   like a white blanket.

4. Mr. Fency is . . .   as slippery as worms.

5. Oysters are . . .   as pretty as a china doll.

Name _____

Like . . . a Simile!

In the sentences below, underline the two objects, persons, etc., being compared. In the blank, write if the comparison is a simile or a metaphor. Remember, a simile uses **like** or **as**; metaphors do not.

1. Angel was as mean as a wild bull. _____

2. Toni and Mattie were like toast and jam. _____

3. Mr. Ashby expected the students to be as busy as beavers. _____

4. The pin was a masterpiece in Mattie's mind. _____

5. The park's peacefulness was a friend to Mattie. _____

6. The words came as slow as molasses into Mattie's mind. _____

7. Mrs. Stamps's apartment was like a museum. _____

8. Mrs. Benson was as happy as a lark when Mattie won the contest.

   _____

9. Mr. Phillip's smile was a glowing beam to Mattie and Mrs. Benson.

   _____

10. Mattie ran as fast as the wind to get her money. _____

11. Angel's mean words cut through Charlene like glass. _____

12. Mr. Bacon was a fairy godmother to Mattie. _____

13. The gingko tree's leaves were like fans. _____

Complete the following sentences using similes.

1. Matt was as artistic as _____

2. Hannibal's teeth were like _____

3. Toni's mind worked fast like _____

4. Mattie was as sad as _____

5. Mrs. Stamps was like _____

Name _____

Snacking in the U.S.A.

Ned's award for losing weight was a trip to Disney World. Travel to these vacation spots in the U.S.A. and list the foods you could eat there that begin with the same first letter as the place. For example, Disney World = Doritos, doughnuts, dill pickles.

Niagara Falls
1. _____
2. _____
3. _____

Hollywood
1. _____
2. _____
3. _____

Grand Canyon
1. _____
2. _____
3. _____

Washington, D.C.
1. _____
2. _____
3. _____

Mount Rushmore
1. _____
2. _____
3. _____

Disneyland
1. _____
2. _____
3. _____

Busch Gardens
1. _____
2. _____
3. _____

Statue of Liberty
1. _____
2. _____
3. _____

Rocky Mountains
1. _____
2. _____
3. _____

Lincoln Memorial
1. _____
2. _____
3. _____

Pike's Peak
1. _____
2. _____
3. _____

Empire State Building
1. _____
2. _____
3. _____

Carlsbad Caverns
1. _____
2. _____
3. _____

Indianapolis Speedway
1. _____
2. _____
3. _____

Sea World
1. _____
2. _____
3. _____

Name _____

Abracadabra Magical Sentences

Make magical sentences by using words that begin with each of the letters in the animal names given below.

For example: FROG = Foxes Run Over Grasslands.
BEAR = Blue Elephants Are Rare!

1. SNAKE = _____
_____

2. LION = _____
_____

3. GORILLA = _____
_____

4. CROW = _____

5. SHEEP = _____
_____

6. PIG = _____
_____

7. PYTHON = _____
_____

8. RABBIT = _____
_____

9. HORSE = _____
_____

10. WOLF = _____
_____

11. CAMEL = _____
_____

12. MOUSE = _____
_____

13. HAMSTER = _____
_____

Challenge: Illustrate your best abracadabra sentences on drawing paper.

Name _____

R.I.P.

Not all epitaphs are serious or sentimental. Some are humorous. Below are two examples.

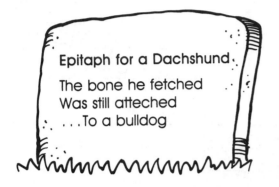

Epitaph for a Dachshund

The bone he fetched
Was still atteched
. . .To a bulldog

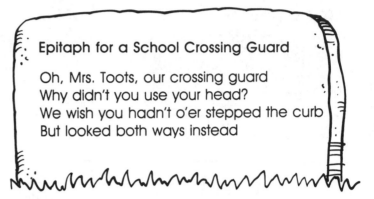

Epitaph for a School Crossing Guard

Oh, Mrs. Toots, our crossing guard
Why didn't you use your head?
We wish you hadn't o'er stepped the curb
But looked both ways instead

Try your hand at writing an epitaph. Here are some ideas of characters for whom you might write:

a sports announcer
a waiter or waitress
a carpenter
a professional wrestler
a talkative parrot

a bank teller
an aerial performer
a pet boa constrictor
a lawyer
a minister, rabbi or priest

Here lies _____
name

_____ - _____
born   died
(month, day, year)   (month, day, year)

epitaph

_____

_____

_____

_____

_____

Name _____

Publishing House

Theodor Seuss Geisel was best known by his pen name, Dr. Seuss. His children's books are usually written in verse and combine nonsense with humor. Draw a picture of a nonsensical being in the box below. Give it a name. Then, write a poem about it on the lines to the right.

_____

_____

_____

_____

_____

_____

_____

_____

_____

_____

Norman Rockwell was an illustrator of everyday people involved in everyday situations. His pictures told stories. They were filled with actions, feeling and details. Think of something you just did with your family, or a feeling you just experienced. Draw a detailed account of the situation in the box to the right.

Name _____

Dear . . .

november 30,

dear mr henshaw

   i would like to learn how to right letters like leigh botts. can we be pun plas two   i ve never red Moose on Toast or Weighs to Amuse a Dog, but i will soon i liked when you signed that letter Messing a round have you written eny more books lately who is your favrit author i will sind you a story with this letter. right back and tell me how you like it

yours 'til niagara falls,

Follow the directions to correct this letter to Mr. Henshaw. Use colored pencils or crayons. Put a check in each box as you correct each item.

☐ 1. Put periods and question marks in the letter where needed in **red**.

☐ 2. Add commas and apostrophes in **green**.

☐ 3. Underline any misspelled words in **orange**.

☐ 4. Circle in **purple** letters that should be capitals.

☐ 5. Write the year after the date in pencil.

☐ 6. Write your name in cursive for the signature.

☐ 7. Circle the entire body of this letter in **yellow**.

☐ 8. Draw a **brown** box around the greeting of the letter.

☐ 9. Underline the closing with **blue**.

☐ 10. Draw two **pink** lines under the signature.

☐ 11. Draw a **red** happy face above the date.

Bonus

On another paper write a story to send to Mr. Henshaw.

Name _____

Mistake'n Letter

The letter below has several mistakes in punctuation, capitalization, and in form. Write it correctly below.

september 9 1868

dear laura.

I was so sorry to hear of your move to virginia we used to have so much fun together i will really miss the opportunity to spend time with you i hope you will enjoy living with your aunt and uncle I hope you return soon in the meantime please write often

sincerely joel.

_____

_____

_____

_____

_____

_____

_____

_____

_____

_____

Name _____

Matching Before and After

Match the first part of each sentence with its last part. Write the matching parts on the lines below the boxes.

First Part   **Before**   Second Part

| Call the store to see if they have turkey |
| It's better to have insurance |
| I had my hair cut |
| My room was cleaned |
| Refill the water jar |

| you need it. |
| hot weather set in. |
| you could count to three. |
| we drive there to get it. |
| you put it back in the refrigerator. |

_____ before _____
_____ before _____
_____ before _____
_____ before _____
_____ before _____

First Part   **After**   Second Part

| We had plenty of hot water |
| Let's have a party |
| My mom and dad ordered new carpet |
| We were suntanned |
| Sam's golf game improved by several points |

| he took some hitting lessons. |
| we finish our tests. |
| we bought a larger water heater. |
| we came back from a long vacation. |
| the puppy was trained. |

_____ after _____
_____ after _____
_____ after _____
_____ after _____
_____ after _____

• Write what comes next.

at bat cat eat fat hat _____

Name _____

When Do You Do It?

Write the listed activities that you do under the appropriate heading. If you do any activities more than once a day, write them more than once. Cross out the ones you don't do.

Activities		
make my bed	take care of a pet	turn off alarm clock
go to school	carry out trash	organized sports
go to scouts	go to dentist	go to lunchroom
eat brunch	watch cartoons	play with friend after school
homework	take bath or shower	sleep a long time
do the dishes	go to Sunday school	go home from school
go to bed	have pleasant dreams	go to dance lessons
have lunch recess	play after school	kiss mom and/or dad goodnight

Between Dinner and Breakfast

_____

_____

_____

_____

_____

Between Breakfast and Lunch

_____

_____

_____

_____

Between Lunch and Dinner

_____

_____

_____

_____

_____

• Write what comes next.

      _____

Name _____

If – Then

Match the sentence parts that go together best. Write the number of the first sentence part on the line in front of the last sentence part for each one.

1. If you baby-sit for me Saturday night
2. If you are nice
3. If we leave work by 4:30
4. If you leave a note on your door
5. If you don't have enough money for the movie
6. If my father isn't too tired
7. If the wind keeps up
8. If you want to get a seat at the concert
9. If our neighbor cuts the grass early Sunday morning
10. If the plant doesn't feel damp
11. If my house were painted white
12. If everyone talked at the same time
13. If you don't get a haircut
14. If the tea kettle whistles
15. If no one answers the door
16. If the little boy crosses the street
17. If the horse is tired
18. If you have a long fork
19. If you don't want any dessert
20. If a king comes into a room
21. If it snows a lot tomorrow

____ the delivery man will leave the package.
____ it needs to be watered.
____ you could roast marshmallows.
____ probably no one is at home.
____ everyone will rise.
____ I'll pay you double.
____ the water is boiling.
____ tomorrow will be a great kite-flying day.
____ let him rest.
____ no one could hear directions.
____ we will avoid rush hour.
____ say "No thank you."
____ the noise will wake me up.
____ we can build an igloo.
____ he said he would show me how to shoot baskets.
____ it would look like a miniature White House.
____ I'll loan you the rest.
____ he must hold onto his mother's hand.
____ you will have many friends.
____ you will have to be at the auditorium early.
____ you will have long hair.

• Write what comes next.

A ʙ ɔ ◠ E _____

Name _____

What Made It Happen?

Each set of sentences includes a cause and an effect. Remember, the cause is what makes something happen, and the effect is the result. Write the cause on the line, and circle the effect.

1. The snow came down harder than anyone could ever remember. For days the people of the village were housebound.

   _____

2. Many of the soldiers decided to learn to ski. The children called one soldier "Lieutenant Sit-Down" because he fell down more than he stood on his skis.

   _____

3. The Commandant kept kicking the snowman covering the gold. Peter threw a snowball to distract the Commandant from discovering the gold.

   _____

4. Per Garson was skiing in crazy patterns around and around the Lundstrom's house. Uncle Victor had been there earlier on his skis.

   _____

5. Peter was sailing down the slope at high speed. In his path he could see approaching soldiers. Peter was going so fast he could not stop his sled. The soldiers scattered to let Peter through.

   _____

6. Mrs. Holms seemed very excited to see the Lundstroms coming to her home. She acted as though she could not wait to speak. Earlier in the day a German soldier had been in the Holm's barn.

   _____

Name _____

Time for Titles

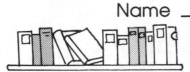

Choose the word or phrase from the Word Box that best completes the heading for each group of words.

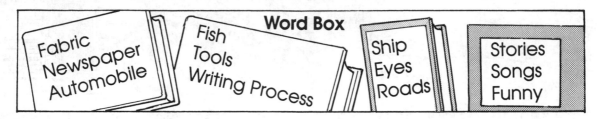

Word Box

Fabric
Newspaper
Automobile

Fish
Tools
Writing Process

Ship
Eyes
Roads

Stories
Songs
Funny

Parts of a . . .	Kinds of . . .	Things for . . .
_____	_____	_____
helm	boulevard	goggles
rudder	freeway	spectacles
gunwale	avenue	contacts
Other words for . . .	Parts of an . . .	Kinds of . . .
_____	_____	_____
witty	headlight	satin
hilarious	windshield	velvet
humorous	seatbelt	flannel
Kinds of . . .	Kinds of . . .	Parts of a . . .
_____	_____	_____
legend	pliers	headline
myth	chisel	column
parable	crowbar	article
Kinds of . . .	Part of the . . .	Kinds of . . .
_____	_____	_____
lullaby	edit	flounder
anthem	proofread	sardine
hymn	revise	salmon

Name _____

Row, Row, Row Your Boat

In the wordsearch, circle words from the list that name **types of boats**. Cross out words that do not belong in that category. Words may go → ← ↑ ↓ ↗.

ark	schooner	battleship	boat	canoe
dory	destroyer	dinghy	liner	sarong
skiff	submarine	mirage	sloop	kayak
raft	rowboat	sailboat	ferry	barge
ship	freighter	carrier	yacht	hinge
tug	tanker	steamer		

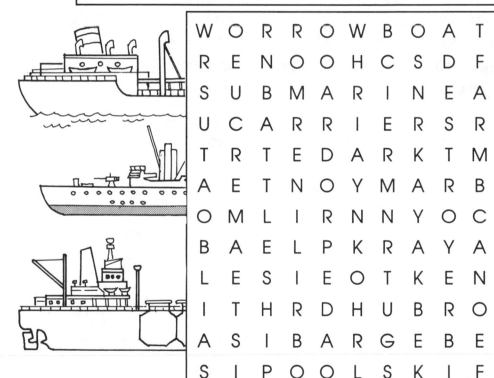

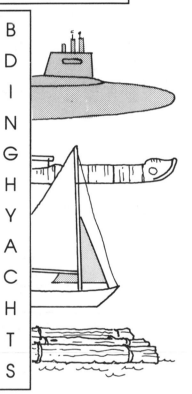

```
W O R R O W B O A T A B
R E N O O H C S D F E D
S U B M A R I N E A T I
U C A R R I E R S R R N
T R T E D A R K T M E G
A E T N O Y M A R B T H
O M L I R N N Y O C H Y
B A E L P K R A Y A G A
L E S I E O T K E N I C
I T H R D H U B R O E H
A S I B A R G E B E R T
S I P O O L S K I F F S
```

Use a dictionary to help answer the questions.

1. Which boat has the ability to travel underwater: a skiff or a submarine?

_____

2. Which boat would more likely be used in a war: a carrier or a liner?

_____

3. Which boat is more like a canoe: a sloop or a kayak? _____

4. Which vessel is a type of fishing boat: a barge or a dory? _____

51   Daily Learning Drills Grade 4

Name _____

Classification

Read the paragraph. Write each sentence in the correct category.

The civilians of the town had a strange disease. The disease was somewhat like scarlet fever, and it spread through the town like a plague. However, the disease only affected small children. All of the small children who had the disease had to be quarantined. The children did not lose their appetite and did not have a temperature. The Commandant ordered that they keep a careful quarantine. He was afraid his infantrymen might contract the disease. The German army had ammunition, but none to fight this type of war. The lieutenant did not want his sentries around the diseased children, so they did not go into town. The witty doctor created a disease for the children and it was a success! The children moved the gold safely.

Sentences relating to the townspeople

_____

_____

_____

_____

_____

_____

Sentences relating to the German army

_____

_____

_____

_____

_____

_____

Name _____

Scaredy-Cat!

What do you fear? Rate these fears from greatest to least, with one being the greatest.

Fear	Rating
dark	_____
fire	_____
strangers	_____
thunder	_____
snakes	_____
school grades	_____
not having friends	_____
monsters	_____
bees	_____
dogs	_____
death	_____
moving	_____
cemeteries	_____
superstitions	_____
crying in public	_____
being unloved	_____

Think about a fear that you have now or might have in the future. Write a diary entry describing this fear.

date _____

Dear Diary,

_____

_____

_____

_____

_____

_____

_____

In Other Words . . .

On the line in front of each sentence, write the letter of the phrase that best defines, describes or explains the underlined part of each sentence.

_____ 1. Mom decided it was a perfect day to <u>capture Minnesota on film</u>.

_____ 2. Lenny thought Huckleberry Heights looked like <u>uncharted territory</u>.

_____ 3. Once they got the door open, they could see that Huckleberry Heights looked like a <u>desert of snow</u>.

_____ 4. Aunt Fluffy always said, "<u>Let's sleep on it</u>."

_____ 5. Edgar thought Mr. Cummings had <u>bitten off more than he could chew</u>.

_____ 6. When Lenny walked Gladys onto the stage, it <u>brought the house down</u>.

_____ 7. Mom said that little Rosalie should be <u>welcomed into their circle</u>.

_____ 8. Tony brushed Smiley's fur so that he <u>shone like tinsel</u>.

_____ 9. Aunt Fluffy's new boyfriend was the <u>last cloud hanging over Tony's holidays</u>.

_____ 10. The whole house <u>smelled like Christmas</u>.

A. think about something overnight and see how you feel about it in the morning

B. the air was filled with scents that remind you of Christmas

C. to make everyone feel like they belong

D. take photographs of Minnesota

E. took on a project that is more than he can handle

F. the audience clapped and cheered

G. was very shiny

H. somewhere no one has ever been before

I. a gloomy thing to think about

J. there was snow everywhere

I guess we're just a pair of "good skates."

A NOW . . . D   A "good skate" is someone who is cooperative and gets along well with other people. Choose a classmate who you think is a good skate and write down reasons that explain why you feel this way. Share these "warm fuzzies" (nice thoughts) with your class.

Name _____

What a Tragedy!

Drama is a play performed by actors. A drama tells a story. Drama can be serious, or funny, or sometimes both. There are three basic kinds of drama: tragedy, comedy and melodrama.

A tragedy is a drama about a serious subject. Tragedies often deal with the meaning of life, and how people treat each other.

A comedy is a drama that uses feelings of joy. Comedy can also show very exaggerated and ridiculous behavior.

A melodrama is a drama which tells a story of good against evil. A melodrama features an evil villain who tries to destroy the good characters.

Drama is believed to have begun in ancient Greece. The

Greeks performed their plays in outdoor theaters. Many of the Greek tragedies were about myths. Drama was later popular in many countries: Italy, England, Spain, France, India, China and Japan. Today, drama is popular in practically every country in the world.

Circle and check.

Drama

. . . is a costume / play performed by actors.

. . . tells a: ☐ joke ☐ part ☐ story

. . . can be serious, or funny, or both. T F

Write.

Drama is believed to have begun in ancient _____ .

The Greeks performed their dramas in _____ theaters.

Many of the Greek tragedies were about _____ .

• Write a plot or story for each of the three kinds of drama.

Name _____

Scrambled Words

Unscramble the letters in parentheses to spell a word that makes sense in each sentence.

1. Cookies don't _____ to me; I prefer candy.
(papale)

2. The desert is a good place to see a _____ .
(saccut)

3. When is Halley's _____ supposed to appear again?
(tomec)

4. Take a deep breath and then _____ .
(elahex)

5. Place the _____ in the can before pouring the gasoline.
(nenulf)

6. I am learning how to do _____ tricks.
(gicam)

7. "I don't have a _____ thing to wear!" complained Jill.
(gilens)

8. An _____ home is made of sun-dried bricks.
(bedoa)

9. Is _____ ice cream your favorite?
(alaviln)

10. This word scramble is _____ too difficult for me.
(splimy)

11. Mother set the china on the _____ tablecloth.
(ennil)

12. I am _____ for chocolate chip cookies.
(gurhyn)

13. I wish you much _____ on your new job.
(usseccs)

14. How many people are employed at that _____ ?
(tarfocy)

15. Hold your breath to help get rid of the _____ .
(spuchic)

Perfect Pairs

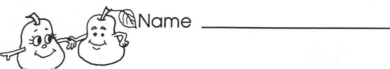

Name _____

Some words just seem to belong together. See how many word pairs you can make by using words from Column B to complete the phrases in Column A.

Example: salt and **pepper**

Column A

1. Rocky and _____
2. cup and _____
3. pencil and _____
4. cookies and _____
5. cats and _____
6. rock and _____
7. hammer and _____
8. Batman and _____
9. mustard and _____
10. song and _____
11. shoes and _____
12. hat and _____
13. ham and _____
14. peanut butter and _____
15. bacon and _____
16. Jack and _____
17. night and _____
18. table and _____
19. comb and _____
20. bread and _____
21. apples and _____
22. fruits and _____
23. bride and _____

Column B

brush
Bullwinkle
butter
chairs
cheese
coat
dance
day
dogs
eggs
vegetables
groom
jelly
Jill
ketchup
milk
nails
oranges
paper
Robin
roll
saucer
socks

Name _____

Babes in Arms

Situation: It's five o'clock p.m., and you are babysitting for a family with three young children. Before the adults leave, what questions should you ask?

Number these questions in importance, listing 1 as the most important.
Cross out any questions you feel are inappropriate.

___ Does your stereo system work well?

___ How much does the job pay?

___ How long do you expect to be out?

___ Where is your telephone?

___ Are you expecting any phone calls?

___ Do you have a VCR?

___ Do I have to wash the dishes?

___ What is an appropriate bedtime for the children?

___ Where do you keep snacks?

___ May I invite a friend over to stay with me?

___ How much money do you make?

___ How might I reach you in an emergency?

___ When was the last time you vacuumed your carpet?

___ What shall I feed the children?

___ Has your dog been tested for rabies?

___ May I share some candy with the children?

Comment on either a question you crossed out as inappropriate or a question you rated very high.

_____

_____

On another sheet of paper, provide a list of ten tips for prospective babysitters.

Ride with the Wind

Name _____

Size: 22-inch frame	Tire Pressure: 65 lbs
Weight: 37 lbs.	Gears: 3
Tire Size: 26" x 1 3/8"	

The tires provide good grip on both wet and dry road surfaces. The narrow tires decrease friction and allow for greater speed.

The side basket is useful for carrying a wide variety of items from newspapers to groceries.

The frame is lighter than most bikes of this time. It is painted maroon or "icky brick."

With the bike's three gears, the rider can easily adjust pedal speed to match the road conditions.

The streamers and raccoon tail are just two ways for a rider to give her or his individual touch.

When these caliper brake levers are depressed, "shoes" or pads on both sides of the wheel rim press in to bring the wheel to a halt.

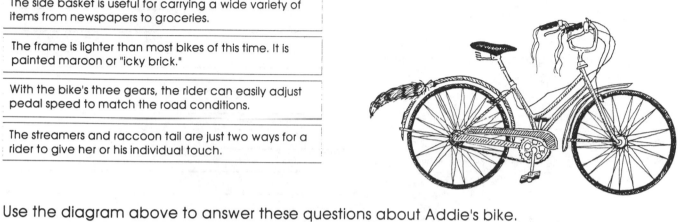

Use the diagram above to answer these questions about Addie's bike.

1. Why does Addie's bike go faster than other children's bikes?_____

_____

2. Where can Addie carry her flowers? _____

3. How many gears does Addie's bike have? _____

4. Where does the raccoon tail hang? _____

5. What is the color of the bike? _____

6. How do the brakes work? _____

_____

7. How heavy is this bike? _____

8. How many more pounds of pressure are in Addie's bike tires than are in Carla Mae's which has 41 pounds of pressure?_____

9. Does this bike have a chain guard? _____ Why does this help?_____

_____

10. How is this bike different from many bikes today? _____

_____

Name _____

Jumping to Conclusions

Write your own conclusion to each situation in the space provided.

Situations	Conclusions

1. Your brother just turned five. He has chocolate all over his face and he looks sheepish.

   _____
   _____
   _____

2. Your parents are gone. It's 9:00 p.m. and you hear a thump and a cry.

   _____
   _____
   _____

3. You are making a cake. You hear the sound of beating wings and a thin, shrill squeal.

   _____
   _____
   _____

4. You are outdoors after dark during summer vacation. You see a sudden flash of light and smell a smoky odor.

   _____
   _____
   _____

5. One morning at school you see your friend looking dreamy-eyed. On her paper, she writes SW + SD.

   _____
   _____
   _____

6. A large column of clouds appears in the western sky, and a strong wind starts blowing.

   _____
   _____
   _____

7. You hear a noise in your parents' bedroom. Then you see a broken window and a baseball rolling across the floor.

   _____
   _____
   _____

8. In the classroom next door you see a desk tipped over, text books scattered, and one boy crying.

   _____
   _____

Challenge: Describe a new situation on another paper. Include four important details and make up a conclusion in your head. Then let a friend read what you've written and guess your conclusion. Does your friend draw the same conclusion?

It's Greek to Me

Name _____

Anti – is a prefix from the Greek word **anti** which means *against.*
Look up each word in the dictionary and write its definition.

1. antibiotic _____
2. antidote _____
3. antiknock _____
4. antipathy _____
5. antiperspirant _____
6. antiseptic _____

Answer the questions in complete sentences.

1. If a person were accidentally poisoned, would he or she be given an antidote or an antiseptic? _____
   _____

2. If you strongly disliked fish, would you have an antibiotic or an antipathy toward it? _____
   _____

3. Which would a person more likely use on his or her body: an antiperspirant or an antipathy? _____
   _____

4. To prevent infection from a cut, would you use an antiperspirant or an antiseptic? _____
   _____

5. Is penicillin an example of an antibiotic or an antiseptic? _____
   _____

Name _____

Borrowed from Abroad

Many words in the English language have come from other languages. For example, **garage** comes from a French word meaning *protect*.

Use a dictionary to find the language from which each of the following words was taken. Write the name of the language and a short meaning for each word.

1. gimlet: _____

   _____

2. hacienda: _____

   _____

3. javelin: _____

   _____

4. jerky: _____

   _____

5. morgue: _____

   _____

6. terrazzo: _____

   _____

Answer the following questions in complete sentences.

1. Which two words above are from Spanish?

   _____

2. Which two words are French in origin?

   _____

3. Which word is the name of something to eat?

   _____

4. Where would you likely find terrazzo – in a morgue or a hacienda?

   _____

5. Which might an athlete use: a javelin or a gimlet?

   _____

Name _____

My Own Secret Kingdom

Create your own kingdom by following these directions. Use a large sheet of drawing paper.

1. Draw a directional compass in the southeast corner of the paper.

2. Draw your castle in the northeast corner of the kingdom. Add plenty of details.

3. There is a river that runs north and south through your kingdom. Color the river blue and write its name beside it.

4. Two bridges cross the river. One crosses the northern section and one crosses the southern section. Draw them.

5. Draw a moat around your castle.

6. Add a large forest south of the castle.

7. Horses and chariots are stabled in a barn surrounded by a corral. The corral is between the forest and the river.

8. There are four lookout towers protecting your land. Place one in each of the corners of the kingdom. Add different colored flags at the top of each.

9. A pond lies in the southeast part of the kingdom, west of the river and east of the tower and directional compass.

10. Your guardian dog, _____ (name), is napping by the pond. He is a _____ (breed).

11. Secret evergreen groves are north of the pond. In the center of the grove is a meeting place built with rocks.

12. In the northwest corner by the tower, draw your kingdom's crest or symbol.

13. Now add four more features to your kingdom. List them here.

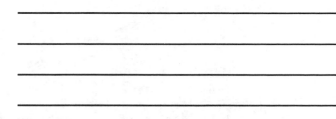

14. Name your kingdom.

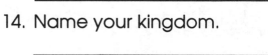

Daily Learning Drills Grade 4

Name _____

Pictures from the Palace

Fold a piece of drawing paper into four parts and draw a picture for each descriptive paragraph below. Number the pictures to match the paragraphs.

1. The Emperor sat on a golden throne. The huge chair was taller than any man and carved with dragons and snakes. Multicolored jewels were embedded in the gold. The Emperor wore a royal blue and gold robe. His hat resembled a blue graduation cap with several strands of multicolored beads hanging from the brim. His shoes were black. He held a paper scroll in both hands.

2. The Princess was beautiful. Her long black hair was knotted into several sections. A pink butterfly hair clip was fastened off to one side. She had black, almond-shaped eyes and rosy cheeks. Her flowered pink, green, and yellow silk gown was tied with a green sash. Pink slippers adorned her feet. She carried a pink fan decorated with Chinese nature scenes.

3. The palace kitchen had a long wooden table in the middle of the room, filled with steaming pots of food. The back wall was made of brick. Long-handled copper and silver pans and skillets hung near the top of this brick wall. Huge ovens covered the left wall. On the right, several cooks chopped and diced fresh vegetables. Vegetable baskets lined the floor.

4. The summer palace was small, built high up on bamboo poles. The roof was made of straw and bamboo with upward curving edges. Its long, vertical windows were covered with paper and colorful Chinese murals. A balcony was built around the outside.

Name _____

Hamsterology

Carefully read the following paragraph about golden hamsters. Then follow the directions.

Native to Central Asia and Europe, the golden hamster is a nocturnal animal that makes its home in complex tunnels under the ground. It is a rodent, related to mice and rats. It eats mostly vegetables, grains and seeds which it stores in its cheek pouches to take back to its tunnel. In the wild, the hamster will also prey upon small animals and birds. It grows to be about 5 inches long and has a short tail. It weighs 4 to 5 ounces and has golden brown fur. The female breeds when she is seven to eight weeks old, producing litters of six to seven babies. Golden hamsters make good pets. Their life span is two to three years.

Directions:
1. Circle in yellow every "hamster" in the paragraph.
2. Make blue boxes around the places where golden hamsters originated.
3. Underline in red the plant foods that golden hamsters eat.
4. Draw an orange **X** over the animals a hamster will eat.
5. Draw a purple, wiggly line under the word that means hamsters sleep during the day and are awake at night.
6. Put a green **R** over the word that tells what type of animal the hamster is.
7. Draw a brown star over the place where hamsters store their food.
8. Make a pink line below the hamster's habitat.
9. Draw a red line on top of the word that describes their tails.
10. Circle in red the number of babies most female hamsters have.
11. Underline in black how long hamsters live.
12. Draw an orange box around how long hamsters grow to be.
13. Put a green heart around the verb that as a noun means an animal eaten by a meat-eating animal.
14. Draw a brown, wiggly line under the color of the hamster's fur.

Challenge: Use the encyclopedia to write a report on field mice, gerbils, kangaroo rats or guinea pigs, comparing them to golden hamsters. Share your findings with the rest of the class.

Name _____

Answering Questions

Within each group draw a line from each question on the left to the answer that matches it best on the right.

Where will you stay if the hotel can't take you?

Who has the lead part in the play?

Why didn't you complete your homework last night?

When was the last time you saw the gerbil?

What time do you want to meet?

How many people will be at the game?

Whenever is best for you.

I had to go to my grandmother's birthday dinner.

I'll make that decision then.

If it's raining, there will be very few.

They are posting the roles after lunch.

Last Friday when he climbed into the wastebasket.

Are there any holes in that sieve?

Why are the dishes still in the sink?

Would you show me how to play?

How well do you know him?

What did you tell her?

Why didn't you go to the concert?

I was too tired.

He has lived next to me for two years.

It's a secret.

It's in perfect condition.

I will when there is time.

Dad said he'd do them.

Why aren't you eating dinner?

What is the boy saying?

Why isn't the new boy playing kickball?

When will it be ready?

Did anyone send a thank-you note to our room mother?

Does she have good handwriting?

I mailed it to her yesterday.

It is supposed to be available now.

We had a late lunch.

He's giving the score.

It's the best I've seen.

He doesn't know how.

Has anyone heard anything about the new play?

How are the flowers?

Why did Tom stay after school?

How old is the antique dresser?

Is there any cake left?

Where did you find the ball?

They need water.

The teacher wanted to see him.

Jean said it was very long.

Barbara finished the crumbs.

It was caught in the fence.

It was my great grandmother's.

Name _____

What's the Point?

Locate and underline the main idea in each group of sentences.

1. Bert returned with half a baked ham, butter, and a jug of milk. Martin had not eaten since the night before last. Laura set the table for their late night snack.

2. When Laura woke up, Martin looked like a different boy. He was wearing a pair of Bert's pants and one of his old shirts. He looked as though he had taken a bath.

3. Humming, Laura began to scrape and stack the dishes. She put water on the stove to heat. Laura enjoyed working in the kitchen.

4. The sheriff and slave hunters stormed through the house. Laura heard the crash of a chair. They searched every room and closet. The men were look-ing for a fugitive slave.

5. The field behind the vegetable garden was aglow with goldenrod and wild flowers. The autumn sun shone brightly in the yard. Laura looked out the window. She longed to go outside on this beautiful autumn day.

Now write one detail sentence from each group on the lines below.

1. _____

2. _____

3. _____

4. _____

5. _____

Name _____

Camp Rules

Donald, Arnold and Jack are all at Camp Explore-It-All this week. They think camp is a lot of fun, but they have also learned from their instructors that there are some very important rules all campers must obey so that everyone has a good time.

All campers had to take swimming tests to see what depth of water they will be allowed to swim in. Donald and Jack passed the advanced test and can swim in the deep water. Arnold, however, only passed the intermediate test. He is supposed to stay in the area where the water is waist deep. When it is time to swim, Arnold decides to sneak into advanced with Donald and Jack. After all, he has been swimming in deep water for three years. No way is he going to stay in the shallow water with the sissies.

Donald and Jack don't think Arnold should come into the deep water, but they can't tell him anything. So the boys jump into the water and start swimming and playing. Fifteen minutes later, Arnold is yelling, "Help!" He swam out too far and is too tired to make it back in. The lifeguard jumps in and pulls him out. Everyone stops to see what is happening. Arnold feels very foolish.

Check.

The main idea of this story is . . .

☐ Arnold ends up feeling foolish.　　　　☐ Camp is fun.

☐ All campers take swimming tests.　　　☐ Rules are made for good reasons.

☐ You can learn a lot from instructors.　　☐ Rules are made to be broken.

Underline.

Arnold got himself into a(n) _____ situation.

　　amusing　　　　　　　funny　　　　　　　dangerous　　　　　ambiguous

Circle.

Arnold thought the guys in the shallow area were (bullies/sissies). However, he should

have (stayed with them/gone to the advanced area).

Write.

What lesson do you think Arnold learned? _____

_____

What do you think the other campers learned? _____

_____

Name _____

From Whose Point of View?

Read each sentence below. Decide if it is the first or third person's point of view. If It Is a first person's point of view, rewrite the sentence to make it a third person's point of view. If it is a third person's point of view, rewrite it to make it a first person's point of view.

1. I wanted to tell Anh and Thant the secret of our leaving, but I had given my word.

   _____

2. The grandmother did not want to go aboard the boat.

   _____

3. The people on shore were pushing to get on the deck of the boat.

   _____

4. Though I had worked many days in the rice paddies watching planes fly over, I never thought I'd be on one.

   _____

5. Loi made a net from pieces of string and caught a turtle with his new device.

   _____

6. I know of a place where we can wash our clothes.

   _____

7. The officer looked at them with great interest.

   _____

8. When I looked into the harbor, I could see the shape of the sampan boats.

   _____

9. This is my duck and I choose to share it with everyone on the boat for the celebration of Tet.

   _____

Name _____

Make Your Mark Here

Use the proofreader marks shown to the right to correct the sentences below.

apostrophe $\vee$	end marks ⊙ ⑦ ①
quotation marks " "	comma $\wedge$
capitalize ☰	

1. lucy wailed i can t go to the party i told everyone what a great costume i was going to have

2. carla said okay meet me at my place the basement apartment of the eucalyptus arms do you know where that is

3. are you a real vampire lucy demanded

4. hold it lucy i dropped my fangs down your neck mumbled the embarrassed knievel

5. knievel howled don t you have more that s the best chocolate cupcake i ever ate why it s got everything

6. stay right there squeaked the rabbit i ll get you something don t move

7. where s the tv questioned susannah looking around   i m sure i heard one before we came in

8. mr mordecai rubbed his hands and smiled shyly i ll be back he whispered then he vanished

9. i m pretty sure knievel got the poisoned candy when he was with us susannah said i don t think he had done any trick-or-treating before he met us

10. forgot my key shouted aunt louise how are you girl where s that niece of mine

Draw a picture to go with one of the quotes above. Write the quote next to it.

Quote: _____

_____

_____

Name _____

Fish Facts

All of the fourth graders in Miss Freed's class did reports on animals. Jackie did hers on fish. She learned so much about these fascinating animals. She can't wait to share the information with her class.

Jackie didn't know much about fish when she started. She has since learned that fish are vertebrates because they have backbones. She was also amazed to learn that there are more kinds of fish than all other kinds of water and land vertebrates put together. The kinds of fish differ so greatly In shape, color and size that Jackie can hardly believe they all belong to the same group of animals.

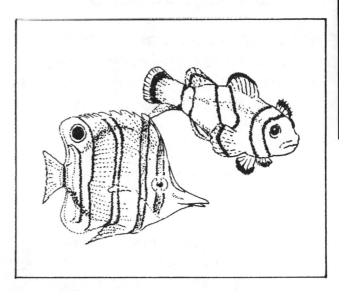

Some fish, Jackie found out, look like lumpy rocks. Others look like wriggly worms. Some can blow themselves up like balloons, and others are as flat as pancakes. Fish can be all the colors of the rainbow, and also striped and polka-dotted. The one fish Jackie definitely never wants to run into is the stonefish. Though it is small, it can kill a person in a few minutes. The subject of fish turned out to be a lot more interesting than Jackie ever imagined.

Circle.

Fish are (invertebrates/vertebrates) because they (do not have/have) backbones.

Underline.

Fish differ greatly in . . .

taste.   size.   shape.   color.   length.

Check.

Fish can be . . .

☐ lumpy.   ☐ depressed.   ☐ colorful.   ☐ striped.

☐ smart.   ☐ flat.   ☐ polka-dotted.   ☐ sad.

Write.

Describe the kinds of fish found in aquariums. Use adjectives relating to size, shape and color.

_____

_____

What kinds of fish have you eaten? _____

_____

Name _____

Mixed-Up Recipe

In the story, Laura decides to make a batch of homemade applesauce. Below is a recipe she may have followed. However, by looking at the directions, it is easy to see that something is mixed-up. Read the recipe, compare it to others if you wish, then rewrite it correctly.

Applesauce

12 to 16 medium apples
1 cup water
1 to 1 1/2 cups of sugar

Directions:
Heat to boiling. Add 1 cup water. Peel and slice the apples into quarters. Simmer over low heat for 20 to 30 minutes or until soft. Stir occasionally. Stir in sugar and heat through. Add 1 teaspoon of cinnamon if you wish.

Makes 12 servings.

Correct Directions:

_____

_____

_____

_____

_____

_____

_____

_____

Name _____

Weekend Fun

Number each group of sentences in the correct order.

____ I had a hamburger, but everyone else had a salad.

____ My parents picked us up after the movie.

____ A horse-drawn carriage took us for a ride through the park to the zoo.

____ I didn't buy any popcorn during the movie.

____ We spent a couple of hours at the zoo before we took a bus to meet our friends for lunch.

____ We walked to the movie after lunch.

____ A wind lifted the kite high in the air.

____ Father let out the string while I ran with the kite.

____ The park was crowded with people flying kites when we got there.

____ We found a spot to fly the kite away from the other people.

____ Father and I took a kite to the park.

____ We had to tie a tail on the kite before it was ready to be flown.

____ I took an atlas home with me on Friday.

____ I wrote down important facts about each country.

____ I turned in my report on Monday morning.

____ After I watched cartoons Saturday morning, I looked up England and Germany in the atlas.

____ I wrote a report about England and Germany from my notes.

____ Friday morning the teacher said our reports on different countries were due on Monday.

____ We decided what kind of cones we wanted while standing in line.

____ Larry fell down and the cone flew into the air.

____ While walking down the street with our cones, a large dog charged Larry.

____ There was a long line at the ice-cream shop when Larry and I got there.

____ The dog caught the cone and ran away with it.

____ We stood behind the last person in line.

Name _____

Putting Them in Order

Rewrite the sentences in each paragraph below in the correct order.

There was a loud crack and the ice Elizabeth was on began to sink. Her mother warned her not to go too far out on the ice, but she forgot. Elizabeth asked her mother if she could go skating on the pond. Elizabeth's cries for help were answered, and some other skaters pulled her to safety.

_____
_____
_____
_____
_____
_____
_____
_____
_____

When Marcy and Tony were walking home from school he suggested they go a different way. The stream twisted and turned, and it eventually led them back to school. They followed the stream in the direction they thought would take them home. They cut across a farmer's field and down a hill to a stream.

_____
_____
_____
_____
_____
_____
_____
_____
_____

• Write what comes next.

VI VOI VOIVI _____

Name _____

Moving Time

David's family is buying a new house. Their old house is just too small. However, there are two houses that they like equally as much. The first one is in the neighborhood in which they live now. David's family would still be around all their same friends, and David could still ride to school with his best friend. The only problem is that this house doesn't have a playroom where David and his friends could go, which was one of the reasons for moving. It also needs a lot of painting, which David's dad is not happy about. But, it's a good buy.

The second house is across town. David could still go to the same school, but he wouldn't be close to his old friends. This house is really big with a huge playroom, and it has just been freshly painted. Even though it costs more than the other one, it's still a good deal.

So now David's family has to decide if they want less room, more work and the same neighborhood, or more room and less work. Both houses have 3 bedrooms and big family rooms, so his parents are happy about that. What a decision!

Underline.

David and his family have found two houses that they like . . .

equally as well.   almost as much as their old one.   in his neighborhood.   a little.

Circle.

David would want to buy the second house except that it . . .

has a big playroom.   needs to be painted.   isn't close to his friends.

Check.

The first house is different from the second one because it . . .

☐ has three bedrooms.   ☐ has a family room.

☐ is in David's same neighborhood.   ☐ needs to be painted.

☐ doesn't have a play room.   ☐ is a good buy.

Write.

List at least 3 reasons David's family is having a hard time deciding which house to buy.

1. _____

2. _____

3. _____

If you ever had to move, how would you feel about it? List five positive things and five negative things about moving.

Name _____

Yesterday and Today

Read each sentence. If it tells about a past event, write **THEN** on the line. If it tells about an event that is happening in the present, write **NOW** on the line.

_____ The forest fire is burning out of control.

_____ We sent money to help feed and clothe the flood victims.

_____ The river rushing past my window keeps me up at night.

_____ I am taking a series of tennis lessons on Wednesdays.

_____ Glaciers covered over one-fifth of the world.

_____ The student council sets rules for the student body to follow.

_____ I bought enough glue to last a lifetime.

_____ The third grade had the best attendance record.

_____ The picnic was cancelled because of the heavy downpour.

_____ I belong to the scouts.

_____ The forest floor is covered with ferns and moss.

_____ The Hopi Indians live within the Navajo Indian nation.

_____ My aunt and uncle stayed with us for a week.

_____ The day started out sunny.

_____ My grade in penmanship indicates great improvement.

_____ I baked banana bread for the room mother's tea.

_____ I watch television every night for an hour before going to bed.

_____ Melissa is the fastest runner in the class.

_____ I made a deposit in my savings account.

_____ I cut my birthday cake after I blew out all the candles.

_____ The patrol boys and girls help younger children cross the street.

_____ The snow is continuing to fall.

_____ I save my pennies for rainy days.

_____ The chandelier swayed during the earthquake.

_____ We fastened our seat belts before father started the car.

_____ The native dancers' clothes were colorful.

• Write what comes next.

BA   ED   IH   ON   _____

Name _____

Keeping in Touch

On the lines next to the letter, write the correct category **(who, what, when, where** or **why)** for each underlined word or phrase in Genevieve's letter.

Dear Mom and Dad,

I have been very busy (1) <u>here in the United States</u> taking care of Lucas and the twins. (2) <u>A few weeks ago</u> (3) <u>Lucas and his friends</u> (4) <u>climbed up onto the roof</u> of the Cotts' home (5) <u>to get a better view of the neigh-borhood</u>. (6) <u>He</u> has spent a lot of time with me (7) <u>since then</u>.

(8) <u>Today</u>, I (9) <u>taught him how to dance</u> (10) <u>so he can have a girlfriend</u> (11) <u>when he gets older</u>. (12) <u>Julio</u> danced with us (13) <u>in the living room</u>, too. (14) <u>I</u> miss you both.

Love,

Genevieve

1. _____
2. _____
3. _____
4. _____
5. _____
6. _____
7. _____
8. _____
9. _____
10. _____
11. _____
12. _____
13. _____
14. _____

**A
NOW . . .
D**
Write an essay titled, "The Importance of Being Trustworthy." Share it with your classmates and discuss what each of you thinks about *being* trustworthy and *expecting* trust from others.

Name _____

Are You Mixed Up?

Unscramble the letters on the left to create words which match the meanings on the right.

	Word	Word Meaning
1. degfti	_____	To move restlessly or nervously
2. spygy	_____	A member of a wandering people believed to have come out of India
3. pureto	_____	A group of actors or dancers
4. tayjun	_____	Having a self-confident manner
5. nastioyrta	_____	Not capable of being moved
6. caottitep	_____	A woman's slip or underskirt
7. ever	_____	To swerve
8. rylub	_____	Heavy, strong and muscular
9. merba	_____	A brownish-yellow color
10. laiggnl	_____	Very annoying

Write sentences using four of the words you unscrambled.

1. _____
   _____

2. _____
   _____

3. _____
   _____

4. _____
   _____

Name _____

Say It Again

Add a letter to each word to make a new word. Use letters from the Letter Bank and the clues to help. The letter may be added anywhere to the word.

Example:

word	letter	new word	clue
hove	+ l =	hovel	a hut

Word	Letter	New Word	Clue
gain	_____	_____	Small seed
rate	_____	_____	Used in fireplaces
par	_____	_____	A fruit
rip	_____	_____	Ready for harvest
sing	_____	_____	To burn at the edges
tick	_____	_____	Slow witted
pear	_____	_____	Weapon that can be thrown
ad	_____	_____	Fuss or bother
mat	_____	_____	Important to sailing ships
boar	_____	_____	Two-by-four
die	_____	_____	Urgent
men	_____	_____	Sign of a future event
yarn	_____	_____	To want
tool	_____	_____	Place to sit
toe	_____	_____	To carry
single	_____	_____	Roofing material

Letter Bank
d   d   e   e   e   e   g   h   h   o   o   r   r   s   s   s   t

Name _____

Guide-Worthy Words

Use a pencil to write ten vocabulary words from the Word Bank under each of the guide words. Remember to put them in alphabetical order.

Reflection	Syllable

Abrupt	Authority

Babyhood	Crest

Defense	Exult

Word Bank

burrow	commence	cordial	corporal	accustom
accidentally	barracks	barometer	explosive	schoolmaster
stealth	allow	calamity	stance	defiant
epidemic	ancient	scowl	discard	ammunition
disturbance	subside	salute	reindeer	consternation
assign	demoralize	disposition	appoint	beneficial
resolute	enormous	ashamed	retort	entirely
earthenware	additional	commotion	almanac	surpass

Name _____

Hey, Look Me Over

Use the dictionary pronunciations to answer the questions below.

concoction (kən kok′ shən) *noun.* something prepared by mixing ingredients.

1. Which syllable is accented? _____

2. How many syllables have a "schwa" sound? _____

3. How many syllables are in "concoction?" _____

hover (huv′ ər) *verb. hovered hovering.* to flutter over or about.

1. How many syllables are in *hover*? _____

2. Which syllable is accented? _____

3. How many syllables are found in *hovering*? _____

Rattlesnake stew is one nasty concoction!

eternity (i tur′ nə tē) *noun.* an endless length of time.

1. Which syllable has a long "e" sound? _____

2. Which syllable is accented? _____

3. How many syllables are in *eternity*? _____

honeysuckle (hun′ ē suk′ əl) *noun.* a climbing shrub with pleasant-smelling flowers.

1. How many syllables are in "honeysuckle?" _____

2. Which syllable has a primary accent? _____

3. Which syllable has a secondary accent? _____

4. Which syllable has a "schwa" sound? _____

5. Which two syllables have the same vowel sound? _____

Challenge: Write the phonetic spellings of these words.

audible _____   camouflage _____

pneumonia _____   municipal _____

supernatural _____

Name _____

Weird Words

Use a dictionary to help you answer the questions using complete sentences.

1. Which would you use to treat a sore throat: a **gargoyle** or a **gargle**?

   _____

2. Which might be used on a gravestone: an **epiphyte** or an **epitaph**?

   _____

3. Which is an instrument: **calligraphy** or a **calliope**?

   _____

4. Would a building have a **gargoyle** or an **argyle** on it?

   _____

5. If you trick someone, do you **bamboozle** him or **barcarole** him?

   _____

6. if you studied handwriting, would you learn **calligraphy** or **cajolery**?

   _____

7. What would a gondolier sing: a **barcarole** or an **argyle**?

   _____

8. If you tried to coax someone, would you be using **cajolery** or **calamity**?

   _____

9. Which might you wear: **argyles** or **calliopes**?

   _____

10. In Venice, Italy, would you travel in a **gondola** or a **calamity**?

    _____

Name _____

From the Diary of Milo

Use a dictionary to help you circle the correct definition for each underlined word. In the space, write the dictionary page number.

_____ 1. We saw <u>debris</u> scattered everywhere after the fortress fell.

     smoke   rubble   vegetation

_____ 2. The beautiful island <u>beckoned</u> us to its rich bounty.

     warned   darkened   lured

_____ 3. The strange creature <u>doffed</u> his hat and welcomed us to Digitopolis.

     pounded   washed   tipped

_____ 4. We ducked our heads to avoid the cave's <u>stalactites</u>.

     pitfalls   icicle-shaped mineral   dripping water
                        deposits

_____ 5. The soup's pot loosed a <u>savory</u> steam into the air.

     boiling   safe   appetizing

_____ 6. If I continue to add ones, I could count into <u>infinity</u>.

     endlessness   a secret chamber   wee hours of the night

_____ 7. The <u>sheer</u> mountain walls made climbing difficult for our traveling band.

     icy   very steep   sharply spiked

_____ 8. The giant whined <u>peevishly</u> when we asked him to assist us.

     crossly   weakly   foolishly

_____ 9. As the demons drew near, we noted their <u>loathsome</u> odors.

     powerful   angry   disgusting

_____ 10. The ugly demon, whose <u>bulbous</u> nose honked constantly, fell from his perch.

     reddened   wart-covered   bulb-shaped

Name _____

Hang Tough, Student

Write the letter of the resource book which would best help you answer each question.

A. general encyclopedia

ALL ABOUT EVERYTHING (Generally Speaking.)

B. dictionary

C. science encyclopedia

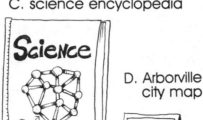

atom

D. Arborville city map

CITY MAP

E. medical encyclopedia

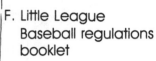

F. Little League Baseball regulations booklet

These are THE RULES

_____ 1. What is a *coati*?

_____ 2. What does a geologist do?

_____ 3. May a runner lead off a base in Little League?

_____ 4. When did the game of soccer originate?

_____ 5. What is the easiest way to get to Sampson Park from the expressway?

_____ 6. Would you say that Mr. and Mrs. Mather were *overtly tactless* with Jim Anderson?

_____ 7. How large is the baseball strike zone?

_____ 8. What causes acne?

_____ 9. How is a lunar eclipse formed?

_____ 10. How far is it from Ferdon Street to the Clinton School diamond?

_____ 11. What are some symptoms of leukemia?

_____ 12. How many states border Michigan?

_____ 13. How long must a pitcher rest between games pitched?

_____ 14. How many calories are found in a meal consisting of two slices of salami on whole wheat bread, a 2-ounce wedge of Swiss cheese, one apple and 14 ounces of milk?

Challenge   Answer one of the above questions using a resource book.

Question Number	Source Used	Page in Source	Answer
_____	_____	_____	_____

Name _____

Jimminy Cricket!

Underline the key word in each question. Then write the encyclopedia volume number you would use to find information to answer each question.

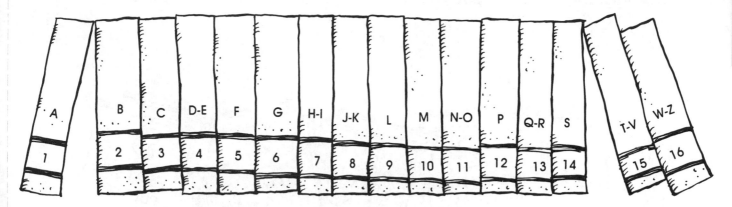

_____ 1. How are cattle branded?

_____ 2. What were some names of early American airplanes?

_____ 3. How should you care for your hair?

_____ 4. How large can a collie become?

_____ 5. Who invented the x-ray machine?

_____ 6. When did Vermont become a state?

_____ 7. What is the life of a cowboy like?

_____ 8. How many ways may a ball be kicked in the game of football?

_____ 9. Which state mines the most tin?

_____ 10. Where was tobacco first grown?

_____ 11. Name the different parts of the corn plant.

_____ 12. Where can daisies be found?

_____ 13. Do tornadoes occur in New England?

_____ 14. When were knickers popular in the United States?

_____ 15. How many bones are found in the human foot?

Challenge

Look up three of the key words from above in an encyclopedia index. How many references are made to it?

_____ (word) _____ (number of references)

_____ (word) _____ (number of references)

_____ (word) _____ (number of references)

Name _____

Furoshiki Bundle

Sadako's mother wrapped all of Sadako's favorite foods in a *furoshiki* bundle. The bundle contained an egg roll, rice, chicken, plums, and bean cakes. List the heading under which you might find information on these foods in a recipe book.

1. Egg roll   _____
2. Plums   _____
3. Rice   _____
4. Chicken   _____
5. Bean cakes   _____

Now, list five foods that someone might bring to you in a *furoshiki* bundle. Then list the heading under which each would be found in a recipe book.

1. _____
2. _____
3. _____
4. _____
5. _____

Name _____

Mumps, Measles, and Other Diseases

Index Sample

diphtheria
   description, 17
   contagion, 19
   recovery rate, 20

measles
   rubella, 61-63
   three-day, 64-65
   treatment, 68

mumps
   description, 72
   prevention, 75

scarlet fever
   cause, 85
   danger, 87
   prevention, 88

small pox
   history, 94-95
   contagion, 96
   prevention, 98

tetanus
   cause, 103
   incubation period, 105

whooping cough
   symptoms, 123
   incubation period, 105
   treatment, 127-128

Use the index sample to write the page numbers you would turn to in order to answer each question below.

_____ 1. How are people treated for whooping cough?

_____ 2. How did small pox affect people 400 years ago?

_____ 3. What is rubella?

_____ 4. How can mumps be prevented?

_____ 5. What are some of the dangers of scarlet fever?

_____ 6. How quickly does a person recover from diptheria?

_____ 7. What is mumps?

_____ 8. How can scarlet fever be prevented?

_____ 9. Is small pox highly contagious?

_____ 10. How does a person become infected with tetanus?

Challenge: Compare the dangers of these seven diseases today. Which diseases are still serious threats in North America? Which are very rare?

Name _Tamanna_

Place Value

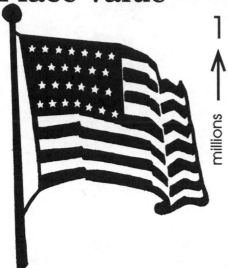

1 , 2 3 4 , 5 6 7

↑ ↑ ↑ ↑ ↑ ↑ ↑
millions hundred-thousands ten-thousands thousands hundreds tens ones

1. The number 8,672,019 has:

    __2__ thousands   __8__ millions

    __1__ ten   __9__ ones

    __6__ hundred-thousands   __7__ ten-thousands

    __0__ hundreds

2. What number has:

    6 ones   9 tens   8 thousands

    3 millions   7 hundreds   5 hundred-thousands

    4 ten-thousands

    The number is ___3,548,796___ .

3. The number 6,792,510 has:

    __9__ ten-thousands   __0__ ones

    __6__ millions   __2__ thousands

    __5__ hundreds   __1__ ten

    __7__ hundred-thousands

4. What number has:

    5 millions   6 thousands   4 ones

    3 tens   1 hundred   8 ten-thousands

    0 hundred-thousands

    The number is ___5,086,134___ .

Name _Tamanna_

The First State

What state is known as the first state? Follow the directions below to find out.

1. Put an A above number 2 if 31,842 rounded to the nearest thousand is 31,000.

2. Put an E above number 2 if 62 rounded to the nearest ten is 60.

3. Put an R above number 7 if 4,234 rounded to the nearest hundred is 4,200.

4. Put an L above number 3 if 677 rounded to the nearest hundred is 600.

5. Put an E above number 5 if 344 rounded to the nearest ten is 350.

6. Put an A above number 4 if 5,599 rounded to the nearest thousand is 6,000.

7. Put an A above number 6 if 1,549 rounded to the nearest hundred is 1,500.

8. Put a W above number 2 if 885 rounded to the nearest hundred is 800.

9. Put an E above number 8 if 521 rounded to the nearest ten is 520.

10. Put an R above number 6 if 74 rounded to the nearest ten is 80.

11. Put an L above number 3 if 3,291 rounded to the nearest thousand is 3,000.

12. Put an R above number 4 if 248 rounded to the nearest hundred is 300.

13. Put a D above number 1 if 615 rounded to the nearest ten is 620.

14. Put a W above number 1 if 188 rounded to the nearest ten is 200.

15. Put a W above number 5 if 6,817 rounded to the nearest thousand is 7,000.

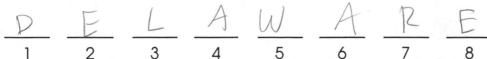

D	E	L	A	W	A	R	E
1	2	3	4	5	6	7	8

Daily Learning Drills Grade 4

Name _____

Underwater Addition

446
+ 489
935

476
+ 527
1003

509
+ 375
884

708
+ 507
1315

438
+ 419
857

334
+ 278
612

251
+ 368
619

464
+ 456
920

589
+ 322
911

288
+ 377
665

811
+ 386
1197

445
+ 476
921

831
+ 483
1314

810
+ 428
1238

531
+ 249
780

714
+ 185
899

767
+ 246
1013

609
+ 475
1084

319
+ 287
706

211
+ 396
607

230
+ 284
514

911
+ 427
1338

Name _____

Grand Prix Addition

Solve each problem. Beginning at 7,000, run through this racetrack to find out the path the race car took. When you reach 7,023, you're ready to exit and gas up for the next race.

3792 + 3225	1838 + 5178	3767 + 3248	1874 + 5140	4809 + 2204
1536 + 5482	3561 + 3458	3771 + 4213	2435 + 5214	1725 + 5287
1157 + 6412	4162 + 2858	4853 + 2156	4123 + 2887	5879 + 1132
3544 + 3478	1273 + 5748	3589 + 3419	5218 + 1789	4658 + 2348
5997 + 1026	5289 + 1713	3698 + 3305	4756 + 2248	4248 + 2757
4853 + 2147	2216 + 4785	3720 + 3698	3612 + 3552	1687 + 5662

Name _____

Fishy Problems

Solve each problem. Locate the fish in the aquarium that has the sum for each problem floating around in its stomach. Write the letter to match each answer in the box above each problem.

1. ☐
31,604
+ 29,217

2. ☐
47,215
+ 23,094

3. ☐
92,185
+ 18,293

4. ☐
20,815
+ 19,903

5. ☐
49,248
+ 27,181

6. ☐
53,614
+ 29,193

7. ☐
21,385
+ 23,492

8. ☐
45,218
+ 12,649

9. ☐
64,218
+ 13,924

10. ☐
81,346
+ 13,497

11. ☐
30,249
+ 28,926

12. ☐
42,618
+ 34,193

13. ☐
50,006
+ 29,999

14. ☐
26,149
+ 81,224

15. ☐
76,415
+ 21,248

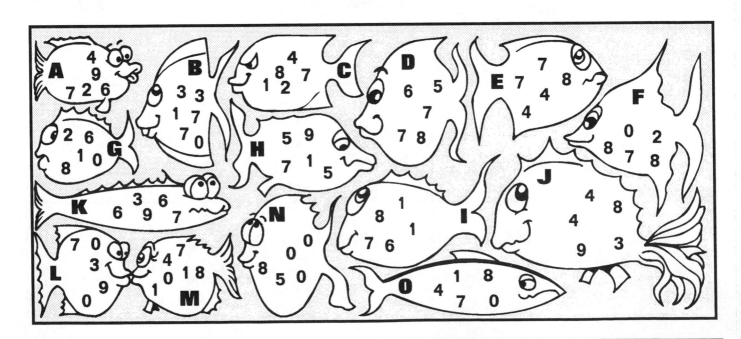

Name _____

Batter Up!

Complete each addition box.

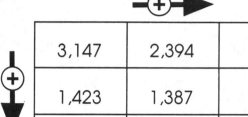

3,147	2,394	
1,423	1,387	

492	224	
118	303	

7,540	2,918	
1,387	2,913	

1,435	2,916	
3,192	2,921	

721	519	
908	286	

5,642	1,829	
2,819	6,425	

4,256	1,487	
1,842	2,143	

Name _____

Addition Slides

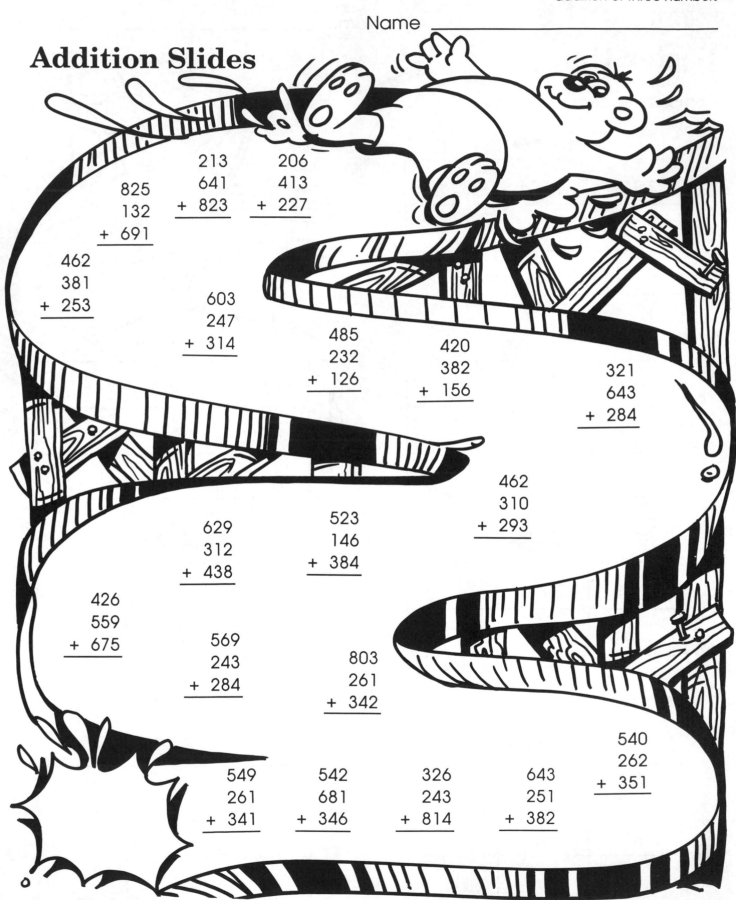

```
           213     206
    825    641     413
    132  + 823   + 227
  + 691
```

```
  462
  381            603
+ 253            247
               + 314        485              420
                            232              382                321
                          + 126            + 156              643
                                                            + 284
```

```
                                                              462
                                                              310
                            523                             + 293
                  629       146
                  312     + 384
                + 438
```

```
  426
  559       569
+ 675       243            803
          + 284            261
                         + 342
```

```
                                                              540
                                                              262
          549       542       326       643                 + 351
          261       681       243       251
        + 341     + 346     + 814     + 382
```

Name _____

Pinball Mathematics
Solve the problems in the pinball machine.

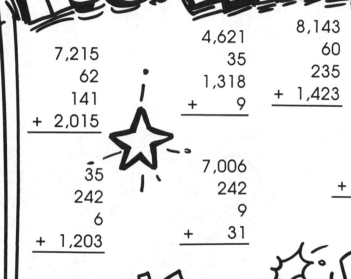

```
  7,215        4,621        8,143
     62           35           60
    141        1,318          235
+ 2,015      +     9      + 1,423
```

```
     35        7,006          521
    242          242        3,134
      6            9           64
+ 1,203      +    31      +   243
```

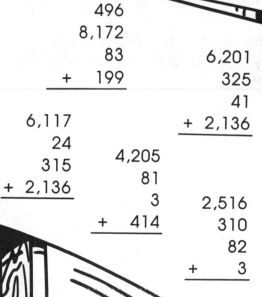

```
    496
  8,172      6,201        5,242        4,162        6,425
     83        325          342          328           41
+   199         41            8           41          324
            + 2,136      +    51      +   503      +     3
  6,117
     24      4,205
    315         81
+ 2,136          3        2,516
             +  414        310        5,426        2,481        3,204
                            82        310          2,514          182
                         +     3      512              2           23
                                    +     4      +    43      +     5
```

Name _____

Knowing When to Add

Circle the key addition words and solve the problems.

1. The choir at Madison School is made up of 26 girls and 18 boys. What is the total choir membership?

   ____ ◯ ____ = ____

2. The band at Madison School is composed of 19 girls and 22 boys. How many band members are there in all?

3. There are 214 girls and 263 boys attending Madison School. How many students altogether attend Madison School?

4. Next fall, in addition to the 477 students already at Madison, 248 more will be bussed in. Altogether, how many students will be at Madison School?

5. Mr. Mill's bus route is 14 miles long. Mrs. Albert's route is 17 miles long. Ms. Byrne's route is 15 miles long. How many miles altogether do these 3 bus routes cover?

6. The book rental at Madison is $8.00. The supplies cost $14.00. The locker fee is $3.00. What is the sum of these expenses?

7. The staff at Madison is made up of 24 teachers, 3 custodians and 2 administrators. How many staff members in all are there?

Name _____

Math Cranes

Across

2. 517
    − 228

3. 428
    − 249

4. 562
    − 274

5. 924
    − 348

6. 923
    − 346

7. 535
    − 248

8. 857
    − 389

9. 561
    − 247

11. 845
    − 599

13. 325
    − 186

14. 356
    − 168

4. 582
    − 346

8. 721
    − 240

Down

1. 421
    − 342

2. 627
    − 348

3. 362
    − 194

5. 824
    − 247

6. 921
    − 346

7. 926
    − 718

10. 768
    − 292

12. 826
    − 337

13. 247
    − 129

Timely Zeros

Name _____

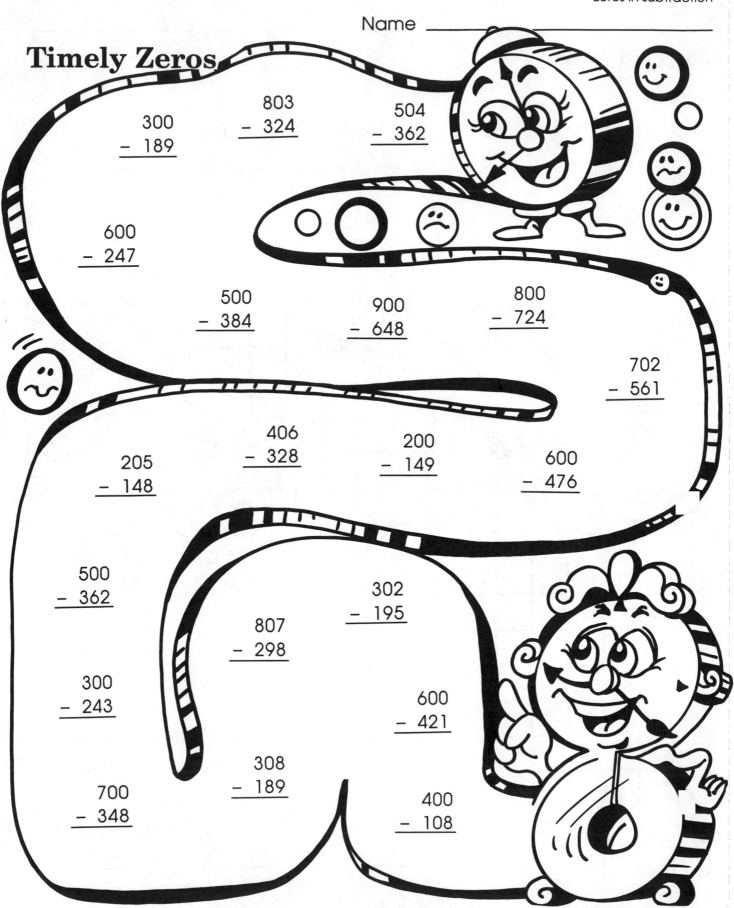

$$\begin{array}{r} 300 \\ -\ 189 \\ \hline \end{array}$$

$$\begin{array}{r} 803 \\ -\ 324 \\ \hline \end{array}$$

$$\begin{array}{r} 504 \\ -\ 362 \\ \hline \end{array}$$

$$\begin{array}{r} 600 \\ -\ 247 \\ \hline \end{array}$$

$$\begin{array}{r} 500 \\ -\ 384 \\ \hline \end{array}$$

$$\begin{array}{r} 900 \\ -\ 648 \\ \hline \end{array}$$

$$\begin{array}{r} 800 \\ -\ 724 \\ \hline \end{array}$$

$$\begin{array}{r} 702 \\ -\ 561 \\ \hline \end{array}$$

$$\begin{array}{r} 205 \\ -\ 148 \\ \hline \end{array}$$

$$\begin{array}{r} 406 \\ -\ 328 \\ \hline \end{array}$$

$$\begin{array}{r} 200 \\ -\ 149 \\ \hline \end{array}$$

$$\begin{array}{r} 600 \\ -\ 476 \\ \hline \end{array}$$

$$\begin{array}{r} 500 \\ -\ 362 \\ \hline \end{array}$$

$$\begin{array}{r} 807 \\ -\ 298 \\ \hline \end{array}$$

$$\begin{array}{r} 302 \\ -\ 195 \\ \hline \end{array}$$

$$\begin{array}{r} 300 \\ -\ 243 \\ \hline \end{array}$$

$$\begin{array}{r} 600 \\ -\ 421 \\ \hline \end{array}$$

$$\begin{array}{r} 700 \\ -\ 348 \\ \hline \end{array}$$

$$\begin{array}{r} 308 \\ -\ 189 \\ \hline \end{array}$$

$$\begin{array}{r} 400 \\ -\ 108 \\ \hline \end{array}$$

Name _____

Subtraction Maze

Work problems.

4172 − 1536	6723 − 2586	547 − 259	834 − 463	562 − 325	7146 − 3498
9427 − 6648	8149 − 5372	5389 − 1652	421 − 275	7456 − 3724	818 − 639
772 − 586	6529 − 4538	5379 − 2835	6275 − 3761	5612 − 1505	8355 − 5366

Shade in answers to find path.

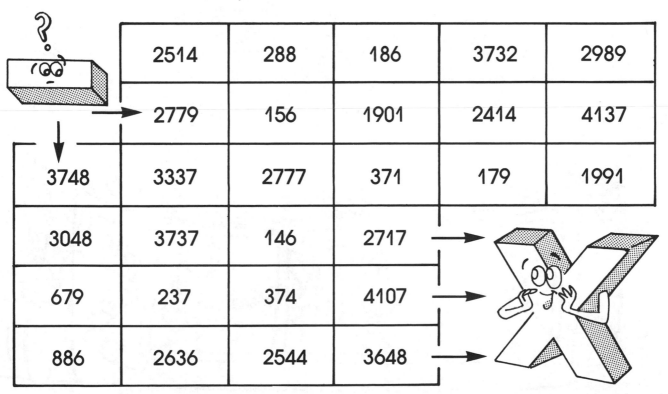

2514	288	186	3732	2989
2779	156	1901	2414	4137
3748	3337	2777	371	179	1991
3048	3737	146	2717		
679	237	374	4107		
886	2636	2544	3648		

Daily Learning Drills Grade 4

Name _____

High Class Math

$$\begin{array}{r} 3,270 \\ -\ 1,529 \\ \hline \end{array}$$

$$\begin{array}{r} 8,248 \\ -\ 1,513 \\ \hline \end{array}$$

$$\begin{array}{r} 7,648 \\ -\ 3,291 \\ \hline \end{array} \qquad \begin{array}{r} 4,321 \\ -\ 1,809 \\ \hline \end{array} \qquad \begin{array}{r} 8,241 \\ -\ 3,516 \\ \hline \end{array} \qquad \begin{array}{r} 3,002 \\ -\ 1,231 \\ \hline \end{array}$$

$$\begin{array}{r} 9,200 \\ -\ 3,146 \\ \hline \end{array}$$

$$\begin{array}{r} 8,254 \\ -\ 3,187 \\ \hline \end{array} \qquad \begin{array}{r} 7,265 \\ -\ 2,134 \\ \hline \end{array} \qquad \begin{array}{r} 3,846 \\ -\ 1,359 \\ \hline \end{array} \qquad \begin{array}{r} 8,006 \\ -\ 3,084 \\ \hline \end{array}$$

$$\begin{array}{r} 5,017 \\ -\ 2,408 \\ \hline \end{array}$$

$$\begin{array}{r} 6,265 \\ -\ 4,189 \\ \hline \end{array} \qquad \begin{array}{r} 4,824 \\ -\ 1,913 \\ \hline \end{array} \qquad \begin{array}{r} 6,205 \\ -\ 1,054 \\ \hline \end{array} \qquad \begin{array}{r} 5,253 \\ -\ 4,428 \\ \hline \end{array}$$

$$\begin{array}{r} 3,084 \\ -\ 1,926 \\ \hline \end{array}$$

$$\begin{array}{r} 9,205 \\ -\ 3,187 \\ \hline \end{array} \qquad \begin{array}{r} 5,809 \\ -\ 3,913 \\ \hline \end{array} \qquad \begin{array}{r} 5,642 \\ -\ 2,408 \\ \hline \end{array}$$

Name _____

Under the Big Top!

43	x	4	=	
x				
2	x	58	=	
=	⧄	x		
	x	7	=	
		=		

65	x	4	=	
x	⧄	x		
5	x	77	=	
=		=		

Name _____

More Multiplication

Put numbers in the □ 's to get correct answer.

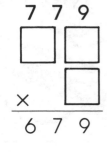

4 7 5	7 7 9	8 7 9
×	×	×
3 7 8	6 7 9	6 3 2

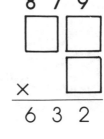 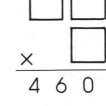

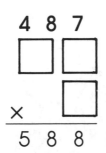

4 8 7	7 6 3	6 9 4	7 3 9	5 2 9
×	×	×	×	×
5 8 8	4 3 8	5 6 4	3 3 3	4 6 0

9 5 6	2 7 5	4 5 6	5 7 6	3 6 9
×	×	×	×	×
3 4 5	1 7 5	2 2 4	3 8 0	2 3 4

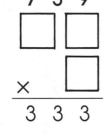 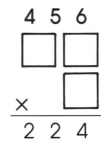 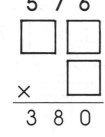 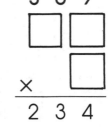

4 8 7	6 6 7	5 5 4	2 3 3	7 8 4
×	×	×	×	×
3 3 6	4 0 2	2 7 0	9 6	5 9 2

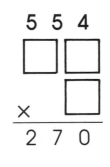 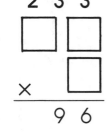 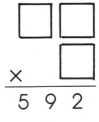

6 5 7	9 4 2	3 8 4	7 8 4	3 8 2
×	×	×	×	×
3 8 0	9 8	3 4 4	5 9 2	1 8 4

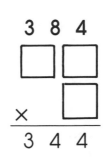 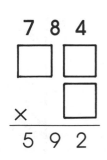

Name _____

Solve It!

What set of ridges, loops and whirls are different on every person? To find out, solve the following problems and put the corresponding letter above the answer at the bottom of the page.

I. 303
    x 3

R. 214
    x 2

N. 413
    x 2

N. 142
    x 2

R. 211
    x 4

F. 104
    x 2

T. 131
    x 2

E. 301
    x 2

I. 134
    x 1

G. 244
    x 2

S. 334
    x 2

P. 232
    x 3

208   909   826   488   602   844   696   428   134   284   262   668

Name _____

Space Math

Complete this space-walking mission!

817
x 6

923
x 2

326
x 5

281
x 4

406
x 3

204
x 8

231
x 6

262
x 7

214
x 2

218
x 5

126
x 9

306
x 7

241
x 8

329
x 6

310
x 5

421
x 6

431
x 3

814
x 9

231
x 4

624
x 7

896
x 1

742
x 8

525
x 4

606
x 7

Name _____

Amazing Arms

What will happen to a starfish that loses an arm? To find out, solve the following problems and put the corresponding letter above the answer at the bottom of the page.

O.   2,893
     x 4

W.   1,763
     x 3

W.   7,665
     x 5

A.   1,935
     x 6

W.   3,097
     x 3

E.   2,929
     x 4

G.   6,366
     x 5

T.   7,821
     x 8

L.   6,283
     x 7

I.   5,257
     x 3

R.   3,019
     x 6

N.   2,908
     x 7

I.   6,507
     x 8

N.   5,527
     x 2

L.   6,626
     x 3

O.   7,219
     x 9

E.   3,406
     x 6

____ ____   ____ ____ ____ ____   ____ ____ ____ ____
52,056 62,568   5,289 15,771 43,981 19,878   31,830 18,114 64,971 9,291

                                                             !

  ____   ____ ____ ____   ____ ____ ____
  11,610   20,356 20,436 38,325   11,572 11,054 11,716

Name _____

Multiplication Drill

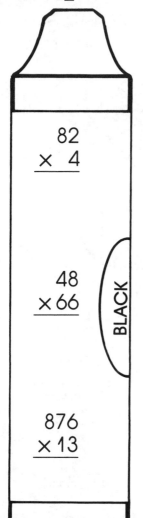
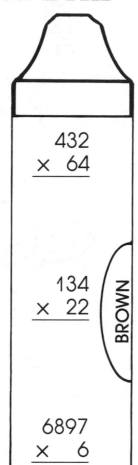

```
  82
×  4
```

```
  48
× 66
```
BLACK

```
 876
× 13
```

```
 432
×  64
```

```
 134
×  22
```
BROWN

```
6897
×   6
```

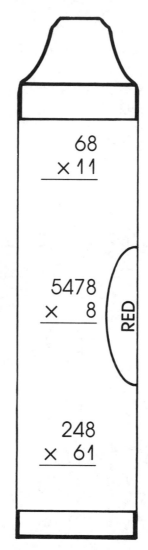

```
  68
× 11
```

```
5478
×   8
```
RED

```
 248
×  61
```

```
6798
×   5
```

```
  79
× 86
```
BLUE

```
 694
×  38
```

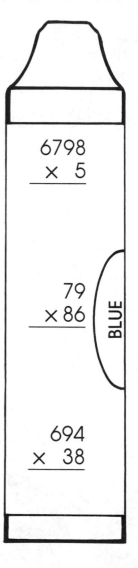

Color picture by matching answers with crayons.

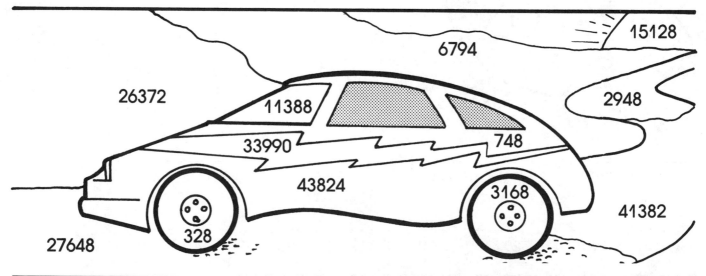

15128

6794

26372   11388   2948

33990   748

43824

                                   3168

27648   328   41382

Name _____

Elephant Escapades

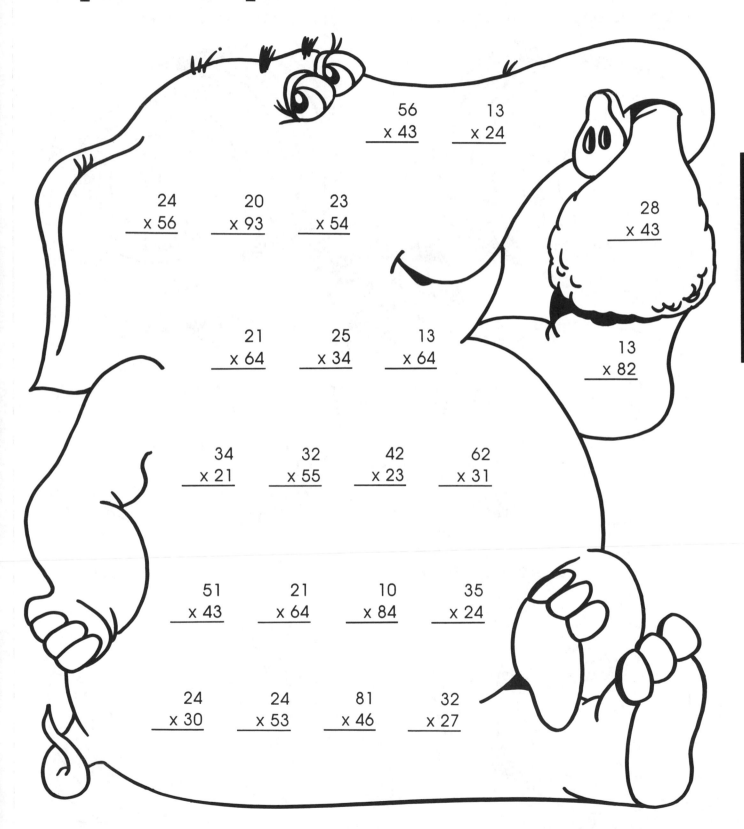

| 56 | 13 |
| x 43 | x 24 |

| 24 | 20 | 23 |
| x 56 | x 93 | x 54 |

| 28 |
| x 43 |

| 21 | 25 | 13 |
| x 64 | x 34 | x 64 |

| 13 |
| x 82 |

| 34 | 32 | 42 | 62 |
| x 21 | x 55 | x 23 | x 31 |

| 51 | 21 | 10 | 35 |
| x 43 | x 64 | x 84 | x 24 |

| 24 | 24 | 81 | 32 |
| x 30 | x 53 | x 46 | x 27 |

MATH

Name _____

Wheels of Wonder

Solve the following problems by multiplying each number by the power of 10 in the center.

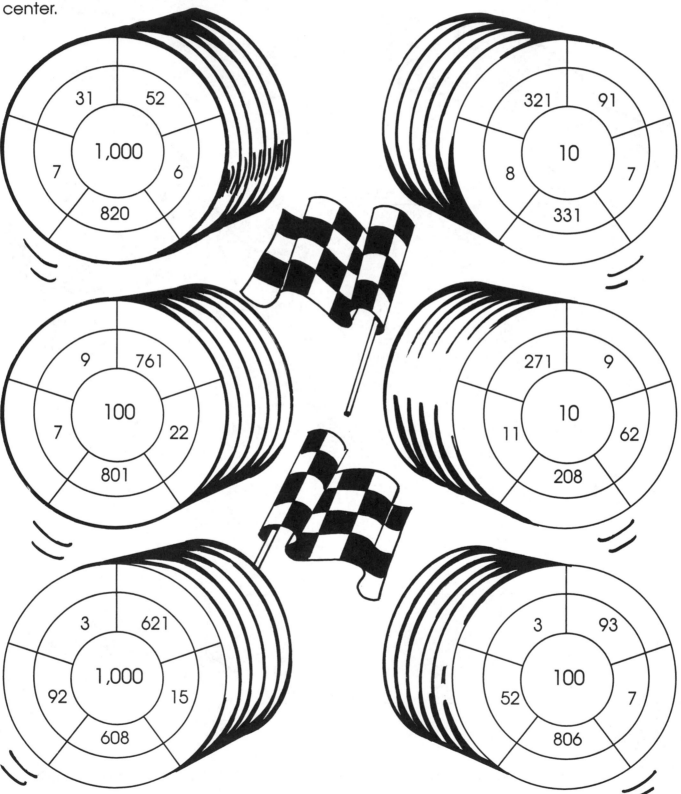

Name _____

Step by Step

Read the problems below. Solve each in the space provided.

Work space

1. Mr. Lundstrom knew they would have to be careful moving the gold. He had the Defense Club only move a small amount at a time. They moved 137 gold bars on Monday and on Tuesday. On Wednesday they moved 150 gold bars. They moved 121 gold bars on Thursday, on Friday, and on Saturday. How many bars were moved in the entire week? _____

2. The German soldiers moved quickly into Norway on the night of the blackout. 1,259 troops came in by parachute, 2,067 came to shore by boat, and 1,099 came in by truck. How many troops came to Norway on that first night? _____

3. Pretend that Peter and Helga could each carry 25 bars of gold on their sleds. They made 35 trips down to the fiord with their loads. How many bars did they move? _____

4. The children saw many small groups of soldiers marching. In one group they counted 53 soldiers. In another group, they counted 69 soldiers. In each of three groups, they counted 77. How many soldiers did they see?

_____

Name _____

Wacky Waldo's Snow Show

Wacky Waldo's Snow Show is an exciting and fantastic sight. Waldo has trained whales and bears to skate together on the ice. There is a hockey game between a team of sharks and a pack of wolves. Elephants ride sleds down steep hills. Horses and buffaloes ski swiftly down mountains.

1. Wacky Waldo has 4 ice-skating whales. He has 4 times as many bears who ice skate. How many bears can ice skate?

2. **Waldo's Snow Show** has 4 shows on Thursday, but it has 6 times as many shows on Saturday. How many shows are there on Saturday?

3. The Sharks' hockey team has 3 white sharks. It has 6 times as many tiger sharks. How many tiger sharks does it have?

4. The Wolves' hockey team has 4 gray wolves. It has 8 times as many red wolves. How many red wolves does it have?

5. Waldo taught 6 buffaloes to ski. He was able to teach 5 times as many horses to ski. How many horses did he teach?

6. Buff, a skiing buffalo, took 7 nasty spills when he was learning to ski. His friend Harry Horse fell down 8 times as often. How many times did Harry fall?

Name _____

Molly Mugwumps

Molly Mugwumps is the toughest kid in school. She picks fights with kindergarteners and spends more time in the office than the principal does.

1. Molly is the toughest football player in her school. She ran for 23 yards on one play and went 3 times as far on the next play. How far did she run the second time?

2. Molly keeps a rock collection. She has 31 rocks in one sack. She has 7 times as many under her bed. How many rocks are under her bed?

3. Molly had 42 marbles when she came to school. She went home with 4 times as many. How many did she go home with?

4. Molly stuffed 21 sticks of gum in her mouth in the morning. In the afternoon, she crammed 9 times as many sticks into her mouth. How many sticks did she have in the afternoon?

5. Molly got 51 problems wrong in math last week. This week, she missed 8 times as many. How many did she miss this week?

6. Molly was sent to the office 21 days last year. This year, she was sent 7 times as often. How many days did she go this year?

Daily Learning Drills Grade 4

Name _____

Snowball Bash

Help Pete climb down this
mound of giant snowballs!

7 ⟌ 84   5 ⟌ 75

3 ⟌ 45   9 ⟌ 99   4 ⟌ 88   5 ⟌ 80

4 ⟌ 64 3 ⟌ 57   3 ⟌ 78   3 ⟌ 72   8 ⟌ 96

2 ⟌ 86   2 ⟌ 38 6 ⟌ 66   5 ⟌ 65   4 ⟌ 52

4 ⟌ 68   6 ⟌ 78   7 ⟌ 91   2 ⟌ 42 6 ⟌ 72

Name _____

Scaling the Heights

Work the problems. To find the path to the top, the answers should match the problem number. Color the path.

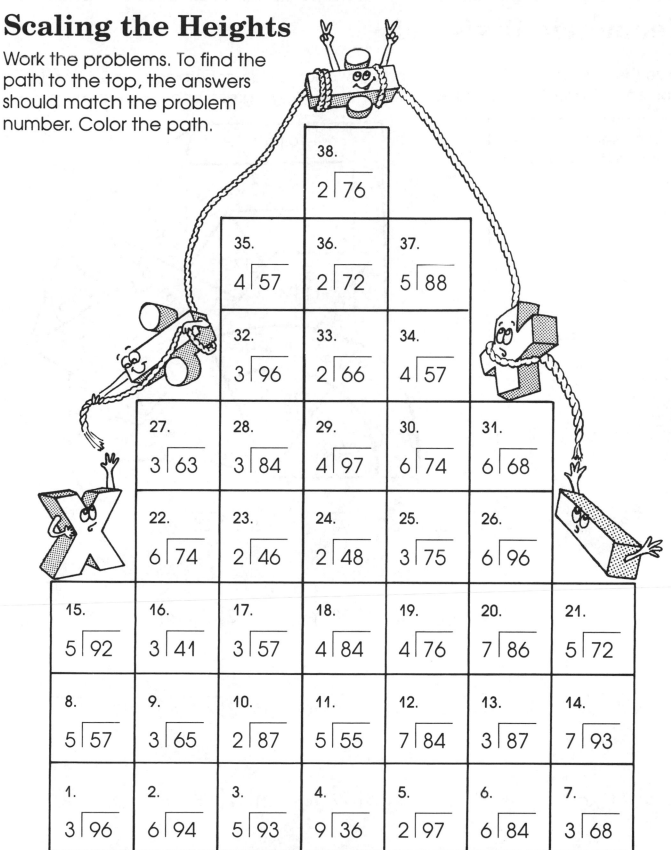

38.
$2\overline{)76}$

35.
$4\overline{)57}$

36.
$2\overline{)72}$

37.
$5\overline{)88}$

32.
$3\overline{)96}$

33.
$2\overline{)66}$

34.
$4\overline{)57}$

27.
$3\overline{)63}$

28.
$3\overline{)84}$

29.
$4\overline{)97}$

30.
$6\overline{)74}$

31.
$6\overline{)68}$

22.
$6\overline{)74}$

23.
$2\overline{)46}$

24.
$2\overline{)48}$

25.
$3\overline{)75}$

26.
$6\overline{)96}$

15.
$5\overline{)92}$

16.
$3\overline{)41}$

17.
$3\overline{)57}$

18.
$4\overline{)84}$

19.
$4\overline{)76}$

20.
$7\overline{)86}$

21.
$5\overline{)72}$

8.
$5\overline{)57}$

9.
$3\overline{)65}$

10.
$2\overline{)87}$

11.
$5\overline{)55}$

12.
$7\overline{)84}$

13.
$3\overline{)87}$

14.
$7\overline{)93}$

1.
$3\overline{)96}$

2.
$6\overline{)94}$

3.
$5\overline{)93}$

4.
$9\overline{)36}$

5.
$2\overline{)97}$

6.
$6\overline{)84}$

7.
$3\overline{)68}$

MATH

Name _____

Geometric Division!

Solve the division problems below and color each shape according to the matching problem and quotient (b = blue, r = red, y = yellow, g = green and p = purple).

Name seven shapes that are in the design.
1. _____
2. _____
3. _____
4. _____
5. _____
6. _____
7. _____

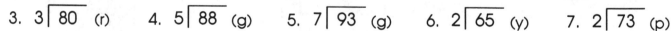

19 R3
14 R1
13 R2
23 R1
47 R1
21 R2
17 R3
11 R4
18 R1
12 R3
24 R1
15 R3
14 R3
32 R1
31 R2
32 R1
38 R1
17 R2
26 R2
36 R1
27 R2
14 R4

1. $2\overline{)65}$ (b)   2. $4\overline{)86}$ (b)

3. $3\overline{)80}$ (r)   4. $5\overline{)88}$ (g)   5. $7\overline{)93}$ (g)   6. $2\overline{)65}$ (y)   7. $2\overline{)73}$ (p)

8. $4\overline{)79}$ (y)   9. $3\overline{)55}$ (y)   10. $6\overline{)88}$ (g)   11. $2\overline{)77}$ (r)   12. $3\overline{)70}$ (y)

13. $6\overline{)70}$ (g)   14. $5\overline{)73}$ (y)   15. $4\overline{)57}$ (p)   16. $2\overline{)49}$ (b)   17. $4\overline{)70}$ (r)

18. $5\overline{)78}$ (r)   19. $3\overline{)95}$ (y)   20. $8\overline{)99}$ (p)   21. $2\overline{)95}$ (r)   22. $3\overline{)83}$ (p)

Name _____

On-Stage Division

6) 888   2) 956   2) 712

4) 860   6) 750   9) 999

8) 968   3) 774   5) 735   8) 920   5) 845

7) 805   8) 984   4) 500   2) 846   4) 712

6) 810   7) 882

3) 642   3) 477

Name _____

Puzzling Problems

Solve the following problems. Write the answers in the puzzle.
Hint: Remainders (R) take up their own box.

Across

2. $2\overline{)917}$ 4. $6\overline{)830}$

7. $4\overline{)975}$ 8. $2\overline{)859}$

12. $2\overline{)779}$ 14. $3\overline{)475}$

16. $3\overline{)680}$ 17. $8\overline{)988}$

18. $3\overline{)971}$ 19. $5\overline{)927}$

Down

1. $3\overline{)776}$ 3. $7\overline{)948}$ 5. $3\overline{)740}$

6. $7\overline{)897}$ 9. $4\overline{)751}$ 10. $5\overline{)714}$

11. $4\overline{)639}$ 13. $6\overline{)749}$ 15. $5\overline{)634}$

Name _____

Division Checklist

Work the problems. Draw a line
from the division problem to the
matching checking problem.

$3\overline{)56}$ ————— $\begin{array}{r} 18 \\ \times\ 3 \\ \hline \end{array}$ $3\overline{)64}$ $\begin{array}{r} 92 \\ \times\ 3 \\ \hline \end{array}$ $3\overline{)276}$

$3\overline{)127}$ $\begin{array}{r} 59 \\ \times\ 3 \\ \hline \end{array}$ $3\overline{)178}$ $\begin{array}{r} 21 \\ \times\ 3 \\ \hline \end{array}$ $3\overline{)175}$

$\begin{array}{r} 42 \\ \times\ 3 \\ \hline \end{array}$ $3\overline{)236}$ $\begin{array}{r} 10 \\ \times\ 3 \\ \hline \end{array}$ $3\overline{)32}$ $\begin{array}{r} 58 \\ \times\ 3 \\ \hline \end{array}$

$\begin{array}{r} 28 \\ \times\ 3 \\ \hline \end{array}$ $3\overline{)86}$ $\begin{array}{r} 78 \\ \times\ 3 \\ \hline \end{array}$ $3\overline{)247}$ $\begin{array}{r} 82 \\ \times\ 3 \\ \hline \end{array}$

MATH

Name _____

From Cocoons to Butterflies

Work problems. Draw line connecting cocoon with butterfly.

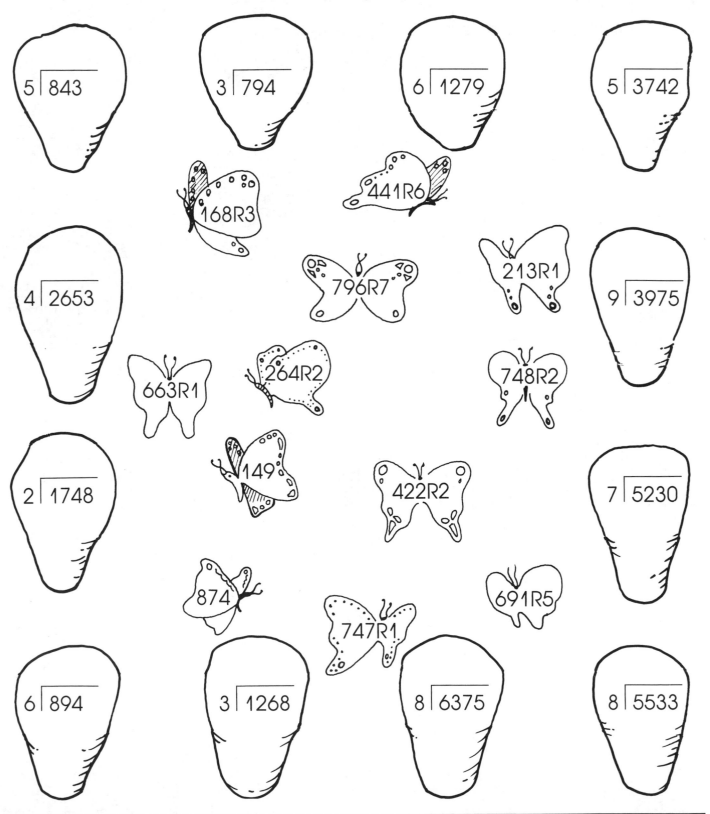

Name _____

Marty's Mania

Help Marty eat all the cheese by traveling the route.

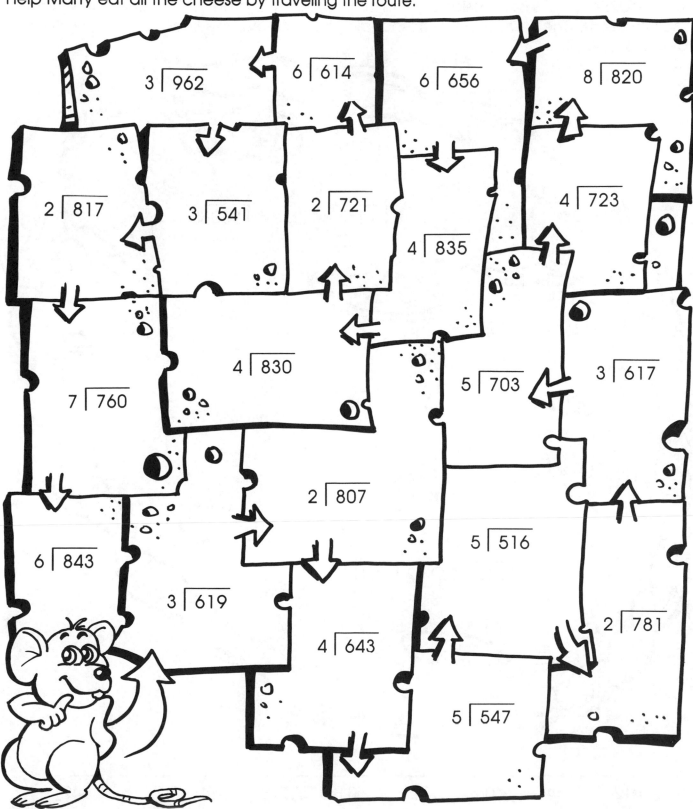

Name _____

Yum! Yum!

What edible fungus is occasionally found on pizzas or in omelets? To find out, solve the problems. Then, write the corresponding letter above the answer at the bottom of the page.

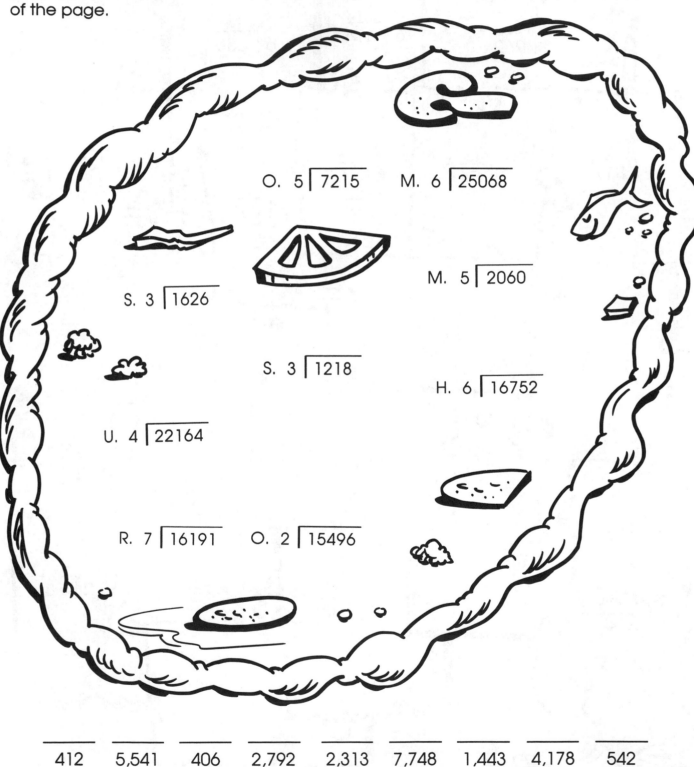

O. 5 ⟌ 7215   M. 6 ⟌ 25068

S. 3 ⟌ 1626

M. 5 ⟌ 2060

S. 3 ⟌ 1218

H. 6 ⟌ 16752

U. 4 ⟌ 22164

R. 7 ⟌ 16191   O. 2 ⟌ 15496

| 412 | 5,541 | 406 | 2,792 | 2,313 | 7,748 | 1,443 | 4,178 | 542 |

Name _____

Flying High

Solve the problems in this incredible dragon kite!

18 ⟌ 130   45 ⟌ 140   13 ⟌ 92

24 ⟌ 164

53 ⟌ 320   42 ⟌ 90   24 ⟌ 98   22 ⟌ 70

17 ⟌ 104   35 ⟌ 42   18 ⟌ 75

41 ⟌ 92

26 ⟌ 80

12 ⟌ 75   19 ⟌ 100   43 ⟌ 221

61 ⟌ 185

32 ⟌ 193

16 ⟌ 90   23 ⟌ 74

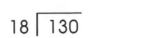

Daily Learning Drills Grade 4

Name _____

Lizzy the Lizard Bags Her Bugs

Lizzy the Lizard is a great hunter
of insects. She separates her
bugs into separate bags so that
her lunch is ready for the week.
Help her decide how to divide
the bugs.

1. Lizzy bagged 45 cockroaches.
She put 5 into each bag. How
many bags did she use?

2. Lizzy found 32 termites. She
put 4 into each bag. How
many bags did she need?

3. Lizzy captured 49 stinkbugs.
She put them into 7 bags. How
many stinkbugs were in each
bag?

4. Lizzy captured 27 horn
beetles. She used 3 bags.
How many beetles went into
each bag?

5. Lizzy lassoed 36 butterflies.
She put 9 into each bag. How
many bags did she need?

6. Lizzy went fishing and caught
48 water beetles. She used 6
bags for her catch. How many
beetles went into each bag?

Name _____

Bargain Bonanza at Pat's Pet Place

Pat is having a gigantic sale at his place. Help him divide his animals into groups for the sale.

1. Pat got 84 rabbits. He is putting 4 rabbits in each cage. How many cages does he need?

2. Pat sells guppies in plastic bags with 5 guppies in each bag. He has 195 guppies. How many plastic bags does he need?

3. Pat has 392 white mice. They are kept in cages of 7 mice each. How many cages does Pat need?

4. Pat has 324 goldfish. If he puts 6 goldfish in each bag, how many plastic bags will he need?

5. Pat received 116 hamsters. He keeps them in cages of 4 each. How many cages does he need for his hamsters?

6. Pat has 120 parrots. They live in bird cages with 3 to each cage. How many bird cages does Pat need?

MATH

Daily Learning Drills Grade 4

Name _____

Number Puzzles

1

Write your age. _____

Multiply it by 3. _____

Add 18. _____

Multiply by 2. _____

Subtract 36. _____

Divide by 6. (your age) _____

2

Write any number. _____

Double that number. _____

Add 15. _____

Double again. _____

Subtract 30. _____

Divide by 2. _____

Divide by 2 again. _____

3

Write any two-digit number. _____

Double that number. _____

Add 43. _____

Subtract 18. _____

Add 11. _____

Divide by 2. _____

Subtract 18. _____

4

Write the number of children in your class. _____

Double that number. _____

Add 15. _____

Double it again. _____

Subtract 30. _____

Divide by 4. _____

Name _____

Which Problem Is Correct?

One of the methods of solution at the left is correct for the problem. Pick the correct method of solution and finish solving the problem.

1.
$$\begin{array}{r} 56 \\ +17 \\ \hline \end{array} \qquad \begin{array}{r} 56 \\ -17 \\ \hline \end{array}$$
Bill and his friends collect baseball cards. Bill has 17 fewer cards than Mack. Bill has 56 cards. How many baseball cards does Mack have?

2.
$$\begin{array}{r} 54 \\ \times\ 3 \\ \hline \end{array} \qquad 3\ \overline{)54}$$
Amos bought 54 baseball cards. He already had 3 times as many. How many baseball cards did Amos have before his latest purchase?

3.
$$\begin{array}{r} 3.80 \\ +3.50 \\ \hline \end{array} \qquad \begin{array}{r} 3.80 \\ -3.50 \\ \hline \end{array}$$
Joe paid $3.50 for a "Mickey Mantle" baseball card. "Ted Williams" cost him $3.80. How much more did he pay for "Ted Williams" than for "Mickey Mantle"?

4.
$$\begin{array}{r} 3.60 \\ \times\ 9 \\ \hline \end{array} \qquad 9\ \overline{)3.60}$$
Will bought 9 baseball cards for $3.60. How much did he pay per card?

5.
$$\begin{array}{r} 8.00 \\ +\ .50 \\ \hline \end{array} \qquad \begin{array}{r} 8.00 \\ -\ .50 \\ \hline \end{array}$$
"Babe Ruth" baseball cards were selling for $8.00. "Herb Score" baseball cards sold for 50¢. "Herb Score" cards sold for how much less than "Babe Ruth" cards?

6.
$$\begin{array}{r} 0.75 \\ \times\ 8 \\ \hline \end{array} \qquad 8\ \overline{)0.75}$$
Andy bought 8 baseball cards at 75¢ each. How much did Andy pay in all?

Name _____

Identifying Operations

Decide which sign is correct for
each problem and put in blank.

5 ◯ 5 = 10   14 ◯ 59 = 73   21 ◯ 9 = 30   36 ◯ 63 = 99

9 ◯ 9 = 81   56 ◯ 17 = 73   64 ◯ 8 = 8   6 ◯ 9 = 54

56 ◯ 8 = 48   40 ◯ 5 = 8   7 ◯ 8 = 56   33 ◯ 57 = 90

91 ◯ 16 = 75   9 ◯ 3 = 27   76 ◯ 19 = 57   27 ◯ 3 = 9

54 ◯ 6 = 9   29 ◯ 37 = 66   43 ◯ 7 = 50   63 ◯ 9 = 54

28 ◯ 17 = 11   6 ◯ 5 = 30   4 ◯ 9 = 36   8 ◯ 38 = 46

25 ◯ 5 = 5   36 ◯ 5 = 31   48 ◯ 8 = 6   2 ◯ 9 = 18

72 ◯ 9 = 63   56 ◯ 8 = 7   9 ◯ 1 = 9   55 ◯ 37 = 92

64 ◯ 8 = 56   7 ◯ 1 = 7   45 ◯ 5 = 9   81 ◯ 9 = 9

36 ◯ 4 = 9   57 ◯ 9 = 48   36 ◯ 27 = 63   80 ◯ 17 = 63

45 ◯ 5 = 40   7 ◯ 6 = 42   48 ◯ 6 = 42   32 ◯ 4 = 8

82 ◯ 9 = 91   8 ◯ 8 = 64   9 ◯ 8 = 72   71 ◯ 15 = 86

17 ◯ 77 = 94   40 ◯ 6 = 34   47 ◯ 38 = 9   56 ◯ 9 = 47

36 ◯ 6 = 30   15 ◯ 38 = 53   3 ◯ 6 = 18   6 ◯ 6 = 36

72 ◯ 8 = 9   43 ◯ 48 = 91   27 ◯ 18 = 45   5 ◯ 9 = 45

49 ◯ 7 = 7   7 ◯ 7 = 49   8 ◯ 3 = 24   16 ◯ 16 = 32

Name _____

Work It Out

The average is the result of dividing the sum of addends by the number of addends. Match the problem with its answer.

62
79
+ 87
228

$$3\overline{)228}$$ 76

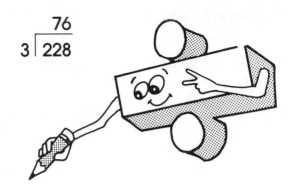

1. 80 + 100 + 90 + 95 + 100 •   A.   53

2. 52 + 56 + 51 •   B.   190

3. 85 + 80 + 95 + 95 + 100 •   C.   410

4. 782 + 276 + 172 •   D.   91

5. 125 + 248 + 214 + 173 •   E.   93

6. 81 + 82 + 91 + 78 •   F.   55

7. 40 + 60 + 75 + 45 •   G.   83

8. 278 + 246 •   H.   33

9. 75 + 100 + 100 + 70 + 100 •   I.   3

10. 0 + 0 + 0 + 0 + 15 •   J.   262

11. 21 + 34 + 44 •   K.   89

12. 437 + 509 + 864 + 274 •   L.   94

13. 80 + 80 + 100 + 95 + 95 •   M.   8

14. 4 + 6 + 7 + 12 + 11 •   N.   90

15. 75 + 100 + 100 + 100 + 95 •   O.   521

MATH

Name _____

Sport Problems

Work problems by averaging. Shade in answers.

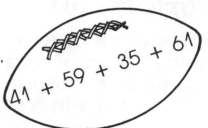

$41 + 59 + 35 + 61$

$54 + 75 + 16 + 28 + 32$

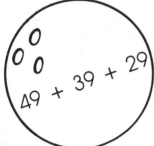

$49 + 39 + 29$

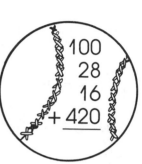

$$100$$
$$28$$
$$16$$
$$+ \ 420$$

$25 + 30 + 68$

$95 + 103 + 78$

$$18$$
$$27$$
$$34$$
$$28$$
$$33$$
$$+ \ 16$$

$$13$$
$$19$$
$$17$$
$$12$$
$$+ \ 14$$

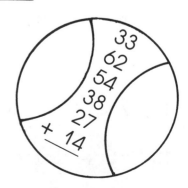

$$33$$
$$62$$
$$54$$
$$38$$
$$27$$
$$+ \ 14$$

Name _____

What Fraction Am I?

Identify the fraction for each shaded section.

A. _____

B. _____   H. _____

C. _____   I. _____

D. _____   J. _____

E. _____   K. _____

F. _____   L. _____

G. _____   M. _____

Name _____

Picture the Problem

Draw a picture of each problem. Then solve the problem.

1. Andy had two ropes of the same length. He cut one rope into 2 equal parts and gave the 2 halves to Bill. The other rope he cut into 4ths and gave 2 of the 4ths to Sue. Who got the most rope?

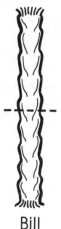 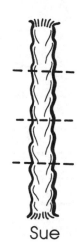

Bill   Sue

2. Henry cut an 8-foot log into 4 equal pieces and burned 2 of them in the fireplace. Joseph cut an 8-foot log into 8 equal pieces and put 3 of them in the fireplace. Who put the most wood in the fireplace?

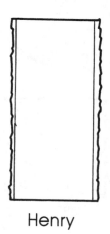 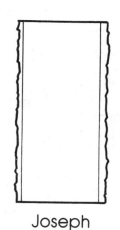

Henry   Joseph

3. Mr. Johns built an office building with an aisle down the middle. He divided one side into 6 equal spaces. He divided the other side into 9 equal spaces. The Ace Company rented 5 of the 9ths. The Best Company rented 4 of the 6ths. Which company rented the larger space?

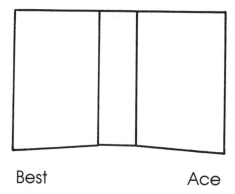

Best   Ace

4. The 4-H Club display area at the state fair was divided into 2 equal areas. One of these sections had 12 booths, the other 9 booths. The flower display covered 3 of the 9ths, and the melon display covered 4 of the 12ths. Which display had the most room?

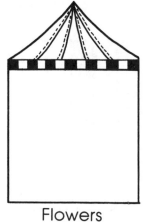 

Flowers   Melons

Name _____

Dare to Compare

Compare the fractions below. Use >, < and =.

$\frac{1}{8}$ ◯ $\frac{1}{16}$ $\frac{3}{4}$ ◯ $\frac{3}{4}$ $\frac{3}{6}$ ◯ $\frac{2}{3}$

$\frac{1}{5}$ ◯ $\frac{3}{10}$ $\frac{4}{7}$ ◯ $\frac{3}{7}$ $\frac{3}{8}$ ◯ $\frac{2}{8}$

$\frac{1}{2}$ ◯ $\frac{3}{6}$ $\frac{1}{3}$ ◯ $\frac{1}{2}$ $\frac{1}{4}$ ◯ $\frac{5}{8}$

$\frac{1}{2}$ ◯ $\frac{3}{4}$ $\frac{4}{6}$ ◯ $\frac{4}{6}$ $\frac{2}{5}$ ◯ $\frac{2}{10}$

$\frac{3}{8}$ ◯ $\frac{6}{8}$ $\frac{5}{6}$ ◯ $\frac{3}{4}$

Daily Learning Drills Grade 4

Name _____

More Than Peanuts

Use >, < and = to compare the fractions below.

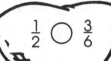

$\frac{3}{8} \bigcirc \frac{2}{8}$

$\frac{1}{2} \bigcirc \frac{3}{6}$

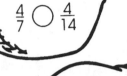

$\frac{2}{3} \bigcirc \frac{3}{6}$

$\frac{3}{6} \bigcirc \frac{1}{2}$

$\frac{4}{7} \bigcirc \frac{4}{14}$

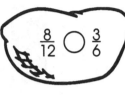

$\frac{7}{14} \bigcirc \frac{1}{2}$

$\frac{7}{10} \bigcirc \frac{2}{5}$

$\frac{8}{12} \bigcirc \frac{3}{6}$

$\frac{1}{3} \bigcirc \frac{6}{9}$

$\frac{4}{7} \bigcirc \frac{3}{7}$

$\frac{3}{4} \bigcirc \frac{3}{4}$

$\frac{4}{8} \bigcirc \frac{8}{16}$

$\frac{1}{3} \bigcirc \frac{2}{6}$

$\frac{2}{8} \bigcirc \frac{1}{2}$

$\frac{4}{7} \bigcirc \frac{4}{14}$

$\frac{1}{5} \bigcirc \frac{3}{10}$

$\frac{6}{11} \bigcirc \frac{5}{11}$

$\frac{6}{12} \bigcirc \frac{1}{2}$

$\frac{2}{3} \bigcirc \frac{2}{6}$

$\frac{7}{12} \bigcirc \frac{2}{4}$

$\frac{5}{6} \bigcirc \frac{1}{3}$

$\frac{7}{10} \bigcirc \frac{3}{10}$

$\frac{1}{2} \bigcirc \frac{8}{12}$

$\frac{1}{5} \bigcirc \frac{8}{10}$

$\frac{7}{8} \bigcirc \frac{2}{4}$

$\frac{1}{3} \bigcirc \frac{5}{6}$

$\frac{3}{8} \bigcirc \frac{1}{4}$

$\frac{2}{5} \bigcirc \frac{5}{10}$

$\frac{5}{6} \bigcirc \frac{2}{3}$

$\frac{6}{10} \bigcirc \frac{2}{5}$

$\frac{6}{10} \bigcirc \frac{3}{10}$

$\frac{3}{6} \bigcirc \frac{6}{12}$

$\frac{1}{8} \bigcirc \frac{1}{4}$

$\frac{1}{2} \bigcirc \frac{1}{4}$

$\frac{5}{6} \bigcirc \frac{2}{3}$

$\frac{5}{8} \bigcirc \frac{1}{4}$

Name _____

Match the Fractions

Under each bar, write a fraction for the shaded part. Then, match each fraction on the left with its equivalent fraction on the right.

1. _____   a. _____

2. _____   b. _____

3. _____   c. _____

4. _____   d. _____

5. _____   e. _____

6. _____   f. _____

7. _____   g. _____

8. _____   h. _____

Name _____

Oh, My!

Draw the correct mouths on the animals by finding the whole number for each fraction.

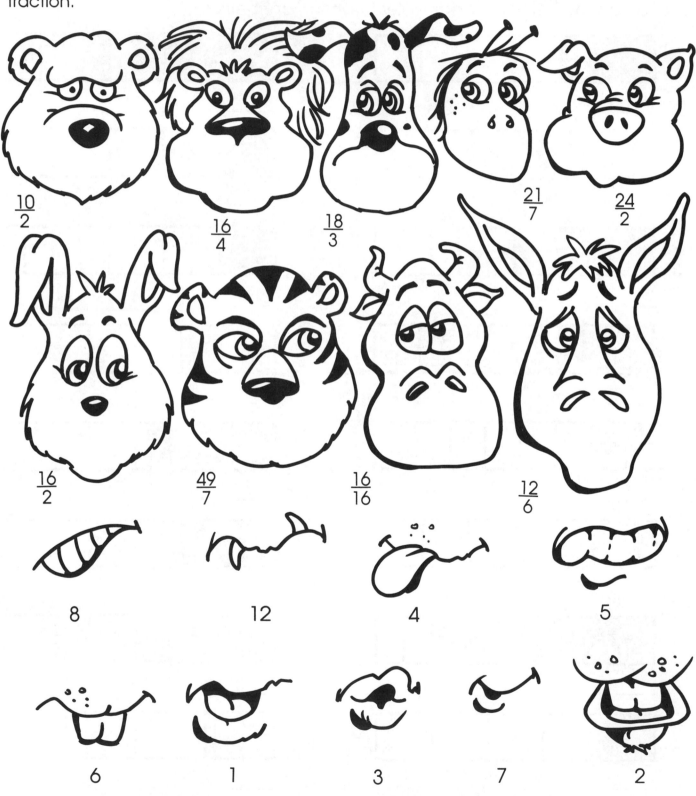

$\frac{10}{2}$

$\frac{16}{4}$

$\frac{18}{3}$

$\frac{21}{7}$

$\frac{24}{2}$

$\frac{16}{2}$

$\frac{49}{7}$

$\frac{16}{16}$

$\frac{12}{6}$

8

12

4

5

6

1

3

7

2

Name _____

Reduce the Fat Grams

Help this reducing machine function properly! Reduce each fraction.

$\frac{5}{25}$ = $\frac{8}{16}$ = $\frac{12}{18}$ = $\frac{10}{25}$ = $\frac{12}{30}$ = $\frac{3}{30}$ =

$\frac{6}{30}$ = $\frac{12}{20}$ = $\frac{3}{18}$ = $\frac{3}{9}$ = $\frac{4}{26}$ = $\frac{4}{28}$ =

$\frac{7}{21}$ = $\frac{16}{20}$ = $\frac{2}{10}$ = $\frac{3}{27}$ = $\frac{5}{60}$ =

$\frac{21}{35}$ = $\frac{3}{12}$ = $\frac{24}{40}$ = $\frac{8}{24}$ =

$\frac{16}{40}$ = $\frac{9}{36}$ = $\frac{15}{25}$ = $\frac{7}{35}$ =

Name _____

"Gator Aid"

Climb these obstacle ledges to the top.

$$\frac{3}{7} = \frac{}{21}$$

$$\frac{4}{5} = \frac{}{20}$$

$$\frac{4}{6} = \frac{}{18}$$

$$\frac{1}{3} = \frac{}{24}$$

$$\frac{2}{3} = \frac{}{15}$$

$$\frac{2}{3} = \frac{4}{}$$

$$\frac{1}{2} = \frac{6}{}$$

$$\frac{5}{7} = \frac{}{49}$$

$$\frac{7}{9} = \frac{14}{}$$

$$\frac{2}{3} = \frac{}{12}$$

$$\frac{4}{9} = \frac{}{27}$$

$$\frac{1}{6} = \frac{}{24}$$

$$\frac{4}{7} = \frac{}{28}$$

$$\frac{1}{2} = \frac{4}{}$$

$$\frac{1}{6} = \frac{}{36}$$

$$\frac{5}{10} = \frac{}{20}$$

$$\frac{1}{8} = \frac{}{16}$$

$$\frac{1}{3} = \frac{}{12}$$

$$\frac{2}{5} = \frac{4}{}$$

$$\frac{4}{9} = \frac{}{27}$$

$$\frac{2}{3} = \frac{}{9}$$

$$\frac{1}{2} = \frac{}{16}$$

$$\frac{3}{8} = \frac{}{24}$$

$$\frac{2}{5} = \frac{}{25}$$

$$\frac{1}{4} = \frac{4}{}$$

$$\frac{2}{7} = \frac{}{14}$$

$$\frac{3}{6} = \frac{}{12}$$

Name _____

Figure It Out

Work problems. Connect the
dots in order of answers.

1. $3\frac{3}{4} = \frac{\quad}{4}$

2. $\frac{9}{2} = 4\frac{\quad}{2}$

3. $\frac{30}{11} = 2\frac{\quad}{11}$

4. $8\frac{1}{2} = \frac{\quad}{2}$

5. $\frac{10}{6} = 1\frac{\quad}{6}$

6. $4\frac{3}{8} = \frac{\quad}{8}$

7. $4\frac{1}{5} = \frac{\quad}{5}$

8. $\frac{11}{3} = 3\frac{\quad}{3}$

9. $\frac{13}{7} = 1\frac{\quad}{7}$

10. $3\frac{5}{6} = \frac{\quad}{6}$

11. $1\frac{5}{6} = \frac{\quad}{6}$

12. $\frac{13}{5} = 2\frac{\quad}{5}$

13. $4\frac{1}{3} = \frac{\quad}{3}$

14. $\frac{12}{7} = 1\frac{\quad}{7}$

15. $2\frac{2}{5} = \frac{\quad}{5}$

16. $6\frac{2}{5} = \frac{\quad}{5}$

17. $1\frac{1}{9} = \frac{\quad}{9}$

18. $\frac{13}{8} = 1\frac{\quad}{8}$

19. $1\frac{2}{5} = \frac{\quad}{5}$

20. $1\frac{1}{8} = \frac{\quad}{8}$

• 3 • 5

23 •   • 32

2 •   • 5

• 9

• 8   • 15

35 •

17 •   1 •

• 4

7 •

• 21

10 •

• 6

12 •   • 13   • 11

Name _____

Make the Move

Lighten the load by solving the puzzle.

Down

1. $\frac{3}{4}$ of 12

3. $\frac{1}{5}$ of 25

5. $\frac{8}{9}$ of 27

6. $\frac{3}{6}$ of 18

7. $\frac{3}{8}$ of 16

12. $\frac{2}{11}$ of 22

13. $\frac{3}{4}$ of 24

15. $\frac{1}{8}$ of 16

Across

2. $\frac{3}{10}$ of 20

4. $\frac{9}{10}$ of 20

8. $\frac{1}{3}$ of 15

9. $\frac{7}{9}$ of 9

10. $\frac{1}{3}$ of 12

11. $\frac{1}{8}$ of 16

12. $\frac{7}{8}$ of 16

14. $\frac{1}{5}$ of 15

15. $\frac{1}{6}$ of 18

16. $\frac{2}{5}$ of 10

Name _____

Make a Wish

Begin this acrobatic challenge of mathematics and skill. Work your way to the top and make a little magic for Marty the mouse.

$\frac{7}{8}$ of 16 $\frac{3}{7}$ of 49 $\frac{4}{6}$ of 60

$\frac{3}{6}$ of 54 $\frac{6}{8}$ of 24 $\frac{9}{12}$ of 36

$\frac{9}{12}$ of 24 $\frac{2}{5}$ of 25 $\frac{3}{8}$ of 32

$\frac{5}{7}$ of 42 $\frac{3}{4}$ of 48 $\frac{3}{7}$ of 35

$\frac{7}{9}$ of 36 $\frac{6}{8}$ of 64 $\frac{8}{9}$ of 81

$\frac{3}{6}$ of 24 $\frac{5}{6}$ of 30 $\frac{9}{10}$ of 40

$\frac{6}{8}$ of 72 $\frac{9}{11}$ of 33 $\frac{3}{8}$ of 48

Name _____

The Ultimate Adding Machine

Find the sum for each problem. Reduce to lowest terms.

$\frac{1}{9} + \frac{3}{9}$

$\frac{7}{9} + \frac{1}{9}$

$\frac{4}{12} + \frac{3}{12}$

$\frac{3}{6} + \frac{2}{6}$

$\frac{4}{10} + \frac{2}{10}$

$\frac{3}{6} + \frac{2}{6}$

$\frac{5}{9} + \frac{3}{9}$

$\frac{2}{5} + \frac{1}{5}$

$\frac{5}{11} + \frac{5}{11}$

$\frac{3}{7} + \frac{2}{7}$

$\frac{4}{8} + \frac{1}{8}$

$\frac{4}{12} + \frac{1}{12}$

$\frac{5}{8} + \frac{2}{8}$

$\frac{6}{12} + \frac{4}{12}$

$\frac{4}{11} + \frac{4}{11}$

$\frac{5}{8} + \frac{1}{8}$

$\frac{2}{5} + \frac{2}{5}$

$\frac{1}{9} + \frac{2}{9}$

$\frac{7}{10} + \frac{2}{10}$

$\frac{4}{6} + \frac{1}{6}$

Name _____

Bubble Math

Reduce each sum to a whole number or a mixed number in lowest terms.

$\frac{6}{9} + \frac{6}{9}$

$\frac{5}{11} + \frac{8}{11}$

$\frac{3}{4} + \frac{2}{4}$

$\frac{8}{11} + \frac{8}{11}$

$\frac{2}{5} + \frac{3}{5}$

$\frac{4}{5} + \frac{6}{5}$

$\frac{5}{9} + \frac{5}{9}$

$\frac{8}{9} + \frac{3}{9}$

$\frac{4}{8} + \frac{6}{8}$

$\frac{4}{3} + \frac{2}{3}$

$\frac{5}{7} + \frac{6}{7}$

$\frac{2}{4} + \frac{2}{4}$

$\frac{3}{6} + \frac{3}{6}$

$\frac{5}{4} + \frac{2}{4}$

$\frac{4}{8} + \frac{4}{8}$

$\frac{8}{11} + \frac{3}{11}$

$\frac{3}{12} + \frac{10}{12}$

$\frac{6}{12} + \frac{8}{12}$

$\frac{7}{14} + \frac{8}{14}$

$\frac{7}{12} + \frac{7}{12}$

$\frac{6}{8} + \frac{6}{8}$

$\frac{5}{12} + \frac{8}{12}$

$\frac{3}{9} + \frac{7}{9}$

$\frac{7}{11} + \frac{7}{11}$

$\frac{5}{12} + \frac{10}{12}$

$\frac{7}{13} + \frac{6}{13}$

$\frac{13}{16} + \frac{7}{16}$

$\frac{8}{15} + \frac{14}{15}$

$\frac{5}{7} + \frac{6}{7}$

$\frac{4}{11} + \frac{9}{11}$

Daily Learning Drills Grade 4

Name _____

Bug Me!

Solve the puzzle.

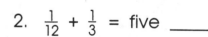

Across

2. $\frac{1}{12} + \frac{1}{3}$ = five ____

3. $\frac{5}{10} + \frac{2}{5}$ = nine ____

5. $\frac{7}{15} + \frac{1}{5}$ = ____ thirds

6. $\frac{1}{2} + \frac{2}{6}$ = ____ sixths

8. $\frac{1}{6} + \frac{1}{2}$ = ____ thirds

9. $\frac{1}{5} + \frac{4}{10}$ = ____ fifths

10. $\frac{1}{3} + \frac{3}{6}$ = ____ sixths

12. $\frac{2}{7} + \frac{1}{14}$ = five ____

13. $\frac{8}{14} + \frac{2}{7}$ = ____ sevenths

Down

1. $\frac{1}{15} + \frac{2}{5}$ = ____ fifteenths

4. $\frac{2}{12} + \frac{2}{6}$ = one ____

5. $\frac{3}{10} + \frac{7}{20}$ = thirteen ____

7. $\frac{1}{8} + \frac{1}{4}$ = three ____

8. $\frac{3}{6} + \frac{1}{12}$ = seven ____

9. $\frac{3}{9} + \frac{1}{3}$ = two ____

11. $\frac{1}{8} + \frac{2}{16}$ = ____ fourth

Name _____

Soaring Subtraction

Solve each subtraction problem. Reduce each difference to lowest terms.

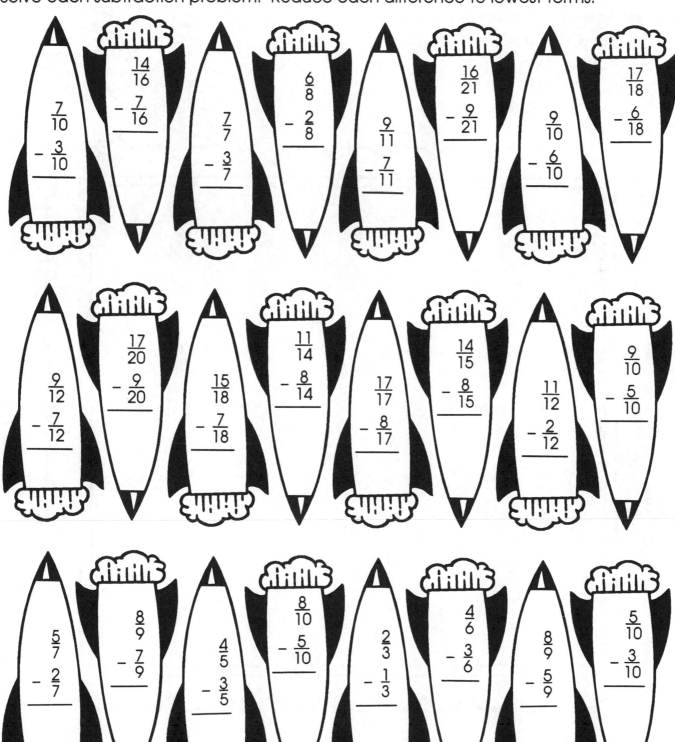

$$\frac{7}{10} - \frac{3}{10}$$

$$\frac{14}{16} - \frac{7}{16}$$

$$\frac{7}{7} - \frac{3}{7}$$

$$\frac{6}{8} - \frac{2}{8}$$

$$\frac{9}{11} - \frac{7}{11}$$

$$\frac{16}{21} - \frac{9}{21}$$

$$\frac{9}{10} - \frac{6}{10}$$

$$\frac{17}{18} - \frac{6}{18}$$

$$\frac{9}{12} - \frac{7}{12}$$

$$\frac{17}{20} - \frac{9}{20}$$

$$\frac{15}{18} - \frac{7}{18}$$

$$\frac{11}{14} - \frac{8}{14}$$

$$\frac{17}{17} - \frac{8}{17}$$

$$\frac{14}{15} - \frac{8}{15}$$

$$\frac{11}{12} - \frac{2}{12}$$

$$\frac{9}{10} - \frac{5}{10}$$

$$\frac{5}{7} - \frac{2}{7}$$

$$\frac{8}{9} - \frac{7}{9}$$

$$\frac{4}{5} - \frac{3}{5}$$

$$\frac{8}{10} - \frac{5}{10}$$

$$\frac{2}{3} - \frac{1}{3}$$

$$\frac{4}{6} - \frac{3}{6}$$

$$\frac{8}{9} - \frac{5}{9}$$

$$\frac{5}{10} - \frac{3}{10}$$

Daily Learning Drills Grade 4

Name _____

Take a Closer Look

| What is a stamp collector called? |

To find out, solve the following subtraction problems, reduce to lowest terms, and then put the letter above its corresponding answer at the bottom of the page.

I. $\frac{10}{11} - \frac{9}{11}$ H. $\frac{12}{12} - \frac{3}{12}$ E. $\frac{13}{14} - \frac{8}{14}$

A. $\frac{6}{8} - \frac{4}{8}$ I. $\frac{6}{7} - \frac{5}{7}$ P. $\frac{6}{6} - \frac{2}{6}$

T. $\frac{13}{14} - \frac{6}{14}$ L. $\frac{17}{20} - \frac{8}{20}$ S. $\frac{10}{14} - \frac{6}{14}$

T. $\frac{8}{10} - \frac{2}{10}$ L. $\frac{14}{18} - \frac{8}{18}$

$\frac{2}{3}$ $\frac{3}{4}$ $\frac{1}{7}$ $\frac{1}{3}$ $\frac{1}{4}$ $\frac{1}{2}$ $\frac{5}{14}$ $\frac{9}{20}$ $\frac{1}{11}$ $\frac{2}{7}$ $\frac{3}{5}$

Name _____

Numeral Nibblers

Finish these number sentences.

$$\frac{15}{16} \quad - \quad \frac{1}{2} \quad = \quad \boxed{}$$

$-$

$$\frac{3}{4} \quad - \quad \frac{10}{16} \quad = \quad \boxed{}$$

$= \quad \text{(shaded)} \quad -$

$$\boxed{} \quad - \quad \frac{1}{8} \quad = \quad \boxed{}$$

$= \qquad -$

$$\frac{2}{3} \quad - \quad \frac{2}{12} \quad = \quad \boxed{} \qquad \frac{1}{48}$$

$- \qquad\qquad =$

$$\frac{2}{9} \qquad \frac{21}{24} \quad - \quad \frac{5}{6} \quad = \quad \boxed{}$$

$= \qquad - \quad \text{(shaded)} \quad -$

$$\boxed{} \qquad \frac{3}{4} \quad - \quad \frac{7}{12} \quad = \quad \boxed{}$$

$= \qquad =$

Name _____

Figuring Distance

Find the perimeter of each figure.

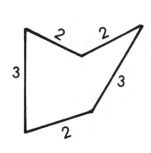

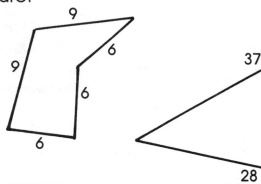

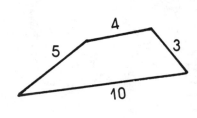

_____

_____

_____

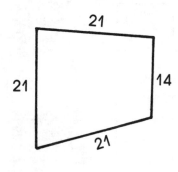

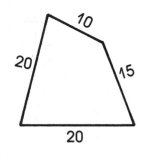

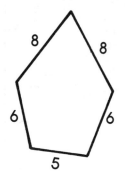

_____

_____

_____

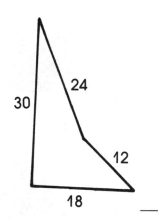

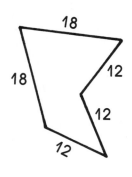

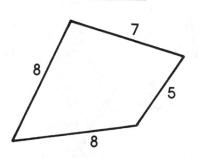

_____

_____

_____

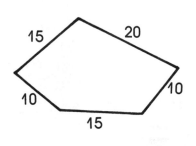

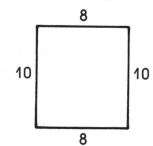

_____

_____

_____

Name _____

Quilt Math

Find the perimeter and area of each quilt.

1.

perimeter _____ area _____

2.

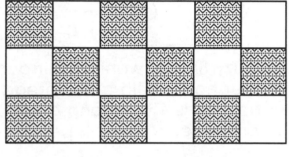

perimeter _____ area _____

3.

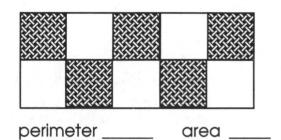

perimeter _____ area _____

4.

perimeter _____ area _____

5.

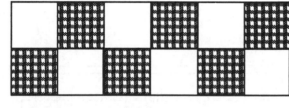

perimeter _____ area _____

6.

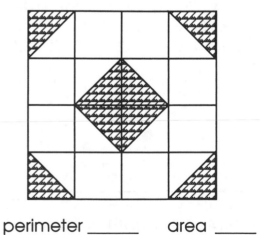

perimeter _____ area _____

7.

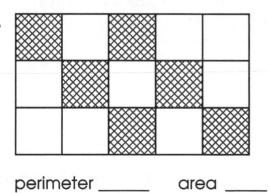

perimeter _____ area _____

8. What did you notice about the perimeter in problems 4, 5, 6 and 7? _____

9. On the back of this paper, lay out and then sketch a quilt so that it has 30 blocks in it.

10. On the back, lay out and sketch a quilt that has a perimeter of 14 units.

Daily Learning Drills Grade 4

Name _____

Suzy Spider, Interior Decorator

Suzy Spider is decorating her house. She is a very clever decorator, but she needs your help figuring out the area and perimeter.

1. Suzy is putting a silk fence around her garden. It is 12 cm long and 10 cm wide. What is the perimeter of the garden?

2. Suzy Spider wants to surround her house with a silk thread. Her house is 17 cm long and 12 cm wide. What is its perimeter?

3. Suzy wants to carpet her living room. It is 5 cm long and 4 cm wide. How much carpet should she buy for her living room?

4. Suzy wants to put wallpaper on a kitchen wall. The wall is 7 cm tall and 4 cm wide. What is its area?

5. Suzy has decided to hang a silk thread all the way around her porch. The porch is 4 cm long and 3 cm wide. How long should the thread be?

6. Suzy's bedroom is 6 cm long and 5 cm wide. How much carpet should she buy for it?

Name _____

Turn Up the Volume

The **volume** is the measure of the inside of a space figure. Find the volume. Count the boxes.

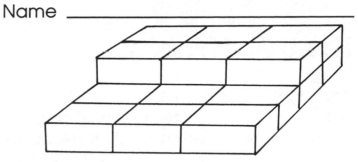

_____

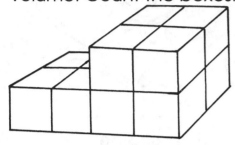

_____

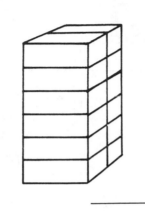

_____

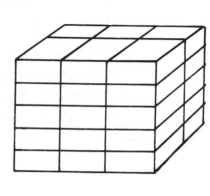

_____

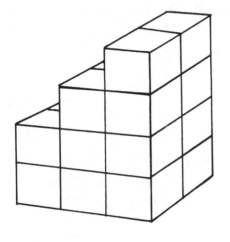

_____

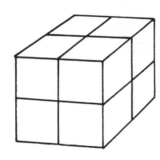

_____

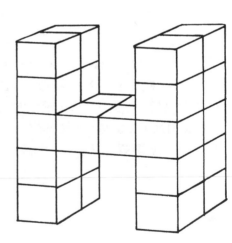

_____

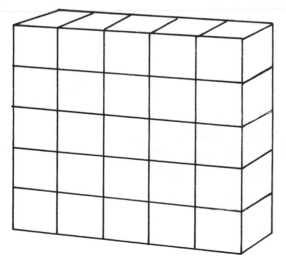

_____

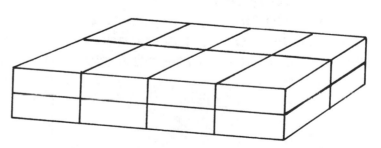

_____

MATH

Name _____

Krab E. Krabby

Krab E. Krabby carries a yardstick
with him everywhere he goes, and
he measures everything that he can.

Key Facts:
   12 inches = 1 foot
   36 inches = 3 feet = 1 yard

1. Krab E. Krabby wanted to measure the length of a grasshopper. Would he use a ruler or a yardstick?

2. Krab E. Krabby scolded Rollo Rattlesnake because Rollo wouldn't straighten out and cooperate. Should Krab E. Krabby use a ruler or a yardstick to measure Rollo?

3. Mr. Krabby measured a garter snake that was 44 inches long. How many yards and inches was this?
_____ yard _____ inches left over

4. Krab E. measured a tomato hornworm that was 5 inches long. How many inches less than a foot was this?

5. Mr. Krabby measured a monarch butterfly that was 4 inches wide. How many inches less than a foot was the butterfly?

6. Krab E. Krabby measured a lazy tuna that was 1 foot 11 inches long. How many total inches was the tuna?

Name _____

Animal Math

The chart below lists some of the body statistics of 15 endangered animals. Use these measurements to solve the problems below the chart.

Animal	Height	Weight	Length
Mountain gorilla	6 feet	450 pounds	
Brown hyena	25 inches	70 pounds	3 feet
Black rhinoceros	5.5 feet	4000 pounds	12 feet
Cheetah	2.5 feet	100 pounds	5 feet
Leopard	2 feet	150 pounds	4.5 feet
Spectacled bear	2.5 feet	300 pounds	5 feet
Giant armadillo		100 pounds	4 feet
Vicuna	2.5 feet	100 pounds	
Central American tapir	3.5 feet	500 pounds	8 feet
Black-footed ferret		1.5 pounds	20 inches
Siberian tiger	38 inches	600 pounds	6 feet
Orangutan	4.5 feet	200 pounds	
Giant panda		300 pounds	6 feet
Polar Bear		1600 pounds	8 feet
Yak	5.5 feet	1200 pounds	

Problems to solve:

1. What is the total height of a mountain gorilla, a vicuna and a yak? _____

2. What is the total weight of a leopard, a cheetah and a polar bear? _____

3. What is the total weight of a giant panda and a giant armadillo? _____

4. Add the lengths of a black rhinoceros, a spectacled bear and a Siberian tiger. _____

5. Add the heights of two leopards, three yaks and four orangutans. _____

6. Subtract the height of a vicuna from the height of a cheetah. _____

7. Multiply the height of a Central American tapir by the height of a mountain gorilla. _____

8. Add the heights of a brown hyena and a Siberian tiger. _____

9. Add the weights of all the animals. _____

10. For the animals whose lengths are given, arrange the lengths of the animals from longest to shortest on another sheet of paper.

Name _____

It Suits Me to a Tee!

How many centimeters from the tee to the flag? Stay on "course"!

Example

12 cm

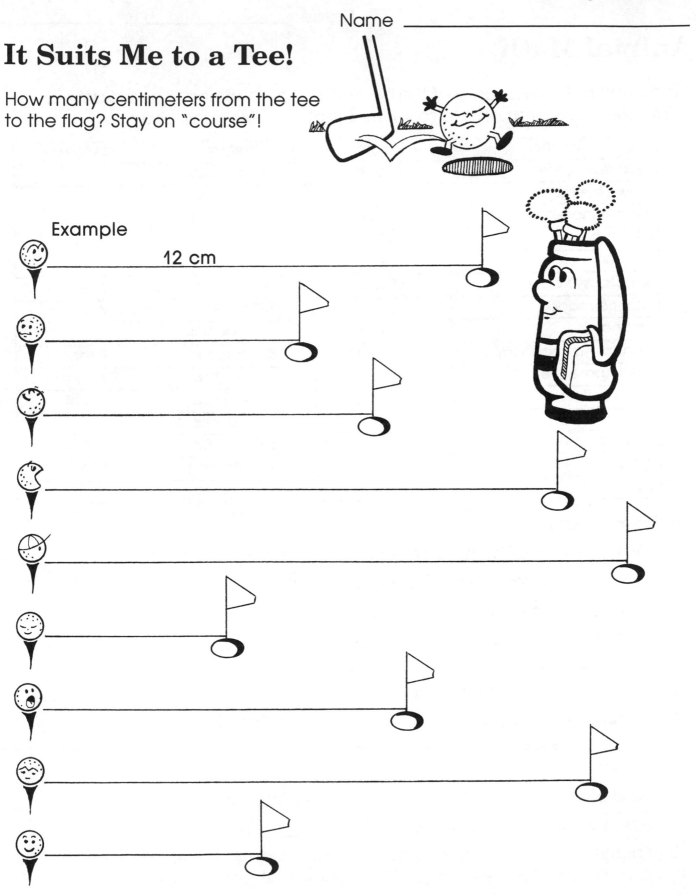

Name _____

Digging for Lost Treasure

While vacationing on Octopus Island in the Caribbean Sea, you discover an old treasure map in a bottle on the beach. Using a metric ruler, follow the directions below by plotting your movements to the location of the buried treasure using vertical and horizontal lines. Mark the spot on the map where you locate the treasure. You will be rewarded if you are correct!

1. From the starting point, go 8 centimeters east.
2. Go 6 centimeters north.
3. Go 9 centimeters east.
4. Go 3 centimeters south.
5. Go 7 centimeters west.
6. Go 5 centimeters north.
7. Go 7.5 centimeters west.
8. Go 2 centimeters north.
9. Go 9.5 centimeters east.
10. Go 10 centimeters south. Dig for treasure!

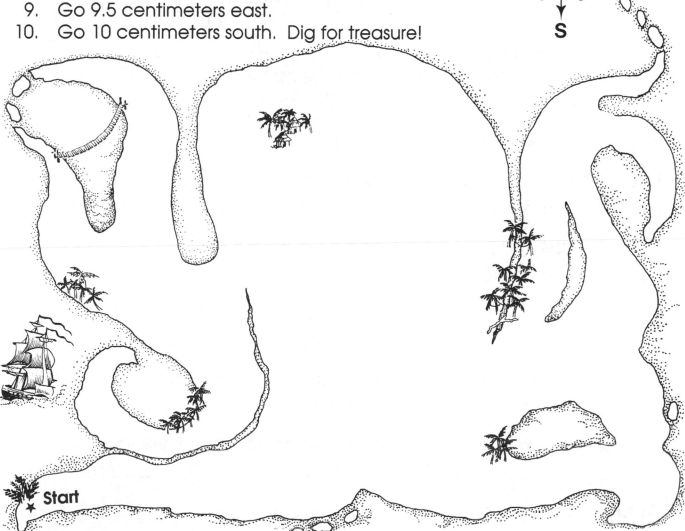

MATH

Name _____

Discovering Metric Equivalents

Isn't it fun to estimate and guess? How many times a day do you guess how much bubble gum it will take to fill that hole, or how much oatmeal it will take to fill that crack? How about how much milk it will take to cover your crunchy, poppity cereal? We're always making guesses!

Materials Needed

1 cup capacity measuring cup
500 mL capacity measuring cup
2 one-gallon capacity plastic jugs
water

Directions

Set the 2 one-gallon jugs beside each other. Fill one with water. You will then take turns filling the measuring cups with water from one jug to determine the number of cups, pints, quarts and gallons of water it will take to fill the other jug.

1 cup - How many mL do you think it will take? _____
The actual amount _____

1 pint (2 cups) - How many mL do you think it will take? _____
_____ The actual amount _____

1 quart (2 pints) - How many L and mL do you think it will take?
_____ L _____ mL The actual amounts _____ L _____ mL

1 half gallon (2 quarts) - How many L and mL do you think it will take?
_____ L _____ mL The actual amounts _____ L _____ mL

1 gallon (4 quarts) - How many L and mL do you think it will take?
_____ L _____ mL The actual amounts _____ L _____ mL

Were you close in your estimates? _____

Name _____

Gliding Graphics

Draw the lines as directed from point to point for each graph.

Draw a line from:
F,7 to D,1
D,1 to I,6
I,6 to N,8
N,8 to M,3
M,3 to F,1
F,1 to G,4
G,4 to E,4
E,4 to B,1
B,1 to A,8
A,8 to D,11
D,11 to F,9
F,9 to F,7
F,7 to I,9
I,9 to I,6
I,6 to F,7

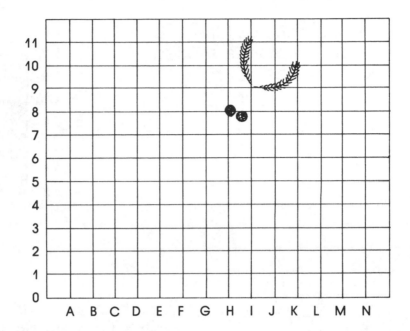

Draw a line from:
J,☉ to N,☾
N,☾ to U,☾
U,☾ to Z,■
Z,■ to X,♡
X,♡ to U,☾
U,☾ to S,☆
S,☆ to N,☾
N,☾ to N,☆
N,☆ to J,☉
J,☉ to L,●
L,● to Y,●
Y,● to Z,■
Z,■ to L,■
L,■ to J,☉

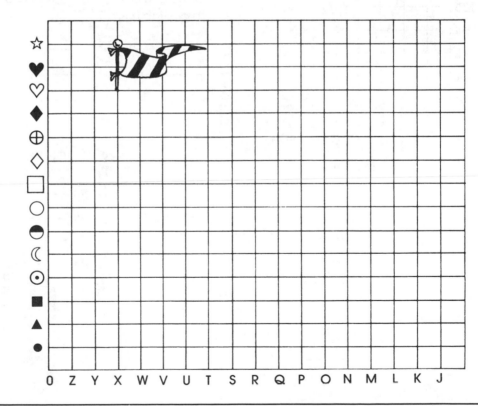

• Write what comes next.

SAD   SBF   SCH   SDJ   SEL   _____

MATH

Name _____

School Statistics

Read each graph and do as directed.

List the names of the students from the shortest to the tallest.

1. _____ 4. _____

2. _____ 5. _____

3. _____ 6. _____

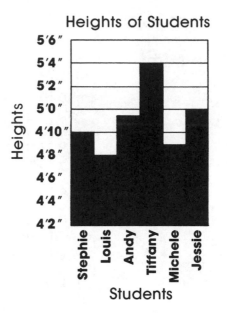

Heights of Students

List the names of the students from the heaviest to the lightest.

1. _____ 5. _____

2. _____ 6. _____

3. _____ 7. _____

4. _____ 8. _____

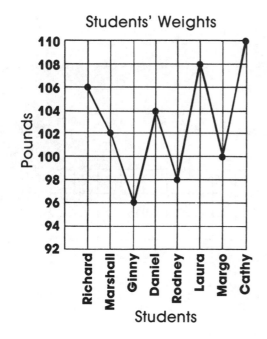

List the months in the order of the least number of absences to the greatest number of absences.

1. _____ 4. _____ 7. _____

2. _____ 5. _____ 8. _____

3. _____ 6. _____ 9. _____

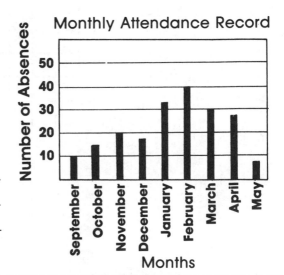

Monthly Attendance Record

• Draw what comes next.

    _____

Name _____

It's About Time!

Write the letter of the card that matches the clock on the line under the clock.

Example

H

_____

_____

_____   _____   _____

_____   _____   _____   _____

A 4:05	**B** 5:40	**C** 11:10	**D** 10:15	**E** 8:25
F 12:55	**G** 5:20	**H** 2:50	**I** 3:20	**J** 1:45

Daily Learning Drills Grade 4

Name _____

Father Time Teasers

Father Time doesn't want to tease you with these. He just wants you to work a little harder to figure out: "What time was it?" or "What time will it be?"

Example

25 minutes ago
5:35
____

10 minutes later
____

40 minutes ago
____

35 minutes ago
____

50 minutes later
____

15 minutes ago
____

20 minutes later
____

45 minutes ago
____

5 minutes ago
____

30 minutes later
____

55 minutes later
____

25 minutes ago
____

Name _____

Time "Tables"

"Set" these tables by drawing the hands on these clocks.

Example

10 minutes **before**

12:17

36 minutes **after**

8:19

8 minutes **before**

1:05

21 minutes **after**

8:40

16 minutes **before**

4:30

46 minutes **after**

10:11

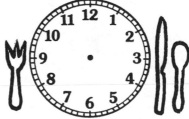

32 minutes **before**

5:25

11 minutes **after**

3:16

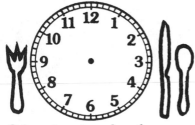

24 minutes **before**

12:30

17 minutes **after**

1:31

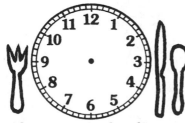

43 minutes **before**

2:01

18 minutes **after**

6:45

MATH

Daily Learning Drills Grade 4

Name _____

Time Problems

Draw the hands on the clocks to show the starting time and the ending time.
Then write the answer to the problem.

1. The bike race started at 2:55 p.m. and lasted 2 hours and 10 minutes. What time did the race end?

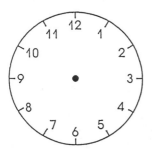

Answer: _____

2. Sherry walked in the 12-mile Hunger Walk. She started at 12:30 p.m. and finished at 4:50 p.m. How long did she walk?

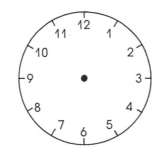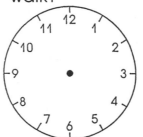

Answer: _____

3. The 500-mile auto race started at 11:00 a.m. and lasted 2 hours and 25 minutes. What time did the race end?

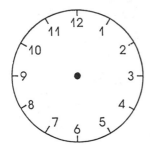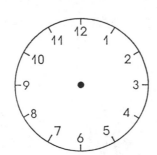

Answer: _____

4. The train left Indianapolis at 7:25 a.m. and arrived in Chicago at 10:50 a.m. How long did the trip take?

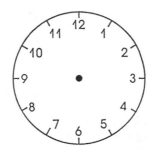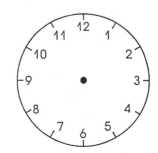

Answer: _____

5. The chili cook-off started at 10:00 a.m., and all the chili was cooked by 4:30 p.m. How long did it take to cook the chili?

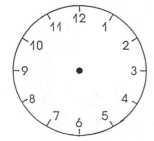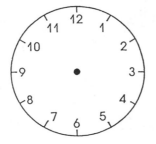

Answer: _____

6. The chili judging began at 4:30 p.m. After 3 hours and 45 minutes the chili had all been eaten. At what time was the chili judging finished?

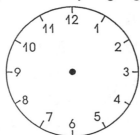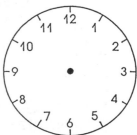

Answer: _____

Name _____

Super Savers!

Adding money means you're saving money! Keep saving. It adds up. Here are a few success stories. Add 'em up!

Sam's Account	Debbie's Account	Sarah's Account	Roberto's Account	Cheryl's Account
$8.03	$45.32	$85.42	$41.46	$54.26
.84	2.41	12.58	+ 8.89	3.04
+ 5.47	+ 34.28	+ 2.21		+ .25

Alex's Account	Eva's Account	Bill's Account	Monica's Account	David's Account
$ 4.06	$89.42	$62.41	$20.04	$56.04
81.23	3.06	3.84	3.42	2.81
+ 2.84	+ .94	+ 64.21	+ 25.81	+ .94

Tom's Account	Andy's Account	Earl's Account	Mark's Account	Michele's Account
$ 8.05	$ .47	$50.42	$21.46	$ .55
21.21	31.24	3.84	20.00	30.24
+ .98	+ 2.38	+ .98	+ 5.58	+ 3.49

Katelyn's Account	Kimberly's Account	Gwen's Account
$ .42	$ 5.42	$60.42
.59	40.64	3.84
+ 3.42	+ 3.89	+ 21.25

Whose account is the largest?

_____

Whose is the smallest?

_____

Whose is closest to $50?

_____

Name _____

Match the $ale

Which item did each of the kids purchase? Calculate the amount. Write the
purchase price in each blank.

Jessica:

$17.43
 -
_____
$9.14

Tammy:

$43.21
 -
_____
$34.86

Heather:

$10.06
 -
_____
$1.64

Mark:

$52.46
 -
_____
$14.17

Eva:

$65.04
 -
_____
$36.94

Roger:

$3.45
 -
_____
$2.56

Monica:

$6.99
 -
_____
$3.56

Katelyn:

$9.06
 -
_____
$5.24

David:

$15.25
 -
_____
$6.82

Curt:

$63.45
 -
_____
$46.16

Michele:

$32.45
 -
_____
$13.50

Carolyn:

$18.46
 -
_____
$14.49

Gwen:

$19.24
 -
_____
$6.38

Thomas:

$9.43
 -
_____
$5.59

$8.35

$28.10

$3.43

$18.95

$8.43

$3.84

$3.82

$12.86

$3.97

.89

$17.29

$8.29

$8.42

$38.29

Name _____

McMealworm

McMealworm's is the latest restaurant of that famous fast food creator, Buggs I. Lyke. His McMealworm Burger costs $1.69. An order of Roasted Roaches costs $.59 for the regular size and $.79 for the large size. A Cricket Cola is $.89.

1. You buy a McMealworm Burger and a regular order of Roasted Roaches. What is the total?

2. Your best friend in class orders a McMealworm Burger, a large order of Roasted Roaches and a Cricket Cola. How much will it cost?

3. Your teacher buys a Cricket Cola and a regular order of Roasted Roaches. What does it cost?

4. The principal is very hungry, so his bill comes to $14.37. How much change will he get from $20.00?

5. Your mom goes to McMealworm's to buy your dinner. She spends $3.37. How much change does she get from a $5.00 bill?

6. You have $1.17 in your bank. How much more do you need to pay for a McMealworm Burger?

Name _____

One-Stop Shopping

Stash McCash is shopping! Find the total cost of the items. Then find how much change Stash should receive.

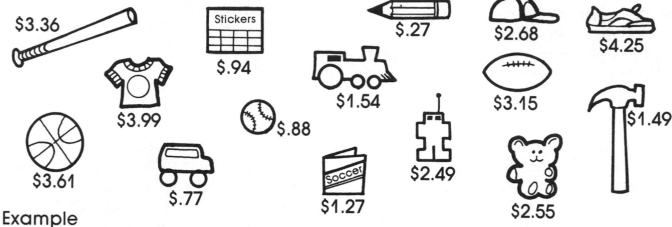

$3.36   Stickers $.94 $.27 $2.68 $4.25

$3.99 $.88 $1.54 $3.15 $1.49

$3.61 $.77   Soccer $1.27 $2.49 $2.55

Example

Stash has $5.00	Stash has $8.50	Stash has $7.04	Stash has $9.00
Buys	Buys	Buys	Buys
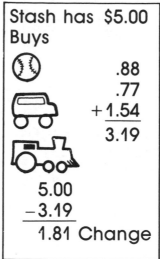 .88 .77 +1.54 3.19 5.00 −3.19 1.81 Change	 Change	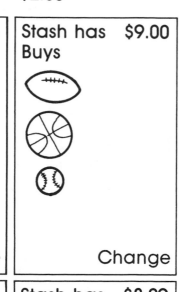 Change	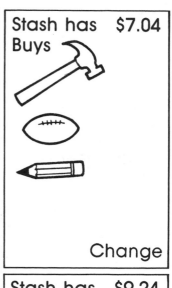 Change

Stash has $10.95	Stash has $10.00	Stash has $9.24	Stash has $8.09
Buys	Buys	Buys	Buys
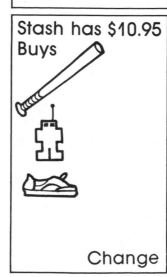 Change	 Change	 Change	 Change

Name _____

Shifty Sam's Shop

Shifty Sam's store is a messy jumble of things. Anything a child could want is there if it can be found under the piles of junk and stuff. But be careful if you buy anything. Check Sam's multiplication!

1. Mighty Man comics cost 13¢ at Shifty Sam's. You buy 4 of these comics. How much should you pay?

2. Your sister decides to buy 2 copies of the latest hit record by the Bird Brains. Each copy costs 89¢. How much will she pay?

3. Your best friend bought 9 marbles at Shifty's. Each marble cost 19¢. How much money did he spend?

4. Crazy stickers cost 21¢ each at Sam's. You buy 7 of them. How much should you pay?

5. Baseball cards are 11¢ each at Shifty Sam's. How much will it cost you for 8 cards?

6. Stinky Stickers have a skunk odor. Your best friend bought 7 Stinky Stickers which cost 18¢ each. How much did he spend?

Name _____

What a Great Catch!

This is "fishy" business! Use your money "sense" to solve these problems.

Buy fish	$2.47
A, C and H.	2.18
	+2.54
Total Cost	$7.19

You have $4.00.
Buy fish D.
How much money
is left?

You have $10.00.
Buy fish E and J.
How much money
is left?

Buy 4 of fish I.

Total Cost

You have $5.75
Buy fish G and C.

How much money
is left?

Buy fish
D, F, J and B.

Total Cost

Buy 6 of fish E.

Total Cost

Buy 3 of fish J
and 6 of fish D.

Total Cost

You have $10.76
Buy 3 of fish A.

How much money
is left?

Name _____

Money Math

$3.42 x 27	$2.45 x 34	$6.42 x 56	$8.43 x 30

$5.41 x 24	$1.24 x 48	$5.42 x 28	$2.43 x 17

$.49 x 56	$2.53 x 41	$8.21 x 37	$4.21 x 36	$5.41 x 42	$.21 x 84

$1.06 x 93	$3.42 x 26	$1.23 x 46	$5.43 x 24

$.89 x 32	$4.25 x 31

Name _____

Sam Sillicook's Doughnut Shoppe

Sam Sillicook believes that you should put a little jelly in your belly. He has invented the Super Duper Jelly Doughnuts that are so full of jelly, they leak. His Twisted Circles are drenched in sugar. He has also invented the Banana Cream Doughnut and Jam-jammed Cream Puffs.

1. Your teacher bought 32 Jam-jammed Cream Puffs. They cost $.89 each. How much did your teacher spend?

2. Harry D. Hulk bought 14 Banana Cream Doughnuts for his breakfast at $.65 each. How much did they cost Harry?

3. Your best friend bought 12 Twisted Circles at $.29 each. How much did he spend?

4. You love Jam-jammed Cream Puffs. Your mother buys 17 for your birthday party at $.89 each. How much do they cost?

5. Your principal decided to treat the teachers. He bought 24 Super Duper Jelly Doughnuts at $.49 each. What was the total cost?

6. Your class was treated to 40 Banana Cream Doughnuts which cost $.65 each. What was the total?

Name _____

Perplexing Problems

Heather and Gwen went to the water park. How much did each of them pay?

Total: $9.68 $ _____

On Saturday, James, Gary, Ted and Raul went to the zoo. What was their individual cost to get in?

Total: $8.72 $ _____

Mark, David, Curt and Sam rented a motorized skateboard for 1 hour. What was the cost for each of them — split equally 4 ways?

Total: $7.36 $ _____

Five students pitched in to buy Mr. Jokestopper a birthday gift. How much did each of them contribute?

Total: $9.60 $ _____

All 6 members of the volleyball team received a special shirt for being in the final game. What was the amount of each shirt?

Total: $8.16 $ _____

Mary, Cheryl and Betty went to the skating rink. What was their individual cost?

$ _____

Total: $7.44

Carol, Katelyn and Kimberly bought lunch at their favorite salad shop. What did each of them pay for lunch?

Total: $8.52 $ _____

Debbie, Sarah, Michele and Kelly earned $6.56 altogether for collecting cans. How much did each of them earn individually?

Total: $6.56 $ _____

Five friends went to the Hamburger Hot Spot Cafe for lunch. They all ordered the special. What did it cost?

Total: $7.45 $ _____

Lee and Ricardo purchased an awesome model rocket together. What was the cost for each of them?

Total: $9.52 $ _____

The total fee for Erik, Bill and Steve to enter the science museum was $8.76. What amount did each of them pay?

Total: $8.76 $ _____

Name _____

Too Much Information

Underline the **distractor** and solve the problems.

1. All 20 of the students from Sandy's class went to the movies. Tickets cost $1.50 each. Drinks cost 55¢ each. How much altogether did the students spend on tickets?

2. Of the students, 11 were girls and 9 were boys. At $1.50 per ticket, how much did the boys' tickets cost altogether?

3. While 5 students had ice cream, 12 others had candy. Ice cream cost 75¢ per cup. How much did the students spend on ice cream?

4. 7 of the 20 students did not like the movie. 3 of the 20 students had seen the movie before. How many students had not seen the movie before?

5. Mary paid 55¢ for an orange drink and 65¢ for a candy bar. Sarah paid 45¢ for popcorn. How much did Mary's refreshments cost her?

6. 6 of the students spent a total of $16.50 for refreshments and $9.00 for their tickets. How much did each spend for refreshments?

7. 10 of the students went back to see the movie again the next day. Each student paid $1.50 for a ticket, 45¢ for popcorn and 55¢ for a soft drink. How much did each student pay?

Name _____

Get the Point

When you add or subtract decimals, remember to "include the point."	Add	Subtract
	3.6	6.8
	+ 3.3	− 2.6
	6.9	4.2

4.2 + 5.2	6.4 + 1.4	3.1 + 7.8	4.7 + 3.2	4.9 + 2.0	3.4 + 1.2
5.9 − 3.2	6.7 − 5.6	7.8 − 2.5	5.8 − 3.3	3.9 − 1.5	5.8 − 2.2
.23 + .25	.43 + .16	.26 + .42	.64 + .15	.68 + .31	.26 + .31
.87 − .42	.98 − .35	.79 − .15	.87 − .67	.83 − .12	.96 − .12
3.13 + 2.26	4.72 + 1.15	6.87 + 2.11	4.98 − 2.32	5.97 − 2.54	5.89 − 1.35
4.86 − 1.76	5.86 − 3.83	6.98 − 1.45	6.73 + 1.15	4.27 + 5.52	3.46 + 2.31

Name _____

Doing Decimals

DECIMAL POINT—A dot placed between the ones place and the tenths place

 .2 is read as two tenths.

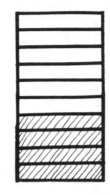 .4 four tenths

Write answer as decimal for shaded parts.

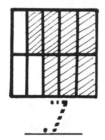

_.7_

_____

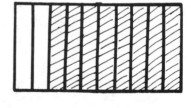

_____

_____

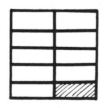

_____

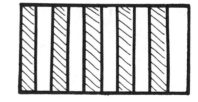

_____

Color parts that match decimals.

.4

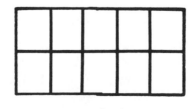

.3

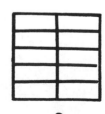

.2

Name _____

Animal Trivia

1. A wood rat has a tail which is 23.6 cm long. A deer mouse has a tail 12.2 cm long. What is the difference?

2. A rock mouse is 26.1 cm long. His tail adds another 14.4 cm. What is his total length from his nose to the tip of his tail?

3. A spotted bat has a tail 4.9 cm long. An evening bat has a tail 3.7 cm long. What is the difference?

4. A pocket gopher has a hind foot 3.5 cm long. A ground squirrel's hind foot is 6.4 cm long. How much longer is the ground squirrel's foot?

5. A cottontail rabbit has ears which are 6.8 cm long. A jackrabbit has ears 12.9 cm long. How much shorter is the cottontail's ear?

6. A porcupine has a tail 30.0 cm long. A possum has a tail 53.5 cm long. How much longer is the possum's tail?

7. The hind foot of a river otter is 14.6 cm long. The hind foot of a hog-nosed skunk is 9.0 cm long. What is the difference?

MATH

Name _____

Living History Books

You can learn a lot about a tree by reading its special calendar of rings. Every year a tree grows a new layer of wood. This makes the tree trunk get fatter and fatter. The new layer makes a ring.

You can see the rings on a freshly cut tree stump. When the growing season is wet, the tree grows a lot and the rings are wide. When the season is dry, the tree grows very little. Then the rings are narrow.

This tree was planted in 1973. Use the picture clues to color the rings of the tree stump. Where will the very first ring be?

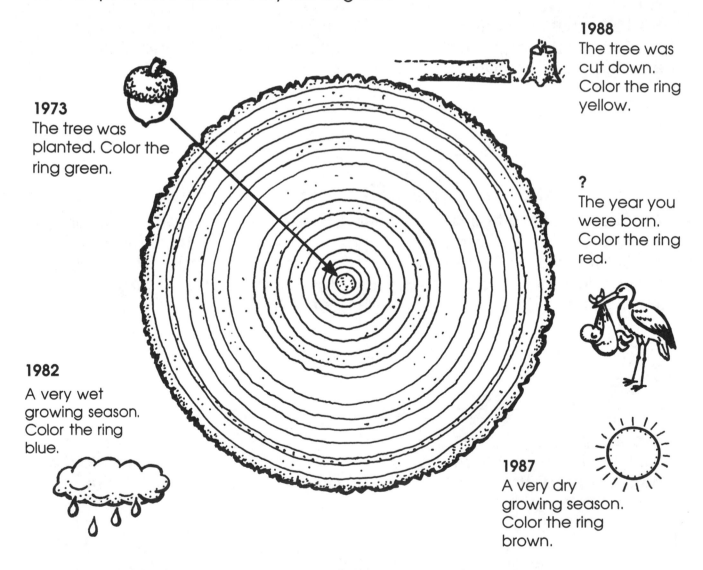

1988
The tree was cut down. Color the ring yellow.

1973
The tree was planted. Color the ring green.

?
The year you were born. Color the ring red.

1982
A very wet growing season. Color the ring blue.

1987
A very dry growing season. Color the ring brown.

Many of the giant sequoia trees in California are more than 2,000 years old. How many rings would a 2,000-year-old tree have?

Name _Tocanna_

Jogging Geraniums

You will probably never see a flower running down the sidewalk, but you might see one climbing a fence. Most plants are rooted in one place, but they still move.

Roots, stems, leaves, and even flowers move in different ways. The leaves grow toward the light. Roots will grow toward water. Even gravity will make a plant grow straight up in the air, away from the center of the earth.

Look at the three plants below. Tell what made the plants "move" or grow the way they did.

The roots are coming twords the water

The leeve are coming twords the sun

The Gravity is making it grow straight up.

Scientists give special names to the three kinds of plant movements above. The names come from combining two words. Put the correct puzzle pieces together to make the new word. Write the new word. Label the pictures above with the correct new word.

	New Word	Meaning
photo "light" + tropism "turn"	Phototroism	To turn toward the light.
geo "earth" + tropism "turn"	geo tropism	To turn because of of earth's gravity.
hydro "water" + tropism "turn"	hydro tropim	To turn toward the water.

Daily Learning Drills Grade 4

SCIENCE

Name _Thurania_

Cruising Coconuts

"Look at this coconut!" Amy called to Matt as they walked along the beach. Safe inside its thick husk, the coconut had floated across the water. Once it washed up on shore, the green leaves sprouted from this large seed.

Seeds travel in many ways. Below are five ways that seeds travel. Tell how each seed travels.

People planting them

getting carried by waves/water

getting carried by people/animals

getting carried by wind

getting carried by birds

Fun Fact

Blast Off
The seed pod of the "touch-me-not" swells as it gets ripe. Finally the seed pod bursts and launches seeds in all directions.

Name _____

Corny Medicine

Use the words from the Word Bank to complete the puzzle. Cross out each word in the Word Bank as you use it. The remaining words in the Word Bank will help you answer the "Corny Medicine" riddle.

Across

4. Deep growing type of root
6. Beautiful, seed-making part of plant
7. Brightly colored "leafy" parts of the flower
9. Large part of seed that supplies food
10. Sweet food made by the leaves

Down

1. Making food with the help of light
2. Green food-making material in a leaf
3. Plant's "food factory"
5. Plant's anchor
8. Plants get their energy from the _____.

Corny Medicine
Why did the cornstalk go to the doctor's office?

Because it had an ear ache

Word Bank				
~~petals~~	because	~~cotyledon~~	it	~~root~~
had	~~flower~~	~~leaf~~	an	~~sugar~~
~~chlorophyll~~	~~sun~~	~~photosynthesis~~	ear	~~tap~~
ache				

Name _____

Guess What?

Use the following hints and the Word Bank to decide what insect each riddle describes.

1. I have stout, spiny forelegs.
   I eat insects, including some of my own kind.
   I camouflage well in my surroundings.
   My forelegs make me appear to be praying.

   What am I? ____praying mantis____

2. I have clear wings.
   My body is quite round.
   The males of my species make long, shrill sounds in summer.
   Some of us take 17 years to develop.

   What am I? ____cicada____

3. I have two pairs of long, thin wings.
   I eat mosquitoes and other small insects.
   I live near lakes, ponds, streams and rivers.
   My abdomen is very long . . . as long as a darning needle.

   What am I? ____dragonfly____

4. I am a type of beetle.
   My young are often called glowworms.
   My abdomen produces light.

   What am I? ____lightning bug____

5. I like warm, damp and dark places and come out at night.
   Humans hate me.
   I am a destructive household pest.
   I am closely related to grasshoppers and crickets.

   What am I? ____cockroach____

Word Bank			
lightning bug	cicada	dragonfly	termite
mosquito	ladybug	aphid	praying mantis
bumblebee	cockroach		

Challenge: Research an insect. Draw a detailed picture and write a report about it.

Name _____

Going Places

Looking at a bird's feet can tell you a lot about how they are used. Look at the bird's feet below. Unscramble the bird's name. Write the bird's name by the best sentence. Can you match the pictures with the names?

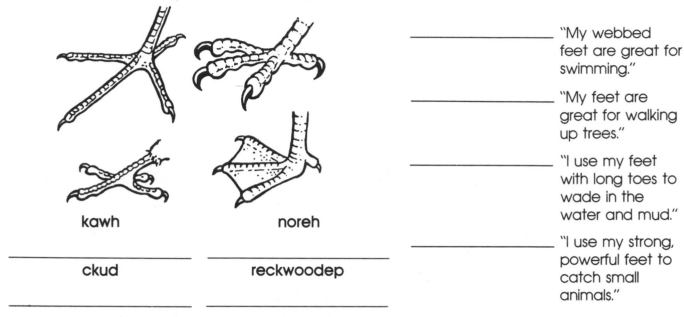

kawh

noreh

_____
ckud

_____
reckwoodep

_____

_____

_____ "My webbed feet are great for swimming."

_____ "My feet are great for walking up trees."

_____ "I use my feet with long toes to wade in the water and mud."

_____ "I use my strong, powerful feet to catch small animals."

Can the shape of a bird's bill tell you anything about what it eats? Look closely at the bills below. Unscramble the bird's name. Write the bird's name by the best sentence. Can you match the pictures with the names?

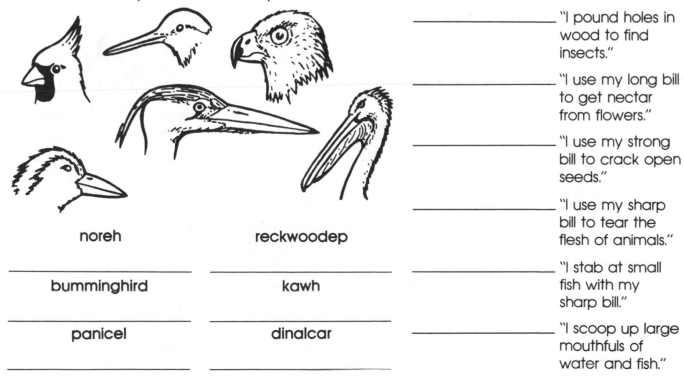

noreh

reckwoodep

_____
bumminghird

_____
kawh

_____
panicel

_____
dinalcar

_____

_____

_____ "I pound holes in wood to find insects."

_____ "I use my long bill to get nectar from flowers."

_____ "I use my strong bill to crack open seeds."

_____ "I use my sharp bill to tear the flesh of animals."

_____ "I stab at small fish with my sharp bill."

_____ "I scoop up large mouthfuls of water and fish."

SCIENCE

Name _____

Family Ties

Unscramble the names of the mom, pop, and baby of these animal families. The coordinates in front of each scrambled name tell where to write it on the chart.

(J-2) nhe ✓   (B-2) woc ✓   (A-1) obc ✓   (C-1) roba ✓
(E-2) ckdu ✓   (G-3) ignolgs ✓   (B-3) plewh ✓   (I-1) arm ✓
(F-2) exvin ✓   (D-3) wfna ✓   (I-3)balm ✓   (G-1) greadn ✓
(I-2) wee ✓   (C-2) ows ✓   (A-3)gentyc ✓   (E-1) kared ✓
(H-2 ream ✓   (D-1) bcku ✓   (F-3) ucb ✓   (J-1) mot ✓
(H-3) loaf ✓   (B-1) lulb ✓   (G-2) sogeo ✓   (A-2) nep ✓
(D-2) eod ✓   (C-3) buc ✓   (J-3) tupol ✓   (H-1) lastonil ✓
(E-3) gludcink ✓   (F-1) odg ✓

		1 Male	2 Female	3 Baby
A	swan	cob	pen	cygnet
B	seal	bull	cow	whelp
C	bear	boar	sow	cub
D	deer	buck	doe	fawn
E	duck	drake	duck	duckeling
F	fox	dog	vixen	cub
G	goose	gander	goose	gosling
H	horse	stallion	mare	foal
I	sheep	ram	ewe	lamb
J	turkey	tom	hen	poult

Challenge: Find the group names of these animals and write them on another sheet of paper.

Name _____

Adopt an Animal

The seas of the world are filled with an amazing variety of life. Starfish, crabs, flying fish, angelfish, worms, turtles, sharks and whales all make their home underwater. The shape, color and size of most sea animals depend on their lifestyle and where they live in the seas. Select a sea animal and become an expert on it. Research your animal and complete the profile below.

Common Name _____

Scientific Name _____

Description

weight:

length:

body shape:

tail shape:

color:

unusual characteristics:

Picture

Behaviors

Description of Habitat: _____

_____

_____

Food and Feeding Habits: _____

_____

_____

Migration (if applicable): _____

_____

_____

SCIENCE

Name _____

Food Chains

All living things in the seas depend on each other for food. The food chain begins with sea plants called phytoplankton. A huge variety of tiny animals called zooplankton, feed on the phytoplankton. These animals include shrimp, copepods, and jellyfish. Some of the most common fish—herring, anchovies, and sprats—feed on zooplankton. These fish are eaten by others, such as tuna and mackerel, which in turn are eaten by the superpredators, such as sharks and dolphins. This pattern of eating is called a food chain.

Use the diagram to answer the following questions on another piece of paper.

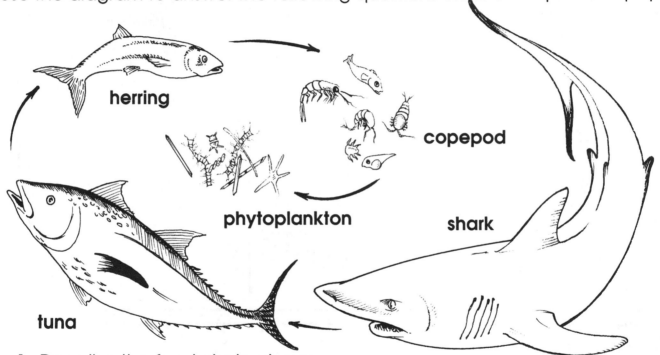

1. Describe the food chain above.

2. If there was a decrease in the copepod population, what would happen to the herring population? Why?

3. What would happen to the phytoplankton population? Why?

4. If the tuna population became endangered, what would the result be?

5. What does it mean when we say, "The death of one species in the food chain upsets the rest of the chain"?

6. An example of a land food chain might be fly-spider-bird-cat. Give an – other example of a land food chain.

7. Draw another sea food chain. Explain and give an example for each step.

Name _____

Polluting Our Seas

The seas provide us with many resources that we need to survive and to keep our industries going. Fish, shellfish, seaweeds, and minerals are just a few of the seas' resources. How long these will last depends on if and how badly we continue to pollute the seas.

For hundreds of years, people have been throwing garbage into the seas. Every day, billions of tons of waste, such as poisonous chemicals, radioactive waste, and plastics, are dumped into the seas. One of the worst sources of pollution is an oil spill. This results when tankers collide with each other or crash into rocks. There are thousands of oil spills every year. Most are small and are not reported, but some are huge. The biggest was in February, 1991, when oil was spilled into the Persian Gulf. It is thought that more than 1.2 million tons of oil spilled into the sea. It was more than 20 times bigger than the *Exxon Valdez* oil spill in 1989 off the coast of Alaska.

The seas cannot continue to be polluted without endangering the sea life. As the world population increases, people will be looking more to the seas to find products and resources.

Pretend you are a reporter. Use the headline below to write an article about pollution of the seas. Research to find interesting facts to back up your story.

SCIENCE

Save Our Seas

Name _____

Animal Comparisons

A Venn diagram is a great way to compare things. Use the one below to compare two animals of the seas. Fill in the circle below the dolphin with characteristics common only to this animal. Fill in the circle below the shark with characteristics common only to the shark. Where the circles overlap, fill in characteristics both animals share. Write a story about your findings on another piece of paper.

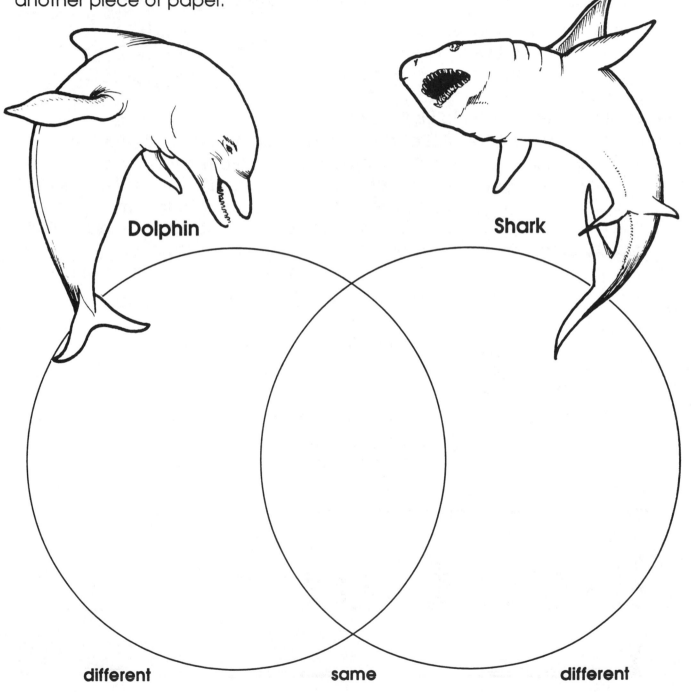

Dolphin

Shark

different   **same**   **different**

Name _____

Danger Ahead!

You will never see a dodo bird or a saber-tooth tiger. These animals are gone forever. They are **extinct.**

The animals on this page are not extinct, but they are in danger of becoming extinct. They are **endangered.** There may not be enough of them to reproduce. They are endangered because of the way people live.

There are many reasons why some animals are endangered. The signs on this page give clues to three main reasons.

Look at the signs. What do you think the three reasons are? Write them below.

1. _____

_____

2. _____

_____

3. _____

_____

Unscramble the names of these endangered animals.

dalb gleae   nereg teltur   lueb laweh   bremit lofw

• There are more than 100 endangered animals in North America. Find the name of one that lives near your area. Make a poster to help people become aware of this animal and the danger it is in.

Name _____

Threatened and Endangered Animals

Many of the earth's animals are threatened or extinct. Use the names of the animals to build a puzzle. Only use the bold-faced words.
Hint: Build off **rhinoceros**.

Word Box

brown **hyena**	Darwin's **rhea**	red **wolf**	black-footed **ferret**
Spanish **lynx**	Philippine **eagle**	**gavial**	ring-tailed **lemur**
giant **panda**	blue **whale**	**numbat**	resplendent **quetzal**
Arabian **oryx**	Grevy's **zebra**	**kakapo**	Galapagos **penguin**
Indian **python**	wild **yak**	**dugong**	

Use an encyclopedia to answer each question.

1. Which animal above is related to the manatee? _____

2. Which is the cousin of the crocodile? _____

3. Which is related to the ostrich? _____

Name _____

Animal Magic

Read Column A. Choose an answer from Column B. Write the number of the answer in the Magic Square. The first one has been done for you.

Column A	**Column B**
A. grizzly bear	1. large bear of the American grasslands
B. koala	2. lives on dry grasslands of South Africa
C. peregrine falcon	3. the most valuable reptile in the world
D. California condor	4. largest soaring bird of North America
E. black-footed ferret	5. the tallest American bird
F. cheetah	6. the fastest animal on land
G. orangutan	7. the only great ape outside Africa
H. giant panda	8. large aquatic seallike animal
I. Florida manatee	9. large black and white mammal of China
J. kit fox	10. small, fast mammal; nocturnal predator
K. blue whale	11. largest animal in the world
L. whooping crane	12. member of the weasel family
M. red wolf	13. has interbred with coyotes in some areas
N. green sea turtle	14. also called a duck hawk; size of a crow
O. brown hyena	15. eats leaves of the eucalyptus tree
P. jaguar	16. known as *el tigre* in Spanish

A _1_	B ___	C ___	D ___
E ___	F ___	G ___	H ___
I ___	J ___	K ___	L ___
M ___	N ___	O ___	P ___

Add the numbers across, down and diagonally. What answer do you get? ____

Why do you think this is called a magic square? _____

Name _____

Bald Eagle Puzzler

Read each statement about the bald eagle. If the statement is false, darken the letter in the circle to the left of that statement. The letters not darkened spell out the name of the chemical that affected the bald eagle's food supply.

(P) Due to federal protection, the bald eagle population is increasing.

(R) It is legal to shoot this bird today.

(E) This bird has keen eyesight and strong wings.

(N) The wingspan of this bird is about 3 feet.

(A) The nest of a bald eagle is made of mud and rocks.

(S) This bird eats mainly fish.

(T) This bird likes to eat only berries and seeds.

(T) The bald eagle is found only in North America.

(B) Only four bald eagles exist today in the United States.

(M) An injured bald eagle may be kept as a pet.

(I) Chemical poisons in the bald eagle's food caused its eggs to crack before incubation could be completed.

(C) The nest of a bald eagle is built high on a cliff or in a tree.

(I) This bird is the national symbol of the United States.

(L) The bald eagle is noted for its bright orange head.

(D) The bald eagle has a hooked beak.

(E) The nest of a bald eagle is called an aerie.

What is the type of chemical? ___ ___ ___ ___ ___ ___ ___ ___ ___

Name _____

Nippers, Rippers, and Grinders

 1.  2.  3.

Scientists tell us that some of the dinosaurs were meat-eaters and others were plant-eaters. But how do the scientists know? By looking at the teeth of certain dinosaur fossils, scientists can tell what those dinosaurs ate. Meat-eaters had sharp, saw-edged teeth (figure 1), for cutting and ripping flesh. Plant-eating dinosaurs had either peg-like teeth (figure 2), for nipping plants, or flat grinding teeth (figure 3), to munch tough twigs or leaves.

1. Match the dinosaur to its teeth by writing its name in the space provided.
2. Circle either "M" for meat-eater or "P" for plant-eater.

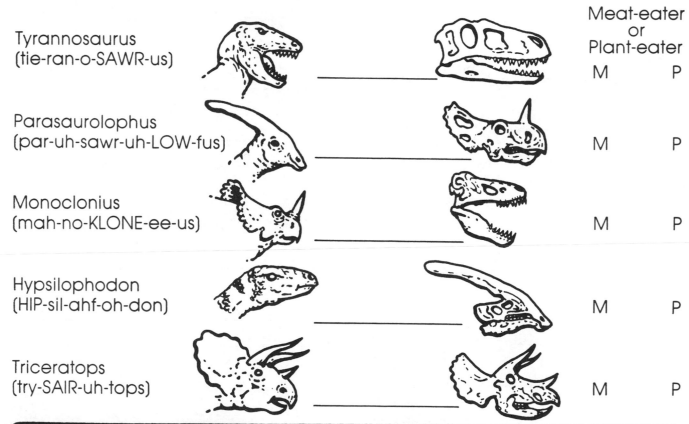

Tyrannosaurus (tie-ran-o-SAWR-us) — M P

Parasaurolophus (par-uh-sawr-uh-LOW-fus) — M P

Monoclonius (mah-no-KLONE-ee-us) — M P

Hypsilophodon (HIP-sil-ahf-oh-don) — M P

Triceratops (try-SAIR-uh-tops) — M P

Meat-eater or Plant-eater

Fantastic Fact

The **Tyrannosaurus**, whose name means "king of the tyrant lizards," was the largest meat-eater. It weighed over 8 tons and was over 15 meters long. Its teeth were over 15 cm long and had edges like a steak knife.

Name _____

Dinosaur Defense

How did the plant-eating dinosaurs protect themselves from the attacks of the fierce meat-eating dinosaurs? One way was to travel in groups. But they also had other ways to defend themselves. For example, some had horns and some could run very fast.

• Look at the plant-eating dinosaurs below. Find the features of their bodies that gave them protection from their enemies. Explain in the space provided.

Stegosaurus
(steg-uh-SAWR-us)

_____
_____
_____
_____

Ankylosaurus
(ang-KILE-uh-sawr-us)

_____
_____
_____
_____

Laosaurus
(LAY-uh-sawr-us)

_____
_____
_____

Triceratops
(try-SAIR-uh-tops)

_____
_____
_____
_____

Name _____

Dino-Find

Find the hidden words in the puzzle below. The words may be written forward, backward, up, down or diagonally. Circle the words. When you have located and circled all the words, write the remaining letters at the bottom of the page to spell out a message.

ALLOSAURUS	**BIRD HIP**	**FOSSIL**	**PLANT-EATER**
APATOSAURUS	**COELURUS**	**JURASSIC**	**PLATED**
ARMORED	**DINOSAUR**	**MEAT-EATER**	**SAUROPOD**
ARCHAEOPTERYX	**DIPLODOCUS**	**PALEONTOLOGIST**	**STEGOSAURUS**

```
S  D  B  U  R  L  I  S  S  O  F  I  S  M  N
G  U  I  T  H  I  S  P  E  R  I  O  T  E  T
J  D  R  U  A  S  O  N  I  D  S  H  E  A  S
U  A  D  U  L  D  L  O  S  E  W  S  G  T  I
R  E  H  A  A  S  O  U  C  R  O  V  O  E  G
A  E  I  R  E  S  R  P  D  O  M  U  S  A  O
S  C  P  H  O  U  O  F  O  M  N  O  A  T  L
S  R  T  H  L  A  M  T  E  R  R  I  U  E  O
I  C  A  E  A  N  D  E  A  A  U  U  R  R  T
C  R  O  O  D  E  T  A  L  P  P  A  U  E  N
A  C  N  D  R  A  I  N  S  C  A  A  S  M  O
E  X  Y  R  E  T  P  O  E  A  H  C  R  A  E
T  O  T  H  D  I  P  L  O  D  O  C  U  S  L
R  E  T  A  E  T  N  A  L  P  E  D  E  S  A
E  R  A  L  L  O  S  A  U  R  U  S  T  S  P
```

SCIENCE

Hidden message:

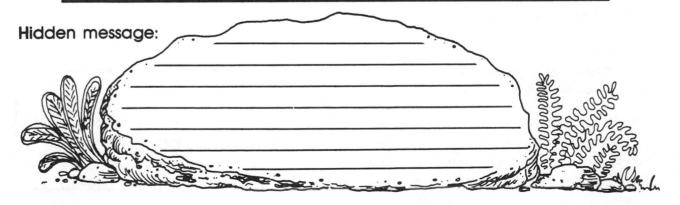

Name _____

Body Building Blocks

Just as some houses are built with bricks, your body is built with cells. Your body is made up of about 500 trillion cells.

Cells differ in **size** and **shape**, but they all have a few things in common. All cells have a nucleus. The **nucleus** is the center of the cell. It controls the cell's activities. Cells can **divide** and become two cells exactly like the original cell.

Your body has many kinds of cells. Each kind has a special job. **Muscle** cells help you move. Nerve cells carry messages between your brain and other parts of your body. Blood cells carry **oxygen** to other cells in your body.

Complete each sentence using the words in bold from above.

The __ __ __ __ __ __ __ controls the cell's
　　　3
activities.

Cells differ in __ __ __ __ and __ __ __ __ __.
　　　　　　　2　　　　　1

One cell can __ __ __ __ __ __ into two cells.
　　　　　　　　　　6

__ __ __ __ __ __ cells help you move.
　　　5

Blood cells carry __ __ __ __ __ __ to other
cells in your body.　　　4

muscle cell

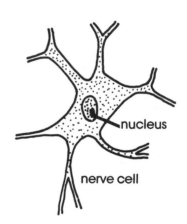
nucleus

nerve cell

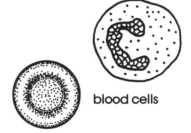
blood cells

Unscramble the numbered letters above to discover this amazing fact.

You began life as a __ __ __ __ __ __ cell!
　　　　　　　　　　1　2　3　4　5　6

Fun Facts

People and most animals are made of billions or even trillions of cells. But some animals are made of only one cell. To find out more about these animals, look up "protozoans" in your library.

Name _____

Bone Up on Your Bones!

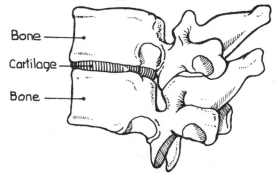

When you were born, your skeleton was made of soft bones called cartilage. As you grew, most of that cartilage turned into bone. However, all people still have some cartilage in their bodies. Our noses and our ears are cartilage, and there are pads of cartilage between sections of our backbone that act as cushions.

Besides supporting the body, the bones also serve other important purposes. They are storage houses for important minerals like calcium and phosphorous and the center of the bone, called bone marrow, produces new blood cells for our bodies.

Try the experiment below to discover more about bones.

Materials Needed
soup bones from a butcher
(Shin bones are ideal. Have
him/her saw it in half for you.)

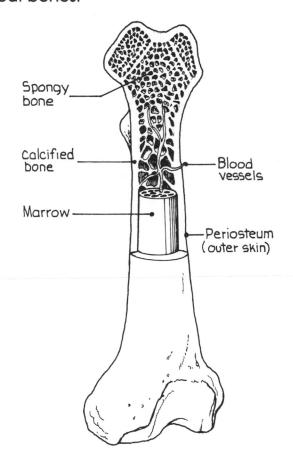

1. Look at the end of the whole bone. Find the parts labeled on the diagram to the right.

2. Now, separate the bone. Look inside the cavity which is filled with marrow. Write 5 adjectives to describe the marrow.

   _____

   _____

3. Pull away the skin covering the bone. What is the name for this outer skin?

   _____

   If the bone is fresh, you will see small red dots where blood vessels enter the bone. Name two types of blood vessels.

   _____

4. Carefully scoop out the bone marrow. Your teacher will now boil the bone to get it really clean. What do you see now? Write three facts about bones.

   _____

   _____

   _____

SCIENCE

Name _____

A Heart-y Puzzle for You

Use the clues to fill in the crossword puzzle about the heart.

Word Box

aorta	artery	atrium	capillary	cardiovascular
heart	vein	valves	ventricle	heartbeat

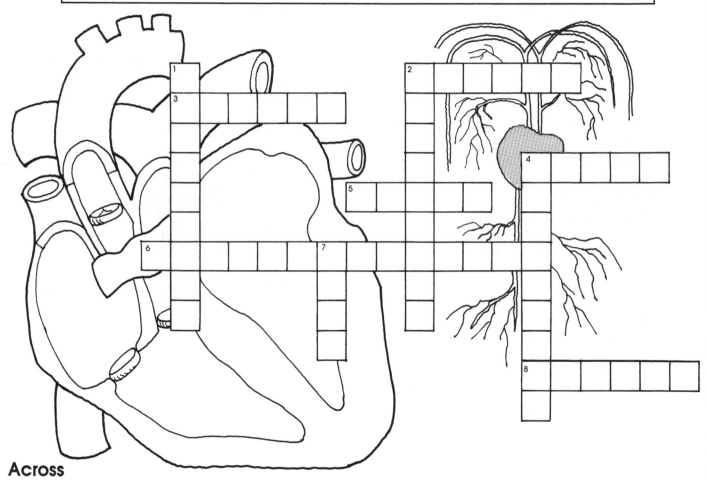

Across

2. control the flow of blood
3. a blood vessel that carries blood away from the heart
4. a muscular organ that circulates blood
5. the main artery
6. pertaining to the heart and blood vessels
8. receives blood into the heart

Down

1. a blood vessel that connects an artery to a vein
2. pumps blood out of the heart
4. a complete pulsation
7. a blood vessel that carries blood into the heart

Name _____

I Can Feel My Heartbeat

Each time your heart pumps the blood through veins and arteries, you can feel it! It's called a pulse. You can feel your pulse in two places where the arteries are close to your skin. Gently, place two fingers on the inside of your wrist or on your neck next to your windpipe. Silently count the pulses and complete the chart below.

*Teacher should time and direct each part. Time for 6 seconds, then multiply by 10.

Pulse Rate	Sitting	Walking Around Room for 1 Minute	Wait 2 Minutes, Then Standing	After 25 Jumping Jacks	Wait 1 Minute, Then Lying Down	After Jogging in Place for 2 Minutes	After Resting for 5 Minutes
in 6 seconds							
in 1 minute							

You should have found that your heart beats faster when you are active. That's because your body uses more oxygen when it exercises, and the blood must circulate faster to get more oxygen! Now, in a group of four, compare pulse rates and find the average for your group (using the 1 minute rate).

Pulse Rate	Sitting	After Walking	After Standing	After Jumping	After Lying Down	After Jogging	After Resting
You							
Person #2							
Person #3							
Person #4							
Total							
÷ 4 to find average							

SCIENCE

Name _____

Our Busy Brains

Your body's central nervous system includes your brain, spinal cord, and nerves that transmit information. It is responsible for receiving information from your senses, analyzing this information, and deciding how your body should respond. Once it has decided, it sends instructions triggering the required actions.

The central nervous system makes some simple decisions about your body's actions within the spinal cord. These are called spinal reflexes and include actions like pulling your hand away from a hot object. For the most part, however, the majority of decisions involve the brain.

Your brain, which weighs about three pounds, controls almost all of the activities in your body. It is made up of three major parts—the cerebrum, the cerebellum, and the brain stem. The cerebrum is divided into two hemispheres which are responsible for all thought and learning processes. The cerebellum is also divided into two parts, and they control all voluntary muscle movement. The brain stem, which is about the size of your thumb, takes care of all involuntary functions. Look around your classroom. Everyone's brain is telling him/her to do things. Fill in the jobs of each part of the brain and then answer the questions below.

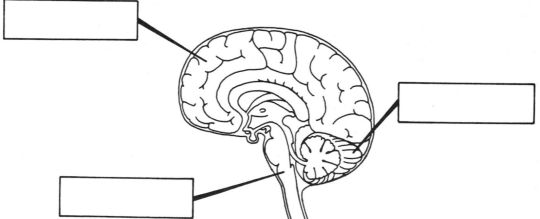

Name someone in your room who is using his/her cerebellum. _____

What is he/she doing? _____

Name someone who is using his/her brain stem. _____

What is he/she doing? _____

Name someone in your room who is using his/her cerebrum. _____

What is he/she doing? _____

Name _____

Find Your Brain Dominance

The two sides of the cerebellum work to control all voluntary movements. These include walking, running, writing and all other movements that we consciously want to do. One side of the cerebellum is usually dominant, or depended upon more heavily. The side that is dominant depends on the person. The left side of the brain controls the right side of your body and vice versa. That means that if a person writes with his/her right hand, he/she is probably left-brain dominant. Answer these questions to find your dominance.

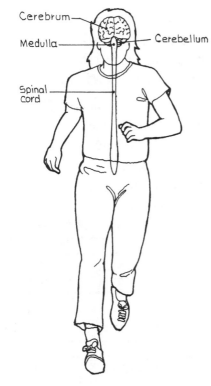

Try This:	Right	Left
Clasp your hands together. Which is on top?		
Pick up a pencil to write. Which hand do you use?		
Take 3 steps. Which foot did your start with?		
Try to do the splits. Which leg is in front?		
Hold your arms. Which arm is on top?		
Blink your eye. Which one did you wink?		
Pick up a fork. Which hand do you eat with?		
Hop 5 times on one foot. Which foot did you use?		
Look through a camera, telescope or microscope. Which eye did you use?		

How many times did you use your right? _____

How many times did you use your left? _____

Which side of your brain is probably more dominant? _____

(Be careful . . . they're opposite.)

*Make a class graph showing dominant sides.

Name _____

Your Pizza's Path

The digestive system is the group of organs that work together to gain fuel from the foods we eat and discard the unwanted waste. This system breaks down food into simple substances your body's cells can use. It then absorbs these substances into the bloodstream and any leftover waste matter is eliminated.

When you eat pizza (or any food), each bite you take goes through a path in the human body called the alimentary canal, or the digestive tract. This canal consists of the mouth, esophagus, stomach, and small and large intestines. It is in this path that foods are broken down, vitamins are saved and poisons are discarded. Study the path below.

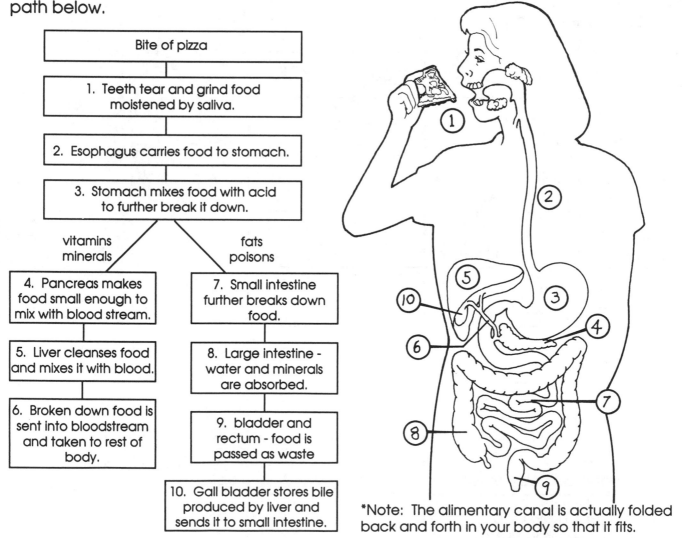

```
Bite of pizza

1. Teeth tear and grind food
   moistened by saliva.

2. Esophagus carries food to stomach.

3. Stomach mixes food with acid
   to further break it down.
```

vitamins   fats
minerals   poisons

```
4. Pancreas makes         7. Small intestine
food small enough to      further breaks down
mix with blood stream.         food.

5. Liver cleanses food    8. Large intestine -
and mixes it with blood.   water and minerals
                            are absorbed.

6. Broken down food is    9. bladder and
sent into bloodstream      rectum - food is
and taken to rest of       passed as waste
body.

                          10. Gall bladder stores bile
                          produced by liver and
                          sends it to small intestine.
```

*Note: The alimentary canal is actually folded back and forth in your body so that it fits.

1. Use a black crayon to trace the path of the healthy parts of the pizza.
2. Use a blue crayon to trace the path of the unhealthy parts of the pizza.
3. Name 3 parts of the pizza that are healthy. _____
4. Name 3 parts of the pizza that are unhealthy. _____

Name _____

Oh, Yes, I See Now!

One of the most sensitive nerves in your body is the optic nerve. It connects your eyes to your brain. The optic nerve receives messages from other nerves that surround your eyes in the retina. As light is caught in the pupils of your eyes, it is sent to the retina, then to the optic nerve, and at last to the brain. Try this experiment to watch your pupils change!

1. Close your eyes and cover them with your hands. Count to 100, open your eyes, and immediately observe them in a mirror. Draw how your eyes look.

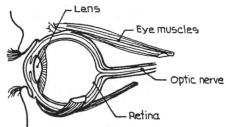

2. Now look at a light in your classroom. Count to 100 and then draw your eyes again.

3. How did your pupils change from one experiment to another? _____

_____

4. Why do you think they changed? _____

_____

5. Why do people wear sunglasses? _____

_____

Daily Learning Drills Grade 4

SCIENCE

Name _____

Energy Savers

Fats give you twice as much energy as protein or carbohydrates. Your body uses fats to save energy for future use. The fats we eat come from animals in the form of meat, eggs, milk, and much more. We also get fats from some plants like beans, peanuts, and corn. But not all plants give us fats in our diet.

Look at the pictures.
Circle the foods which are rich in fat.
Then list them on the chart.

Fat Food Sources	
Animal	Plant

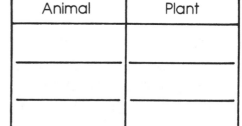

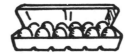
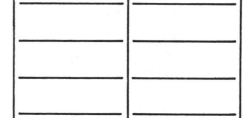

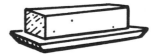

Find Out

Here is a simple test to tell if a food has fat.
1. Cut a brown paper bag into several four-inch squares.
2. Rub a piece of food on a square until it looks wet.
3. Label the paper.
4. Let the paper dry overnight.
5. Hold the paper up to the window the next day. If there is a grease spot, the food contains fat.

Name _____

You Are What You Eat!

Having a nutritious diet helps your body fight diseases. Write the foods from the Word Bank in their correct category(s). Use references if necessary.

Word Bank				
tomatoes	bread	eggs	milk	potatoes
oranges	sugar	fish	cereal	green beans
chicken	margarine	cheese	noodles	rice
butter	apples	red meat		

Carbohydrates

_____ _____

_____ _____

_____ _____

_____ _____

_____ _____

Proteins

_____ _____

_____ _____

_____ _____

_____ _____

Fats

_____ _____

_____ _____

_____ _____

Minerals

_____ _____

_____ _____

_____ _____

Below is a list of the food groups. Write what you ate yesterday in each group. Did you get enough servings of each?

Milk and milk-equivalent foods Group
(2 to 3 cup servings a day)

_____

_____

Fruit & Vegetable Group
(3 to 5 cup servings a day)

_____

_____

Grain Group (4 to 6 oz. servings a day)

_____

Beans and Meat Group (3 to 5 oz. servings a day)

_____

SCIENCE

Name _____

What's in a Label?

Labels give us all kinds of information about the foods we eat. The ingredients of a food are listed in a special order. The ingredient with the largest amount is listed first, the one with the next largest amount is listed second, and so on.

Complete the "Breakfast Table Label Survey" using information from the label on this page.

Breakfast Table Label Survey

1. What does R.D.A. mean? _____

2. Calories per serving with milk _____

3. Calories per serving without milk _____

4. Calories per ½ cup serving of milk _____

5. Protein per serving with milk _____

6. Protein per serving without milk _____

7. Protein in ½ cup serving of milk _____

8. Percentage U.S. R.D.A. of Vitamin C _____

9. First ingredient _____

10. Is sugar a listed ingredient? _____

    If yes, in what place is it listed? _____

11. Were any vitamins added? _____

12. What preservative was added? _____

Find Out: What food product has this ingredient label? "Carbonated water, sugar, corn sweetener, natural flavorings, caramel color, phosphoric acid, caffeine."

Nutrition Information Per Serving

Serving Size: 1 OZ. (About 1⅓ Cups) (28.35 g)
Servings Per Package: 14

	1 OZ. (28.35 g) Cereal	with ½ Cup (118mL) Vitamin D Fortified Whole Milk
Calories	110	190
Protein	1 g	5 g
Carbohydrate	25 g	31 g
Fat	1 g	5 g
Sodium	195 mg	255 mg

Percentages Of U.S. Recommended Daily Allowances (U.S. RDA)

Protein	2%	8%
Vitamin A	25%	30%
Vitamin C	*	*
Thiamine	25%	30%
Riboflavin	25%	35%
Niacin	25%	25%
Calcium	*	15%
Iron	10%	10%
Vitamin D	10%	25%
Vitamin B_6	25%	30%
Folic Acid	25%	25%
Vitamin B_{12}	25%	30%
Phosphorus	2%	10%
Magnesium	2%	6%
Zinc	10%	15%
Copper	2%	4%

*Contains less than 2% of the U.S. RDA for these nutrients.

Ingredients: Corn Flour, Sugar, Oat Flour, Salt, Hydrogenated Coconut and/or Palm Kernel Oil, Corn Syrup, Honey and fortified with the following nutrients: Vitamin A Palmitate, Niacinamide, Iron, Zinc Oxide (Source of Zinc), Vitamin B_6, Riboflavin (Vitamin B_2), Thiamine Mononitrate (Vitamin B_1), Vitamin B_{12}, Folic Acid and Vitamin D_2. BHA added to packaging material to preserve freshness.

Carbohydrate Information

	1 OZ. (28.35 g) Cereal	With ½ Cup (118 mL) Whole Milk
Starch and Related Carbohydrates	14 g	14 g
Sucrose and Other Sugars	11 g	17 g
Total Carbohydrates	25 g	31 g

Name _____

I'm Tired

Do you feel tired after raking the lawn? You feel tired then because work takes a lot of energy. **Energy** is the ability to do work.

There are many forms of energy. Food contains **chemical energy**. Your television uses **electrical energy**. The furnace in your house gives you **heat energy**. The moving parts of your bicycle have another form of energy called **mechanical energy**. Anything that moves has mechanical energy.

Energy can be changed from one form to another. Your radio changes electrical energy into sound energy. Your parents' car may change chemical energy into heat energy and the heat energy into mechanical energy.

_____

_____

- Complete the puzzle using the clues below.
  1. A fire gives us __ __ __ __ energy.
  2. Anything that moves has

     __ __ __ __ __ __ __ __ __ __ energy.
  3. __ __ __ __ __ __ is the ability to do work.
  4. Energy can be __ __ __ __ __ __ __ from one form into another form.
  5. Food contains __ __ __ __ __ __ __ __ energy.

Daily Learning Drills Grade 4

Name _____

Energy in Motion

"Mom, how can I knock down more pins?" Matt asked. "You are bowling straight enough, Matt. Try rolling the ball faster, or try using a heavier ball," his mom replied.

The bowling ball is doing work by knocking over the pins. The ball has kinetic energy. **Kinetic energy** is the energy of motion.

If the ball had more kinetic energy, it could do more work and knock down more pins. If you increase the mass of the ball or its speed, you would increase its kinetic energy.

Just before Matt rolled the ball, he was standing still and not moving. Matt's body had stored energy that would turn into kinetic energy once he started swinging the ball. This stored energy is called **potential energy.**

- Write **P** next to the pictures that show potential energy and **K** next to the pictures that show kinetic energy.

- Look back at the picture of Matt getting ready to bowl.
  1. At what point will the ball have the most potential energy?_____
  2. At what point will the ball have the most kinetic energy?_____
  3. At what point will the ball have the least kinetic energy?_____
  4. At what point will the ball have the least potential energy?_____

  Challenge: A roller-coaster car with people in it will travel much faster than an empty car. Why?

Name _____

Around and Around

A doorknob is a simple machine you use every day. It is a **wheel and axle machine.** The wheel is connected to the axle. The axle is a center post. When the wheel moves, the axle does too.

Opening a door by turning the axle with your fingers is very hard. But by turning the doorknob, which is the "wheel," you use much less force. The doorknob turns the axle for you. The doorknob makes it easy because it is much bigger than the axle. You turn the doorknob a greater distance, but with much less force.

Sometimes the "wheel" of a wheel and axle machine doesn't look like a wheel. But look at the path the doorknob, a wheel, makes when it is turned. The path makes a circle, just like a wheel.

• Color just the wheels of the wheel and axle machines below.

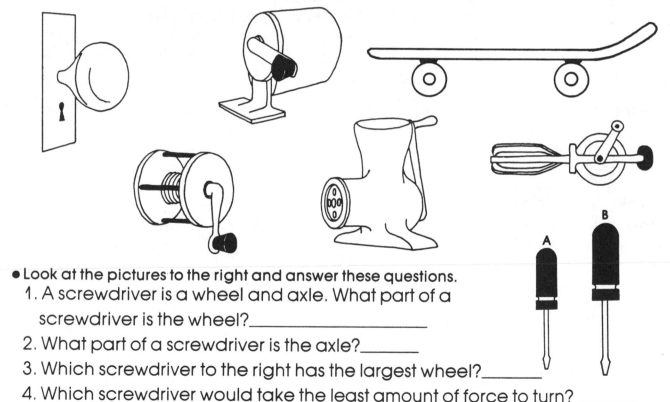

• Look at the pictures to the right and answer these questions.
  1. A screwdriver is a wheel and axle. What part of a screwdriver is the wheel?_____
  2. What part of a screwdriver is the axle?_____
  3. Which screwdriver to the right has the largest wheel?_____
  4. Which screwdriver would take the least amount of force to turn?_____
  5. Which screwdriver must travel the greatest distance?_____

Stumper

Why is the crank on a meat grinder larger than the crank on a pencil sharpener?
Why is the steering wheel on a truck larger than the steering wheel on a car?

Name _____

Levers

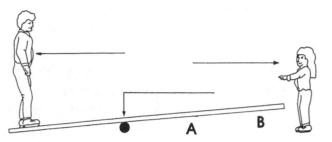

- **Use the words from the Word Bank to complete the sentences.**

     Mandy wants to try to lift her dad off the ground. Where should Mandy stand on the board? By standing on point __, Mandy can lift her dad.

     The board resting on the log is an example of a _ _ _ _ _ _ _ machine called a lever. A **lever** has three parts–the **force,** the **fulcrum,** and the **load.** Mandy is the force. The point on which the lever turns is called the _ _ _ _ _ _ _ _ . And Mandy's dad, the object to be lifted, is called the _ _ _ _ _. The greater the _ _ _ _ _ _ _ _ _ between the _ _ _ _ _ _ and the fulcrum, the _ _ _ _ _ _ _ it is to lift the load. The closer the distance between the **force** and the **fulcrum,** the harder it is to lift the load.

- **Label the picture of Mandy and her father with these words: load, force,** and **fulcrum.**

Fulcrum far away from load   Fulcrum close to load

     The distance between the **load** and the **fulcrum** also affects the force needed to lift a load. The closer the fulcrum is to the load, the easier it is to lift the load.

- **Look at the pictures above to answer these questions.**

  1. Matt wants to move a large rock with a lever. Which lever would let him use the least amount of force to move the rock?_____

  2. Which lever would have to be moved the greatest distance to move the rock?_____

  3. Why is a lever called a simple machine? _____

- **Label the force, fulcrum,** and **load** of the levers below.

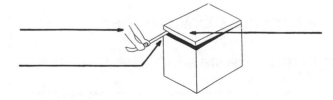

Name _____

Dancing Parsley

Investigate

Run a comb through your hair 30 times. Go only one way. Hold the comb next to some parsley flakes. What happened? _____
_____

Run the comb through your hair 30 times again. Hold it next to some shredded tissue. What happened? _____
_____

Rub the comb 30 times against the hairs on your arm, on a woolen sweater or on a shiny shirt or blouse. Rub only one way. Hold the comb next to the parsley flakes.
Did the comb pick them up? _____
Hold the comb next to the shredded tissue.
Did the comb pick up the tissue? _____

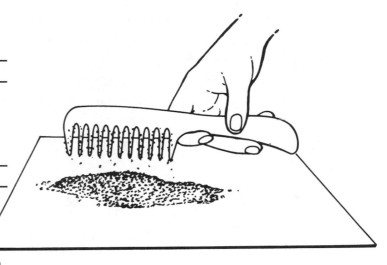

Extending the Concept

Tear another tissue into long, thin strips. Run the comb through your hair 30 times. Hold the comb next to one of the strips of tissue.
Did the comb attract the tissue? _____

Dancing Cereal

Arrange two long rows of puffed rice cereal next to each other. Run the comb through your hair 30 times. Hold the comb between the rows of cereal.
What happened? _____
Hold the comb with the cereal stuck to it in the air and wait 2 minutes.
What happened? _____

Name _____

Charge It!

Have you ever scuffed your feet as you walked across the carpet and then brought your finger close to someone's nose? Zap!! Did the person jump? The spark you made was **static electricity.**

Static electricity is made when objects gain or lose tiny bits of electricity called **electrical charges.** The charges are either positive or negative.

Objects that have electrical charges act like magnets, attracting or repelling each other. If two objects have **like charges** (the same kind of charges), they will repel each other. If two objects have **unlike charges** (different charges), the objects will attract each other.

Find out more about static electricity by unscrambling the word(s) in each sentence.

1. Flashes of (ghtlining) _____ in the sky are caused by static electricity in the clouds.

2. Electrical charges are either (ospivite) _____ or (givnatee) _____.

3. Small units of electricity are called (srgache) _____.

4. Two objects with unlike charges will (arcttat) _____ each other.

5. Sometimes electric charges jump between objects with (unkile) _____ charges. This is what happens when lightning flashes in the sky.

Look at the pictures below to see how static electricity affects objects.
1. Name the two objects that are interacting in each picture.
2. Tell whether the two objects have **like charges** or **unlike charges.**

Objects: _____ _____ _____

_____ _____ _____

Charges: _____ _____ _____

Something Special: Hold this paper against a wall and rub it with 50 quick strokes with the side of your pencil. Take your hand away. Presto! The paper stays on the wall because of the static electricity you have made.

Name _____

Power Paths

    A **circuit** is a path along which electricity travels. It travels in a loop around the circuit. In the circuit pictured below, the electricity travels through the wire, battery, switch, and bulb. The electricity must have a source. What is the source in this circuit? You're right if you said the battery.

    If the wire in the circuit were cut, there would be a **gap**. The electricity wouldn't be able to flow across the gap. Then the bulb would not light. This is an example of an **open circuit**. If there were no gaps, the bulb would light. This is an example of a **closed circuit**.

switch

1. Draw in the wire to the battery, switch, and bulb to make a closed circuit.

 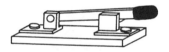

2. Draw in the wire to the battery, switch, and bulb to make an open circuit.

 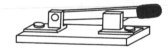

• Unscramble the word at the end of each sentence to fill in the blank.

   3. Even the tiniest _____ can stop the electricity from flowing. (apg)

   4. A _____ is a path along which electricity flows. (ricituc)

   5. If there are no gaps, or openings, a _____ circuit is formed. (sodelc)

   6. A battery is a source of _____ in some circuits. (treleciytci)

Fun Fact

If all of the circuits in a small personal computer were made out of wire and metal switches, the computer would fill the average classroom. Today these circuits are found in tiny chips called microchips.

SCIENCE

Fill the Gap

Name _____

The bulb won't light in the circuit above. What's wrong with the circuit? It has a gap. How could you fill the gap to make a closed circuit? The easiest way would be to connect the two wires, but with what?

What would happen if you placed a paper clip across the gap? How about a nail? The bulb would light up. The nail or paper clip would form a bridge across the gap. The nail and paper clip carry, or **conduct,** electricity. They are both **conductors.**

Some materials will not carry the electricity well enough to make the bulb light. Try a rubber band. The bulb won't light. Rubber is a poor conductor of electricity. It is called an **insulator.**

- Find the different materials hidden in the wordsearch. The materials listed "up and down" are conductors. Those written "across" are insulators. List these materials in the correct group.

```
C O T T O N P
O K G T S O R
P A P E R X K
P L A S T I C
E U D T O R D
R M K E L O S
T I X E R N N
N N G L A S S
R U B B E R Z
K M G R X Z P
```

Insulator

_____

_____

_____

_____

_____

Conductor

_____

_____

_____

_____

- Now that you know which materials make good conductors and which make good insulators, write **C** under each object that is a conductor and **I** under each object that is an insulator.

   Eraser

 Root Beer _____

 _____

 _____

Name _____

Series or Parallel?

You can light several light bulbs with only one cell. In picture **A,** the bulbs are connected in a **series circuit.** What would happen to the circuit if you unscrewed one bulb? All the lights would go out. In picture **B,** the bulbs are connected in a **parallel circuit.** What would happen if you unscrewed a light bulb in a parallel circuit? The other lights would still burn.

Dry cells can also be connected in series and parallel circuits. However, cells are usually connected in series. A series of cells increases the amount of power that flows in a circuit. A series of cells will make a light bulb burn brighter.

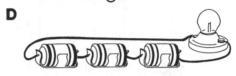

1. In which picture above are the cells connected in a series?_____

2. In which picture above will the bulb light more brightly?_____

3. When one light burned out on Sally's Christmas tree, the rest of the lights went out, too. In what kind of circuit were the bulbs connected?_____

4. Do you think the electric lights in your house are connected in a series circuit or a parallel circuit?_____ Why? _____

   _____

5. How are the batteries connected in the flashlight below? In a series or parallel?_____

6. Some flashlights have four or five cells. How would the brightness of the light from this kind of flashlight compare with one that only has one or two cells?

_____

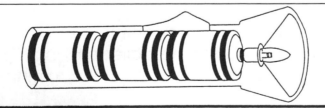

> **Fun Fact**
>
> A single dry cell is often called a battery, but it really isn't a battery. A battery is two or more cells connected together. You can buy batteries that look like a single cell, but they are really two or more cells connected together and put inside one case.

Name _____

Powered Up

Where does the electricity that is in your house come from? It all begins at a large **power plant.** The power plant has a large **turbine generator.** High pressure steam spins the turbines and the generator that is attached to the turbine shaft. As the generator spins, it produces hundreds of megawatts of electricity.

- Below is a picture of a power plant where electricity is generated. Label each part using the terms found in the Power Bank below.

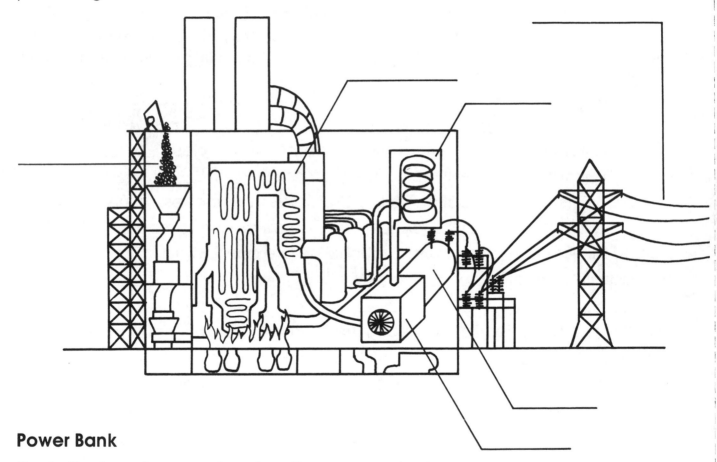

Power Bank

Fuel – Fuel, such as coal, enters the power plant.

Boiler – The burning fuel heats water in the boiler, making high pressure steam.

Turbine – High pressure steam spins the blades of the turbine up to 3,000 times a minute.

Condenser – Steam is cooled in the condenser and is turned back into water. The water is sent back to the boiler.

Generator – The generator attached to the turbine turns, producing hundreds of megawatts of electricity.

Power Lines – Electricity is sent to your home through wires.

Name _____

Portable Power

Steve and Lenny really enjoyed listening to the radio while they fished. Radios need electricity to work. Where did Steve's radio get its power? From a **dry cell battery,** of course. Dry cells are sources of portable power.

Most portable radios use dry cells. A dry cell makes electricity by changing chemical energy into electrical energy. Chemicals in the dry cell act on each other and make **electrons** flow. The flow of electrons is called **electricity.**

● Use the words from the Word Bank to label the parts of the dry cell. You can use your science book to help, but first try to figure out each part by yourself.

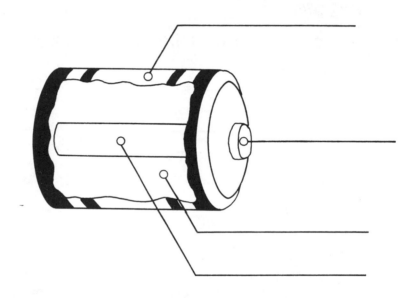

Word Bank

chemical paste
carbon rod
zinc case
terminal

Portable Power Inventory

List the appliances, tools, or toys in your house that are powered with dry cells.

_____   _____
_____   _____
_____   _____
_____   _____
_____   _____
_____   _____

Find Out

Before batteries were invented, scientists did all their experiments with static electricity. Find out who made the first battery and when it was made.

SCIENCE

Name _____

Magnetic Attraction

Try to pick up each of these objects with your magnet. Circle the ones which it picks up.

scissors   eraser   ruler   pencil   crayon

paper clip   thumbtack   toothpick   pen

A magnet will only pick up an object made of _____.

Investigate

List all the objects you can find which your magnet picks up or is attracted to.

1. _____   6. _____
2. _____   7. _____
3. _____   8. _____
4. _____   9. _____
5. _____   10. _____

Is the magnet attracted to any non-metal object? _____

Extending the Concept

Hold a piece of tagboard between the magnet and each object you listed in the "Investigate" section. List each one the magnet is still attracted to.

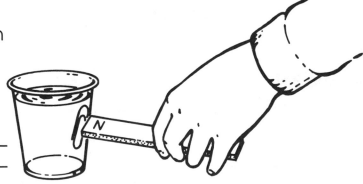

_____

_____

Place each of the objects the magnet is still attracted to in a cup of water.
Hold the magnet against the outside of the cup.

Which items were the magnet still able to attract? _____

_____

What other materials can a magnet attract objects through, besides tagboard and water? _____

Name _____

Working with Electromagnets

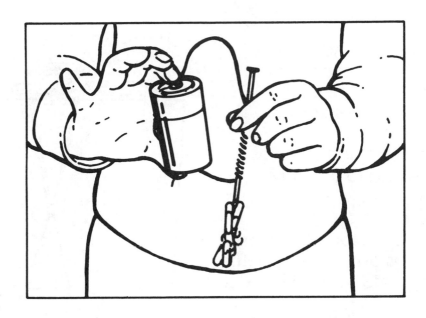

Investigate

1. Strip 1 inch of insulation from each end of a 2-foot-long piece of thin wire.
2. Wrap the wire around a nail 30 times, leaving most of the extra wire dangling at one end.
3. Touch one bare end of the wire to the top of the battery.
4. Touch the other bare end of the wire to the bottom of the battery.
5. Hold the nail near some paper clips.
   How many paper clips did the electromagnet pick up? _____

Making the Electromagnet Stronger

Wrap the wire around the nail 30 more times.
How many paper clips will the electromagnet pick up now? _____
Tape two batteries together with the top of one battery touching the bottom of the other.
How many paper clips will the electromagnet pick up now? _____
Wrap as many coils around the nail as you can.
How many paper clips can you pick up now? _____
Name two ways to make an electromagnet stronger. _____

SCIENCE

Name _____

Weight and Gravity

Making a Scale

1. Use a hole punch or scissors to punch two holes at the top of a clear plastic cup. Make the holes exactly opposite each other.
2. Cut a piece of fish line 6 inches long. Tie one end to one hole and the other end to the opposite hole.
3. Tape a ruler to the top of your desk so one end hangs over the edge. Then tape a piece of tagboard to the side of the desk.
4. Wrap a rubber band around the fish line and loop it inside itself. Now hang the rubber band from the ruler. The cup should hang in front of the tagboard.

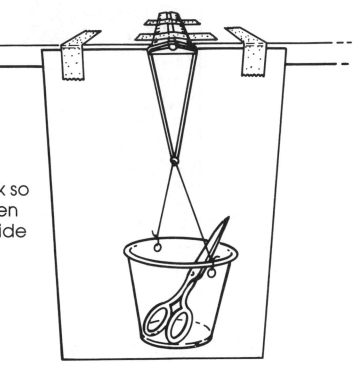

Comparing Weights

To weigh an object, place it in the cup. The heavier the object, the lower the cup will sag. To record its weight, put a mark on the tagboard even with the bottom of the cup and write the name of the object next to the mark.

Weigh these objects. Then number them from lightest to heaviest.

_____scissors _____water _____pencil _____coin
_____stone _____crayon box _____eraser _____magnifying glass

Extending the Concept

Why is gravity important to man? _____
_____

What would happen if there were no gravity? _____
_____

Name _____

Great Gravity Changes

The gravity that pulls on the moon is ⅙ as strong as the pull on Earth. This means that you could jump up and stay in the air six times longer than you can now! Work with a partner to find the measurements below. Record them and then multiply them by six to see how different life would be on the moon.

Activity/Object	Measurement on Earth	Measurement on Moon (Earth x 6)
Distance you can jump with running start (in inches)		
Height you can jump (in inches)		
Distance you can throw a ball (in feet)		
Distance you can kick a ball (in feet)		
Number of books you can pick up at one time		

The gravitational pull on the sun is 28 times stronger than that on Earth. This means that everything would weigh 28 times more if it were on the sun. Below are several objects. Use a scale to find their approximate weight on the sun by multiplying them by 28. To find their weight on the moon, divide their Earth-weight by 6 because the gravitational pull of the moon is that much less than Earth's.

Object	Weight on Earth	Weight on Sun (Earth x 28)	Weight on Moon (Earth ÷ 6)
your math book			
your book bag (full)			
yourself			
(object of your choice)			
(object of your choice)			
(object of your choice)			

SCIENCE

Name _____

A Lo-o-o-ong Trip

What is the longest trip you have ever taken? Was it 100 km? 500 km? Maybe it was more than 1,000 km. You probably didn't know it, but last year you traveled 1 billion kilometers.

The Earth travels in a path around the sun called its **orbit**. Earth's orbit is almost 1 billion kilometers. It takes 1 year, or 365 days, for the Earth to orbit or **revolve** around the sun.

Look at the picture of
Earth's orbit.
It is not a perfect circle.
It is a special shape
called an **ellipse.**

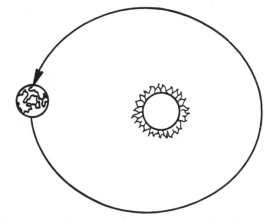

1. How long does it take for the Earth to revolve around the sun? _____

2. How many times has the Earth revolved around the sun since you were born?

_____

3. How many kilometers has the Earth traveled in orbit since you were born?

_____

4. Put an "X" on Earth's orbit to show where it will be in six months.

Experiment

You can draw an ellipse. Place two straight pins about 8 cm apart in a piece of cardboard. Tie the ends of a 25 cm piece of string to the pins. Place your pencil inside the string. Keeping the string tight, draw an ellipse.

Make four different ellipses by changing the length of the string and the distance between the pins. How do the ellipses change?

Fun Fact

Hold on tight. The Earth travels at a speed of 100,000 km per hour in its orbital path around the sun.

Name _____

"Lift-off"

"3-2-1, lift-off!" With a mighty roar, the Saturn V **rocket** leaves the **launch pad**.

Riding high on top of the Saturn V in the **Command Module** are the three Apollo astronauts. Below their Command Module is a Lunar Landing Module that will land two of the astronauts on the moon's surface.

Below this, the Saturn V has three parts, or **stages**. It takes a lot of power to escape the Earth's pull, called **gravity**. The space-craft must reach a speed of almost 40,000 km per hour. The bottom, or first stage, is the largest. After each stage uses up its **fuel**, it drops off and the next stage starts. Each stage has its own fuel and **oxygen**. The fuels need oxygen in order to burn.

The astronauts are now on their 3-day journey to the moon.

Color each Saturn V section a different color. Color the key to match each section.

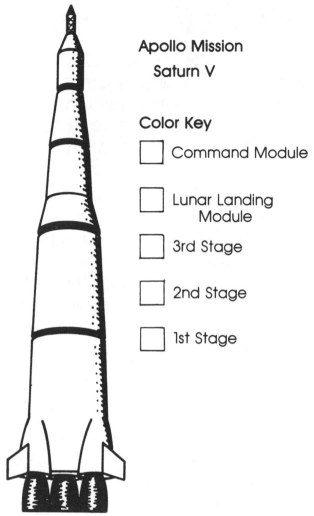

Apollo Mission
Saturn V

Color Key

☐ Command Module

☐ Lunar Landing Module

☐ 3rd Stage

☐ 2nd Stage

☐ 1st Stage

SCIENCE

Fill in the spaces with the words in bold from above. Then use the numbered letters to answer the question.

1. The Saturn V __ __ __ __ __ has three main parts, or __ __ __ __ __ __.
                        13   1   5

2. Rocket engines burn __ __ __ __ and __ __ __ __ __.
                          10   8   6   16   7

3. The Earth's pull is called __ __ __ __ __ __ __.
                                16 11   14

4. "Lift-off." The Saturn V leaves the __ __ __ __ __ __ __.
                                         9   2   12

5. The Apollo astronauts ride in the __ __ __ __ __ __ __ __ __ __ __.
                                                     3 15   4

What were the first words spoken from the surface of the moon on July 20, 1969?

"__ __ __ __ __, __,
  1 2 3 1 5   6 7 8   5 4 3 9 9   5 1 8 12   10 6 11   4 3 7

__ __."
 6 7 8   16 14 3 7 1   9 8 3 12   10 6 11   4 3 7 13 14 7 15

Neil Armstrong, Apollo II Commander

Name _____

"Live Via Satellite"

"This program is brought to you live via satellite from halfway around the world." Satellites are very helpful in sending TV messages from one side of the world to the other. But this is only one of the special jobs that satellites can do.

Most satellites are placed into orbit around the Earth by riding on top of giant rockets. Only recently have some satellites been carried into orbit by a space shuttle. While orbiting the Earth, the giant doors of the shuttle are opened, and the satellite is pushed into orbit.

This satellite relays TV signals from halfway around the world.

Satellites send information about many things. Use the code to find the different kinds of messages and information satellites send.

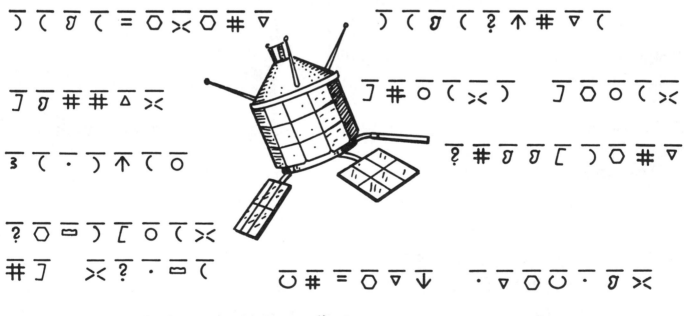

. ! ▭ △ (⅃ ↓ ↑ ○ + : ♉ ∪ ▽ # ? □ ○ ⤬) [= ₃ 𝒪 ⊣⋔

A B C D E F G H I J K L M N O P Q R S T U V W X Y Z

Find Out

Satellites in space need power to send messages. Find out where satellites get their power.

Name _____

Just Imagine . . .

Earth is a very special planet because it is the only planet known to have life. Only Earth has the necessities to support life—water, air, moderate temperatures, and suitable air pressure. Earth is about 92,960,000 miles from the sun and is 7,926 miles in diameter. Its highest recorded temperature was 136° F in Libya and the lowest was -127° F in Antarctica.

Venus is known as Earth's "twin" because the two planets are so similar in size. At about 67,230,000 miles from the sun, Venus is 7,521 miles in diameter. Venus is the brightest planet in the sky, as seen from Earth, and is brighter even than the stars. The temperature on the surface of this planet is about 850° F.

Mercury is the planet closest to the sun. It is about 35,980,000 miles from the sun and is 3,031 miles in diameter. The temperature on this planet ranges from -315° F to 648° F.

Pretend you were going to Venus or Mercury for spring break. Make a list of the things you would bring (you may have to invent them in order to survive) and draw a picture of the vehicle that would take you there. Write about your experiences on another sheet of paper.

SCIENCE

Things I Need to Take	**Vehicle**
_____	
_____	
_____	
_____	
_____	
_____	
_____	
_____	
_____	
_____	
_____	
_____	

Name _____

The Large Planets

Jupiter is the largest planet in the solar system. The diameter at its equator is about 88,836 miles. It was named after the king of the Roman gods and is the fifth closest planet to the sun at about 483,600,000 miles away. This large planet also spins faster than any other. It makes a complete rotation in about 9 hours and 55 minutes.

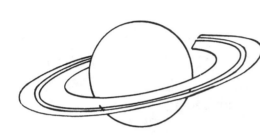

The surface of Jupiter cannot be seen from Earth because of the layers of dense clouds surrounding it. Jupiter has no solid surface but is made of liquid and gases that are held together by gravity.

One characteristic unique to Jupiter is the Great Red Spot that is about 25,000 miles long and about 20,000 miles wide. Astronomers believe the spot to be a swirling, hurricane-like mass of gas.

Saturn, the second largest planet, is well known for its seven thin, flat rings encircling it. Its diameter is about 74,898 miles at the equator. It was named for the Roman god of agriculture. Saturn is the sixth planet closest to the sun and is about 888,200,000 miles away from it. Like Jupiter, Saturn travels around the sun in an oval-shaped (elliptical) orbit, and it takes the planet about 10 hours and 39 minutes to make one rotation.

Scientists believe Saturn is a giant ball of gas that also has no solid surface. Like Jupiter, they believe it too may have an inner core of rocky material. Whereas Saturn claims 23 satellites, Jupiter has only 16 known satellites.

Fill in the chart below to compare Jupiter and Saturn. Make two of your own categories.

Categories	Jupiter	Saturn
1. diameter		
2. origin of name		
3. distance from sun		
4. rotations		
5. surface		
6. unique characteristics		
7.		
8.		

Name _____

The Twin Planets

1. Uranus and Neptune are similar in size, rotation time, and temperature. Sometimes they are called twin planets. Uranus is about 1,786,400,000 miles from the sun. Neptune is about 2,798,800,000 miles from the sun. What is the difference between these two distances? _____

2. Neptune can complete a rotation in 18 to 20 hours. Uranus can make one in 16 to 28 hours. What is the average time it takes Neptune to complete a rotation? _____ Uranus? _____

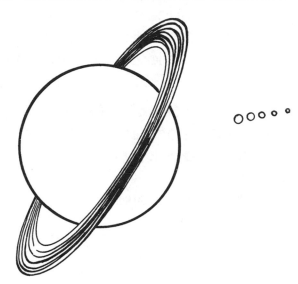

3. Can you believe that it is about -353° F on Neptune, and about -357° F on Uranus? Brrr! that's cold! What is the temperature outside today in your town? _____

   How much warmer is it in your town than on Neptune? _____ Uranus? _____

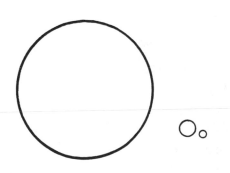

4. Uranus has at least five small satellites moving around it. Their names are Miranda, Ariel, Umbriel, Tatania and Oberon. They are 75, 217, 155, 310 and 280 miles in diameter respectively. What is the average diameter of Uranus' satellites? _____

5. Neptune was first seen in 1846 by Johanna G. Galle. Uranus was first discovered by Sir William Herschel in 1781. How many years ago was Neptune discovered? _____ Uranus? _____

   About how many years later was Uranus discovered than Neptune? _____

6. Both Uranus and Neptune have names taken from Greek and Roman mythology. Use an encyclopedia to find their names and their origins.

   _____

   _____

   _____

   _____

SCIENCE

Name _____

Pluto and Planet X

Pluto, 1,430 miles in diameter, is the smallest planet. It is also the farthest planet from the sun at 3,666,200,000 miles away. However, this is not always true! Pluto's orbit forms a long, thin oval shape that crosses the path of Neptune's orbit every 248 years. So, for about 200 Earth-years, Pluto is actually closer to the sun than Neptune! It is closer now and won't return to its outer position until 1999. Try this art project:

Materials Needed

construction paper
crayons or chalk
glue
yarn (various colors)
pencil

Directions

1. Use a crayon to draw the sun in the center of the paper.
2. Use your pencil to draw the orbit of each planet, being careful to cross Pluto's with Neptune's.
3. Color the planets along the orbits.
4. Trace the orbits in glue, then lay yarn on top.

*Only Pluto's and Neptune's orbits should cross.

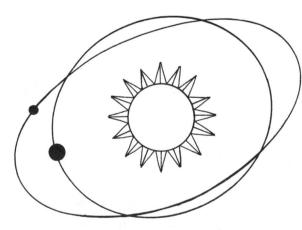

Although there are only nine known planets, it is possible that another exists beyond Pluto. Some people refer to it as Planet X. Write a name for it below and use information about the other planets to estimate and create answers in the chart.

Planet Name	Diameter	Distance from Sun	Revolution	Rotation	Satellites	Symbol

Name _____

Keeping the Order

Nine planets orbit the sun. These planets are arranged in order according to their distance from the sun. Do you know which planet is closest and which is farthest from the sun?

Number the planets in order below with number one being the planet closest to the sun. Use the mean (average) distances in miles to help you.

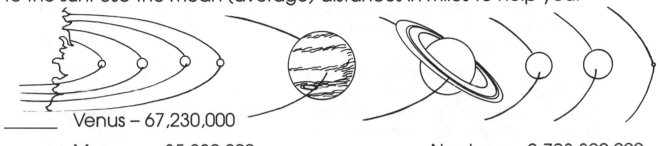

_____ Venus – 67,230,000

_____ Mercury – 35,980,000   _____ Neptune – 2,798,800,000

_____ Earth – 92,960,000   _____ Uranus – 1,786,400,000

_____ Pluto – 3,666,200,000   _____ Jupiter – 483,600,000

_____ Mars – 141,000,000   _____ Saturn – 888,200,000

To help you remember the order of the planets, write a sentence. Use the first letter of each planet, in order from the planet closest to the sun to the one farthest from it, to write words to make a sentence. **Note:** To help you get started, write the planets in order on the lines below and then write down some words on each line that begin with the first letter of that planet.

_____

_____

_____

_____

_____

_____

_____

Your sentence: _____

SCIENCE

Name _____

Star Search

On a clear dark night, you can look up in the sky and see about 2,000 stars without the help of a telescope. But unless you know which stars form constellations, all you will be seeing are stars.

Carefully poke holes in the *Constellation Patterns* sheet using a sharp pencil. Then tonight, when it is dark, hold a flashlight behind the paper to make the constellations appear.

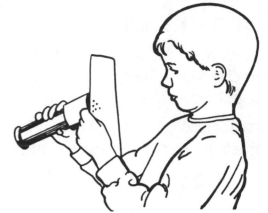

Below are star charts to further help you recognize the constellations. To use the charts, turn them until the present month is at the bottom. Depending on your latitude and the time of night, you should be able to see most of the constellations in the middle and upper part of the chart.

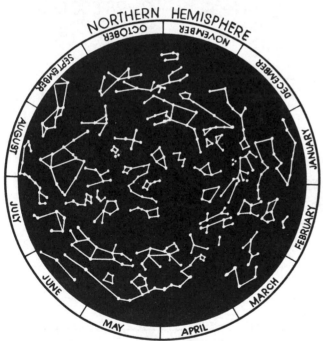

1. Using the *Constellation Patterns* sheet to help you, label as many of the constellations in the chart as you can.

2. Which constellations should you be able to see tonight? _____

_____

_____

3. When it is dark, go outside to look for constellations.

4. Which ones do you actually see?

_____

_____

_____

5. On the back of this paper, draw the night sky you see. Put a small X in the center. This should be the point in the sky directly above you.

Name _____

Constellation Patterns

See pages 226 (*Star Search*) and 228 (*Class Constellation*) for directions.

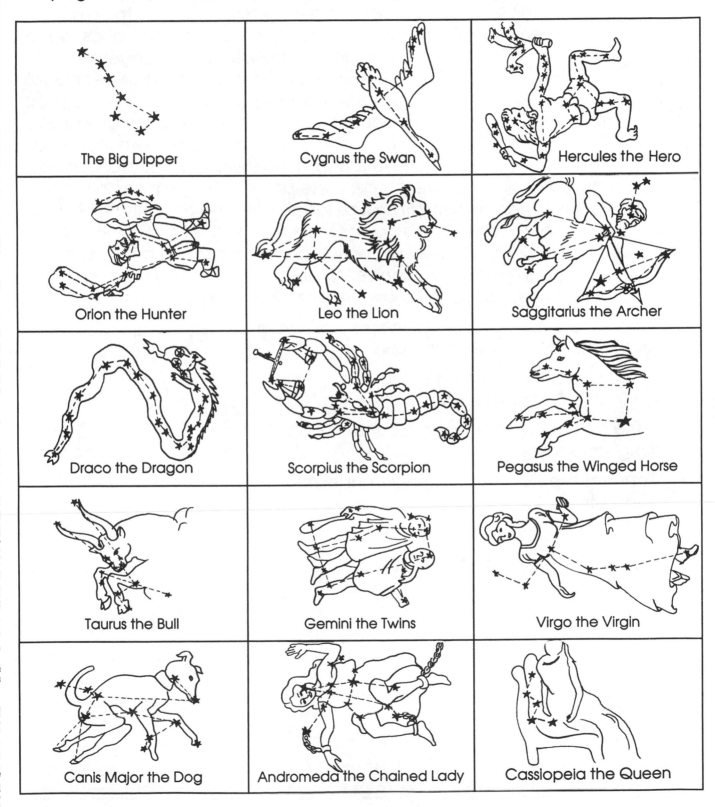

The Big Dipper

Cygnus the Swan

Hercules the Hero

Orion the Hunter

Leo the Lion

Saggitarius the Archer

Draco the Dragon

Scorpius the Scorpion

Pegasus the Winged Horse

Taurus the Bull

Gemini the Twins

Virgo the Virgin

Canis Major the Dog

Andromeda the Chained Lady

Cassiopeia the Queen

SCIENCE

Daily Learning Drills Grade 4

Name _____

Class Constellation

Thousands of years ago, people believed that there were many gods in the heavens above. They believed that the gods made the sun rise, the weather change, the oceans move, and even made people fall in love! The people made up stories (myths) about the gods and their great powers. Many of the characters in these myths can be found in the shapes of the stars. These "star pictures" are called constellations. There are 88 constellations in the sky, but not all of them can be seen from one location. Some are only visible in the Southern Hemisphere while others can only be seen in the Northern Hemisphere. Some are also best observed only in certain seasons. Look at some of the constellations on page 227, *Constellation Patterns*. Pick one or create your own and write a myth about it. Follow the directions below.

1. On a lined sheet of 8 ½"x 11" paper, write your name, the title of your myth, and the myth.

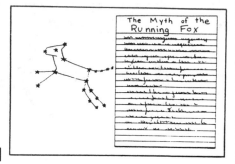

2. Glue the paper on the right side of a 12" x 18" piece of black construction paper.

3. In the box below, design your constellation using star stickers.

4. Connect the stars to show your constellation and add details.

5. Cut out and glue your constellation on the left side of the construction paper.

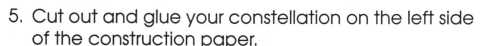

Name _____

Read My Mind

Pretend you have been contacted by NASA
to serve as an astronaut on a secret mission.
Because of its secrecy, NASA cannot give you your
destination. Instead, you must figure it out using the
clues below. After each clue, check the possible
answers. Your destination will soon be evident.

Destination Clues	Mercury	Venus	Earth	Mars	Jupiter	Saturn	Uranus	Neptune	Pluto
It is part of our Solar System.									
It is a bright object in the sky.									
It is less than 2,000,000,000 miles from the sun.									
It orbits the sun.									
It has less than 15 known satellites.									
There is weather here.									
It rotates in the opposite direction of Earth.									
It is the hottest planet.									
Its years are longer than its days.									
It is called "Earth's twin."									
It is closest to Earth.									

Secret Mission Destination is _____

I know this because _____

_____

SCIENCE

Name _____

Space Snowballs

Planets and moons are not the only objects in our solar system that travel in orbits. Comets also orbit the sun.

A **comet** is like a giant dirty snowball from 1 to 5 kilometers wide. It is made of frozen gases, dust, ice, and rocks.

As the comet gets closer to the sun, the frozen gases

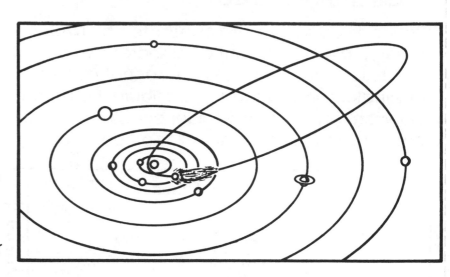

melt and evaporate. Dust particles float in the air. The dust forms a cloud called a **coma**. The "wind" from the sun blows the coma away from the sun. The blowing coma forms the comet's tail.

There are more than 800 known comets. Halley's Comet is the most famous. It appears about every 76 years. The year 1985 was the last scheduled appearance in this century. When will it appear next?

Find the words from the Word Bank in the wordsearch. When you are finished, write down the letters that are not circled. Start at the top of the puzzle and go from left to right.

Word Bank	
dust	orbit
Halley	tail
coma	ice
snowball	sky
melt	shining
solar system	

```
S P M E L T L A N H E
O T S S H A C O M A V
L E N O R D B I T L S
A L O I K U E C I L R
R C W L E S S C O E M
S E B T S T H A V Y E
Y O A R O R B I T B I
S T L S S H A P E D L
T I L K T A I L E A F
E O O T I C E B A L L
M S K Y S H I N I N G
```

___ ___ ___ ___ ___ ___ ___ ___   ___ ___ ___ ___   ___ ___ ___ ___ ___   ___ ___ ___ ___   ___ ___ ___

___ ___ ___ ___ ___,   ___ ___ ___ ___ ___   ___ ___ ___   ___ ___ ___ ___ ___

___ ___ ___ ___ ___   ___ ___ ___ ___   ___ ___ ___ ___ ___ ___ ___ ___.

Name _____

Amazing Asteroids

Asteroids are extremely small planets that revolve around the sun. They are also called minor planets or planetoids. These small planets travel mainly between the orbits of Mars and Jupiter. There are thousands of them, and new ones are constantly being discovered.

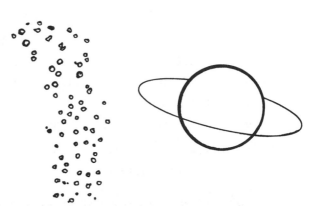

Many asteroids are made of dark, rocky material, have irregular shapes and range widely in size. Ceres, the largest and first-known asteroid, is about 600 miles in diameter. Eros, another asteroid, is only about $\frac{9}{10}$ of a mile in diameter.

Because the asteroids' orbits change slowly due to the gravitational attraction of Jupiter and other large planets, asteroids sometimes collide with each other. Fragments from these collisions can cause other collisions. Any resulting small fragments that reach the surface of Earth are called meteorites.

Try your hand at personification. Personification means giving an inanimate (non-living) object human qualities. Draw a cartoon below of two asteroids colliding with each other. Give the asteroids names and write what they might say to each other.

SCIENCE

1	2
3	4

Daily Learning Drills Grade 4

Name _Tumehna_

Star Light, Star Bright

Lay on your back. Gaze up into the night sky. Which star is the brightest? On a clear night you can see hundreds of stars—some are bright and others are dim.

Why are some stars brighter than others? Let's try to find out by looking at the picture on this page.

1. Look at the two streetlights in the picture. Which streetlight appears the brightest?

   ___The close one___

   Why? ___Its closer___

2. Look at the bicycle and the truck. Which headlights appear the brightest? ___Car___

   Why? ___more light___

3. Some stars appear brighter than others for the same reasons as those stated above. What are the two reasons?

   a. ___Closeness___

   b. ___Size___

Color Me Hot

Stars differ not only in brightness but also in color. As a star gets hotter, its color changes.

Refer to the chart to color these stars.

Star Color	
Temperature	**Color**
20,000° C	Blue
10,500° C	White
5,500° C	Yellow
3,000° C	Red

Blue

Spica
20,000°C

White

Sirius
10,500°C

Yellow

Sun
5,500°C

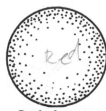

Red

Betelgeuse
3,000°C

Name _Tamanna_

Pass the Profiles

How much do your classmates know about you? Give copies of this sheet to a few other students. Tell them to fill out the information about you. Fill in the blanks that they cannot complete.

Full name: _Tamanna_ _Chollampat_

How my name was chosen: _Movie Star_

Address: _____

Other places I have lived: _India_

Parents' names: _Nedlufer and Siju_

Parents' occupations: _____

Brothers' and sisters' names: _____

Pets (kinds and names/ present or past): _____

Kinds of clothes I like: _? ?_

Fun things I like to do: _Piano, Swimming_

Favorite foods: _____

Favorite songs: _____

Favorite videos and TV shows: _____

Someday I'd like to be… _____

I'm really good at… _____

My favorite expression is… _____

States I've visited: _____

My hero or heroine: _____

Some of my closest friends: _____

What I like to do with friends: _____

Someday I'd like to try to… _____

My birthday is… _____

My favorite restaurant is… _____

Things at school I'm good at: _____

SOCIAL STUDIES

Daily Learning Drills Grade 4

Name _____

List Bliss!

Making lists helped Harvey cope. Try some lists of your own. Each school day for one month, make a list from one of the titles given below. Keep your lists together in a special notebook or binder. You'll be surprised how well you get to know yourself in one month! Check off each list as you've used it. Make up new list titles if you run out.

1. Big Events in My Life
2. Things That Worry Me
3. Projects I've Liked in School
4. Things I Like about Me
5. Bad Things That Have Happened to Me
6. Things I Like to Make
7. My Favorite Things To Do
8. Jobs I'd Like To Do When I'm Older
9. Gifts I Got That I Didn't Want
10. Sad Moments I Remember
11. Places I've Visited
12. Songs I've Always Liked
13. Important People in My Life
14. Months and Dates Special to Me
15. Foods I Just Don't Like
16. Games That I Play Well
17. Books I've Enjoyed
18. Things I Wish For
19. Animals I'd Like to Have
20. Things That Make Me Happy

Name _____

It's a Shame!

With which children are you most likely to sympathize? Rate these characteristics from the greatest to the least with number **1** drawing the greatest amount of sympathy.

Characteristics	Rating
no father at home	____
teacher's pet	____
poor eating habits	____
overweight	____
cries easily	____
death in the family	____
rich	____
little self-control	____
poor health	____
ignorance	____
bad reputation	____
very thin	____
poor	____
adults have high expectations of	____
uncoordinated	____
little adult guidance	____

Should you be more sympathetic with some people?
Write a contract in which you make a promise you can keep.

– –

Sympathy Contract

I, _____ , do hereby promise to be more understanding and sympathetic to
    (your name)
those who _____ . I hope to show consideration by _____

_____

_____

_____ _____
    (signature)   (date)

Give this contract to a trustworthy friend or adult who will help you be more caring.

SOCIAL STUDIES

Name _____

Emily Post Says . . .

Emily Post's book *Etiquette,* published in 1922, established behavior guidelines for all sorts of situations. She believed good manners were based on common sense and feelings for others. She kept up with the changing times and wrote ten editions of her book during her lifetime. People still refer to it when they have a question about proper behavior in social situations. Post also gave advice in a newspaper column and on the radio.

Write a column and give advice for the following situations.

1. Jane wants to have a party. There are ten boys and twelve girls in her class. She wants to invite everyone in the class except two of the girls. She also wants to ask her neighbors Emily and Bridgette, but her Mom says she can only have fifteen guests including herself. Who should she ask? How should they be asked? Answer these questions and give reasons for your answers.

   _____

   _____

   _____

   _____

2. Tim is one of the lucky invited guests, but he knows his best friend, Tom, was not asked. What should Tim tell Tom when Tom asks him to spend the night on the night the party is being given? Why?

   _____

   _____

   _____

3. Michael was pleased because he got one of the leading roles in the school play, but Joe was very disappointed because he did not get a part. What can Michael do to not hurt Joe further and perhaps help ease his disappointment?

   _____

   _____

   _____

Personality Plus Write a question you have concerning the polite thing to do in a certain situation. Put your question in a box with the questions of your classmates. The questions may be discussed in a small group or as a class.

Name _____

Me and My Shadow

Addie can hardly wait to have a friend. Tilla becomes that friend even though the two are different in many ways. In the chart below, compare yourself to one of your friends. You may wish to compare such things as hair color, eye color, family size, hobbies, favorite songs, and so on.

Myself	My friend	Alike or different?

SOCIAL STUDIES

Daily Learning Drills Grade 4

Name _____

Families

One of the things people all over the world have in common is the need to give and receive love. Love is given when you help, talk, listen and share with another person. Family members are often the ones who do these things to show love for each other.

1. List ways your family cares for you.

    _____

    _____

    _____

    _____

2. What do you do to show your family you care? _____

    _____

    _____

3. Do you have specific chores to do at home daily or weekly? _____

    If yes, what are they? _____

4. Does your parents giving you chores to do show that they care about you?_____

    Why or why not? _____

    _____

5. List things a family member has taught you. _____

    _____

    _____

6. List things you have taught or could teach a member of your family. _____

    _____

    _____

7. List ways a family member helps you deal with a variety of emotions. _____

    _____

8. Members of a family often take on certain roles within the family structure.
    Which member of your family is usually the disciplinarian? _____

9. It is often said that a parent's love for a child is unconditional. What do you think
    unconditional love is? _____

    _____

10. On the back of this page, write two positive statements about each member
    of your family. Share these with the person on a day when he/she needs
    cheering up.

Name _____

It's All in the Family!

Write the names of family members with whom you live. _____

_____

Write the names of the members of your immediate family. _____

_____

Write the names of your extended family on the correct lines in the diagram below. Fill in the names of your immediate family in the box.

great-grandparents

_____ _____ _____ _____

_____ _____ _____ _____

grandparents

_____ _____ _____

mother   _____   _____   father

you and your sisters and/or brothers

_____

aunts and uncles   aunts and uncles

_____ _____ _____ _____

_____ _____ _____ _____

_____ _____ _____ _____

cousins   cousins

_____ _____

_____ _____

_____ _____

_____ _____

_____ _____

SOCIAL STUDIES

Name _____

Uniforms

People on all continents wear some type of covering on their bodies. Originally, clothing was used merely to protect a person from climatic conditions. Today, the clothes a person wears tell something about his/her lifestyle or status in society. While many businesses allow people to wear their own clothes to work, others require workers to wear a uniform. Why do you think people in some jobs must wear uniforms? _____

_____

_____

List several jobs that require workers to wear uniforms.

_____

_____

_____

Cut out pictures of people wearing uniforms from old catalogs, magazines, or newspapers. Glue the pictures on a piece of construction paper or posterboard to make a collage of uniforms.

Pretend that you are the president or CEO of your own company. Decide what your company will sell or produce. In the space below, show examples of the uniforms you would require the following workers to wear: 1) clerical; 2) executive officers; 3) assembly line; 4) maintenance.

Should you, as president of the company, have to wear a uniform? _____

Why, or why not? _____

Name _____

Places to Live

Shelters provide a place in which people can live and keep their possessions. Early man took shelter in places provided by nature, such as a cave, hollow or hole in the ground. One of the first shelters devised by humans is still in use today — the tent. As man improved his tools and learned to farm, permanent homes were built. Today, people throughout the world live in a wide variety of homes. List as many different types of shelter as you can think of on the lines below.

_____

_____

_____

_____

Make a list of the different types of shelter the students in your class occupy. Use the information to complete the graph below.

Types of Housing

	1	2	3	4	5	6	7	8	9	10	11	12	13	14	15	16	17	18	19	20	21	22	23	24	25	26	27	28	29	30
House																														
Apartment																														
Mobile Home																														
Condominium																														
Houseboat																														
Cabin																														
Other																														

Use the list of homes above to complete this next activity. Some types of shelter are better suited to hot climates. Others are designed for cold climates. Write the name of each type of home under the correct heading. Some may be suitable for both types of climate.

HOT CLIMATES	COLD CLIMATES	BOTH CLIMATES

SOCIAL STUDIES

Name _____

Picture Your Life in Time

Though you have only lived a short time, many significant events have happened in your life and in the world around you. Record some of these events on this page and the next.

Write the year you were born on the first line under **YEAR**. Write every year thereafter up to the current year. Before each year, the age you were during that year is written in parentheses. On the first line after each year, use a blue pen to write something signifcant you did that year. (You may have to ask a family member to help you with this.) On the second and third lines, use a red pen to write an important event that happened in the world during that year. (You may refer to an almanac or another reference.) Try to find a coin minted during each year of your life. Tape it in the circle to the right of the corre-sponding year.

AGE   **YEAR**

(0-1) _____   _____

_____

_____

(1-2) _____   _____

_____

_____

(2-3) _____   _____

_____

_____

(3-4) _____   _____

_____

_____

Name _____

Picture Your Life in Time (cont.)

(4-5) _____ _____

_____

_____

(5-6) _____ _____

_____

_____

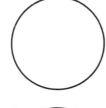

(6-7) _____ _____

_____

_____

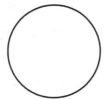

(7-8) _____ _____

_____

_____

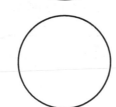

(8-9) _____ _____

_____

_____

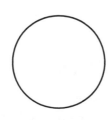

(9-10) _____ _____

_____

_____

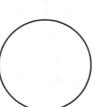

(10-11) _____ _____

_____

_____

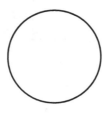

Name _____

Customs and Traditions

1. List several special days or occasions
    you observe, such as holidays or birthdays.
    _____
    _____

2. Pick one of the above that you celebrate with
    your family. Write a paragraph on the back of this page about what you
    and your family did to celebrate this special event the last time it occurred.

    Was the celebration the same as it always has been or were there some
    differences? Write what was the same and what was different.

    Same   Different
    _____   _____
    _____   _____
    _____   _____

3. Write the name of a holiday that you observed in the past year. _____
    With whom did you observe it? _____
    What did you do to celebrate? _____
    _____

    Name three things associated with the holiday that are a traditional part
    of its celebration. _____
    _____

4. List some traditions you and/or your family have. _____
    _____

5. What custom do you carry on today that you would like to see changed
    or dropped? _____
    Why? _____

6. What custom do you intend to carry on when you have a family? _____
    _____

7. What customs observed by the general population do you no longer see
    a need for and why? _____
    _____

8. What would you like to see become a custom and why? _____
    _____

Name _____

U.S. Patriotic Holidays

Memorial Day	Flag Day	Columbus Day	Presidents' Day
Bill of Rights Day	Labor Day	Veterans Day	Independence Day

Use the list of holidays above to write each holiday in the appropriate blank in each sentence or paragraph below.

1. _____ , on the third Monday in February, honors two United States Presidents, George Washington and Abraham Lincoln, born in the month.

2. _____ originally was celebrated May 30 and honored the war dead of the Civil War. It now is observed on the last Monday in May and is dedicated to the memory of all war dead. It is also known as Decoration Day because graves of service people are often decorated.

3. _____ , December 15, honors the date in 1791 on which Congress made them law. They are the first ten amendments of the U.S. Constitution.

4. _____ , on the second Monday in October, commemorates the discovery of America by honoring the man who sailed near its shores in 1492.

5. _____ commemorates the act of Congress on June 14, 1777, that adopted America's stars and stripes as the country's official banner.

6. _____ , observed the first Monday in September in all states, honors America's backbone, its workers.

7. _____ , on July 4, perhaps the most patriotic of all America's holidays, is celebrated in all states. It observes the adoption of the Declaration of Independence.

8. _____ was once called Armistice Day. It began in 1926 to commemorate the signing of the armistice that ended World War I in 1918. In 1954, the holiday's name was changed to honor all men and women who have served their country in the armed services.

Select one of the above holidays. Then, on another sheet of paper, do one of the following:
- Design a stamp to honor its observance.
- Write a poem about the holiday.
- Draw a mural of a parade honoring that holiday.

SOCIAL STUDIES

Name _____

An Interview

Person interviewed _____ Date of interview _____

1. Were you my age about 20, 30, 40, 50, 60, 70 or 80 years ago? _____

2. Where did you live when you were my age? _____
   If not here, how long ago did you move here? _____

3. How has the community changed? _____
   _____

4. What time did you get up when you were my age? _____
   What was your morning schedule? _____

5. What did you do after school? _____
   _____

6. What was your bedtime when you were my age? _____

7. What sort of things did you eat when you were my age? _____
   _____ _____

8. What toys did you have? What were your favorites? _____
   _____

9. What chores did you have, if any? _____
   _____

10. Did you get an allowance? _____ How much was it? _____
    Did you earn any money when you were my age? _____ Doing what? _____
    _____ About what did you make in an hour? _____

11. How did you spend your money? _____
    _____

12. What was your most favorite thing to do during "free time"? _____
    _____ Tell about it. _____
    _____
    _____

13. What games did you play?
    _____
    _____

14. What did you study at school?
    _____
    _____
    _____

Name _____

An Interview (cont.)

15. How did you get to school? _____
16. What was school like? What did you have that was the same? Different?
    (i.e. physical education, cafeteria, etc.) _____
    _____
    _____
    _____

17. Do you remember any rhymes or songs? _____
    Name one. _____
18. Did you ever get in trouble? _____ Tell about one time. _____
    _____

    What happened to you when you got in trouble? _____
    _____

19. What was the best thing that ever happened to you? _____
    _____
    _____

    What was the worst? _____
    _____
    _____

20. What were some of your family customs or traditions (i.e.: birthdays,
    holidays, games, jokes, etc)? _____
    _____
    _____

21. What are some of the biggest changes you have seen during your lifetime?
    _____
    _____
    _____

Write additional questions or information given that was not asked for below or
on another sheet of paper.

_____
_____
_____
_____

SOCIAL STUDIES

Daily Learning Drills Grade 4

Name _____

Other Ways to Communicate

For those people who are hearing impaired, vocal communication is not possible. People who cannot hear use sign language. Even those who can hear but do not speak the same language often use a modified form of sign language. You will often see visitors in a foreign land trying to sign to be understood.

Using the alphabet to the right, learn to sign your name, your hometown and the name of your school. Try to have a conversation with a friend using only sign language.

Braille is a system of printing and writing for the blind. It was developed by Louis Braille, a blind Frenchman, in the 1820's. Braille uses raised dots on a page. A blind person reads dots by touching with his/her fingertips. The Braille symbols are large and thick, so they can be felt easily.

Using the alphabet below, write a paragraph about your favorite hobby. After you finish, answer these questions.

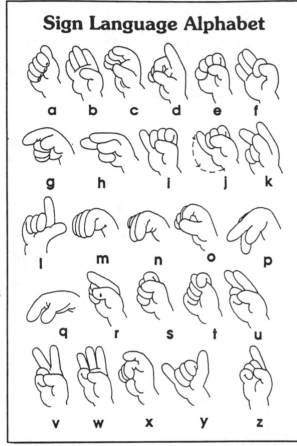

Sign Language Alphabet

1. What is unusual about the symbols used for the numbers? _____

   _____

2. The American Printing House for the Blind in Louisville, KY, issues Braille textbooks for free. Why do you think the federal government pays for the publication of these books but does not pay for your textbooks? _____

   _____

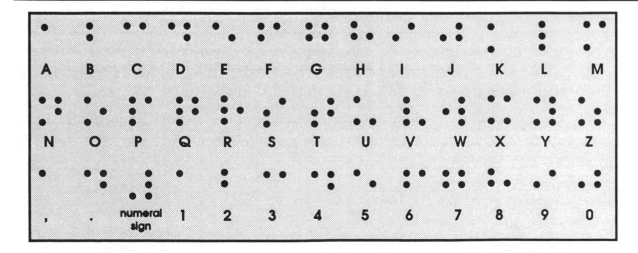

Name _____

Got the Message?

Hieroglyphics is a form of writing used by the ancient Egyptians in which picture symbols represented ideas and sounds. It was the Rosetta Stone, a decree carved on stone with hieroglyphics, that gave the world the key to understanding this writing when it was found in 1799.

Use the hieroglyphics below to write a secret message to your friend. Have him/her decipher your message and write a response to it in hieroglyphics. Then, write your message and his/her response in English. **Note:** There were no vowels in hieroglyphics. Use capital vowels to represent a vowel sound. Note also that there were many variations of this type of writing.

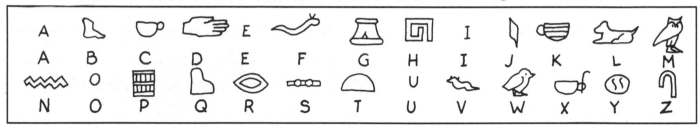

Your message:

Your friend's response:

Translation: _____

In Egyptian archaeology, an oval frame containing the name or symbol of a ruler written in hieroglyphics is called a cartouche. They are often seen on monuments as nameplates of ancient rulers. Use hieroglyphics to make cartouches for the names listed below. Write the name in English on the line under each oval. Again, use capital vowels for vowel sounds.

your first name

_____

your best friend's name

_____

your teacher's name

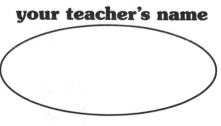

_____

SOCIAL STUDIES

Name _____

Community Needs

Mother Teresa of Calcutta has dedicated her life to helping "the poorest of the poor." Mother Teresa and the members of her congregation, the Missionaries of Charity, aid poor, sick, and abandoned children and adults around the world.

Think about your community. List three of its social problems or needs.

_____

_____

_____

_____

_____

Tell how you think each problem might be solved. Include what you might do to help in each solution.

_____

_____

_____

_____

_____

_____

_____

_____

_____

_____

_____

Follow the Leader   Find out about an organization in your community that works to solve some of the problems you listed above. How do they work to solve the problem? Is there any way you can get involved? Share your information with the class.

Name _____

Community Workers

Ask several men and women in your community what their occupations are (e.g., doctor, farmer, maintenance worker). Record their answers, without names, on another sheet of paper.

When you have completed your survey, plot the two bar graphs below. If you have too many different responses, you may want to group them by categories, such as Medical, Sales, Government, and Service.

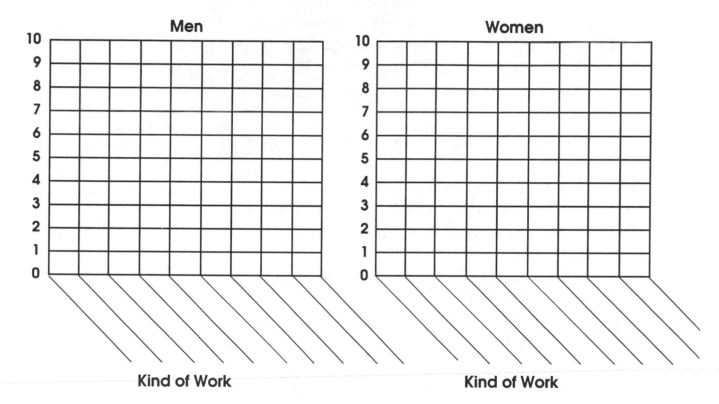

Men

Women

Kind of Work

Kind of Work

Answer these questions to draw some conclusions from your graphs.

What kinds of jobs do most of the community's population have? _____

_____

Are most workers skilled or non-skilled? _____

Are there differences between jobs held by men and women? _____

_____

What types of workers are needed in the community? _____

_____

What else have you observed? _____

_____

SOCIAL STUDIES

Name _____

What Kind of Community?

Read the definitions of three different types of communities below.

Rural Community country; large amount of open space; rustic; agriculture predominates	**Urban Community** big city or town; often at least 50,000 people; crowded with buildings and people; business center	**Suburban Community** largely residential; often near a large city; often incorporated separately

Read the sentences on this page and page 253. Underline only the sentences that describe your community. Then, answer this: In what kind of a community do you live? _____

1. All that can be seen from a rooftop is land criss-crossed by dirt roads and fences.

2. Neighbors may sometimes wake neighbors if they mow their lawns too early in the morning.

3. There is a feeling of open space, and yet there are shopping malls, supermarkets, schools, etc.

4. The sounds of elevated trains and honking horns are heard almost twenty-four hours a day.

5. Many families who work in the city live here because it is quieter, and the commute to the city every day is not too long.

6. During the summer, neighborhood children set up lemonade stands, and families have picnics and barbecues in their back yards.

7. Homes are very close together. Many are stacked one on top of one another in buildings called apartments.

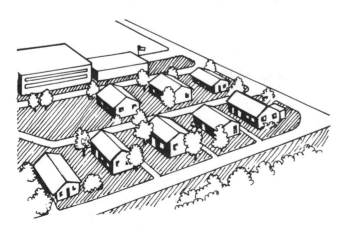

8. Streets and sidewalks are crowded with workers going to and from work and shoppers looking in store front windows.

9. Many people work at farming.

10. Mailboxes are often very far from the houses.

11. Neighbors are often miles apart.

12. It is on the outskirts of a city.

Name _____

What Kind of Community? (cont.)

13. Residents of the community seldom see one another, so a community gathering is a real social event.

14. Hotels provide a place for visitors to stay who come for meetings at the convention center.

15. The population is over 50,000.

16. The high school's students come from several outlying communities and must ride the bus because distances are great.

17. Nights are quiet except for the occasional sound of an animal.

18. Children play in parks rather than in back yards.

19. There is a feeling of country with the conveniences of a city.

Write two or three paragraphs about your community on the lines below. Ideas to include: its population, contact with neighbors, and availability of services.

_____

_____

_____

_____

_____

_____

_____

_____

_____

_____

_____

_____

SOCIAL STUDIES

Name _____

Waste Materials

Next to each picture on this page and the next, write one or two sentences about what is pictured that is harmful for the environment. Tell why or how it is harmful. Then, write ways to correct the problem.

_____
_____
_____
_____
_____
_____
_____
_____

_____
_____
_____
_____
_____
_____

_____
_____
_____
_____
_____
_____

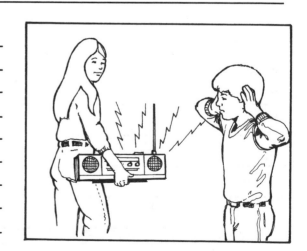

Name _____

Waste Materials (cont.)

_____
_____
_____
_____
_____
_____
_____
_____

_____
_____
_____
_____
_____
_____
_____
_____

_____
_____
_____
_____
_____
_____
_____

_____
_____
_____
_____
_____
_____
_____
_____
_____

SOCIAL STUDIES

Name _____

Money Sources

Ask four people of different ages how they get their money. When they answer yes to a category, check the line in front of it. A person may answer yes to more than one category. Many of the categories may not apply and therefore will not be checked. If the category is "other," write the source.

Ask someone between **8-11** years old: **How do you get your money?**

_____ allowance _____ gifts _____ full-time job _____ part-time job
_____ interest _____ dividends _____ borrowed _____ pension
_____ other: _____

Ask someone between **15-18** years of age: **How do you get your money?**

_____ allowance _____ gifts _____ full-time job _____ part-time job
_____ interest _____ dividends _____ borrowed _____ pension
_____ other: _____

Ask someone between **35-45** years of age: **How do you get your money?**

_____ allowance _____ gifts _____ full-time job _____ part-time job
_____ interest _____ dividends _____ borrowed _____ pension
_____ other: _____

Ask someone over **65** years of age: **How do you get your money?**

_____ allowance _____ gifts _____ full-time job _____ part-time job
_____ interest _____ dividends _____ borrowed _____ pension
_____ other: _____

Compare findings with other class members. Tally where people's money comes from in the different age groups. If desired, make a bar graph for each group.

	8-11	15-18	35-45	65 or over
allowance	_____	_____	_____	_____
gifts	_____	_____	_____	_____
full-time job	_____	_____	_____	_____
part-time job	_____	_____	_____	_____
interest	_____	_____	_____	_____
dividends	_____	_____	_____	_____
borrowed	_____	_____	_____	_____
pension	_____	_____	_____	_____
other	_____	_____	_____	_____

Name _____

Where Money Goes

Ask four people of different ages on what they spend their money. When they answer yes to a category, put a check mark on the line in front of it. A person may answer yes to more than one, or some of the categories may not apply and therefore will not get checked. If the category is "other," write how that money is spent.

Ask someone between **8-11** years old: **On what do you spend your money?**

____ rent/mortgage	____ clothing	____ food	____ utilities
____ transportation	____ vacation	____ taxes	____ savings
____ entertainment	____ insurance	____ dates	____ school
____ investments	____ presents	____ treats	____ supplies
____ medical/doctors	____ eating out	____ sports	____ hobbies
____ other: _____			

Ask someone between **15-18** years of age: **On what do you spend your money?**

____ rent/mortgage	____ clothing	____ food	____ utilities
____ transportation	____ vacation	____ taxes	____ savings
____ entertainment	____ insurance	____ dates	____ school
____ investments	____ presents	____ treats	____ supplies
____ medical/doctors	____ eating out	____ sports	____ hobbies
____ other: _____			

Ask someone between **35-45** years of age: **On what do you spend your money?**

____ rent/mortgage	____ clothing	____ food	____ utilities
____ transportation	____ vacation	____ taxes	____ savings
____ entertainment	____ insurance	____ dates	____ school
____ investments	____ presents	____ treats	____ supplies
____ medical/doctors	____ eating out	____ sports	____ hobbies
____ other: _____			

Ask someone over **65** years of age: **On what do you spend your money?**

____ rent/mortgage	____ clothing	____ food	____ utilities
____ transportation	____ vacation	____ taxes	____ savings
____ entertainment	____ insurance	____ dates	____ school
____ investments	____ presents	____ treats	____ supplies
____ medical/doctors	____ eating out	____ sports	____ hobbies
____ other: _____			

Compare class findings. On another page, tally how the age groups spend money.

SOCIAL STUDIES

Name _____

Needs for Your "Full Circle"

We all have **physical**, **intellectual**, **emotional** and **social** needs to live a happy and healthy life. Read each statement from the text and decide which need is being met. Write it on the blank.

1. Mattie finished the test before anyone else and turned her paper over on her desk. She reached inside for a book. _____

2. Matt had dinner started when Mattie got home—salad and leftover spaghetti. _____

3. Mr. Ashby had outdone himself this weekend. His homework assignments included math, spelling, a social studies essay, a book report, and vocabulary words. He was determined to make his fifth graders work.

   _____

4. "But Mattie, I do love you," said Mrs. Benson with tears in her eyes.

   _____

5. When the telephone rang in the living room, Matt called to his sister. It was Toni. _____

6. Humming softly, Mattie sat up, reached in her back pocket and unwrapped her favorite photograph. She had decided to carry it with her today, and her father's strength seemed to reach out and hold her.

   _____

7. Mattie started dinner—chili, rice, and salad. _____

8. "Oh, Toni, this sounds like a lot of maybes. I'm going to Stern's on Saturday and stopping in to see Mrs. Stamps. I wanted you to come with me."

   _____

Name _____

Do You Speak My Language?

It is estimated that there are about 3,000 spoken languages in use today by the people of the world. This is not a precise figure because linguists disagree as to what constitutes a spoken language and what constitutes a dialect. A dialect is usually considered to be a variation within a language.

Language influences all aspects of a culture, including social behavior. If people can understand each other, human society tends to function smoothly. If people are not able to understand one another, society often grinds to a halt.

To the right are the most widely spoken languages in the world and the percent of the world's population that speaks each one. Use the list to complete the graph below.

Language	
German	1.5
French	1.5
Japanese	2.0
Portuguese	2.0
Arabic	2.0
Spanish	3.0
Russian	3.5
Hindi	4.5
English	6.0
Mandarin	20.0

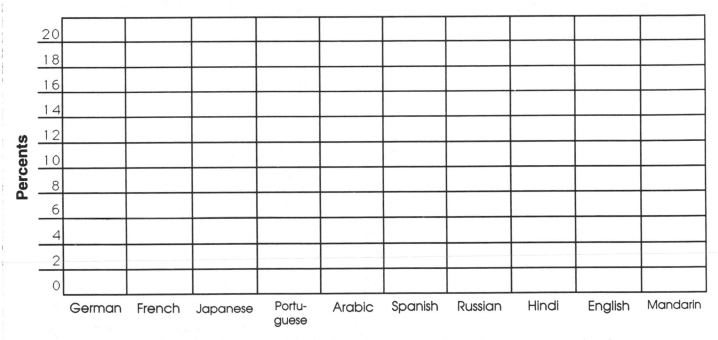

As communication between countries has increased and as companies have increasingly traded with and established branches in other nations, educators have recognized a greater need for students in this country to learn a second language. Most high schools today require students to learn a foreign language. Some elementary schools are also teaching a foreign language.

Survey 15 people who are high school graduates. Ask each person if he/she took a foreign language in school. If the answer is yes, what language did he/she study? Compile your information into a graph similar to the one above.

What career do you plan to pursue when you are an adult? Do you think you will need to know a foreign language for this career? Why, or why not?

Daily Learning Drills Grade 4

Name _____

Where Is Wheat Grown?

Wheat grows best in dry temperate regions. The ideal climate includes a cool, moist spring, a warm dry harvest period and an annual rainfall of 9 to 30 inches. There are nine areas of the world which provide a wheat-growing climate.

I. Locate these wheat-growing areas on the map by writing the number beside each area in the correct blank on the map.

1. Central United States
2. Central Canada
3. Southern Russia
4. Danube River region of Europe
5. Northwest India
6. Northcentral China
7. Argentina
8. Australia
9. Mediterranean region

II. Label the seven continents on the map by placing the letter beside each in the correct location.

A. Europe   B. Asia   C. Australia   D. Africa
E. North America   F. South America   G. Antarctica

III. Label each of these bodies of water by writing the name in the correct location on the map: Mediterranean Sea, Pacific Ocean, Atlantic Ocean, Indian Ocean, Arctic Ocean.

IV. On the map, draw a compass rose which shows all cardinal and intermediate directions.

Name _____

The Beginning of Rome

The earliest Roman settlers were mostly shepherds. Their settlements, mainly in the Roman hills, eventually joined to form the city of Rome. It is believed Romulus and Remus were the legendary founders of Rome, but no one knows for sure if they really existed. However, their story exemplifies strength, a quality admired by ancient Romans. There are several versions of the Romulus and Remus legend. Read the one below. Follow the directions after the story.

Romulus and Remus were twin sons of the war god, Mars. They were set adrift in a basket on the Tiber River by a wicked uncle who hoped they would die. But they survived. A she-wolf heard their cries and rescued them. She nursed them until they grew to be young boys. Then, Faustulus, a shepherd, adopted them. Along with his wife, he raised them as if they were his own. When Romulus and Remus became young men, they set out to found a city. The brothers argued about where their city should be located. Then, supposedly, Romulus killed Remus, named Rome after himself, and became Rome's first king.

1. List the things in the story that symbolize or are examples of strength.

   _____

   _____

2. Name places in the story that are real. _____

3. Do you think this is a true story?_____   Give reasons for your opinion. _____

   _____

   _____

   _____

4. Write a pretend story about the founders of your city/town.

   _____

   _____

   _____

   _____

   _____

   _____

SOCIAL STUDIES

Name _____

Two Great Statues

Two of the Seven Wonders of the World are statues. Both of them were in Greece: The Statue of Zeus at Olympia and The Colossus of Rhodes, near the harbor of the island in the Aegean Sea.

The statue of Zeus was made by the Greek sculptor Phidias around 435 B.C. It was dedicated to Zeus, the king of gods. It showed Zeus seated on his throne and was forty feet tall. Zeus' robe and ornaments were made out of gold and his flesh was made of ivory. In his right hand, he held a figure of his messenger, Nike. In his left hand, he held a scepter with an eagle.

Imagine a conversation the statue of Zeus might have had with an athlete at an Olympic Game. Choose an athlete and write the conversation below.

_____

_____

_____

_____

_____

The Colossus of Rhodes, a bronze statue of the sun god, Helios, stood about 120 feet tall. It took the Greek sculptor Chares about twelve years to complete it in the early 200's B.C. The statue did not stand very long as it was destroyed in an earthquake around 224 B.C. It lay in ruins until 653 A.D. when its remains were sold as scrap metal. Imagine what the Colossus of Rhodes would tell you if it could talk. Write about a conversation between you and it below.

_____

_____

_____

_____

Name _____

Comparing Civilizations

A Venn diagram is a great way to compare things. Use the one below to compare two leaders, gods, or civilizations of Ancient Greece or Rome. Write the names of the two things you are comparing on the lines provided. Fill in the unshared portion of each circle with characteristics common only to the subject. In the overlapped portion, write down characteristics the two subjects share. Then write a story about your findings on the lines below.

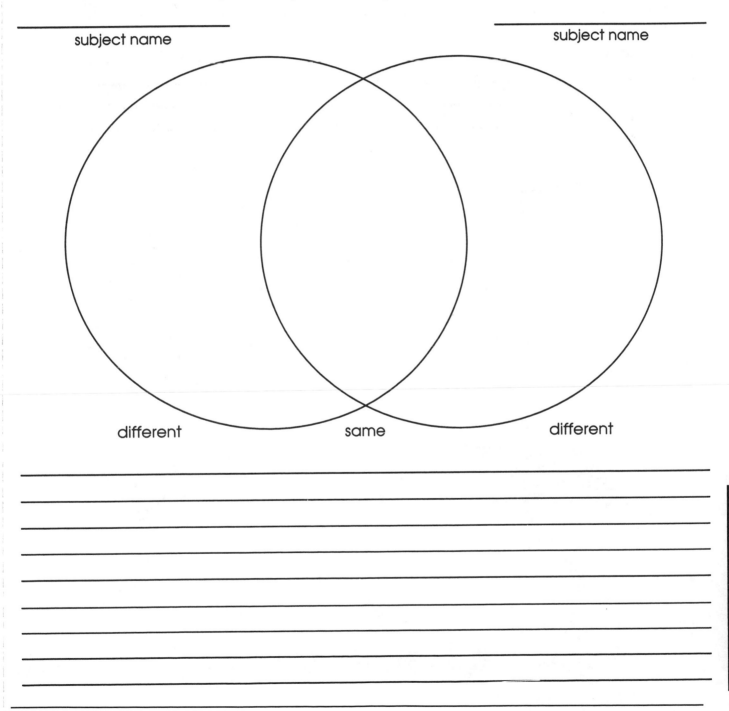

_____
subject name

_____
subject name

different   same   different

_____

_____

_____

_____

_____

_____

_____

_____

SOCIAL STUDIES

Name ______________________

How!

How many of these Indian names can you identify as state names? Write the name of the state by each Indian name. Then draw the matching symbol of that state on the United States map where it belongs.

- Ute ____________
- Emissourita ____________
- Wishdonsing ____________
- Mishigamaw ____________
- Massaadchueset ____________
- Misisipi ____________
- Oheo ____________
- Idaho ____________
- Dakotas ____________
- Alakshak ____________
- Arizonac ____________
- Minisota ____________
- Iliniwek ____________
- Arkansaw ____________
- Alibamu ____________
- Tanasi ____________

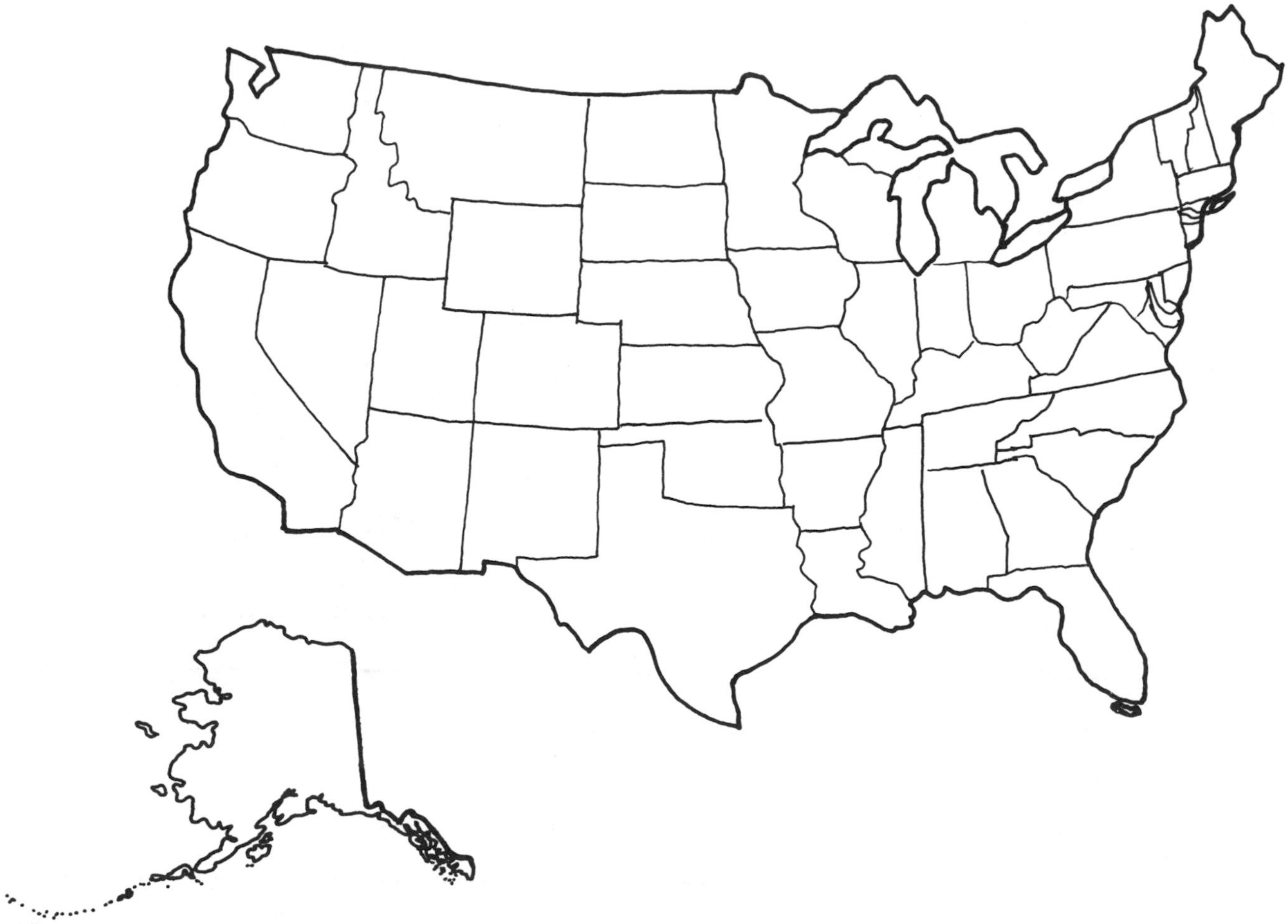

Name _____

Decision-Making Map

As the United States government began forcing the Sioux off their land, the Sioux fought to keep it. They took great care of the land and believed that it belonged to them. The white settlers believed that they were smarter and more deserving of the land. The battles between the two sides resulted in the death of many men, women, and children.

Was there a better way they could have used to solve the problem? Find the best solution by working with a partner to complete the chart below.

Problem:	→	Goal:

Choices:	1.	2.	3.
Pros for each choice:			
Cons for each choice:			

Decision:	Reason:

SOCIAL STUDIES

Name _____

Welcome to the Union

The fifty United States are listed below alphabetically. The date each one entered the Union is given after it. On the line to the left of each state, write the number that tells in what order the state joined the Union.

____ Alabama	Dec. 14, 1819		____ Montana	Nov. 8, 1889
____ Alaska	Jan. 3, 1959		____ Nebraska	Mar. 1, 1867
____ Arizona	Feb. 14, 1912		____ Nevada	Oct. 31, 1864
____ Arkansas	June 15, 1836		____ New Hampshire	June 21, 1788
____ California	Sept. 9, 1850		____ New Jersey	Dec. 18, 1787
____ Colorado	Aug. 1, 1876		____ New Mexico	Jan. 6, 1912
____ Connecticut	Jan. 9, 1788		____ New York	July 26, 1788
____ Delaware	Dec. 7, 1787		____ North Carolina	Nov. 21, 1789
____ Florida	Mar. 3, 1845		____ North Dakota	Nov. 2, 1889
____ Georgia	Jan. 2, 1788		____ Ohio	Mar. 1, 1803
____ Hawaii	Aug. 21, 1959		____ Oklahoma	Nov. 16, 1907
____ Idaho	July 3, 1890		____ Oregon	Feb. 14, 1859
____ Illinois	Dec. 3, 1818		____ Pennsylvania	Dec. 12, 1787
____ Indiana	Dec. 11, 1816		____ Rhode Island	May 29, 1790
____ Iowa	Dec. 28, 1846		____ South Carolina	May 23, 1788
____ Kansas	Jan. 29, 1861		____ South Dakota	Nov. 2, 1889
____ Kentucky	June 1, 1792		____ Tennessee	June 1, 1796
____ Louisiana	Apr. 30, 1812		____ Texas	Dec. 29, 1845
____ Maine	Mar. 15, 1820		____ Utah	Jan. 4, 1896
____ Maryland	Apr. 28, 1788		____ Vermont	Mar. 4, 1791
____ Massachusetts	Feb. 6, 1788		____ Virginia	June 25, 1788
____ Michigan	Jan. 26, 1837		____ Washington	Nov. 11, 1889
____ Minnesota	May 11, 1858		____ West Virginia	June 20, 1863
____ Mississippi	Dec. 10, 1817		____ Wisconsin	May 29, 1848
____ Missouri	Aug. 10, 1821		____ Wyoming	July 10, 1890

• Draw what comes next.   _____

Name _____

Figure Out Freedom

In 1861, 19 states declared themselves "Free States." People in these states were opposed to slavery. Unscramble each name to find out which states were considered "Free."

EIMNA __ __ __ __ __

EWN SEERJY __ __ __   __ __ __ __ __

TREOVMN __ __ __ __ __ __ __

WNE ROYK __ __ __   __ __ __ __

LFIINAAORC __ __ __ __ __ __ __ __ __ __

WIOA __ __ __ __

EGROON __ __ __ __ __ __

NESNOMITA __ __ __ __ __ __ __ __ __

IICHAGMN __ __ __ __ __ __ __ __

DAANIIN __ __ __ __ __ __ __

SILLIONI __ __ __ __ __ __ __ __

SASNKA __ __ __ __ __ __

CHASETSUTSMAS __ __ __ __ __ __ __ __ __ __ __ __ __

NOSSCIIWN __ __ __ __ __ __ __ __ __

HIOO __ __ __ __

CCUTTCIENON __ __ __ __ __ __ __ __ __ __ __

HODER SLANDI __ __ __ __ __   __ __ __ __ __ __

VANPIASENYNL __ __ __ __ __ __ __ __ __ __ __ __

WNE SHEPRAMIH __ __ __   __ __ __ __ __ __ __ __ __

SOCIAL STUDIES

Topical Titles

Name _____

Pick the best title for each paragraph. Be certain to capitalize the first, last and all important words in each title. You will not use all choices listed.

the gregorian calendar	schools in england
george washington's birthday	lieutenant colonel george washington
the french and indian war	mount vernon

1. _____

In 1754, the Governor of Virginia made George Washington a lieutenant colonel and sent him and his troops into the Ohio River Valley to claim the land for Britain. Although the French and their Indian allies fought hard to keep this land, when the war ended in 1763, Britain was the victor.

2. _____

Augustine Washington had three farms. When his son, Lawrence, returned home from school in England, Augustine asked him to manage one of the plantations for him. Lawrence later renamed his plantation "Mount Vernon" in honor of his hero, Admiral Edward Vernon, and both he and George loved living there.

3. _____

George Washington was actually born on February 11. But in 1752, the British adopted a new calendar, and this changed his birthday to February 22. George, however, always considered February 11 to be his date of birth and preferred to celebrate his birthday on that date.

A NOW ... D   The picture at the top of this page shows Mount Rushmore, a national memorial that has the largest figures of any statue in the entire world. If you were going to design such a memorial, which four faces would you choose to include? Then draw a picture of what your memorial would look like.

Name _____

Personality Profiles

All the fourth graders are doing reports on famous Americans. Jackie has gathered lots of information on John Adams. Now all she has to do is pull it together. Help her out by numbering the events below in chronological order.

☐ After teaching school for awhile, Adams studied law. He began practicing in 1758.

☐ Adams was elected by the people of Braintree to help write what became the Massachusetts Constitution of 1780.

☐ John Adams was born in Braintree, Massachusetts, on October 30, 1735.

☐ When Adams was about 20, he was graduated from Harvard College. He was one of the best students in the class.

☐ In 1778, Congress sent Adams to Paris to help Benjamin Franklin and Arthur Lee strengthen American ties with the French.

☐ Adams died on July 4, 1826. He lived longer than any other U.S. President.

☐ In 1789, Adams was named Vice-President under George Washington.

☐ Adams was chosen as one of the four Massachusetts delegates to the First Continental Congress in 1774.

☐ In 1764, Adams married Abigail Smith. Their eldest son, John Quincy, became our 6th President.

☐ John Adams became our 2nd President in 1797. He was the first President to live in the White House.

•SOMETHING EXTRA•
Cut the above facts apart. Glue each of them on a piece of paper. Illustrate each page. Combine the pages to make a book.

SOCIAL STUDIES

Name _____

What a Trip!

Read the paragraphs below about Meriwether Lewis and William Clark's journey to the Pacific Coast. Then, plot their journey on the map below.

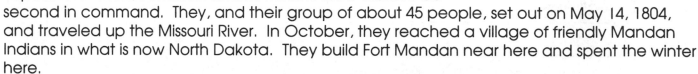

Lewis and Clark led the first expedition across our country's vast northwestern wilderness. It began in 1804 and lasted more than two years. The expedition covered almost 7,700 miles.

President Thomas Jefferson chose Lewis to lead the expedition. Then, Jefferson and Lewis selected Clark to be second in command. They, and their group of about 45 people, set out on May 14, 1804, and traveled up the Missouri River. In October, they reached a village of friendly Mandan Indians in what is now North Dakota. They build Fort Mandan near here and spent the winter here.

On April 17, 1805, the journey resumed. By summer, the group made the hardest part of the trip - they crossed the Rocky Mountains. This took them about a month. From here, they reached the Clearwater River in what is now Idaho. They built new canoes and then paddled toward the Columbia River which they reached in October. The expedition continued on in hopes of reaching the Pacific Coast. They succeeded and arrived at the coast in November 1805.

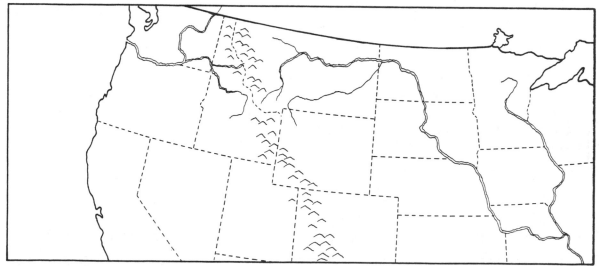

1. Label the areas that are now states through which Lewis and Clark journeyed.
2. Label the rivers on which the expedition traveled.
3. Label the Rocky Mountains.
4. Label the Pacific Ocean.
5. Put a star where the group met the Mandan Indians.

Personality Plus   Pretend you are a news reporter and you get to interview Lewis and Clark about their journey. Write the questions you would ask them and their responses.

Name _____

Down with Slavery

Rewrite the sentences in the paragraph below in the correct order.

John Brown

Brown was tried for and convicted of treason. He rented a farm near Harper's Ferry, Virginia from which he led an armed group of eighteen men. They seized the town and the United States Arsenal there. John Brown spent much of his adult life opposing slavery, but he is best remembered for his final act in 1859. He was hanged in Charleston, South Carolina. Within twenty-four hours the raid was over. Brown's forces were either killed or captured by the United States Marines led by Robert E. Lee.

_____
_____
_____
_____
_____
_____
_____
_____
_____
_____
_____

• Nat Turner is another black man who was important in American history. What did he do?

_____
_____
_____
_____

SOCIAL STUDIES

Name _____

Nuts About Nuts!

A famous American was responsible for the recognition of the peanut as a crop. This brilliant and creative person was George Washington Carver. Carver's research lead to the development of over 300 products made with peanuts!

To find out the influence of peanuts on our lives, complete the activities below.

1. Find 10 food products that contain a form of peanuts. **Example:** Tortilla chips contain peanut oil.

   _____ _____
   _____ _____
   _____ _____
   _____ _____
   _____ _____

2. List 4 non-edible items that contain a form of peanuts. **Example:** A derivative of peanuts is used to make plastic.

   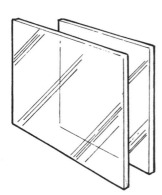

   _____
   _____
   _____
   _____

3. Write your favorite recipe below that contains a form of peanuts. Share it with the class.

   _____
   _____
   _____
   _____
   _____
   _____

Personality Plus   Find another person who you think contributed something important to our society. Write what he/she contributed and why you think it was important. Share it with your class.

Name _____

A Point of View

W.E.B. Du Bois and Booker T. Washington were influential black leaders. Though both men were against racial discrimination, their approaches to improving black civil rights were different. Du Bois criticized Washington for his compromising ways. Du Bois believed blacks must speak out against discrimination by demanding voting rights and desegregation of schools, and that educated blacks should lead the civil rights fight. Washington, on the other hand, urged blacks not to make demands but to develop skills and to get along with whites. He believed they would earn equal rights with the economic prosperity hard work would bring them.

Whose approach to promoting civil rights would you take and why?

_____

_____

_____

_____

_____

Taking this approach, write a newspaper editorial calling for civil rights.

Editorial
by _____

_____

_____

_____

_____

_____

_____

_____

_____

_____

_____

_____

_____

_____

_____

SOCIAL STUDIES

Name _____

One Great Inventor

Rewrite the set of sentences in the correct order.
Use the proper paragraph form.

Thomas Edison

1. By the time he was twelve years old, he was selling newspapers to finance his experiments.
2. He sold the firm his patents and used the money from this sale to set himself up as a freelance inventor.
3. Thomas Edison was taught at home by his mother.
4. At the age of twenty-one, while working for a stock-ticker firm, Thomas patented various improvements on the stock ticker.

_____

_____

_____

_____

_____

_____

_____

_____

_____

• What other inventions are Thomas Edison noted for?

_____

_____

• Name one other inventor. Tell what he invented and when.

_____

_____

_____

• Draw what comes next.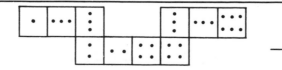

Name _____

Inventions in Time

Use the time line to help decide whether each statement is **true** or **false**.

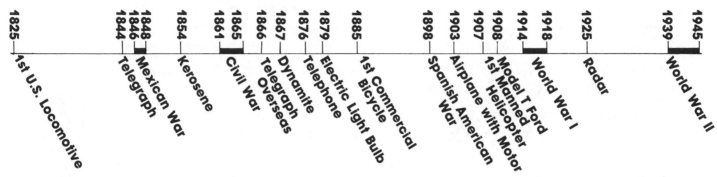

_____ The bicycle as we know it today was used to deliver telegrams during the Civil War.

_____ The helicopter was used during the Spanish American War.

_____ People in New York could talk to people in California on the telephone during the first World War.

_____ Dynamite could have been used during the Civil War by the Union Army.

_____ Kerosene was used before the Civil War.

_____ In 1865 Andrew Johnson was notified by telephone that Lincoln had been shot.

_____ The Spanish American War was the second major war that the United States was involved in since 1840.

_____ When Lincoln studied law in the 1830's he sat by the fire at night in order to have light to read by.

_____ Planes were used in combat during World War II.

_____ Trains were not used until 1878.

_____ America fought in five wars in ninety-nine of the years shown above.

_____ A telegram could be sent between New York and England after the Civil War.

_____ World War I ended four years after it began.

_____ The airplane was invented before the helicopter.

_____ The Model T was used before World War I.

• Draw what comes next.

   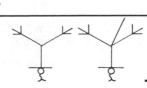 _____

Daily Learning Drills Grade 4

Name _____

Visiting Chile

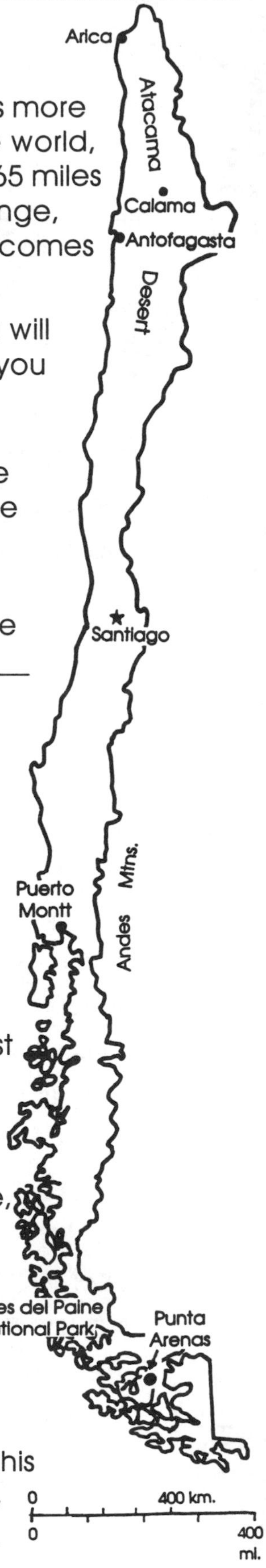

Chile is a long, narrow country on the west coast of South America. It is more than 10 times as long as it is wide. In fact, it is the longest country in the world, stretching 2,650 miles from north to south, yet it averages only about 265 miles from east to west at its widest section. The world's longest mountain range, the Andes Mountains, forms Chile's eastern border. Its name probably comes from the Indian word *chilli* meaning "where the land ends."

Pretend that you are on a trip from the top to the bottom of Chile. You will need your ruler and the map scale shown to figure the distances that you travel.

1. Your trip begins at Arica at the top of the Atacama Desert, one of the driest areas in the world. You travel by Land Rover to Calama near the location of the world's largest open-pit copper mine. You traveled _____ miles.

2. From Calama, you again travel southward to Antofagasta. From there you fly directly to Santiago, the capital. You traveled a total of _____ miles.

3. More than a third of the Chileans live in Santiago. If it has a population of about 4,500,000 people, what is the approximate population of Chile? _____

4. On the outskirts of Santiago, you were surprised to see many grape arbors. You learned that nearly three-fourths of the grapes imported to the U.S. (40 million boxes) come from Chile. How many grapes does the U.S. import altogether? _____

5. While visiting a school in Santiago, you learned that 90 percent of all Chileans 15 years of age and older can read and write. Children must attend school for 8 years. From Santiago you flew to Puerto Montt, a distance of _____ miles.

6. At Puerto Montt, you were surprised to see the German influence. This area was settled largely by Germans in the mid-1800s. From there, you flew into the rugged Archipelago, landing at Punta Arenas. You flew a distance of _____ miles.

7. Northwest of Punta Arenas is Torres del Paine National Park. Since it was only _____ miles away, you traveled by land rover. The park is named after three sheer granite towers. The tallest tower rises 8,530 feet into the sky.

8. This was the end of your journey in Chile. As a final challenge, figure this out: Punta Arenas is 3,800 kilometers west of Chile's most distant spot, Easter Island. About how many miles away is Easter Island? _____

Map labels: Arica, Atacama Desert, Calama, Antofagasta, Santiago, Puerto Montt, Andes Mtns., Torres del Paine National Park, Punta Arenas

Map scale: 0 — 400 km. / 0 — 400 mi.

Name _____

Rich Coast

Costa Rica is located between Nicaragua and Panama in Central America. Christopher Columbus was the first European to see and explore the region on his second voyage in 1502. He and the Spaniards who came after him called it *Costa Rica*, "rich coast." Costa Rica's fertile soil is its chief natural resource. Coffee, bananas, sugar, chocolate, and meat are its leading exports.

Costa Rica is a small, mountainous region. Its coasts have some of the best beaches north of the equator. San José, established in 1737, is the capital and the country's environmental, artistic, educational, and cultural center.

Significant sights include Barva Volcano in Braulio Carrilo National Park, Barra de Matina Beach, site of a leatherback turtle sanctuary, and Bosque Eterno de los Niños, the Children's Eternal Forest. This rain forest has been preserved due to the efforts of school-children around the world who donated time and money.

Choose 10 words from the information above. Write the words on the lines below and then incorporate them into a wordsearch on the Costa Rican flag. Then, lightly color the flag as follows: the top and bottom stripe blue, the center stripe red. Leave the other two stripes white.

_____

_____

_____

_____

_____

_____

_____

_____

_____

_____

SOCIAL STUDIES

Name _____

The Great Sphinx

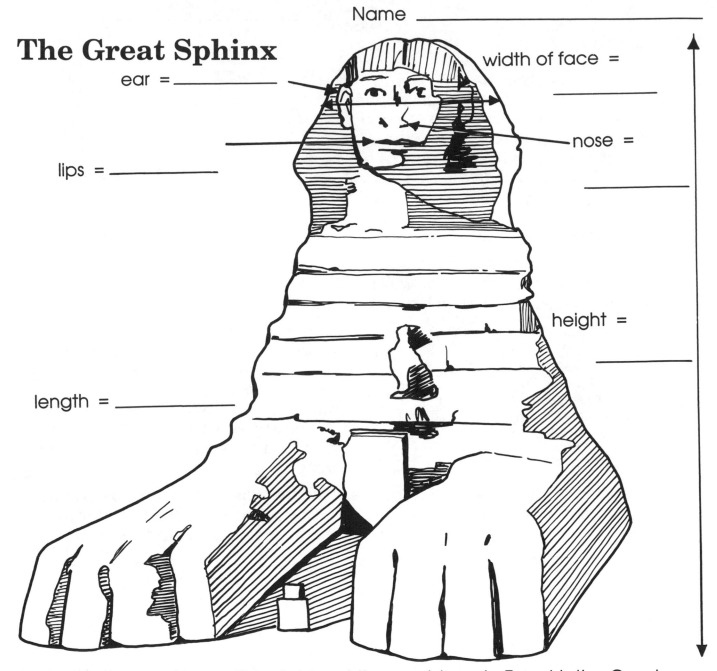

ear = _____

width of face =

_____

lips = _____

nose =

_____

height =

_____

length = _____

Probably the most incredible sight a visitor would see in Egypt is the Great Sphinx. The Great Sphinx has the head of a man and the body of a lion. No one knows for sure which king built the Great Sphinx. Most historians say that this sphinx has the facial features of the Egyptian king, Khafre, and that he had it built.

Convert these measurements from inches to feet. Label the Great Sphinx with the new measurements.

height = 792 inches	ear = 54 inches
width of face = 164 inches	nose = 67 inches
length = 2,880 inches	lips = 91 inches

Name _____

Tour de France

The Tour de France is a 2,000-mile bicycle race that winds around France for over three weeks in July. The route changes from year to year. The map of France below shows the principal cities through which more than 100 professional bicyclists might travel. Pretend you are a rider striving for the yellow jersey. Follow the directions below.

1. You live in Luxembourg. You and your bicycle fly from Luxembourg across Belgium to Lille on July 1st. Draw a solid red line from Luxembourg to Lille. You begin the race here.

2. Next travel to St. Malo. Draw a solid blue line from Lille to St. Malo.

3. Continue on to Tours. Draw a red line from St. Malo to Tours.

4. From Tours, you travel to Bordeaux. Draw a solid red line from Tours to Bordeaux.

5. Draw a blue dotted line from Bordeaux to Agen. This takes you about halfway through the race. What a relief!

6. From Agen, you ride your bicycle down to the border of Spain and back up to Toulouse. Continue your blue dotted line.

7. From Toulouse, you go east to Marseille on the Mediterranean Sea. Draw your route in red and label the sea.

8. Draw a wiggly red line from Marseille through the French Alps to Alpe d´Huez.

9. Your climb to Alpe d´Huez is nine miles long and has 21 hairpin turns. Thousands of spectators are watching you. On the back of your paper, draw what you look like when you reach the top.

10. From there you cycle to just a few miles outside of Paris. Draw a blue dotted line to that point.

11. You are first to cross the finish line! Draw and decorate your yellow T-shirt on construction paper.

Name _____

A Tale of Two Families

A September, 1991, issue of *National Geographic* told a story of the lives of two families who live only 30 miles apart, yet whose lives are worlds apart. The Hapide family, in what was West Germany, live a modest, but comfortable life. The article pictured Eva celebrating her eleventh birthday with friends in the finished basement of their house. Her mother has time for sewing, batik, and a class in jazz dancing. Sometimes Eva's father will pick up chicken, butter, milk, and vegetables as he returns from work at a printing company.

In contrast, the Rabe family in East Germany has few frills in life though Gunther, the father, has his own electrical business. The teenaged son of the family was depicted cutting kindling for the coal furnace that heats their home. For them, raising pigs and chickens and growing a garden is a necessity. Under Communism, they had their jobs, a home and food but they could not speak or travel freely. Time will tell if democracy serves to lessen the gap between these two families.

Let's learn to write a diamante poem. There are seven lines in this type of poem.

- Line 1 is made up of one noun that tells the subject of the poem.
- Line 2 has 2 adjectives describing that noun.
- Line 3 has 3 verbs ending in "ing" that tell what the subject does.
- Next, think of a word that is opposite of or contrasts to line 1. This is line 7.
- Line 6 has 2 adjectives that describe line 7.
- Line 5 usually has 3 verbs ending in "ing" that tell what the word in line 7 does.
- Line 4 has 4 words relating to lines 1 and 7. These are usually nouns.

1	Farms
2	Quiet, Spacious
3	Plowing, Planting, Pruning
4	Tractors, Barns, Cars, Planes
5	Waiting, Walking, Working
6	Noisy, Crowded
7	Cities

In the box to the left, practice writing a diamante poem about Germany. Think of the two nouns first. You could use East and West, Communism and Democracy, or Germany and the U.S. Or, you could be creative and come up with your own pair of nouns! After refining your poem, copy and illustrate it on another sheet of paper.

Name _____

Journey to Japan

Use colored pencils to label the map according to the instructions below.

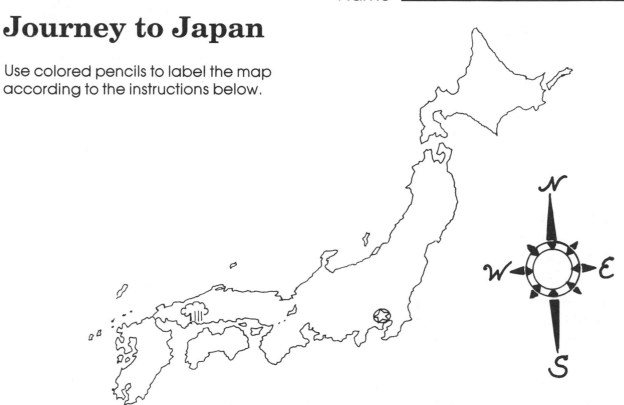

1. Label the islands of Japan from north to south in this order.

   Hokkaido   Honshu   Shikoku   Kyushu

2. Draw brown mountains on all the islands, but not on the east coast of Honshu.

3. Trace the ⛩ red and label Tokyo as the capital of Japan.

4. Color the mushroom atom bomb cloud black. Label the city Hiroshima.

5. Label the water to the northwest of Japan "Sea of Japan" in blue.

6. Label the water to the east of the islands "North Pacific Ocean" in green letters.

7. Place a golden crane in the northwest corner of the map.

8. Draw two orange lines under the Japanese island that has the most vowels.

9. Japan's flag is a white rectangle with a large red circle in the center. Draw it in the northeast corner of the map.

10. Japan's highest mountain, an inactive volcano, is Mount Fuji. Label and draw it on Honshu.

11. Japan is one of the world's greatest fishing countries. Draw and color six different kinds of fish surrounding the islands.

12. Draw 🌸, the symbol for Japan, in the southeast corner of the map.

13. Light a candle for Sadako. Draw a lit candle anywhere on the map. Write the date of Japan's Peace Day, August 6, by the candle.

SOCIAL STUDIES

Name _____

Visiting New Zealand

Laura took a trip to a location deep in the South Pacific—New Zealand. Nearly a thousand miles away from its neighbors, Australia and New Caldonia, New Zealand is a land of incredible beauty. Long ago, Rudyard Kipling sang of it as "loneliest, loveliest, exquisite, apart . . . the Happy Isles!" North Island is the site of the largest city, Auckland. It is a modern, cosmopolitan area with hints of the emerald isles in its subtropical climate. South Island, with its snowy, glacier-hung alps and remote deer, sheep and cattle stations, is the site of Wellington, the nation's capital.

Thousands of Pacific Islanders have been coming to Auckland in recent years—Samoans, Tongans and Fijians to name a few. Combined with the native Maori, the first inhabitants of the area, they are making Auckland into one of the largest Polynesian cities in the world. By the year 2000, every third or fourth New Zealander will have a Polynesian ancestor.

About the size of Colorado, New Zealand is nearly equidistant from the South Pole and the equator. Nowhere are you ever more than 80 miles from the sea. The fishermen harvest and export rock lobsters, blue cod, abalone and grouper. Salmon farming is a new, growing industry. The farms are actually out in the open sea with pens on either sides of causeways.

New Zealand offers a free education to all students up to the age of 19. If students live too far away to ride the bus, they receive instruction from the Correspondence School in Wellington. The school mails lessons to the students who then send their homework back.

Fill in the blanks below.

A. Write the names of New Zealand's nearest neighbors. _____

B. From the above paragraph, copy words or group of words meaning the same as the following:
   1. snow-covered mountains (paragraph 1) _____
   2. ranches (paragraph 1) _____
   3. urban (paragraph 1) _____
   4. people who occupy a land (paragraph 2) _____
   5. older relative (paragraph 2) _____
   6. same distance (paragraph 3) _____
   7. schooling (paragraph 4) _____

C. From the list on the right, choose the correct meanings of the words on the left which are in the story.
   1. incredible _____   green
   2. emerald _____   raised roads
   3. location _____   unbelievable
   4. causeways _____   site

D. Find the words in the story that are the opposite of the words below.
   1. sow _____   3. ugliest _____
   2. import _____   4. teachers _____

Name _____

The South American Rainforests

Pretend you just spent a great summer vacation visiting the rainforest in South America. You know you covered a lot of ground and you want to find out just how many miles you traveled. Chart your trip and the miles you covered using a ruler and the map below. Hint: Pretend each centimeter equals 250 miles.

1. You started off your South American rainforest adventure at the basin of the Amazon River. There you saw a jaguar taking a drink. Up in the trees, you see a three-toed sloth casually munching on green leaves. It was hard to leave, but you had to fly westward to Ecuador east of the Andes Mountains. You traveled about _____ miles.

2. The Andes Mountains were beautiful! From there, you flew into Guyana and were surrounded to the west, east, and north by rainforests filled with sound and color. A noisy red-green macaw and a spider monkey watched you from their perches in the canopy. Off in the bush, you were sure you heard a hunting coati. What a great place Guyana was! You traveled about _____ miles.

3. Leaving this part of South America, you flew to the smaller strips of rainforest to the west of the Andes, in Colombia. As you continued observing and photographing the animals, you realized that any animal caught unaware on the forest floor by another animal could become this animal's next meal. While you were thinking about this, you saw butterflies searching for blossoms and a red-eyed tree frog waiting for insects. Your next stop took you back to

   _____.

4. Add three more stops in your trip. You could even venture to one of the rainforests in another land. Use maps to help you!

SOCIAL STUDIES

Name _____

Americans All!

People from many different countries have come to live in the United States. They have brought with them the rich heritage and culture of their native lands.

Build a puzzle with the names of twenty-one countries from which people have emigrated to America. The letters given in the puzzle will help you.

Word Box

China	Egypt	Haiti	India	Italy
Japan	Korea	Spain	France	Mexico
Norway	Poland	Russia	Denmark	England
Ireland	Nigeria	Romania	Vietnam	Tanzania
Hungary				

Name _____

What Happened?

Below you will learn what was happening during the lives of some famous Americans. Shade in the boxes following the events that occurred during the lifetime of each person listed at the bottom of the chart.

Year	Event	Betsy Ross (1752–1836)	Emily Post (1872–1960)	John C. Frémont (1813–1890)	Noah Webster (1758–1843)	Orville Wright (1871–1948)	Eliot Ness (1902–1957)	Pocahontas (1595–1617)	Joseph Pulitzer (1847–1911)	Sacagawea (1786–1812)	Ann S. Macy (1866–1936)	Walter Cronkite (1916–)	Edward R. Murrow (1908–1965)	Norman Thomas (1884–1968)	Sitting Bull (1837–1890)
1972	Gloria Steinem founded *Ms.* magazine.														
1966	Betty Friedan helped found NOW.														
1957	Dr. Tom Dooley helped found MEDICO.														
1955	Rosa Parks helped start Civil Rights Movement.														
1936	Jesse Owens won 4 gold medals at Summer Olympics.														
1896	George W. Carver received a master's degree.														
1889	Jane Addams helped found Hull House.														
1881	Clara Barton established American Red Cross.														
1879	Edison invented the electric light.														
1872	Buffalo Bill first appeared in "Wild West" show.														
1857	Dred Scott Decision														
1839	Horace Mann founded first state normal school in U.S.														
1814	Francis Scott Key wrote "The Star-Spangled Banner."														
1794	Dolley Todd married President Madison.														
1776	Nathan Hale was hung by British as a spy.														
1621	Massasoit made treaty with Plymouth Colony.														

1. Who did not live during any of the events listed above? _____

2. During which event were none of the personalities alive? _____

3. What is NOW? _____

4. Of which of the events listed above would you have liked to have been a part? Why?

Personality Plus   Make a list of 10 important events that have occurred during your lifetime. Share them with the class.

SOCIAL STUDIES

Name _____

Where Did They Come From?

Our country has been shaped by great minds from many states. Use the clues and the Word Bank to discover from which states many American personalities came. Label the map with the appropriate states' names or abbreviations.

Word Bank
Massachusetts
Pennsylvania
New York
Texas
Illinois
California
South Dakota
Tennessee
Ohio
Georgia
Virginia
Alabama

1. Samuel Adams, Susan B. Anthony, W.E.B. Du Bois, Ben Franklin and John Hancock once lived in this state which is now home to Harvard, Martha's Vineyard and the Freedom Trail. _____

2. This Land of Infinite Variety is mainly a farm state and was once home to Hubert Humphrey. _____

3. One of four states officially known as a commonwealth, this Keystone State is where Daniel Boone and George Marshall were born. _____

4. William Tecumseh Sherman and Ulysses S. Grant once called this Buckeye State home. _____

5. Niagara Falls graces this Empire State in which John Jay, John Rockefeller, Elizabeth Cady Stanton and Geraldine Ferraro were born. _____

6. Martin Luther King, Jr. once called this Goober State home. _____

7. The second largest state in the U.S., it was the birthplace of Sandra Day O'Connor, Chester Nimitz and Dwight D. Eisenhower. _____

8. Known as the Mother of Presidents, this state was also home at one time to Booker T. Washington, Robert E. Lee, Henry Clay, Patrick Henry, Sam Houston, Thomas "Stonewall" Jackson and John Marshall. _____

9. President Abraham Lincoln lived much of his life in this state as did William Jennings Bryan. _____

10. Jesse Owens and George Wallace were born in this Heart of Dixie. _____

11. The site of the famous gold rush, George S. Patton, Jr., and Earl Warren were both born in this Golden State. _____

12. Indians once roamed this Volunteer State where Sam Rayburn and Dave Farragut were born. _____

Personality Plus Make a list of some people from your state who you think are famous Americans in history. Tell what they have done.

Name _____

Treasure Hunt in the Rainforest

Tribes living in the rainforest use as many of its treasures as they can for meals, shelter, clothes, medicines, tools and cosmetics. Your home is filled with rainforest products too. Many fruits and nuts and even the domestic chicken originated from the rainforest. And scientists believe that there is much more to learn from the rainforest. To learn more about some of the rainforest's treasures, follow the directions below. You will need another sheet of paper on which to draw your discoveries.

1. Title the top of your map, Rainforest Treasure Hunt.

2. Draw a compass rose in the top left corner.

3. In the southwest corner of your paper, draw an orange and black frog. This is an arrow-poison frog. These tiny rainforest frogs produce a strong poison. This poison is extracted and used on the tips of blowpipe darts when hunting big game.

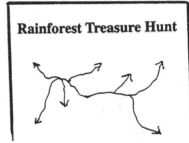

4. Travel northeast to the center of your paper. There is an Amazonian tree that produces a sap very similar to diesel. It can be used as fuel by trucks. Draw a tree with a gas hose coming from it.

5. Heading southeast, you discover plants and animals from which medicines originate. Draw a picture of medicine bottles in this corner.

6. Move up to the northeast corner to see the insects that provide an alternative to expensive pesticides. Three types of wasps were successfully introduced in Florida to control pests that were damaging citrus tree crops. Draw three wasps in this corner.

7. Traveling west, you stop to listen to a scientist estimating that there are at least 1,500 potential new fruits and vegetables growing in the rainforest. Draw a picture of a fruit or vegetable you discovered. Be sure to name it.

8. Return home and discuss with your parents the interesting facts you learned on your treasure hunt.

Daily Learning Drills Grade 4

Name _____

Problems in the Rainforest

In many countries, slash-and-burn agriculture is one of the leading causes of tropical deforestation. Slash-and-burn farmers clear rainforest land to grow their crops. During the first few years, the crops do well, but after the land has been cultivated for a while, the soil becomes worn out and the plot is abandoned. The rains wash away the topsoil and the land becomes difficult to cultivate. What can you do to help the rainforests?

Before solving a problem, it is often helpful to go through it in steps. For example, read the steps below to learn how you can try to help solve the slash-and-burn problem.

1. Restate the problem into a question.
2. State the facts you know about the problem.
3. Brainstorm possible ways to help solve the problem. Remember, in brainstorming, all the ideas you have are written down, even if you aren't sure they will work.

> How can we stop slash-and-burn agriculture?

> 1. Many trees are cut down.
> 2. The soil is only fertile for a short while.
> 3. The land is abandoned.

> 1. Remove the trees with aerial cables instead of heavy logging equipment.
> 2. Allow only certain areas to be cut down one at a time.
> 3. Research to learn more about how rainforests can regenerate.

Read the following problem and fill in your ideas in the graphic organizer to the left. Share your ideas with the class.

Deforestation has a direct impact on tribes native to the rainforest. In many cases, these people are forced to move or relocate through government programs. The people also suffer from diseases brought by "outsiders."

1. Restate the problem into a question.

2. State the facts you know about the problem.

3. Brainstorm possible ways to help solve the problem.

Answer Key

The National Pastime

Print the names of the National League Baseball Teams in ABC order on the lines below. Then write the letters in the circles on the lines at the bottom of the page to decode the message.

1. Ⓐstros
2. BravⒺs
3. Cardinals
4. CⓤbⓢᏚ
5. Dodgers
6. Ⓔxⓟos
7. Ⓖiants
8. MarⒾⓝs
9. Mets
10. Pᗩdres
11. PhⒾⓁⓁies
12. PiraⓉes
13. Rⓔds
14. RockⒾes

These teams belong to the:

Ⓝ Ⓐ Ⓣ Ⓘ Ⓞ Ⓝ Ⓐ Ⓛ   Ⓛ Ⓔ Ⓐ Ⓖ Ⓤ Ⓔ
8² 10 12 9 1 6 11   11 13 2 7 4 6

8¹ = 1st circled letter   8² = 2nd circled letter

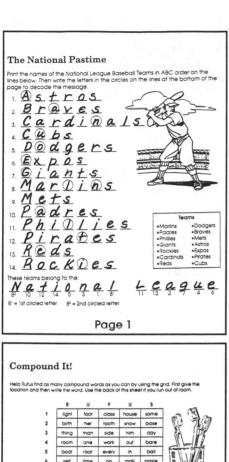

Teams
- Marlins
- Padres
- Phillies
- Giants
- Rockies
- Cardinals
- Reds
- Dodgers
- Braves
- Mets
- Astros
- Expos
- Pirates
- Cubs

Page 1

Are You Alphabetically Inclined?

Below are several groups of words. If the group is in the correct alphabetical order, draw a star around it. If it is incorrect, write it correctly in the blanks provided at the bottom of the page.

slithering	dialect	tomahawk	mingle
Seminole	doleful	thatch	metallic
sorrowful	deafen	tourniquet	mythical
salvage	defiance	turban	muslin

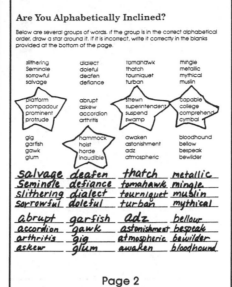

platform	abrupt	strewn	capable
pompadour	askew	superintendent	college
prominent	accordion	suspend	comprehend
protrude	arthritis	swamp	cymbal

gig	hammock	awaken	bloodhound
garfish	hoist	astonishment	bellow
gawk	horde	adz	bespeak
glum	inaudible	atmospheric	bewilder

salvage   deafen   thatch   metallic
Seminole   defiance   tomahawk   mingle
slithering   dialect   tourniquet   muslin
sorrowful   doleful   turban   mythical

abrupt   garfish   adz   bellow
accordion   gawk   astonishment   bespeak
arthritis   gig   atmospheric   bewilder
askew   glum   awaken   bloodhound

Page 2

Compound Checkup

Write the compound word from the Word Box that matches each definition.

1. physical examination – checkup
2. a giant Pacific coast evergreen – redwood
3. difficult thing to bear – hardship
4. an outdoor advertising sign – billboard
5. small metal pot for cooking – saucepan
6. on a lower floor – downstairs
7. a glass container used for measuring time – hourglass
8. a movable ramp to a ship – gangplank
9. to betray – double-cross
10. a person with a quick temper – hothead
11. to intimidate – browbeat
12. delighted – overjoyed
13. a logger – lumberjack
14. lower half of a chicken leg – drumstick
15. a very clever person – mastermind
16. a robbery – holdup
17. a limited-access highway – freeway
18. an insect with brightly-colored wings – butterfly
19. a large area for dancing – ballroom
20. a path in the street marked for pedestrians – crosswalk

Word Box

ballroom	billboard	browbeat	butterfly	checkup
crosswalk	double-cross	downstairs	drumstick	freeway
gangplank	hardship	holdup	hothead	hourglass
lumberjack	mastermind	overjoyed	redwood	saucepan

Page 3

Compound It!

Help Rufus find as many compound words as you can by using the grid. First give the location and then write the word. Use the back of this sheet if you run out of room.

	R	U	F	U	S
1	light	foot	class	house	some
2	birth	her	foot	snow	base
3	thing	man	side	him	day
4	room	one	work	out	bare
5	boat	roar	every	in	ball
6	self	time	no	mail	paste
7	stairs	to	shop	mate	up

location   word
Example: F-2, S-6   toothpaste

	location	word		location	word
1.	R-1, U-1	lighthouse	10.	U-2, U-3	snowman
2.	R-2, S-3	birthday	11.	U-2, S-5	snowball
3.	F-5, R-3	everything	12.	F-5, R-4	ballroom
4.	F-1, R-4	classroom	13.	S-3, R-4	dayroom
5.	U-1, R-5	houseboat	14.	S-3, R-1	daylight
6.	U-3, R-6	herself	15.	S-3, U-6	daytime
7.	U-3, R-6	himself	16.	S-2, S-5	baseball
8.	S-7, R-7	upstairs	17.	F-4, U-4	workout
9.	U-1, S-5	football	18.	F-6, U-4	noone

Bonus   Others possible.

How many of your words can you draw rebus clues for? Trade your drawings with friends and ask them to guess the words.

Example: basketball

Page 4

Words That Break

Divide each word into two words with a slash (/). Then choose one of the two words and combine it with a word from the Word Bank to form a different word.
Example: side/walk—boardwalk   **Others possible.**

1. afternoon   after/noon   backyard
2. junkyard
3. handkerchief   handsome
4. football   baseball
5. downtown   downtown
6. eggshell   seashell
7. undersea   underwear
8. nearbreak   daybreak

9. outgrow   outboard
10. without   within
11. everybody   everywhere
12. inside   backside
13. overlook   overhear
14. teapot   teaspoon
15. lighthouse   daylight
16. cowboy   cowbell

Word Bank

back	day	in	town
base	heat	off	wear
bell	flash	sea	where
board	thought	spoon	some

Take two unrelated words to create a whole new compound word. Then tell what it means and use it in a sentence.
Example: junkfea — a blend of tea made from garbage. We bought our junktea at a reduced price.

1. Sentences will vary.
2. _____
3. _____
4. _____

Page 5

Comma Quandary

Look at the underlined parts in each sentence. If each is a complete thought, place a comma in the box. If it is not a complete thought, place an X in the box.

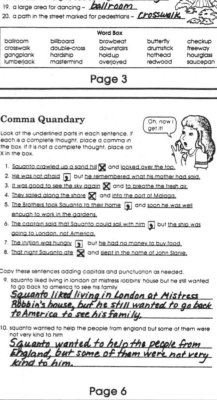
Oh, now I get it!

1. Squanto crawled up a sand hill ☒ and looked over the top.
2. He was not afraid 🔲 but he remembered what his mother had said.
3. It was good to see the sky again ☒ and to breathe the fresh air.
4. They sailed along the shore ☒ and into the port of Malaga.
5. The Brothers took Squanto to their home 🔲 and soon he was well enough to work in the gardens.
6. The captain said that Squanto could sail with him 🔲 but the ship was going to London, not America.
7. The Indian was hungry 🔲 but he had no money to buy food.
8. That night Squanto ate ☒ and slept in the home of John Slanie.

Copy these sentences adding capitals and punctuation as needed.

9. squanto liked living in london at mistress robbins' house but he still wanted to go back to america to see his family
Squanto liked living in London at Mistress Robbin's house, but he still wanted to go back to America to see his family.

10. squanto wanted to help the people from england but some of them were not very kind to him
Squanto wanted to help the people from England, but some of them were not very kind to him.

Page 6

The Prisoner's Sentence Is Imperative!

WANTED RUNAWAY SLAVE

Match each sentence with the correct type by drawing a line.

"I don't want a slave in my room!" ——— interrogative
"Are you a freedman?" ——— declarative
"Go to the cellar and get some food." ——— exclamatory
The fall sunshine felt nice. ——— imperative

Use vocabulary words in the Word Bank to help you write each type of sentence.

Word Bank

apologize	doubtfully	confided	maddening
rudeness	impatiently	enthusiastically	sprawled
cantered	scornfully	dumbfounded	defiantly
convince	lurking	denser	good-humored
collided	exhausted		

Imperative   Sentences will vary.
Declarative _____
Exclamatory _____
Interrogative _____

Page 7

Makin' Room

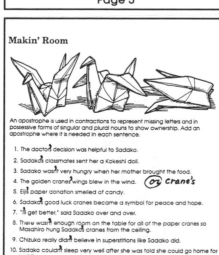

An apostrophe is used in contractions to represent missing letters and in possessive forms of singular and plural nouns to show ownership. Add an apostrophe where it is needed in each sentence.

1. The doctor's decision was helpful to Sadako.
2. Sadako's classmates sent her a Kokeshi doll.
3. Sadako wasn't very hungry when her mother brought the food.
4. The golden cranes' wings blew in the wind. (or crane's)
5. Eiji's paper donation smelled of candy.
6. Sadako's good luck cranes became a symbol for peace and hope.
7. "I'll get better," said Sadako over and over.
8. There wasn't enough room on the table for all of the paper cranes so Masahiro hung Sadako's cranes from the ceiling.
9. Chizuko really didn't believe in superstitions like Sadako did.
10. Sadako couldn't sleep very well after she was told she could go home for a visit.
11. Mrs. Sasaki's slippers slapped softly on the floor.
12. "Here's your first crane," said Chizuko.

Page 8

Keep It Simple

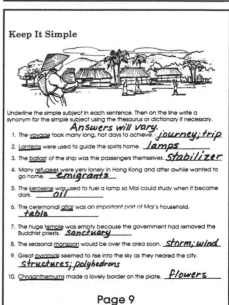

Underline the simple subject in each sentence. Then on the line write a synonym for the simple subject using the thesaurus or dictionary if necessary.
Answers will vary.

1. The voyage took many long, hot days to achieve. journey; trip
2. Lanterns were used to guide the spirits home. lamps
3. The ballast of the ship was the passengers themselves. stabilizer
4. Many refugees were very lonely in Hong Kong and after awhile wanted to go home. emigrants
5. The kerosene was used to fuel a lamp so Mai could study when it became dark. oil
6. The ceremonial altar was an important part of Mai's household. table
7. The huge temple was empty because the government had removed the Buddhist priests. sanctuary
8. The seasonal monsoon would be over the area soon. storm; wind
9. Great pyramids seemed to rise into the sky as they neared the city. structures; polyhedrons
10. Chrysanthemums made a lovely border on the plate. flowers

Page 9

That's Mine!

dog's bones   dogs' bones

Change the underlined word to show possession by adding an apostrophe or apostrophe and s. Write the possessive form on the line.

	Possessive
1. Mother took me to <u>Tony</u> house.	Tony's
2. The <u>chickens</u> eggs were large.	Chickens'
3. <u>Jonathan</u> bicycle needs new brakes.	Jonathan's
4. Follow the <u>team</u> rules.	team's
5. The <u>shoes</u> soles need repair.	shoes'
6. Mrs. <u>Thomas</u> car was in the driveway.	Thomas's
7. My <u>brother</u> story won first prize.	brother's
8. Our <u>neighbors</u> lawns need cutting.	neighbors'
9. <u>Ellen</u> paintings were on display.	Ellen's
10. The truck <u>drivers</u> routes were long.	drivers'
11. The <u>babies</u> toys are put away.	babies'
12. The <u>principal</u> office is small.	principal's
13. The <u>bird</u> nest is empty.	bird's
14. The <u>doctors</u> hours were long.	doctors'
15. The <u>painter</u> brushes were clean.	painter's
16. The <u>skunk</u> scent was not pleasant.	skunk's
17. The <u>aliens</u> spaceship had landed.	aliens'

Page 10

Name _____

Know Your Nouns

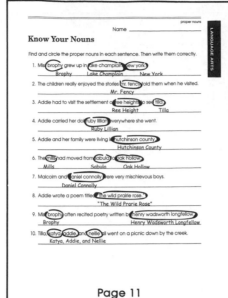

Find and circle the proper nouns in each sentence. Then write them correctly.

1. Miss Brophy grew up in Lake Champlain, New York.
   Brophy   Lake Champlain   New York

2. The children really enjoyed the stories Mr. Fency told them when he visited.
   Mr. Fency

3. Addie had to visit the settlement of Ree Heights to see Tilla.
   Ree Heights   Tilla

4. Addie carried her doll Ruby Lillian everywhere she went.
   Ruby Lillian

5. Addie and her family were living in Hutchinson County.
   Hutchinson County

6. The Mills had moved from Sabula to Oak Hollow.
   Mills   Sabula   Oak Hollow

7. Malcolm and Daniel Connolly were very mischievous boys.
   Daniel Connolly

8. Addie wrote a poem titled "The Wild Prairie Rose."
   "The Wild Prairie Rose"

9. Miss Brophy often recited poetry written by Henry Wadsworth Longfellow.
   Brophy   Henry Wadsworth Longfellow

10. Tilla, Katya, Addie, and Nellie all went on a picnic down by the creek.
    Katya, Addie, and Nellie

Page 11

A View of the Past?

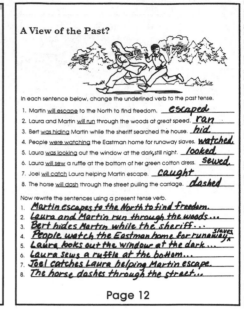

In each sentence below, change the underlined verb to the past tense.

1. Martin <u>will escape</u> to the North to find freedom. — escaped
2. Laura and Martin <u>will run</u> through the woods at great speed. — ran
3. Bert <u>was hiding</u> Martin while the sheriff searched the house. — hid
4. People <u>were watching</u> the Eastman home for runaway slaves. — watched
5. Laura <u>was looking</u> out the window at the dark, still night. — looked
6. Laura <u>will sew</u> a ruffle at the bottom of her green cotton dress. — sewed
7. Joel <u>will catch</u> Laura helping Martin escape. — caught
8. The horse <u>will dash</u> through the street pulling the carriage. — dashed

Now rewrite the sentences using a present tense verb.

1. Martin escapes to the North to find freedom.
2. Laura and Martin run through the woods...
3. Bert hides Martin while the sheriff...
4. People watch the Eastman home for runaway slaves.
5. Laura looks out the window at the dark...
6. Laura sews a ruffle at the bottom...
7. Joel catches Laura helping Martin escape.
8. The horse dashes through the street...

Page 12

Are You in the Past or Present?

Underline the verb in each sentence. On the line after each sentence write if the verb is past or present tense.

1. Sadako <u>ran</u> home from school every day. — past
2. The wind almost <u>blew</u> the light out of the ceremonial lantern on Peace Day. — past
3. Sadako <u>dreamed</u> of good health. — past
4. The wind <u>caught</u> the paper cranes. — past
5. Sadako's gums <u>were</u> swollen. — past
6. Sadako <u>read</u> all of the letters. — past
7. The sun <u>shines</u> brightly on the balcony of the hospital. — present
8. Sadako <u>slept</u> very soundly after the shot of medication. — past
9. Sadako <u>runs</u> faster than almost anyone. — present
10. Kenji <u>knew</u> about leukemia. — past

Page 13

Three Playful Kittens

Rule An **adjective** is a word that describes a noun or a pronoun. It tells **what kind, how many,** or **which one.**

Example All of these adjectives can be used to describe kittens : black, several, these, playful, furry, three, many, young.

Exercise Place an X in the blanks in front of the adjectives. Then complete the sentence with those adjectives.

1. X striped
   X one
   ___ carefully
   ___ soon
   One striped
   zebra ran through the jungle.

2. X powerful
   X ahead
   X two
   ___ cautiously
   Two powerful
   elephants trudged along the path.

3. ___ yesterday
   ___ quickly
   X scaly
   X spotted
   A **scaly , spotted**
   snake darted through the grass.

4. X colorful
   ___ graceful
   ___ happily
   ___ however
   The **colorful , graceful**
   birds soared through the air.

• Underline the nouns in the sentences below. Circle the adjectives.

1. The huge, gray elephant lumbered through the hot jungle.
2. Three swift lions raced through the long, green grass.
3. The playful monkeys swung from the high tree branches.
4. The lazy, green turtle slept under the hot tropical sun.
5. The large, horned rhinoceros slipped into the muddy river.
6. The scaly, old crocodile blinked its large, dark eyes.

Page 14

The Fragrant Flowers

Rule Adjectives answer these specific questions about the nouns they modify.

| Which one? | What kind? | How many? |

Example

| these, those, that, this | tall, colorful, red, majestic | three, many, several, few, one |

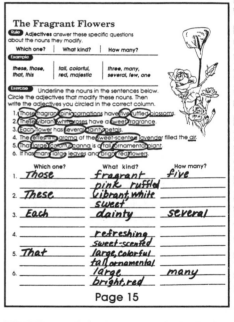

Exercise Underline the nouns in the sentences below. Circle the adjectives that modify these nouns. Then write the adjectives you circled in the correct column.

1. Those fragrant pink carnations have five ruffled blossoms.
2. These vibrant white roses have a sweet fragrance.
3. Each flower has several dainty petals.
4. The refreshing aroma of the sweet-scented lavender filled the air.
5. That large colorful canna is a tall ornamental plant.
6. It has many large leaves and bright, red flowers.

	Which one?	What kind?	How many?
1.	Those	fragrant pink ruffled	five
2.	These	vibrant, white sweet	
3.	Each	dainty	several
4.		refreshing sweet-scented	
5.	That	large, colorful tall ornamental	
6.		large bright, red	many

Page 15

Adverbs Answer

Adverbs modify verbs or adjectives and tell **how, when,** or **where.**

How— I read slowly.
Where— I read inside.
When— I was reading today.

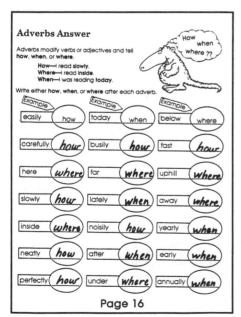

Write either how, when, or where after each adverb.

Example		Example		Example	
easily	how	today	when	below	where
carefully	how	busily	how	fast	how
here	where	far	where	uphill	where
slowly	how	lately	when	away	where
inside	where	noisily	how	yearly	when
neatly	how	after	when	early	when
perfectly	how	under	where	annually	when

Page 16

That's How It's Done!

Adverbs answer the questions **when, where,** and **how.** The adverbs in the sentences below answer how. Underline the adverb(s) in each sentence. Then circle the verb it describes. The first one is done for you.

1. The two boys solemnly shook hands.
2. Chip looked down incredulously at the fallen shingle which landed softly at his feet.
3. "I don't salvage," remarked Rudy calmly when his counselor glared at him.
4. "Rudy," whispered Mike warningly. Chip was glaring in their direction.
5. The door opened and Mr. Warden emerged, smartly dressed in a white tennis outfit.
6. "Harold, you have no soul," explained Rudy pleasantly.
7. "Why do you immediately assume that I'm guilty?" asked Rudy in a hurt tone.
8. "I'd rather go back to arts and crafts," nodded Mike sheepishly.
9. "Tomorrow," Rudy said thoughtfully, "when we carefully daubed pale blue paint onto their creation, "we'll go earlier."
10. Arms flailing wildly, Chip rushed anxiously toward his cabin.
11. "Let's just walk directly away from the lake," decided Rudy.

Write four sentences of your own containing adverbs. Underline the adverbs and circle the verbs that are described.

1. Sentences will vary.
2. _____
3. _____
4. _____

Page 17

They're Coming!

Circle the 24 pronouns in the following story.

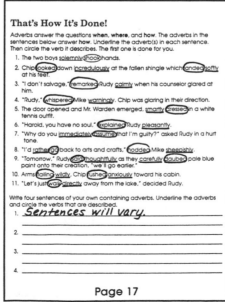

A Scary Dream

"They are coming after us," Rhonda said to her brother, Scott. Believe me, Scott, I saw them with their funny-looking faces. The two of them had long, orange hair, and they had gigantic feet. I thought they could be from Mars because they spoke a funny language.

One of them glared at me with his strange-looking face. The other one looked like she had on her clothes from outer space.

Scott, you can't imagine my, thoughts as I saw them coming after me with their weird looks and their weird clothes.

Finish this story. Use at least six different pronouns. Circle the pronouns you use.

Story endings will vary

_____
_____
_____
_____
_____
_____

Page 18

Listen to the Music

In the sentences below, label each of the following.

N—noun   Adj—adjective
P—pronoun   Adv—adverb
V—verb

Example:
Adj Adj N V   Adv
The little girl ran outside.

1. P V Adj N Adv
   We feed the birds regularly.
2. N V Adj Adj N Adv
   Derek planted a maple tree yesterday.
3. N V P N
   Charles wrote them a letter.
4. P V Adj Adj N
   They have two small dogs.
5. N V Adv
   Rose will be dancing tomorrow.
6. Adj N V Adv
   The toys are everywhere.
7. Adj Adj N V Adv Adv
   The three children are going swimming today.
8. P V P N Adv
   You can eat now.
9. P V Adj N Adv
   They washed the car carefully.
10. Adj Adj N V Adj N
    Several thirsty children drank cold lemonade.
11. P V Adj N Adv
    We run three miles often.
12. Adj N V Adv
    The chorus has been singing beautifully.
13. P V N Adj N
    He gave Chuck five dollars.
14. N V Adj N Adv
    Pam washed the dishes slowly.
15. Adj Adj N V Adv
    That tiny baby was sleeping soundly.

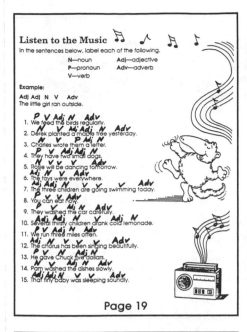

Page 19

Break It Up!

For each word given below, give the base word and the prefix and/or suffix. Remember, some base words' spellings have been changed before adding suffixes. Not all words will have a prefix and a suffix.

Word	Prefix	Base Word	Suffix
resourceful	re	source	ful
accomplishment		accomplish	ment
numbness		numb	ness
convincing		convince	ing
merciless		mercy	less
sturdiest		sturdy	est
disobeying	dis	obey	ing
unmistakable	un	mistake	able
disinfecting	dis	infect	ing
disclaimed	dis	claim	ed
reopening	re	open	ing
inventive		invent	ive
restless		rest	less
precaution	pre	caution	
imitating		imitate	ing

Page 20

Fore and Aft

Fill in the blanks with the appropriate affixes. Some will be used more than once.

Prefixes: dis- im- mis- re- un-   Suffixes: -ful -ish -ist -less -ly -ness -ward

	Meaning	Root Word + Affix	New Word
1.	having no fear	fear _less_	fearless
2.	to vanish	_dis_ appear	disappear
3.	toward a lower level	down _ward_	downward
4.	having no friends	friend _less_	friendless
5.	an error in action	_mis_ take	mistake
6.	to enter again	_re_ enter	reenter
7.	too many to count	count _less_	countless
8.	not happy	_un_ happy	unhappy
9.	perfection seeker	perfection _ist_	perfectionist
10.	quality of being dark	dark _ness_	darkness
11.	not possible	_im_ possible	impossible
12.	having doubts	doubt _ful_	doubtful
13.	without a care	care _less_	careless
14.	sad from being alone	lone _ly_	lonely
15.	not thinking	_un_ thinking	unthinking
16.	without shoes	shoe _less_	shoeless
17.	in a mysterious way	mysterious _ly_	mysteriously
18.	appear again	_re_ appear	reappear
19.	in a quiet manner	quiet _ly_	quietly
20.	call by wrong name	_mis_ call	miscall
21.	somewhat yellow	yellow _ish_	yellowish
22.	cautious	care _ful_	careful
23.	to release	_dis_ engage	disengage

Page 21

Don't Miss This!

The prefix mis– means wrong or wrongly, bad or badly, no or not. Underline the base words in the following list. Then circle the base words in the wordsearch. Words may go → ↑ ↓ ↘ ↗.

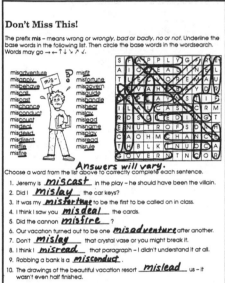

misadventure   misfit
misapply   misfortune
misbehave   misgovern
miscall   misguide
miscast   mishandle
mischance   mishear
misconduct   mislay
miscount   mislead
misdeal   misname
misdeed   misplay
misdirect   misread
misfile   misrule
misfire

Answers will vary.

Choose a word from the list above to correctly complete each sentence.

1. Jeremy was _miscast_ in the play – he should have been the villain.
2. Did I _mislay_ the car keys?
3. It was my _misfortune_ to be the first to be called on in class.
4. I think I saw you _misdeal_ the cards.
5. Did the cannon _misfire_ ?
6. Our vacation turned out to be one _misadventure_ after another.
7. Don't _mislay_ that crystal vase or you might break it.
8. I think I _misread_ that paragraph – I didn't understand it at all.
9. Robbing a bank is a _misconduct_ .
10. The drawings of the beautiful vacation resort _mislead_ us – it wasn't even half finished.

Page 22

Similar in Some Way

Put an X in the circle by the phrase to correctly complete each analogy.

1. conductor is to orchestra as . . .
   ○ scene is to actor
   ⊗ director is to play

2. absent is to present as . . .
   ⊗ adult is to child
   ○ levy is to tax

3. button is to blouse as . . .
   ○ coat is to hat
   ⊗ zipper is to skirt

4. pork is to hog as . . .
   ○ bacon is to eggs
   ⊗ beef is to cattle

5. allow is to permit as . . .
   ⊗ alter is to change
   ○ refute is to confirm

6. mirror is to reflect as . . .
   ⊗ scissors is to cut
   ○ read is to book

7. aide is to assistant as . . .
   ○ brash is to cautious
   ⊗ convince is to persuade

8. autumn is to season as . . .
   ○ winter is to summer
   ⊗ Halloween is to holiday

9. shirt is to collar as . . .
   ○ sock is to shoes
   ⊗ trousers is to cuffs

10. ice cream is to dessert as . . .
    ⊗ cereal is to breakfast
    ○ supper is to dinner

11. graph is to chart as . . .
    ○ present is to past
    ⊗ explore is to investigate

Page 23

Analyzing Analogies

Put an X in the circle by the phrase that correctly completes each analogy.

1. hobo is to tramp as . . .
   ⊗ vagabond is to vagrant
   ○ knight is to serf

2. hopeless is to desperate as . . .
   ○ pessimistic is to optimistic
   ⊗ certain is to confident

3. sow is to reap as . . .
   ○ gather is to pick
   ⊗ plant is to harvest

4. miserly is to generous as . . .
   ⊗ stingy is to extravagant
   ○ mean is to cheap

5. vapid is to taste as . . .
   ○ cool is to touch
   ⊗ odorless is to smell

6. ignite is to kindle as . . .
   ⊗ prattle is to chatter
   ○ gradual is to sudden

7. cloth is to weaver as . . .
   ○ money is to banker
   ⊗ book is to printer

8. mechanic is to automobile as . . .
   ○ pipe is to plumber
   ⊗ electrician is to wiring

9. throw is to football as . . .
   ○ baseball is to toss
   ⊗ fling is to Frisbee

10. quiver is to vibrate as . . .
    ○ shiver is to cold
    ⊗ wiggle is to squirm

Page 24

Let's Change Laura's Disposition

Antonyms are words that mean almost the opposite. Replace the underlined word in each sentence with an antonym from the Word Bank.

1. Laura stood by the door with a mournful look on her face. _happy_
2. Laura retreated at the sound of voices outside the springhouse.
   advanced
3. Laura scornfully accepted the fact that they would be hiding a runaway slave.
   respectfully
4. When Joel asked Laura to read a book of his, she was very resentful.
   cheerful
5. Bert asked Laura to look in the wardrobe for Martin. She was very impatient in her search.
   tolerant
6. Laura swiftly went to her room and firmly closed the door. _sluggishly_
7. Martin quickly descended the stairs when they heard a wagon out front.
   climbed
8. Laura was very indignant about the idea of having Martin hiding in her room.
   gratified

Word Bank			
respectfully	tolerant	cheerful	gratified
sluggishly	happy	climbed	advanced

Choose three of the vocabulary words underlined above and use each one in a sentence.
1. _Answers will vary._
2. _____
3. _____

Page 25

Antonym Action

Using the words from the Word Box, write a word that means the opposite of each numbered word. Then circle each word from the Word Box in the wordsearch. Words may go → ← ↑ ↓ ↘ ↙.

Word Box			
hero	deny	clean	bright	ancient
exit	stale	rebel	compel	divulge
raze	solid	greedy	corrupt	educated

1. approve – _deny_
2. coax – _compel_
3. conform – _rebel_
4. construct – _raze_
5. coward – _hero_
6. dreary – _bright_
7. enter – _exit_
8. fresh – _stale_
9. generous – _greedy_
10. hide – _divulge_
11. honest – _corrupt_
12. ignorant – _educated_
13. liquid – _solid_
14. modern – _ancient_
15. soiled – _clean_

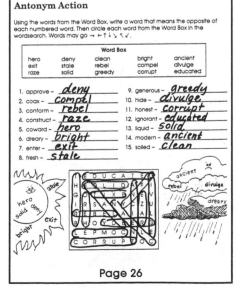

Page 26

Code Names

Use the code to write a synonym for each word.

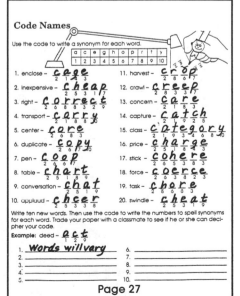

a	c	e	g	h	o	p	r	t	y
1	2	3	4	5	6	7	8	9	10

1. enclose – _cage_ (2 1 4 3)
2. inexpensive – _cheap_ (2 5 3 1 7)
3. right – _correct_ (2 6 8 8 3 2 9)
4. transport – _carry_ (2 1 8 8 10)
5. center – _core_ (2 6 8 3)
6. duplicate – _copy_ (2 6 7 10)
7. pen – _coop_ (2 6 6 7)
8. table – _chart_ (2 5 1 8 9)
9. conversation – _chat_ (2 5 1 9)
10. applaud – _cheer_ (2 5 3 3 8)
11. harvest – _crop_ (2 8 6 7)
12. crawl – _creep_ (2 8 3 3 7)
13. concern – _care_ (2 1 8 3)
14. capture – _catch_ (2 1 9 2 5)
15. class – _category_ (2 1 9 3 4 6 8 10)
16. price – _charge_ (2 5 1 8 4 3)
17. stick – _cohere_ (2 6 5 3 8 3)
18. force – _coerce_ (2 6 3 8 2 3)
19. task – _chore_ (2 5 6 8 3)
20. swindle – _cheat_ (2 5 3 1 9)

Write ten new words. Then use the code to write the numbers to spell synonyms for each word. Trade your paper with a classmate to see if he or she can decipher your code.

Example: deed – _act_ (1 2 9)

1. _Words will vary._   6. _____
2. _____   7. _____
3. _____   8. _____
4. _____   9. _____
5. _____   10. _____

Page 27

Daily Learning Drills Grade 4

The Synonymous Sleuth

Write the synonym for the backwards word in each sentence. Decode and use the backwards synonyms at the bottom.

1. Miss Whitehead's feet look regral this year. **bigger**
2. I kniht Miss Elson is one of those people you don't bother to think about twice. **believe**
3. It's just what Ole Golly says, hcir people are boring. **wealthy**
4. When I look at him, I could tae 1,000 tomato sandwiches. **devour**
5. He looks yppah except I wouldn't like all those cats. **content**
6. Is he a tnereffid person when he's with someone else? **distinct**
7. She snwort when she looks at things close. **scowls**
8. I just feel ynnuf all over. **strange**
9. Spies should not get thguac. **captured**
10. It was just too suoregnad to go there. **risky**
11. Every time I have a dab dream, I feel like leaving town. **terrible**
12. Sometimes Sport is like a little old namow. **lady**
13. I have deman him the boy with the purple socks. **labeled**
14. Maybe they think I'm a gnilkaew, but I'm trained for this kind of fight. **wimp**
15. There is no rest for the yraew. **tired**
16. This cook certainly makes a lot of esion. **racket**
17. Ole Golly is thgir, sometimes you have to lie. **correct**
18. They're trying to lortnoc me and make me give up. **rule**
19. I will never give up this notebook, but it is raelc that they are going to be as mean as they can. **plain**
20. I will be the tseb spy there ever was and I will know everything. **greatest**

Clues
egnarts	ydal	reggib	slwocs	delebal	derit	tekcar
yksir	ruoved	eveileb	yhtlaew	pmiw	elur	tcerroc
tnetnoc	tcnitsid	derutpac	nialp	tsetaerg	elbirret	

Page 28

Super Synonyms

Read each sentence below. Write a synonym for each underlined word. You may want to use a thesaurus. **Words will vary.**

1. Mattie and Toni find a beautiful pin for Mattie's mother. _____
2. Matt is thrilled to be on the basketball team. _____
3. Mrs. Benson works very hard to keep everything done around the apartment building. _____
4. Mrs. Stamps is a friendly person to visit. _____
5. Mr. Ashby tries to be a fair teacher. _____
6. Angel is wicked toward everyone around her. _____
7. The Bacon family really enjoyed Mattie's babysitting service. _____
8. Charlene took the bracelet from Angel because she was envious of Angel. _____
9. Mr. Phillips was amazed by Mattie's story. _____
10. Mattie had been very helpful to her mother. _____

Now use the thesaurus to find an antonym for each synonym you wrote above.

1. _____   6. _____
2. _____   7. _____
3. _____   8. _____
4. _____   9. _____
5. _____   10. _____

Page 29

You Can Count on the Count

Homographs are words that are spelled the same but have different meanings. Write the correct homograph for the underlined word(s) in each sentence.

Word Bank
bank	spruce	pupil
flag	hide	stake
brush	arms	bay

1. She hid the gold by the evergreen tree. **spruce**
2. The soldiers carried weapons. **arms**
3. I have a dark center in my eye. **pupil**
4. The children had a lot of risk if they were caught with the gold. **stake**
5. The kids could signal for help if needed. **flag**
6. The skin on the alligator was thick and dark. **hide**
7. The ship docked in the inlet. **bay**
8. The tentacles on the octopus moved constantly. **arms**
9. The dog suddenly began to howl. **bay**
10. The children could conceal the gold in the snow. **hide**
11. Uncle Victor had a banner hanging in his ship. **flag**
12. Someone was hiding in the bushes by the Snake River. **brush**
13. The land along the river was covered with brush. **bank**
14. She had a close encounter with danger. **brush**
15. The snow pile was as tall as a tree. **bank**
16. She was a quiet student. **pupil**
17. I will help you fix up things around here. **spruce**
18. They drove a post in the ground to mark the spot. **stake**

Page 30

Help with Homophones

Circle the correct homophones in each sentence.

1. I'd like to (halve, **have**) a piece when you (**halve**, have) that apple.
2. Please give me the (**real**, reel) fishing rod (real, **reel**).
3. Our (guessed, **guest**) (**guessed**, guest) the correct answer.
4. I heard (**him**, hymn) sing the (him, **hymn**).
5. The robber was (scene, **seen**) at the (**scene**, seen) of the crime.
6. The (**band**, banned) could not play the (band, **banned**) song.
7. I heard Alex (**moan**, mown) when he was reminded he had not yet (moan, **mown**) the grass.
8. The weather forecaster said the (missed, **mist**) had (**missed**, mist) our area.
9. When the knight hurled his (soared, **sword**) it (**soared**, sword) into the air.
10. It's so (chili, **chilly**) today, let's have (**chili**, chilly) for supper.

On the lines below, write a sentence for each pair of homophones.

ate, eight **Sentences will vary.**

dear, deer _____

we'd, weed _____

hoarse, horse _____

scent, sent _____

Page 31

Homophone Hype

For each word given below find and circle the homophone(s) in the wordsearch. List the homophones in the spaces provided. Then write a sentence using the given word and at least one homophone.

1. Main   **Maine   mane**
   Sentence: **sentences will vary.**
2. Liar   **lyre**
   Sentence:
3. Farrow   **pharoah   faro**
   Sentence:
4. Bridle   **bridal**
   Sentence:
5. I'll   **aisle   isle**
   Sentence:
6. Graze (Hint: plural form of a color)   **grays**
7. Here   **hear**
   Sentence:
8. Way   **weigh   whey**
   Sentence:
9. Do   **due   dew**
   Sentence:
10. Sent   **scent   cent**
   Sentence:

Page 32

Indefatigable Idioms

Use the code to find idioms for each phrase.

1. wasting time
   killing time
   X V Y Y V A T   G V Z R
2. start to think
   wheels begin
   J U R D V   O R T V A
   to turn
   G B   G H E A
3. become weak and weary
   run down
   E H A   Q B J A
4. self-evident
   it goes without
   V G   T B R F   J V G U B H G
   saying
   F N V V A T
5. take back what you said
   eat his words
   R N G   U V F   J B E Q F
6. what a person deserves
   just desserts
   W H F G   Q R F F R E G F
7. she attempts to do too much
   bites off more than
   O V G R F   B S S   Z B E R   G U N A
   she can chew
   F U R   P N A   P U R J
8. poorly planned
   half baked
   U N Y S - O N X R Q

Code
A	N
B	O
C	P
D	Q
E	R
F	S
G	T
H	U
I	V
J	W
K	X
L	Y
M	Z

Challenge: Write a story using as many idioms as possible. You might want to include: play it by ear, child's play, eyes peeled, double cross, ham it up, see red, over a barrel, wound up, down in the dumps, time flies, make ends meet, on the tip of my tongue.

Page 33

Watch for Grandpa's Watch

Each "watch" in the title of this worksheet has a different meaning. One means "to look for," and the other means "time piece." Write two meanings for the words below.

Words will vary.

	Meaning 1	Meaning 2
1. spring		
2. run		
3. ruler		
4. duck		
5. suit		
6. cold		
7. fall		
8. tire		
9. rose		
10. face		
11. train		
12. play		
13. foot		
14. pen		
15. box		
16. dice		
17. fly		
18. seal		
19. bowl		
20. ride		
21. line		

Challenge: Choose some of the above words and illustrate their two meanings on another piece of paper.

Page 34

Double Trouble

Fill in the blanks with the correct definition number for each underlined word.

Example: _3_ I was covered with pitch after climbing the pine tree.

winding	1. having bends or curves
	2. the act of turning something around a central core
wolf	1. to gulp down
	2. a large carnivorous member of the dog family
pitch	1. to sell or persuade
	2. to throw a ball from the mound to the batter
	3. a resin that comes from the sap of pine trees

_1_ 1. Do girl scouts pitch cookies?
_2_ 2. We are winding the top's string tightly.
_2_ 3. The adult wolf returned to her lair.
_2_ 4. Red didn't pitch after the fourth inning.
_1_ 5. The Mather family had a winding driveway.
_1_ 6. The young ball player wolfed down his lunch.

choke	1. to strangle
	2. to bring the hands up on the bat
hitch	1. obstacle
	2. to fasten or tie temporarily
wind-up	1. the swing of the pitcher's arm just before the pitch
	2. to close or conclude

_2_ 1. We hitched the mule to the cart.
_2_ 2. Tip would not choke up on his bat.
_1_ 3. Paul wished to play, but there was just one hitch.
_2_ 4. We wish to wind-up our program with more music.
_1_ 5. Mom was afraid the dog would choke itself on its leash.
_1_ 6. He has a great wind-up and curve ball.

Page 35

Words We Can Hear . . . Onomatopoeia

Words that imitate the sounds that they are associated with are onomatopoeic. Use words from the Word Bank to write a poem or short story.

Word Bank
whack	buzz	hiss	creak	squeal	honk
twang	cuckoo	grind	clink	ping	crack
thump	crash	bow wow	chug	moo	blip
flip flop	squish	beep	smack	chug	chirp
ding dong	rustle	clomp			

_____

Stories will vary.

_____

_____

_____

_____

_____

_____

_____

_____

_____

_____

Page 36

Describe It Please!

Decide in which category each word from the Word Bank belongs.

Word Bank

robust	slimy	sour	energetic	forgiving
aggravated	devoted	enormous	outraged	prickly
affectionate	delighted	tart	spiteful	silky
enraged	happy	gooey	well	depressed
miserable	adorable	fit	ecstatic	
gloomy	gigantic			

Anger
aggravated
enraged
outraged
spiteful

Some answers may vary.

Sadness
miserable
gloomy
depressed

Joy
delighted
happy
ecstatic

Love
affectionate
devoted
delighted
forgiving

Feel (Touch)
slimy
gooey
prickly
silky

Taste
sour
tart

Size
gigantic
enormous

Page 37

As Sharp As a Tack

Similes use **like** or **as** to compare two unlike things that share a characteristic. Draw a red line under the two things being compared in each sentence.

1. The snow reached high into the sky like a mountain peak.
2. The barn door felt like a lost friend.
3. The Connolly brothers are as mean as skunks.
4. The huge hill climbed into the sky like a giant's belly as he lay on his back.
5. The wood stovepipe was as red as a fire engine.
6. Tilla's eyes were as blue as a cornflower.
7. The barn was dark like a cave.
8. The warm cow was like a comfortable blanket.
9. George looked like a coyote peering into a henhouse.
10. Tilla's brother was as strong as an ox.

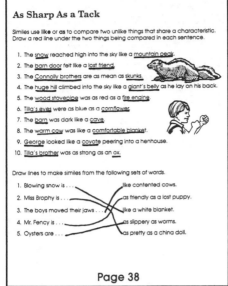

Draw lines to make similes from the following sets of words.

1. Blowing snow is . . .   like contented cows.
2. Miss Brophy is . . .   as friendly as a lost puppy.
3. The boys moved their jaws . . .   like a white blanket.
4. Mr. Fency is . . .   as slippery as worms.
5. Oysters are . . .   as pretty as a china doll.

Page 38

Like . . . a Simile!

In the sentences below, underline the two objects, persons, etc., being compared. In the blank, write if the comparison is a simile or a metaphor. Remember, a simile uses like or as; metaphors do not.

1. Angel was as mean as a wild bull. *simile*
2. Toni and Mattie were like toast and jam. *simile*
3. Mr. Ashby expected the students to be as busy as beavers. *simile*
4. The pin was a masterpiece in Mattie's mind. *metaphor*
5. The park's peacefulness was a friend to Mattie. *metaphor*
6. The words came as slow as molasses into Mattie's mind. *simile*
7. Mrs. Stamps's apartment was like a museum. *simile*
8. Mrs. Benson was as happy as a lark when Mattie won the contest. *simile*
9. Mr. Phillip's smile was a glowing beam to Mattie and Mrs. Benson. *metaphor*
10. Mattie ran as fast as the wind to get her money. *simile*
11. Angel's mean words cut through Charlene like glass. *simile*
12. Mr. Bacon was a fairy godmother to Mattie. *metaphor*
13. The gingko tree's leaves were like fans. *simile*

Complete the following sentences using similes.

1. Matt was as artistic as *Sentences will vary.*
2. Hannibal's teeth were like _____
3. Toni's mind worked fast like _____
4. Mattie was as sad as _____
5. Mrs. Stamps was like _____

Page 39

Snacking in the U.S.A.

Ned's award for losing weight was a trip to Disney World. Travel to these vacation spots in the U.S.A. and list the foods you could eat there that begin with the same first letter as the place. For example, Disney World = Doritos, doughnuts, dill pickles.

Words will vary.

Niagara Falls
1. _____
2. _____
3. _____

Hollywood
1. _____
2. _____
3. _____

Grand Canyon
1. _____
2. _____
3. _____

Washington, D.C.
1. _____
2. _____
3. _____

Mount Rushmore
1. _____
2. _____
3. _____

Disneyland
1. _____
2. _____
3. _____

Busch Gardens
1. _____
2. _____
3. _____

Statue of Liberty
1. _____
2. _____
3. _____

Rocky Mountains
1. _____
2. _____
3. _____

Lincoln Memorial
1. _____
2. _____
3. _____

Pike's Peak
1. _____
2. _____
3. _____

Empire State Building
1. _____
2. _____
3. _____

Carlsbad Caverns
1. _____
2. _____
3. _____

Indianapolis Speedway
1. _____
2. _____
3. _____

Sea World
1. _____
2. _____
3. _____

Page 40

Abracadabra Magical Sentences

Make magical sentences by using words that begin with each of the letters in the animal names given below.
For example: FROG = Foxes Run Over Grasslands.
BEAR = Blue Elephants Are Rare!

1. SNAKE = *Sentences will vary.*
2. LION = _____
3. GORILLA = _____
4. CROW = _____
5. SHEEP = _____
6. PIG = _____
7. PYTHON = _____
8. RABBIT = _____
9. HORSE = _____
10. WOLF = _____
11. CAMEL = _____
12. MOUSE = _____
13. HAMSTER = _____

Challenge: Illustrate your best abracadabra sentences on drawing paper.

Page 41

R.I.P.

Not all epitaphs are serious or sentimental. Some are humorous. Below are two examples.

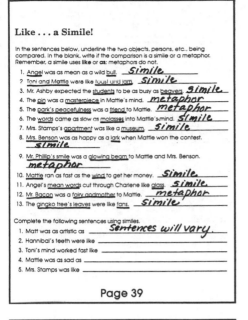

Epitaph for a Dachshund
The bone he fetched
Was still attached
. . . To a bulldog

Epitaph for a School Crossing Guard
Oh, Mrs. Toots, our crossing guard
Why didn't you use your head?
We wish you hadn't o'er stepped the curb
But looked both ways instead

Try your hand at writing an epitaph. Here are some ideas of characters for whom you might write:

a sports announcer
a waiter or waitress
a carpenter
a professional wrestler
a talkative parrot

a bank teller
an aerial performer
a pet boa constrictor
a lawyer
a minister, rabbi or priest

Here lies _____ name
_____ _____
(month, day, year)   (month, day, year)
born   died
epitaph

will vary

Page 42

Publishing House

Theodor Seuss Geisel was best known by his pen name, Dr. Seuss. His children's books are usually written in verse and combine nonsense with humor. Draw a picture of a nonsensical being in the box below. Give it a name. Then, write a poem about it on the lines to the right.

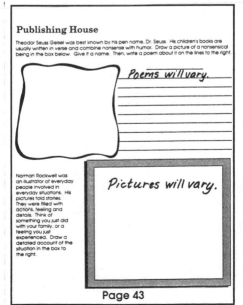

Poems will vary.

_____
_____
_____
_____

Norman Rockwell was an illustrator of everyday people involved in everyday situations. His pictures told stories. They were filled with actions, feeling and details. Think of something you just did with your family, or a feeling you just experienced. Draw a detailed account of the situation in the box to the right.

Pictures will vary.

Page 43

Dear . . .

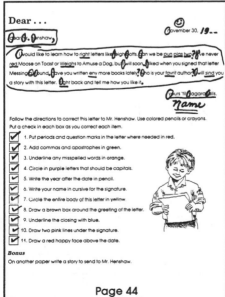

November 30, 19--

Dear Mr. Henshaw,

I would like to learn how to right letters like eight-oughts. Can we be pun pals two ?? I've never red Moose on Toast or Weighs to Amuse a Dog, but I will soon. I liked when you signed that letter Messing a Round. Have you written any more books lately? Who is your favrit author. I will sind you a story with this letter. Right back and tell me how you like it.

Yours 'til Niagara Falls,
Name

Follow the directions to correct this letter to Mr. Henshaw. Use colored pencils or crayons. Put a check in each box as you correct each item.

☑ 1. Put periods and question marks in the letter where needed in red.
☑ 2. Add commas and apostrophes in green.
☑ 3. Underline any misspelled words in orange.
☑ 4. Circle in purple letters that should be capitals.
☑ 5. Write the year after the date in pencil.
☑ 6. Write your name in cursive for the signature.
☑ 7. Circle the entire body of this letter in yellow.
☑ 8. Draw a brown box around the greeting of the letter.
☑ 9. Underline the closing with blue.
☑ 10. Draw two pink lines under the signature.
☑ 11. Draw a red happy face above the date.

Bonus
On another paper write a story to send to Mr. Henshaw.

Page 44

Mistake'n Letter

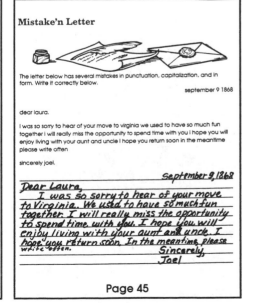

The letter below has several mistakes in punctuation, capitalization, and in form. Write it correctly below.

september 9 1868

dear laura.

I was so sorry to hear of your move to virginia we used to have so much fun together I will really miss the opportunity to spend time with you I hope you will enjoy living with your aunt and uncle I hope you return soon in the meantime please write often

sincerely joel.

September 9, 1868

Dear Laura,
I was so sorry to hear of your move to Virginia. We used to have so much fun together. I will really miss the opportunity to spend time with you. I hope you will enjoy living with your aunt and uncle. I hope you return soon. In the meantime, please write often.
Sincerely,
Joel

Page 45

Daily Learning Drills Grade 4

Matching Before and After

Match the first part of each sentence with its last part. Write the matching parts on the lines below the boxes.

First Part	**Before**	Second Part
Call the store to see if they have turkey		you need it.
It's better to have insurance		not weather set in.
I had my hair cut		you could count to three.
My room was cleaned		we drive there to get it.
Refill the water jar		you put it back in the refrigerator.

Call the store to see if... before *we drive there to get it.*
It's better to have insurance before *you need it.*
I had my hair cut before *hot weather set in.*
My room was cleaned before *you could count to three.*
Refill the water jar before *you put it back in the refrigerator.*

First Part	**After**	Second Part
We had plenty of hot water		he took some hitting lessons.
Let's have a party		we finish our tests.
My mom and dad ordered new carpet		we bought a larger water heater.
We were suntanned		we came back from a long vacation.
Sam's golf game improved by several points		the puppy was trained.

We had plenty of hot water after *we bought a larger water heater.*
Let's have a party after *we finish our tests.*
My mom and dad ordered... after *the puppy was trained.*
We were suntanned after *we came back from...*
Sam's golf game... after *he took some hitting lessons.*

- Write what comes next.
  at bat cat eat fat hat *mat*

Page 46

When Do You Do It?

Write the listed activities that you do under the appropriate heading. If you do any activities more than once a day, write them more than once. Cross out the ones you don't do.

Activities

make my bed	take care of a pet	turn off alarm clock
go to school	carry out trash	organized sports
go to scouts	go to dentist	go to lunchroom
eat brunch	watch cartoons	play with friend after school
homework	take bath or shower	sleep a long time
do the dishes	go to Sunday school	go home from school
go to bed	have pleasant dreams	go to dance lessons
have lunch recess	play after school	kiss mom and/or dad goodnight

Between Dinner and Breakfast
Answers will vary.

Between Breakfast and Lunch

Between Lunch and Dinner

- Write what comes next. △ ▲ △ ▽ ▼ ▽

Page 47

If – Then

Match the sentence parts that go together best. Write the number of the first sentence part on the line in front of the last sentence part for each one.

1. If you baby-sit for me Saturday night
2. If you are nice
3. If we leave work by 4:30
4. If you leave a note on your door
5. If you don't have enough money for the movie
6. If my father isn't too tired
7. If the wind keeps up
8. If you want to get a seat at the concert
9. If our neighbor cuts the grass early Sunday morning
10. If the plant doesn't feel damp
11. If my house were painted white
12. If everyone talked at the same time
13. If you don't get a haircut
14. If the tea kettle whistles
15. If no one answers the door
16. If the little boy crosses the street
17. If the horse is tired
18. If you have a long fork
19. If you don't want any dessert
20. If a king comes into a room
21. If it snows a lot tomorrow

4 the delivery man will leave the package.
10 it needs to be watered.
15 probably no one is at home.
20 everyone will rise.
1 I'll pay you double.
14 the water is boiling.
7 tomorrow will be a great kite-flying day.
17 let him rest.
12 no one could hear directions.
3 we will avoid rush hour.
19 say "No thank you."
9 the noise will wake me up.
21 we can build an igloo.
6 he said he would show me how to shoot baskets.
11 it would look like a miniature White House.
5 I'll loan you the rest.
16 he must hold onto his mother's hand.
2 you will have many friends.
8 you will have to be at the auditorium early.
13 you will have long hair.

- Write what comes next. A ∞ ⊃ ⊃ E **⊓**

Page 48

What Made It Happen?

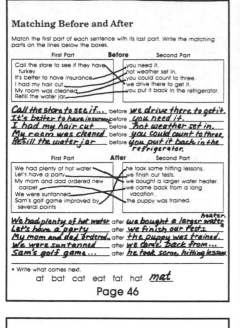

Each set of sentences includes a cause and an effect. Remember, the cause is what makes something happen, and the effect is the result. Write the cause on the line, and circle the effect.

1. The snow came down harder than anyone could ever remember. For days the people of the village were housebound.
   The snow came down harder than anyone could ever remember

2. Many of the soldiers decided to learn to ski. The children called one soldier "Lieutenant Sit-Down" because he fell down more than he stood on his skis.
   he fell down more than he stood on his skis

3. The Commandant kept kicking the snowman covering the gold. Peter threw a snowball to distract the Commandant from discovering the gold.
   The Commandant kept kicking the snowman covering the gold

4. Peter Garson was skiing in crazy patterns around and around the Lundstrom's house. Uncle Victor had been there earlier on his skis.
   Uncle Victor had been there earlier on his skis

5. Peter was sailing down the slope at high speed. In his path he could see approaching soldiers. Peter was going so fast he could not stop his sled. The soldiers scattered to let Peter through.
   Peter was going so fast he could not stop his sled

6. Mrs. Holms seemed very excited to see the Lundstroms coming to her home. She acted as though she could not wait to speak. Earlier in the day a German soldier had been in the Holm's barn.
   Earlier in the day a German soldier had been in the Holm's barn

Page 49

Time for Titles

Choose the word or phrase from the Word Box that best completes the heading for each group of words.

Word Box: Fabric, Newspaper, Automobile, Fish, Tools, Writing Process, Ship, Eyes, Roads, Stories, Songs, Funny

Parts of a . . . *ship*	Kinds of . . . *roads*	Things for . . . *eyes*
helm	boulevard	goggles
rudder	freeway	spectacles
gunwale	avenue	contacts

Other words for . . . *funny*	Parts of an . . . *automobile*	Kinds of . . . *fabric*
witty	headlight	satin
hilarious	windshield	velvet
humorous	seatbelt	flannel

Kinds of . . . *stories*	Kinds of . . . *tools*	Parts of a . . . *newspaper*
legend	pliers	headline
myth	chisel	column
parable	crowbar	article

Kinds of . . . *songs*	Part of the . . . *writing process*	Kinds of . . . *fish*
lullaby	edit	flounder
anthem	proofread	sardine
hymn	revise	salmon

Page 50

Row, Row, Row Your Boat

In the wordsearch, circle words from the list that name **types of** boats. Cross out words that do not belong in that category. Words may go → ← ↑ ↓ ↗.

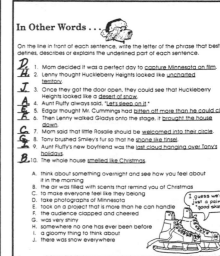

Use a dictionary to help answer the questions.

1. Which boat has the ability to travel underwater: a skiff or a submarine?
   submarine

2. Which boat would more likely be used in a war: a carrier or a liner?
   carrier

3. Which boat is more like a canoe: a sloop or a kayak? *kayak*

4. Which vessel is a type of fishing boat: a barge or a dory? *dory*

Page 51

Classification

Read the paragraph. Write each sentence in the correct category.

The civilians of the town had a strange disease. The disease was somewhat like scarlet fever, and it spread through the town like a plague. However, the disease only affected small children. All of the small children who had the disease had to be quarantined. The children did not lose their appetite and did not have a temperature. The Commandant ordered that they keep a careful quarantine. The German army had ammunition, but none to fight this type of war. The lieutenant did not want his sentries around the diseased children, so they did not go into town. The witty doctor created a disease for the children and it was a success! The children moved the gold safely.

Sentences relating to the townspeople
The civilians of the town had a strange disease.
The disease was somewhat like scarlet fever...
However, the disease only affected small children.
All the small children who had the disease.
The children did not lose their appetite and...
The witty doctor created a disease for...
The children moved the gold safely.

Sentences relating to the German army
The Commandant ordered that they keep...
He was afraid the infantrymen might!...
The German army had ammunition, but...
The lieutenant did not want his sentries...

Page 52

Scaredy-Cat!

What do you fear? Rate these fears from greatest to least, with one being the greatest. *Answers will vary.*

Fear	Rating
dark	
fire	
strangers	
thunder	
snakes	
school grades	
not having friends	
monsters	
bees	
dogs	
death	
moving	
cemeteries	
superstitions	
crying in public	
being unloved	

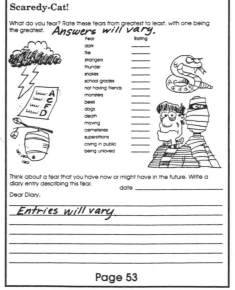

Think about a fear that you have now or might have in the future. Write a diary entry describing this fear.   date _____

Dear Diary,

Entries will vary

Page 53

In Other Words . . .

On the line in front of each sentence, write the letter of the phrase that best defines, describes or explains the underlined part of each sentence.

D 1. Mom decided it was a perfect day to capture Minnesota on film.
H 2. Lenny thought Huckleberry Heights looked like uncharted territory.
J 3. Once they got the door open, they could see that Huckleberry Heights looked like a desert of snow.
A 4. Aunt Fluffy always said, "Let's sleep on it."
E 5. Edgar thought Mr. Cummings had bitten off more than he could chew.
F 6. Then Lenny walked Gladys onto the stage, it brought the house down.
C 7. Mom said that little Rosalie should be welcomed into their circle.
G 8. Tony brushed Smiley's fur so that he shone like tinsel.
I 9. Aunt Fluffy's new boyfriend was the last cloud hanging over Tony's holidays.
B 10. The whole house smelled like Christmas.

A. think about something overnight and see how you feel about it in the morning
B. the air was filled with scents that remind you of Christmas
C. to make everyone feel like they belong
D. take photographs of Minnesota
E. took on a project that is more than he can handle
F. the audience clapped and cheered
G. was very shiny
H. somewhere no one has ever been before
I. a gloomy thing to think about
J. there was snow everywhere

I guess we're just a pair of "good skates."

A NOW . . . D A "good skate" is someone who is cooperative and gets along well with other people. Choose a classmate who you think is a good skate and write down reasons that explain why you feel this way. Share these "warm fuzzies" (nice thoughts) with your class.

Page 54

What a Tragedy!

Drama is a play performed by actors. A drama tells a story. Drama can be serious, or funny, or sometimes both. There are three basic kinds of drama: tragedy, comedy and melodrama.

A tragedy is a drama about a serious subject. Tragedies often deal with the meaning of life, and how people treat each other.

A comedy is a drama that uses feelings of joy. Comedy can also show very exaggerated and ridiculous behavior.

A melodrama is a drama which tells a story of good against evil. A melodrama features an evil villain who tries to destroy the good characters.

Drama is believed to have begun in ancient Greece. The Greeks performed their plays in outdoor theaters. Many of the Greek tragedies were about myths. Drama was later popular in many countries; Italy, England, Spain, France, India, China and Japan. Today, drama is popular in practically every country in the world.

Circle and check.

Drama . . . is a costume / (play) performed by actors.

. . . tells a: ☐ joke ☐ part ☑ story

. . . can be serious, or funny, or both. (T) F

Write.

Drama is believed to have begun in ancient *Greece*.

The Greeks performed their dramas in *outdoor* theaters.

Many of the Greek tragedies were about *myths*.

- Write a plot or story for each of the three kinds of drama.

Page 55

Scrambled Words

Unscramble the letters in parentheses to spell a word that makes sense in each sentence.

1. Cookies don't *appeal* (apaple) to me; I prefer candy.
2. The desert is a good place to see a *cactus* (saccut).
3. When is Halley's *comet* (tomec) supposed to appear again?
4. Take a deep breath and then *exhale* (elahex).
5. Place the *funnel* (nenuif) in the can before pouring the gasoline.
6. I am learning how to do *magic* (gicam) tricks.
7. "I don't have a *single* (glisn) thing to wear!" complained Jill.
8. An *adobe* (bedoa) home is made of sun-dried bricks.
9. Is *vanilla* (alavlin) ice cream your favorite?
10. This word scramble is *simply* (spliniy) too difficult for me.
11. Mother set the china on the *linen* (ennil) tablecloth.
12. I am *hungry* (gurnyh) for chocolate chip cookies.
13. I wish you much *success* (usseccs) on your new job.
14. How many people are employed at that *factory* (tarfocy)?
15. Hold your breath to help get rid of the *hiccups* (spuchic).

Page 56

Perfect Pairs

Some words just seem to belong together. See how many word pairs you can make by using words from Column B to complete the phrases in Column A.

Example: salt and pepper

Column A	Column B
1. Rocky and *Bullwinkle*	brush
2. cup and *saucer*	Bullwinkle
3. pencil and *paper*	butter
4. cookies and *milk*	chairs
5. cats and *dogs*	cheese
6. rock and *roll*	coat
7. hammer and *nails*	dance
8. Batman and *Robin*	day
9. mustard and *ketchup*	dogs
10. song and *dance*	eggs
11. shoes and *socks*	vegetables
12. hat and *coat*	groom
13. ham and *cheese*	jelly
14. peanut butter and *jelly*	Jill
15. bacon and *eggs*	ketchup
16. Jack and *Jill*	milk
17. night and *day*	nails
18. table and *chairs*	oranges
19. comb and *brush*	paper
20. bread and *butter*	Robin
21. apples and *oranges*	roll
22. fruits and *vegetables*	saucer
23. bride and *groom*	socks

Page 57

Babes in Arms

Situation: It's five o'clock p.m., and you are babysitting for a family with three young children. Before the adults leave, what questions should you ask?

Number these questions in importance, listing 1 as the most important.
Cross out any questions you feel are inappropriate. *Answers will vary.*

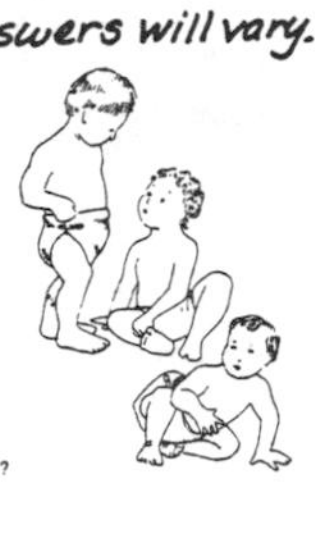

___ Does your stereo system work well?
___ How much does the job pay?
___ How long do you expect to be out?
___ Where is your telephone?
___ Are you expecting any phone calls?
___ Do you have a VCR?
___ Do I have to wash the dishes?
___ What is an appropriate bedtime for the children?
___ Where do you keep snacks?
___ May I invite a friend over to stay with me?
___ How much money do you make?
___ How might I reach you in an emergency?
___ When was the last time you vacuumed your carpet?
___ What shall I feed the children?
___ Has your dog been tested for rabies?
___ May I share some candy with the children?

Comment on either a question you crossed out as inappropriate or a question you rated very high.

On another sheet of paper, provide a list of ten tips for prospective babysitters.

Page 58

Ride with the Wind

Size: 22-inch frame
Weight: 37 lbs.
Tire Size: 26" x 1 3/8"
Tire Pressure: 65 lbs
Gears: 3

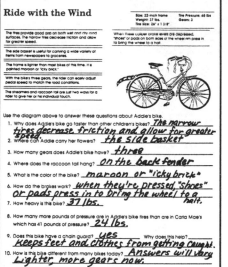

The tires provide good grip on both wet and dry road surfaces. The narrow tires decrease friction and allow for greater speed.

The side basket is useful for carrying a wide variety of items from newspapers to groceries.

The frame is lighter than most bikes of this time. It is painted maroon or "icky brick."

With the bike's three gears, the rider can easily adjust pedal speed to match the road conditions.

The streamers and raccoon tail are just two ways for a rider to give her or his individual touch.

When these caliper brake levers are depressed, "shoes" or pads on both sides of the wheel rim press in to bring the wheel to a halt.

Use the diagram above to answer these questions about Addie's bike.

1. Why does Addie's bike go faster than other children's bikes? *The narrow tires decrease friction and allow for greater speed.*
2. Where can Addie carry her flowers? *the side basket*
3. How many gears does Addie's bike have? *three*
4. Where does the raccoon tail hang? *on the back fender*
5. What is the color of the bike? *maroon or "icky brick"*
6. How do the brakes work? *when they're pressed, "shoes" or pads press in to bring the wheel to a halt.*
7. How heavy is this bike? *37 lbs.*
8. How many more pounds of pressure are in Addie's bike tires than are in Carla Mae's which has 41 pounds of pressure? *24 lbs.*
9. Does this bike have a chain guard? *yes* Why does this help? *Keeps feet and clothes from getting caught.*
10. How is this bike different from many bikes today? *Answers will vary. Lighter, more gears now.*

Page 59

Jumping to Conclusions

Write your own conclusion to each situation in the space provided.

Situations	Conclusions
1. Your brother just turned five. He has chocolate all over his face and he looks sheepish.	*Answers will vary.*
2. Your parents are gone. It's 9:00 p.m. and you hear a thump and a cry.	
3. You are making a cake. You hear the sound of beating wings and a thin, shrill squeal.	
4. You are outdoors after dark during summer vacation. You see a sudden flash of light and smell a smoky odor.	
5. One morning at school you see your friend looking dreamy-eyed. On her paper, she writes SW + SD.	
6. A large column of clouds appears in the western sky, and a strong wind starts blowing.	
7. You hear a noise in your parents' bedroom. Then you see a broken window and a baseball rolling across the floor.	
8. In the classroom next door you see a desk tipped over, text books scattered, and one boy crying.	

Challenge: Describe a new situation on another paper. Include four important details and make up a conclusion in your head. Then let a friend read what you've written and guess your conclusion. Does your friend draw the same conclusion?

Page 60

It's Greek to Me

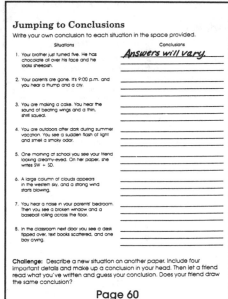

Anti – is a prefix from the Greek word **anti** which means *against*.
Look up each word in the dictionary and write its definition.

Definitions may vary.

1. antibiotic — *a substance able, when diluted, to kill another microbe*
2. antidote — *a remedy to counteract the effects of poison*
3. antiknock — *a substance used to prevent knocking in internal combustion engine*
4. antipathy — *dislike*
5. antiperspirant — *preparation used to check excessive perspiration*
6. antiseptic — *a germicide*

Answer the questions in complete sentences. *Sentences may vary.*

1. If a person were accidentally poisoned, would he or she be given an antidote or an antiseptic? *He or She would be given an antidote.*
2. If you strongly disliked fish, would you have an antibiotic or an antipathy toward it? *You would have an antipathy toward it.*
3. Which would a person more likely use on his or her body: an antiperspirant or an antipathy? *A person would use an antiperspirant on his or her body.*
4. To prevent infection from a cut, would you use an antiperspirant or an antiseptic? *You use an antiseptic to Keep cuts from becoming infected.*
5. Is penicillin an example of an antibiotic or an antiseptic? *Penicillin is an example of an antibiotic.*

Page 61

Borrowed from Abroad

Many words in the English language have come from other languages. For example, **garage** comes from a French word meaning *protect*.

Use a dictionary to find the language from which each of the following words was taken. Write the name of the language and a short meaning for each word. *Meanings may vary.*

1. gimlet: *French; a small tool with a screw point, used for boring holes*
2. hacienda: *Spanish; a large estate, plantation*
3. javelin: *Celt; a slender shaft thrown for distance in a field event*
4. jerky: *Spanish; preserved meat*
5. morgue: *French; a place where bodies of dead persons are kept until identified by relatives*
6. terrazzo: *Italian; a mosaic flooring*

Answer the following questions in complete sentences. *May vary.*

1. Which two words above are from Spanish? *Hacienda and jerky are from Spanish.*
2. Which two words are French in origin? *Gimlet and morgue are French in origin.*
3. Which word is the name of something to eat? *Jerky is the name of something to eat.*
4. Where would you likely find terrazzo – in a morgue or a hacienda? *Terrazzo would likely be found in a hacienda.*
5. Which might an athlete use: a javelin or a gimlet? *An athlete might use a javelin.*

Page 62

My Own Secret Kingdom

Create your own kingdom by following these directions. Use a large sheet of drawing paper. *Kingdoms will vary.*

1. Draw a directional compass in the southeast corner of the paper.
2. Draw your castle in the northeast corner of the kingdom. Add plenty of details.
3. There is a river that runs north and south through your kingdom. Color the river blue and write its name beside it.
4. Two bridges cross the river. One crosses the northern section and one crosses the southern section. Draw them.
5. Draw a moat around your castle.
6. Add a large forest south of the castle.
7. Horses and chariots are stabled in a barn surrounded by a corral. The corral is between the forest and the river.
8. There are four lookout towers protecting your land. Place one in each of the corners of the kingdom. Add different colored flags at the top of each.
9. A pond lies in the southeast part of the kingdom, west of the river and east of the tower and directional compass.
10. Your guardian dog, ____________ (name), is napping by the pond. He is a ____________ (breed).
11. Secret evergreen groves are north of the pond. In the center of the grove is a meeting place built with rocks.
12. In the northwest corner by the tower, draw your kingdom's crest or symbol.
13. Now add four more features to your kingdom. List them here.

14. Name your kingdom.

Page 63

Pictures from the Palace

Fold a piece of drawing paper into four parts and draw a picture for each descriptive paragraph below. Number the pictures to match the paragraphs.

Pictures will vary.

1. The Emperor sat on a golden throne. The huge chair was taller than any man and carved with dragons and snakes. Multicolored jewels were embedded in the gold. The Emperor wore a royal blue and gold robe. His hat resembled a blue graduation cap with several strands of multicolored beads hanging from the brim. His shoes were black. He held a paper scroll in both hands.

2. The Princess was beautiful. Her long black hair was knotted into several sections. A pink butterfly hair clip was fastened off to one side. She had black, almond-shaped eyes and rosy cheeks. Her flowered pink, green, and yellow silk gown was tied with a green sash. Pink slippers adorned her feet. She carried a pink fan decorated with Chinese nature scenes.

3. The palace kitchen had a long wooden table in the middle of the room, filled with steaming pots of food. The back wall was made of brick. Long-handled copper and silver pans and skillets hung near the top of this brick wall. Huge ovens covered the left wall. On the right, several cooks chopped and diced fresh vegetables. Vegetable baskets lined the floor.

4. The summer palace was small, built high up on bamboo poles. The roof was made of straw and bamboo with upward curving edges. Its long, vertical windows were covered with paper and colorful Chinese murals. A balcony was built around the outside.

Page 64

Hamsterology

Carefully read the following paragraph about golden hamsters. Then follow the directions.

Native to Central Asia and Europe, the golden hamster is a nocturnal animal that makes its home in complex tunnels under the ground. It is a rodent, related to mice and rats. It eats mostly grains and seeds which it stores in its cheek pouches to take back to its tunnel. In the wild, the hamster will also prey upon small animals and birds. It grows to be about 5 inches long with a short tail. It weighs 4 to 5 ounces and has golden brown fur. The female breeds when she is seven to eight weeks old, producing litters of six to seven babies. Golden hamsters make good pets. Their life span is two to three years.

Directions:

1. Circle in yellow every "hamster" in the paragraph.
2. Make blue boxes around the place where golden hamsters originated.
3. Underline in red the plant foods that gold hamsters eat.
4. Draw an orange X over the animals a hamster will eat.
5. Draw a purple, wiggly line under the word that means hamsters sleep during the day and are awake at night.
6. Put a green R over the word that tells what type of animal the hamster is.
7. Draw a brown star over the place where hamsters store their food.
8. Make a pink line below the hamster's habitat.
9. Draw a red line on top of the word that describes their tails.
10. Circle in red the number of babies most female hamsters grow to be.
11. Underline in black how long hamsters live.
12. Draw an orange box around how long hamsters grow to be.
13. Put a green heart around the verb that as a noun means an animal eaten by a meat-eating animal.
14. Draw a brown, wiggly line under the color of the hamster's fur.

Challenge: Use the encyclopedia to write a report on field mice, gerbils, kangaroo rats or guinea pigs, comparing them to golden hamsters. Share your findings with the rest of the class.

Page 65

Answering Questions

Within each group draw a line from each question on the left to the answer that matches it best on the right.

Where will you stay if the hotel can't take you?	Whenever is best for you.
Who has the lead part in the play?	I had to go to my grandmother's birthday dinner.
Why didn't you complete your homework last night?	I'll make that decision then.
When was the last time you saw the gerbil?	If it's raining, there will be very few.
What time do you want to meet?	They are posting the roles after lunch.
How many people will be at the game?	Last Friday when he climbed into the wastebasket.

Are there any holes in that sieve?	I was too tired.
Why are the dishes still in the sink?	He has lived next to me for two years.
Would you show me how to play?	It's a secret.
How well do you know him?	It's in perfect condition.
What did you tell her?	I will when there is time.
Why didn't you go to the concert?	Dad said he'd do them.

Why aren't you eating dinner?	I mailed it to her yesterday.
What is the boy saying?	It is supposed to be available now.
Why isn't the new boy playing kickball?	We had a late lunch.
When will it be ready?	He's giving the score.
Did anyone send a thank-you note to our room mother?	It's the best I've seen.
Does she have good handwriting?	He doesn't know how.

Has anyone heard anything about the new play?	They need water.
How are the flowers?	The teacher wanted to see him.
Why did Tom stay after school?	Jean said it was very long.
How old is the antique dresser?	Barbara finished the crumbs.
Is there any cake left?	It was caught in the fence.
Where did you find the ball?	It was my great grandmother's.

Page 66

What's the Point?

Locate and underline the main idea in each group of sentences.

1. Bert returned with half a baked ham, butter, and a jug of milk. Martin had not eaten since the night before last. Laura set the table for their late night snack.

2. When Laura woke up, Martin looked like a different boy. He was wearing a pair of Bert's pants and one of his old shirts. He looked as though he had taken a bath.

3. Humming, Laura began to scrape and stack the dishes. She put water on the stove to heat. Laura enjoyed working in the kitchen.

4. The sheriff and slave hunters stormed through the house. Laura heard the crash of a chair. They searched every room and closet. The men were looking for a fugitive slave.

5. The field behind the vegetable garden was aglow with goldenrod and wild flowers. The autumn sun shone brightly in the yard. Laura looked out the window. She longed to go outside on this beautiful autumn day.

Now write one detail sentence from each group on the lines below.

1. *Answers will vary.*
2. _____
3. _____
4. _____
5. _____

Page 67

Camp Rules

Donald, Arnold and Jack are all at Camp Explore-it-All this week. They think camp is a lot of fun, but they have also learned from their instructors that there are some very important rules all campers must obey so that everyone has a good time.

All campers had to take swimming tests to see what depth of water they will be allowed to swim in. Donald and Jack passed the advanced test and can swim in the deep water. Arnold, however, only passed the intermediate test. He is supposed to stay in the area where the water is waist deep. When it is time to swim, Arnold decides to sneak into advanced with Donald and Jack. After all, he has been swimming in the shallow water for three years. No way is he going to stay in the shallow water with the sissies.

Donald and Jack don't think Arnold should come into the deep water, but they can't tell him anything. So the boys jump into the water and start swimming and playing. Fifteen minutes later, Arnold is yelling, "Help!" He swam out too far and is too tired to make it back in. The lifeguard jumps in and pulls him out. Everyone stops to see what is happening. Arnold feels very foolish.

Check.
The main idea of this story is . . .

☐ Arnold ends up feeling foolish.   ☐ Camp is fun.
☐ All campers take swimming tests.   ☑ Rules are made for good reasons.
☐ You can learn a lot from instructors.   ☐ Rules are made to be broken.

Underline.
Arnold got himself into a(n) _____ situation.

amusing   funny   *dangerous*   ambiguous

Circle.
Arnold thought the guys in the shallow area were (bullies sissies). However, he should have (stayed with them gone to the advanced area).

Write.
What lesson do you think Arnold learned? *Answers will vary.*

What do you think the other campers learned? _____

Page 68

From Whose Point of View?

Read each sentence below. Decide if it is the first or third person's point of view. If it is a first person's point of view, rewrite the sentence to make it a third person's point of view. If it is a third person's point of view, rewrite it to make it a first person's point of view. *Sentences may vary.*

1. I wanted to tell Anh and Thant the secret of our leaving, but I had given my word.
   He wanted to tell Anh and Thant the secret of their leaving, but he had given his word.

2. The grandmother did not want to go aboard the boat.
   I did not want to go aboard the boat.

3. The people on shore were pushing to get on the deck of the boat.
   We were pushing to get on the deck of the boat.

4. Though I had worked many days in the rice paddies watching planes fly over, I never thought I'd be on one.
   Though she had worked many days in the rice paddies watching planes fly over, she had never thought she'd...

5. Loi made a net from pieces of string and caught a turtle with his new device.
   I made a net from pieces of string and caught a turtle with my new device.

6. I know of a place where we can wash our clothes.
   She knew of a place where they could wash their clothes.

7. The officer looked at them with great interest.
   I looked at them with great interest.

8. When I looked into the harbor, I could see the shape of the sampan boats.
   When he looked into the harbor, he could see the shape of the sampan boats.

9. This is my duck and I choose to share it with everyone on the boat for the celebration of Tet.
   This is her duck and she chose to share it with everyone on the boat for the celebration of Tet.

Page 69

Make Your Mark Here

Use the proofreader marks shown to the right to correct the sentences below.

apostrophe	✓
quotation marks	❝❞
capitalize	≡
end marks	⊙❓❗
comma	∧

1. lucy wailed can't go to the party I told everyone what a great costume I was going to have

2. carla said okay meet me at my place the basement apartment of the eucalyptus arms do you know where that is

3. are you a real vampire lucy demanded

4. told ya lucy I dropped my fangs down your neck mumbled the embarrassed knievel

5. knievel howled don't you have more that's the best chocolate cupcake I ever ate

6. stay right there squeaked the rabbit I'll get you something don't move

7. there's the tv questioned susannah looking around I'm sure I heard one before we came in

8. mr mordecai rubbed his hands and smiled shyly I'll be back he whispered then he vanished

9. I'm pretty sure knievel got the poisoned candy when he was with us susannah said I don't think he had done any trick-or-treating before he met us

10. forgot my key shouted aunt louise how are you girls where's that niece of mine

Draw a picture to go with one of the quotes above. Write the quote next to it.

Quote: *Quotes will vary.*

Page 70

Fish Facts

All of the fourth graders in Miss Freed's class did reports on animals. Jackie did hers on fish. She learned so much about these fascinating animals. She can't wait to share the information with her class.

Jackie didn't know much about fish when she started. She has since learned that fish are vertebrates because they have backbones. She was also amazed to learn that there are more kinds of fish than all other kinds of water and land vertebrates put together. The kinds of fish differ so greatly in shape, color and size that Jackie can hardly believe they all belong to the same group of animals.

Some fish, Jackie found out, look like lumpy rocks. Others look like wriggly worms. Some can blow themselves up like balloons, and others are as flat as pancakes. Fish can be all the colors of the rainbow, and also striped and polka-dotted. The one fish Jackie definitely never wants to run into is the stonefish. Though it is small, it can kill a person in a few minutes. The subject of fish turned out to be a lot more interesting than Jackie ever imagined.

Circle.
Fish are (invertebrates vertebrates) because they (do not have have) backbones.

Underline.
Fish differ greatly in . . .

taste.   *size.*   *shape.*   *color.*   *length.*

Check.
Fish can be . . .

☑ lumpy.   ☐ depressed.   ☑ colorful.   ☑ striped.
☐ smart.   ☑ flat.   ☑ polka-dotted.   ☐ sad.

Write.
Describe the kinds of fish found in aquariums. Use adjectives relating to size, shape and color.
Answers will vary.

What kinds of fish have you eaten? _____

Page 71

Mixed-Up Recipe

In the story, Laura decides to make a batch of homemade applesauce. Below is a recipe she may have followed. However, by looking at the directions, it is easy to see that something is mixed-up. Read the recipe, compare it to others if you wish, then rewrite it correctly.

Applesauce

12 to 16 medium apples
1 cup water
1 to 1 1/2 cups of sugar

Directions:
Heat to boiling. Add 1 cup water. Peel and slice the apples into quarters. Simmer over low heat for 20 to 30 minutes or until soft. Stir occasionally. Stir in sugar and heat through. Add 1 teaspoon of cinnamon if you wish.

Makes 12 servings.

Correct Directions:
Peel and slice the apples into quarters. Add 1 cup water. Heat to boiling. Simmer over low heat for 20 to 30 minutes or until soft. Stir occasionally. Stir in sugar and heat through. Add 1 teaspoon of cinnamon if you wish.

Page 72

Weekend Fun

Number each group of sentences in the correct order.

3 I had a hamburger, but everyone else had a salad.
6 My parents picked us up after the movie.
1 A horse drawn carriage took us for a ride through the park to the zoo.
5 I didn't buy any popcorn during the movie.
2 We spent a couple of hours at the zoo before we took a bus to meet our friends for lunch.
4 We walked to the movie after lunch.

6 A wind lifted the kite high in the air.
5 Father let out the string while I ran with the kite.
2 The park was crowded with people flying kites when we got there.
3 We found a spot to fly the kite away from the other people.
1 Father and I took a kite to the park.
4 We had to tie a tail on the kite before it was ready to be flown.

2 I took an atlas home with me on Friday.
4 I wrote down important facts about each country.
6 I turned in my report on Monday morning.
3 After I watched cartoons Saturday morning, I looked up England and Germany in the atlas.
5 I wrote a report about England and Germany from my notes.
1 Friday morning the teacher said our reports on different countries were due on Monday.

3 We decided what kind of cones we wanted while standing in line.
5 Larry fell down and the cone flew into the air.
4 While walking down the street with our cones, a large dog charged Larry.
1 There was a long line at the ice-cream shop when Larry and I got there.
6 The dog caught the cone and ran away with it.
2 We stood behind the last person in line.

Page 73

Putting Them in Order

Rewrite the sentences in each paragraph below in the correct order.

There was a loud crack and the ice Elizabeth was on began to sink. Her mother warned her not to go too far out on the ice, but she forgot. Elizabeth asked her mother if she could go skating on the pond. Elizabeth's cries for help were answered, and some other skaters pulled her to safety.

Elizabeth asked her mother if she could go skating on the pond. Her mother warned her not to go too far out on the ice, but she forgot. There was a loud crack and the ice Elizabeth was on began to sink. Elizabeth's cries for help were answered, and some other skaters pulled her to safety.

When Marcy and Tony were walking home from school he suggested they go a different way. The stream twisted and turned, and it eventually led them back to school. They followed the stream in the direction they thought would take them home. They cut across a farmer's field and down a hill to a stream.

When Marcy and Tony were walking home from school he suggested they go a different way. They cut across a farmer's field and down a hill to a stream. They followed the stream in the direction they thought would take them home. The stream twisted and turned, and it eventually led them back to school.

• Write what comes next.
VI VOI VOIVI VOIVOI

Page 74

Moving Time

David's family is buying a new house. Their old house is just too small. However, there are two houses that they like equally as much. The first one is in the neighborhood in which they live now. David's family would still be around all their same friends, and David could still ride to school with his best friend. The only problem is that this house doesn't have a playroom where David and his friends could go, which was one of the reasons for moving. It also needs a lot of painting, which David's dad is not happy about. But, it's a good buy.

The second house is across town. David could still go to the same school, but he wouldn't be close to his old friends. This house is really big with a huge playroom, and it has just been freshly painted. Even though it costs more than the other one, it's still a good deal.

So now David's family has to decide if they want less room, more work and the same neighborhood, or more room and less work. Both houses have 3 bedrooms and big family rooms, so his parents are happy about that. What a decision!

Underline.
David and his family have found two houses that they like . . .
equally as well. almost as much as their old one. in his neighborhood. a little.

Circle.
David would want to buy the second house except that it . . .
has a big playroom. needs to be painted. (isn't close to his friends.)

Check.
The first house is different from the second one because it . . .
☐ has three bedrooms. ☐ has a family room.
☑ is in David's same neighborhood. ☑ needs to be painted.
☑ doesn't have a play room. ☐ is a good buy.

Write.
List at least 3 reasons David's family is having a hard time deciding which house to buy.
Answers will vary.
1. They like both houses.
2. Both houses are good buys.
3. Both houses have 3 bedrooms.

If you ever had to move, how would you feel about it? List five positive things and five negative things about moving.

Page 75

Yesterday and Today

Read each sentence. If it tells about a past event, write THEN on the line. If it tells about an event that is happening in the present, write NOW on the line.

Now The forest fire is burning out of control.
Then We sent money to help feed and clothe the flood victims.
Now The river rushing past my window keeps me up at night.
Now I am taking a series of tennis lessons on Wednesdays.
Then Glaciers covered over one-fifth of the world.
Now The student council sets rules for the student body to follow.
Then I bought enough glue to last a lifetime.
Then The third grade had the best attendance record.
Then The picnic was cancelled because of the heavy downpour.
Now I belong to the scouts.
Now The forest floor is covered with ferns and moss.
Now The Hopi Indians live within the Navajo Indian nation.
Then My aunt and uncle stayed with us for a week.
Then The day started out sunny.
Now My grade in penmanship indicates great improvement.
Then I baked banana bread for the room mother's tea.
Now I watch television every night for an hour before going to bed.
Now Melissa is the fastest runner in the class.
Then I made a deposit in my savings account.
Then I cut my birthday cake after I blew out all the candles.
Now The patrol boys and girls help younger children cross the street.
Now The snow is continuing to fall.
Now I save my pennies for rainy days.
Then The chandelier swayed during the earthquake.
Then We fastened our seat belts before father started the car.
Then The native dancers' clothes were colorful.

• Write what comes next.
BA ED IH ON VU

Page 76

Keeping in Touch

On the lines next to the letter, write the correct category (**who, what, when, where** or **why**) for each underlined word or phrase in Genevieve's letter.

Dear Mom and Dad,

I have been very busy (1) here in the United States taking care of Lucas and the twins. (2) A few weeks ago (3) Lucas and his friends (4) climbed up onto the roof of the Cotts' home (5) to get a better view of the neighborhood. (6) He has spent a lot of time with me (7) since then.

(8) Today, I (9) taught him how to dance (10) so he can have a girlfriend (11) when he gets older. (12) Julio danced with us (13) in the living room, too. (14) I miss you both.

Love,
Genevieve

1. where
2. when
3. who
4. what
5. why
6. who
7. when
8. when
9. what
10. why
11. when
12. who
13. where
14. who

A NOW . . . D Write an essay titled, "The Importance of Being Trustworthy." Share it with your classmates and discuss what each of you thinks about *being* trustworthy and *expecting* trust from others.

Page 77

Are You Mixed Up?

Unscramble the letters on the left to create words which match the meanings on the right.

	Word	Word Meaning
1. degtti	fidget	To move restlessly or nervously
2. spygy	gypsy	A member of a wandering people believed to have come out of India
3. pureto	troupe	A group of actors or dancers
4. tayjun	jaunty	Having a self-confident manner
5. nastioyrta	stationary	Not capable of being moved
6. caottitep	petticoat	A woman's slip or underskirt
7. ever	veer	To swerve
8. rylub	burly	Heavy, strong and muscular
9. merba	amber	A brownish-yellow color
10. laiggni	galling	Very annoying

Write sentences using four of the words you unscrambled.
1. Sentences will vary.
2.
3.
4.

Page 78

Say It Again

Add a letter to each word to make a new word. Use letters from the Letter Bank and the clues to help. The letter may be added anywhere to the word.

Example:

word		letter		new word	clue
hove	+	l	=	hovel	a hut

Word	Letter	New Word	Clue
gain	r	grain	Small seed
rate	g	grate	Used in fireplaces
par	e	pear	A fruit
rip	e	ripe	Ready for harvest
sing	e	singe	To burn at the edges
tick	h	thick	Slow witted
pear	s	spear	Weapon that can be thrown
ad	o	ado	Fuss or bother
mat	s	mast	Important to sailing ships
boar	d	board	Two-by-four
die	r	dire	Urgent
men	o	omen	Sign of a future event
yarn	e	yearn	To want
tool	s	stool	Place to sit
toe	t	tote	To carry
single	h	shingle	Roofing material

Letter Bank
d e e e e g h h o o r r s s s t

Page 79

Guide-Worthy Words

Use a pencil to write ten vocabulary words from the Word Bank under each of the guide words. Remember to put them in alphabetical order.

Reflection	Syllable
reindeer	scowl
resolute	stance
retort	stealth
salute	subside
schoolmaster	surpass

Abrupt	Authority
accidentally	ammunition
accustom	ancient
additional	appoint
allow	ashamed
almanac	assign

Babyhood	Crest
barometer	commerce
barracks	commotion
beneficial	consternation
burrow	cordial
calamity	corporal

Defense	Exult
defiant	earthenware
demoralize	enormous
discard	entirely
disposition	epidemic
disturbance	explosive

Word Bank

burrow	commence	cordial	corporal	accustom
accidentally	barracks	barometer	explosive	schoolmaster
stealth	allow	calamity	stance	defiant
epidemic	ancient	scowl	discard	ammunition
disturbance	subside	salute	reindeer	consternation
assign	demoralize	disposition	appoint	beneficial
resolute	enormous	ashamed	retort	entirely
earthenware	additional	commotion	almanac	surpass

Page 80

Hey, Look Me Over

Use the dictionary pronunciations to answer the questions below.

concoction (kən kok´ shən) *noun.* something prepared by mixing ingredients.
1. Which syllable is accented? 2nd
2. How many syllables have a "schwa" sound? 2
3. How many syllables are in "concoction?" 3

hover (huv´ ər) *verb. hovered hovering.* to flutter over or about.
1. How many syllables are in hover? 2
2. Which syllable is accented? 1st
3. How many syllables are found in *hovering*? 3

eternity (I tur´ nə tē) *noun.* an endless length of time.
1. Which syllable has a long "e" sound? 4th
2. Which syllable is accented? 2nd
3. How many syllables are in *eternity*? 4

honeysuckle (hun´ ē suk´ əl) *noun.* a climbing shrub with pleasant-smelling flowers.
1. How many syllables are in "honeysuckle?" 4
2. Which syllable has a primary accent? 1st
3. Which syllable has a secondary accent? 3rd
4. Which syllable has a "schwa" sound? 4th
5. Which two syllables have the same vowel sound? 1st, 3rd

Challenge: Write the phonetic spellings of these words. May vary.
audible ô´ də bəl camouflage kam´ ə fläzh
pneumonia nōō mōn´ yə municipal myōō nis´ ə pəl
supernatural sōō pər nach´ ər əl

Page 81

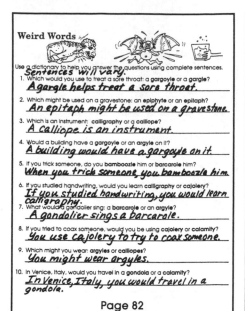

Weird Words

Use a dictionary to help you answer the questions using complete sentences. *Sentences will vary.*

1. Which would you use to treat a sore throat: a gargoyle or a gargle?
   A gargle helps treat a sore throat.

2. Which might be used on a gravestone: an epiphyte or an epitaph?
   An epitaph might be used on a gravestone.

3. Which is an instrument: calligraphy or a calliope?
   A calliope is an instrument.

4. Would a building have a gargoyle or an argyle on it?
   A building would have a gargoyle on it.

5. If you trick someone, do you bamboozle him or barcarole him?
   When you trick someone, you bamboozle him.

6. If you studied handwriting, would you learn calligraphy or cajolery?
   If you studied handwriting, you would learn calligraphy.

7. What would a gondolier sing: a barcarole or an argyle?
   A gondolier sings a barcarole.

8. If you tried to coax someone, would you be using cajolery or calamity?
   You use cajolery to try to coax someone.

9. Which might you wear: argyles or calliopes?
   You might wear argyles.

10. In Venice, Italy, would you travel in a gondola or a calamity?
    In Venice, Italy, you would travel in a gondola.

Page 82

From the Diary of Milo

Use a dictionary to help you circle the correct definition for each underlined word. In the space, write the dictionary page number. *Page numbers vary.*

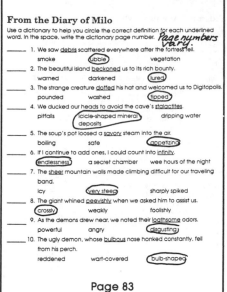

1. We saw debris scattered everywhere after the fortress fell.
   smoke — (rubble) — vegetation

2. The beautiful island beckoned us to its rich bounty.
   warned — darkened — (lured)

3. The strange creature doffed his hat and welcomed us to Digitopolis.
   pounded — washed — (tipped)

4. We ducked our heads to avoid the cave's stalactites.
   pitfalls — (icicle-shaped mineral deposits) — dripping water

5. The soup's pot loosed a savory steam into the air.
   boiling — safe — (appetizing)

6. If I continue to add ones, I could count into infinity.
   (endlessness) — a secret chamber — wee hours of the night

7. The sheer mountain walls made climbing difficult for our traveling band.
   icy — (very steep) — sharply spiked

8. The giant whined peevishly when we asked him to assist us.
   (crossly) — weakly — foolishly

9. As the demons drew near, we noted their loathsome odors.
   powerful — angry — (disgusting)

10. The ugly demon, whose bulbous nose honked constantly, fell from his perch.
    reddened — wart-covered — (bulb-shaped)

Page 83

Hang Tough, Student

Write the letter of the resource book which would best help you answer each question.

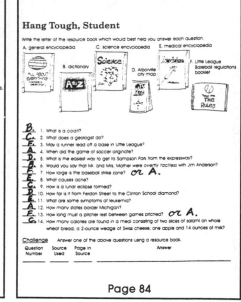

A. general encyclopedia C. science encyclopedia E. medical encyclopedia
B. dictionary D. Arborville city map F. Little League Baseball regulations booklet

B 1. What is a coati?
C 2. What does a geologist do?
F 3. May a runner lead off a base in Little League?
A 4. When did the game of soccer originate?
D 5. What is the easiest way to get to Sampson Park from the expressway?
B 6. Would you say that Mr. and Mrs. Mather were overtly tactless with Jim Anderson?
F 7. How large is the baseball strike zone? *or A.*
E 8. What causes acne?
C 9. How is a lunar eclipse formed?
D 10. How far is it from Ferdon Street to the Clinton School diamond?
E 11. What are some symptoms of leukemia?
D 12. How many states border Michigan?
A 13. How long must a pitcher rest between games pitched? *or A.*
E 14. How many calories are found in a meal consisting of two slices of salami on whole wheat bread, a 2-ounce wedge of Swiss cheese, one apple and 14 ounces of milk?

Challenge Answer one of the above questions using a resource book.

Question Number __ Source Used __ Page in Source __ Answer __

Page 84

Jimminy Cricket!

Underline the key word in each question. Then write the encyclopedia volume number you would use to find information to answer each question.

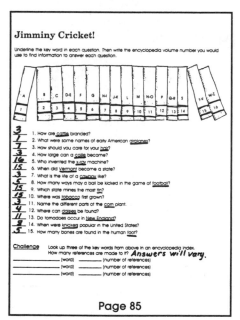

3 1. How are cattle branded?
1 2. What were some names of early American airplanes?
7 3. How should you care for your hair?
3 4. How large can a coala become?
16 5. Who invented the x-ray machine?
15 6. When did Vermont become a state?
3 7. What is the life of a cowboy like?
5 8. How many ways may a ball be kicked in the game of football?
15 9. Which state mines the most tin?
15 10. Where was tobacco first grown?
3 11. Name the different parts of the corn plant.
4 12. Where can daisies be found?
11 13. Do tornadoes occur in New England?
8 14. When were knickers popular in the United States?
5 15. How many bones are found in the human foot?

Challenge Look up three of the key words from above in an encyclopedia index. How many references are made to it? *Answers will vary.*

____ (word) ____ (number of references)
____ (word) ____ (number of references)
____ (word) ____ (number of references)

Page 85

Furoshiki Bundle

Sadako's mother wrapped all of Sadako's favorite foods in a *furoshiki* bundle. The bundle contained an egg roll, rice, chicken, plums, and bean cakes. List the heading under which you might find information on these foods in a recipe book.

Answers may vary.

1. Egg roll *Japanese specialties*
2. Plums *fruits*
3. Rice *breads/grains*
4. Chicken *meats/poultry*
5. Bean cakes *Japanese specialties*

Now, list five foods that someone might bring to you in a *furoshiki* bundle. Then list the heading under which each would be found in a recipe book.

Answers will vary.

1. ____
2. ____
3. ____
4. ____
5. ____

Page 86

Mumps, Measles, and Other Diseases

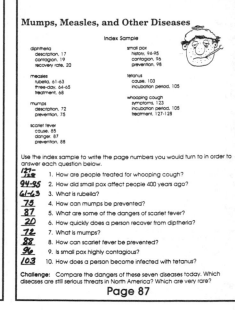

Index Sample

diphtheria
  description, 17
  contagion, 19
  recovery rate, 20

measles
  rubella, 61-63
  three-day, 64-65
  treatment, 68

mumps
  description, 72
  prevention, 75

scarlet fever
  cause, 85
  danger, 87
  prevention, 88

small pox
  history, 94-95
  contagion, 96
  prevention, 98

tetanus
  cause, 103
  incubation period, 105

whooping cough
  symptoms, 123
  incubation period, 105
  treatment, 127-128

Use the index sample to write the page numbers you would turn to in order to answer each question below.

127-128 1. How are people treated for whooping cough?
94-95 2. How did small pox affect people 400 years ago?
61-63 3. What is rubella?
75 4. How can mumps be prevented?
87 5. What are some of the dangers of scarlet fever?
20 6. How quickly does a person recover from diptheria?
72 7. What is mumps?
88 8. How can scarlet fever be prevented?
96 9. Is small pox highly contagious?
103 10. How does a person become infected with tetanus?

Challenge: Compare the dangers of these seven diseases today. Which diseases are still serious threats in North America? Which are very rare?

Page 87

Place Value

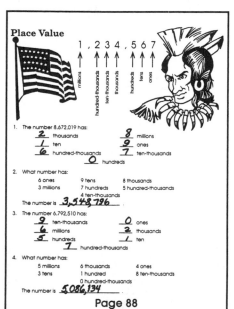

1,234,567
millions / hundred-thousands / ten-thousands / thousands / hundreds / tens / ones

1. The number 8,672,019 has:
   2 thousands   8 millions
   1 ten   9 ones
   6 hundred-thousands   0 ten-thousands   0 hundreds

2. What number has:
   6 ones   9 tens   8 thousands
   3 millions   7 hundreds   5 hundred-thousands
   4 ten-thousands
   The number is 3,548,796

3. The number 6,792,510 has:
   9 ten-thousands   0 ones
   6 millions   2 thousands
   5 hundreds   1 hundred-thousands   7 ten

4. What number has:
   5 millions   6 thousands   4 ones
   3 tens   1 hundred   8 ten-thousands
   0 hundred-thousands
   The number is 5,086,134

Page 88

The First State

What state is known as the first state? Follow the directions below to find out.

1. Put an A above number 2 if 31,842 rounded to the nearest thousand is 31,000.
2. Put an E above number 2 if 62 rounded to the nearest ten is 60.
3. Put an R above number 7 if 4,234 rounded to the nearest hundred is 4,200.
4. Put an L above number 3 if 677 rounded to the nearest hundred is 600.
5. Put an A above number 5 if 344 rounded to the nearest ten is 350.
6. Put an A above number 4 if 5,599 rounded to the nearest thousand is 6,000.
7. Put an A above number 6 if 1,549 rounded to the nearest hundred is 1,500.
8. Put a W above number 2 if 885 rounded to the nearest hundred is 800.
9. Put an E above number 8 if 521 rounded to the nearest ten is 520.
10. Put an R above number 6 if 74 rounded to the nearest ten is 80.
11. Put an L above number 3 if 3,291 rounded to the nearest thousand is 3,000.
12. Put an R above number 4 if 248 rounded to the nearest hundred is 300.
13. Put a D above number 1 if 615 rounded to the nearest ten is 620.
14. Put a W above number 1 if 188 rounded to the nearest ten is 200.
15. Put a W above number 5 if 6,817 rounded to the nearest thousand is 7,000.

D E L A W A R E
1 2 3 4 5 6 7 8

Page 89

Underwater Addition

446 + 489 = 935

476 + 527 = 1003   509 + 375 = 884

708 + 507 = 1215   438 + 419 = 857   334 + 278 = 612

251 + 368 = 619

464 + 456 = 920   589 + 322 = 911   288 + 377 = 665

811 + 386 = 1197

810 + 428 = 1238   831 + 483 = 1314   445 + 476 = 921

531 + 249 = 780   319 + 287 = 606   714 + 185 = 899   767 + 246 = 1013

609 + 475 = 1084   230 + 284 = 514   911 + 427 = 1338

211 + 396 = 607

Page 90

Page 91 — Grand Prix Addition

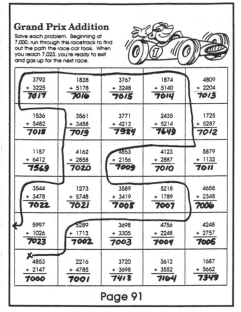

Solve each problem. Beginning at 7,000, run through this racetrack to find out the path the race car took. When you reach 7,023, you're ready to exit and gas up for the next race.

3792 + 3225 = **7017**	1838 + 5178 = **7016**	3767 + 3248 = **7015**	1874 + 5140 = **7014**	4809 + 2204 = **7013**
1536 + 5482 = **7018**	3561 + 3458 = **7019**	3771 + 4213 = **7984**	2435 + 5214 = **7649**	1725 + 5287 = **7012**
1157 + 6412 = **7569**	4162 + 2858 = **7020**	4853 + 2156 = **7009**	4123 + 2887 = **7010**	5879 + 1132 = **7011**
3544 + 3478 = **7022**	1273 + 5748 = **7021**	3589 + 3419 = **7008**	5218 + 1789 = **7007**	4658 + 2348 = **7006**
5997 + 1026 = **7023**	5289 + 1713 = **7002**	3698 + 3305 = **7003**	4756 + 2248 = **7004**	4248 + 2757 = **7005**
4853 + 2147 = **7000**	2216 + 4785 = **7001**	3720 + 3698 = **7418**	3612 + 3552 = **7164**	1687 + 5662 = **7349**

Page 92 — Fishy Problems

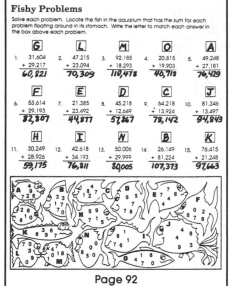

Solve each problem. Locate the fish in the aquarium that has the sum for each problem floating around in its stomach. Write the letter to match each answer in the box above each problem.

1. **G** 31,604 + 29,217 = **60,821**
2. **L** 47,215 + 23,094 = **70,309**
3. **M** 92,185 + 18,293 = **110,478**
4. **O** 20,815 + 19,903 = **40,718**
5. **A** 49,248 + 27,181 = **76,429**
6. **F** 53,614 + 29,193 = **82,807**
7. **E** 21,385 + 23,492 = **44,877**
8. **D** 45,218 + 12,649 = **57,867**
9. **C** 64,218 + 13,924 = **78,142**
10. **J** 81,346 + 13,497 = **94,843**
11. **H** 30,249 + 28,926 = **59,175**
12. **I** 42,618 + 34,193 = **76,811**
13. **N** 50,006 + 29,999 = **80,005**
14. **B** 26,149 + 81,224 = **107,373**
15. **K** 76,415 + 21,248 = **97,663**

Page 93 — Batter Up!

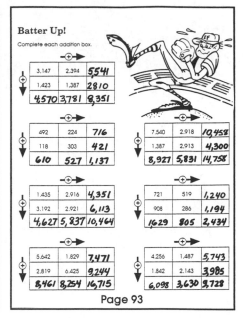

Complete each addition box.

+ →			+ →		
3,147	2,394	**5,541**	7,540	2,918	**10,458**
1,423	1,387	**2810**	1,387	2,913	**4,300**
4,570	**3,781**	**8,351**	**8,927**	**5,831**	**14,758**

492	224	**716**	1,435	2,916	**4,351**
118	303	**421**	3,192	2,921	**6,113**
610	**527**	**1,137**	**4,627**	**5,837**	**10,464**

721	519	**1,240**	5,642	1,829	**7,471**
908	286	**1,194**	2,819	6,425	**9,244**
1,629	**805**	**2,434**	**8,461**	**8,254**	**16,715**

4,256	1,487	**5,743**
1,842	2,143	**3,985**
6,098	**3,630**	**9,728**

Page 94 — Addition Slides

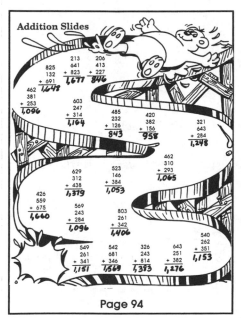

825 132 + 691 = **1,648**	213 641 132 + 691 = **1,677**	206 413 227 = **846**
462 381 253 = **1,096**	603 247 + 314 = **1,164**	485 232 + 126 = **843**
	420 382 + 156 = **958**	321 643 + 284 = **1,248**
629 312 + 438 = **1,379**	523 146 + 384 = **1,053**	462 310 + 293 = **1,065**
426 559 + 675 = **1,660**	569 243 + 284 = **1,096**	803 261 + 342 = **1,406**
549 261 + 341 = **1,151**	542 681 + 346 = **1,569**	326 243 + 814 = **1,383**	643 251 + 382 = **1,276**	540 262 + 351 = **1,153**

Page 95 — Pinball Mathematics

Solve the problems in the pinball machine.

- 7,215 62 141 + 2,015 = **9,433**
- 4,621 35 1,318 9 = **5,573**
- 8,143 60 235 + 1,423 = **9,861**
- 521 3,134 64 + 243 = **3,962**
- 7,006 35 242 6 + 31 = **7,288**
- 35 9 + 1,203 = **1,486**
- 496 8,172 83 + 199 = **8,950**
- 6,201 325 41 + 2,136 = **8,703**
- 5,242 342 8 + 51 = **5,643**
- 4,162 328 41 + 503 = **5,034**
- 6,425 41 324 + 3 = **6,793**
- 6,117 24 315 + 2,136 = **8,592**
- 4,205 81 2,516 + 414 = **4,703**
- 310 82 + 512 = **2,911**
- 5,426 310 512 + 4 = **6,252**
- 2,481 2,514 23 + 43 = **5,040**
- 3,204 182 23 + 3 = **3,414**

Page 96 — Knowing When to Add

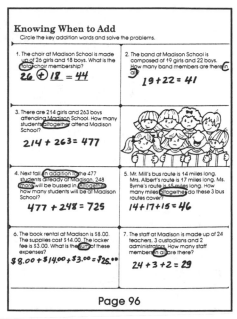

Circle the key addition words and solve the problems.

1. The choir at Madison School is made up of 26 girls and 18 boys. What is the total choir membership?
   26 ⊕ 18 = **44**

2. The band at Madison School is composed of 19 girls and 22 boys. How many band members are there in all?
   19 + 22 = 41

3. There are 214 girls and 263 boys attending Madison School. How many students altogether attend Madison School?
   214 + 263 = 477

4. Next fall in addition to the 477 students already at Madison, 248 more will be bussed in. Altogether how many students will be at Madison School?
   477 + 248 = 725

5. Mr. Mill's bus route is 14 miles long. Mrs. Albert's route is 17 miles long. Ms. Byrne's route is 15 miles long. How many miles altogether do these 3 bus routes cover?
   14 + 17 + 15 = 46

6. The book rental at Madison is $8.00. The supplies cost $14.00. The locker fee is $3.00. What is the sum of these expenses?
   $8.00 + $14.00 + $3.00 = $25.00

7. The staff at Madison is made up of 24 teachers, 3 custodians and 2 administrators. How many staff members in all are there?
   24 + 3 + 2 = 29

Page 97 — Math Cranes

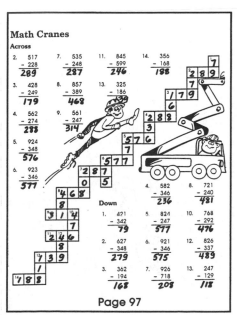

Across

2. 517 − 228 = **289**
3. 428 − 249 = **179**
4. 562 − 274 = **288**
5. 924 − 348 = **576**
6. 923 − 346 = **577**
7. 535 − 248 = **287**
8. 857 − 389 = **468**
9. 561 − 247 = **314**
11. 845 − 599 = **246**
13. 325 − 186 = **139**
14. 356 − 168 = **188**

4. 582 − 346 = **236**
8. 721 − 240 = **481**

Down

1. 421 − 342 = **79**
2. 627 − 348 = **279**
3. 362 − 194 = **168**
5. 824 − 247 = **577**
6. 921 − 346 = **575**
7. 926 − 718 = **208**
10. 768 − 292 = **476**
12. 826 − 337 = **489**
13. 247 − 129 = **118**

Page 98 — Timely Zeros

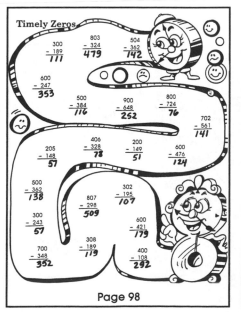

- 300 − 189 = **111**
- 803 − 324 = **479**
- 504 − 362 = **142**
- 600 − 247 = **353**
- 500 − 384 = **116**
- 900 − 648 = **252**
- 800 − 724 = **76**
- 702 − 561 = **141**
- 205 − 148 = **57**
- 406 − 328 = **78**
- 200 − 149 = **51**
- 600 − 476 = **124**
- 500 − 362 = **138**
- 302 − 195 = **107**
- 807 − 298 = **509**
- 300 − 243 = **57**
- 600 − 421 = **179**
- 308 − 189 = **119**
- 700 − 348 = **352**
- 400 − 108 = **292**

Page 99 — Subtraction Maze

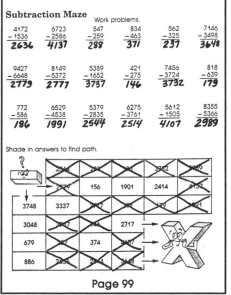

Work problems.

4172 − 1536 = **2636**	6723 − 2586 = **4137**	547 − 259 = **288**	834 − 463 = **371**	562 − 325 = **237**	7146 − 3498 = **3648**
9427 − 6648 = **2779**	8149 − 5372 = **2777**	5389 − 1652 = **3737**	421 − 275 = **146**	7456 − 3724 = **3732**	818 − 639 = **179**
772 − 586 = **186**	6546 − 4538 = **1991**	5379 − 2835 = **2544**	6275 − 3761 = **2514**	5612 − 1505 = **4107**	8355 − 5366 = **2989**

Shade in answers to find path.

		156	1901	2414	
3748	3337				
3048		2717			
679		374			
886					

High Class Math

MATH BLIMPS OF AMERICA, INC.

8,248 − 1,513 = 6,735				3,270 − 1,529 = 1,741
9,200 − 3,146 = 6,054	7,648 − 3,291 = 4,357	4,321 − 1,809 = 2,512	8,241 − 3,516 = 4,725	3,002 − 1,231 = 1,771
5,017 − 2,408 = 2,609	8,254 − 3,187 = 5,067	7,265 − 2,134 = 5,131	3,846 − 1,359 = 2,487	8,006 − 3,084 = 4,922
3,084 − 1,926 = 1,158	6,265 − 4,189 = 2,076	4,824 − 1,913 = 2,911	6,205 − 1,054 = 5,151	5,253 − 4,428 = 825
	9,205 − 3,187 = 6,018	5,809 − 3,913 = 1,896	5,642 − 2,408 = 3,234	

Page 100

Under the Big Top!

43	x	4	=	172
x				
2	x	58	=	116
=		x		
86	x	7	=	602

406

65	x	4	=	260
5	x	77	=	385
=		=		
325		308		

Page 101

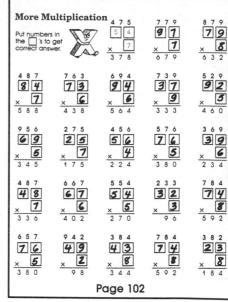

More Multiplication

Put numbers in the □'s to get correct answer.

| 475 × 378 | 779 × 679 | 879 × 632 |

487 ×84 = 588	763 ×73 = 438	694 ×94 = 564	739 ×37 = 333	529 ×92 = 460
956 ×69 = 345	275 ×25 = 175	456 ×56 = 224	576 ×74 = 380	369 ×39 = 234
487 ×48 = 336	667 ×67 = 402	554 ×54 = 270	233 ×32 = 96	784 ×74 = 592
657 ×76 = 380	942 ×49 = 98	384 ×43 = 344	784 ×74 = 592	382 ×23 = 184

Page 102

Solve It!

What set of ridges, loops and whirls are different on every person? To find out, solve the following problems and put the corresponding letter above the answer at the bottom of the page.

I. 303 × 3 = 909	R. 214 × 2 = 428	N. 413 × 2 = 826
N. 142 × 2 = 284	R. 211 × 4 = 844	F. 104 × 2 = 208
T. 131 × 2 = 262	E. 301 × 2 = 602	I. 134 × 1 = 134
G. 244 × 2 = 488	S. 334 × 2 = 668	P. 232 × 3 = 696

F i n g e r p r i n t s
208 909 826 488 602 696 428 134 284 262 668

Page 103

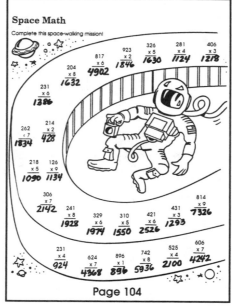

Space Math

Complete this space-walking mission!

817 ×6 = 4902 ... 923 ×2 = 1846 ... 326 ×5 = 1630 ... 281 ×4 = 1124 ... 406 ×3 = 1218

204 ×8 = 1632

231 ×6 = 1386

262 ×7 = 1834 ... 214 ×2 = 428

218 ×5 = 1090 ... 126 ×9 = 1134

306 ×7 = 2142 ... 241 ×8 = 1928 ... 329 ×6 = 1974 ... 310 ×5 = 1550 ... 421 ×6 = 2526 ... 431 ×3 = 1293 ... 814 ×9 = 7326

231 ×4 = 924 ... 624 ×7 = 4368 ... 896 ×1 = 896 ... 742 ×8 = 5936 ... 525 ×4 = 2100 ... 606 ×7 = 4242

Page 104

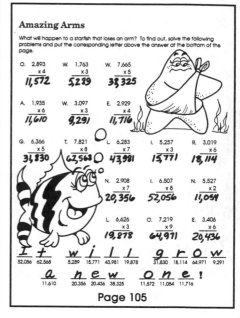

Amazing Arms

What will happen to a starfish that loses an arm? To find out, solve the following problems and put the corresponding letter above the answer at the bottom of the page.

O. 2,893 ×4 = 11,572	W. 1,763 ×3 = 5,289	W. 7,665 ×5 = 38,325
A. 1,935 ×6 = 11,610	W. 3,097 ×3 = 9,291	E. 2,929 ×4 = 11,716
G. 6,366 ×5 = 31,830	T. 7,821 ×8 = 62,568	L. 6,283 ×7 = 43,981	L. 5,257 ×3 = 15,771	R. 3,019 ×6 = 18,114
N. 2,908 ×7 = 20,356	I. 6,507 ×8 = 52,056	N. 5,527 ×2 = 11,054
L. 6,626 ×3 = 19,878	O. 7,219 ×9 = 64,971	E. 3,406 ×6 = 20,436

I t w i l l g r o w
52,056 62,568 5,289 15,771 43,981 19,878 31,830 18,114 64,971 9,291

a n e w o n e !
11,610 20,356 20,436 38,325 11,572 11,054 11,716

Page 105

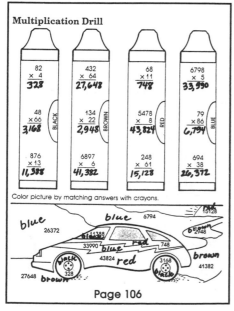

Multiplication Drill

82 × 4 = 328	432 × 64 = 27,648	68 × 11 = 748	6798 × 5 = 33,990
48 × 66 = 3,168 BLACK	134 × 22 = 2,948 BROWN	5478 × 8 = 43,824 RED	79 × 86 = 6,794 BLUE
876 × 13 = 11,388	6897 × 6 = 41,382	248 × 61 = 15,128	694 × 38 = 26,372

Color picture by matching answers with crayons.

blue 26372 ... blue 6794 ... blue ... brown 2948
6141388 ... 33990 ... blue ... red 748 ... brown
43824 ... red ... 3168 brown
27648 ... brown ... 41382 ... black 328

Page 106

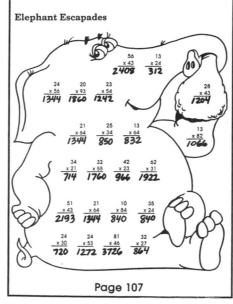

Elephant Escapades

56 × 43 = 2408	13 × 24 = 312
24 × 56 = 1344	20 × 93 = 1860	23 × 54 = 1242	28 × 43 = 1204
21 × 64 = 1344	25 × 34 = 850	13 × 64 = 832	13 × 82 = 1066
34 × 21 = 714	32 × 55 = 1760	42 × 23 = 966	62 × 31 = 1922
51 × 43 = 2193	21 × 64 = 1344	10 × 84 = 840	35 × 24 = 840
24 × 30 = 720	24 × 53 = 1272	81 × 46 = 3726	32 × 27 = 864

Page 107

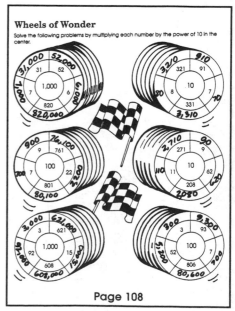

Wheels of Wonder

Solve the following problems by multiplying each number by the power of 10 in the center.

1,000: 31 → 31,000 ... 52 → 52,000 ... 820 → 820,000

10: 321 → 3,210 ... 91 → 910 ... 331 → 3,310

100: 761 → 76,100 ... 801 → 80,100

10: 271 → 2,710 ... 9 → 90 ... 208 → 2,080

1,000: 621 → 621,000 ... 608 → 608,000

100: 93 → 9,300 ... 806 → 80,600

Page 108

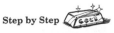

Step by Step

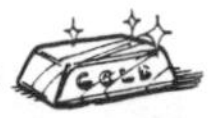

Read the problems below. Solve each in the space provided.

Work space

1. Mr. Lundstrom knew they would have to be careful moving the gold. He had the Defense Club only move a small amount at a time. They moved 137 gold bars on Monday and on Tuesday. On Wednesday they moved 150 gold bars. They moved 121 gold bars on Thursday, on Friday, and on Saturday. How many bars were moved in the entire week? 787

137 + 137 + 150 + 121 + 121 + 121 = 787

2. The German soldiers moved quickly into Norway on the night of the blackout. 1,259 troops came in by parachute, 2,067 came to shore by boat, and 1,099 came in by truck. How many troops came to Norway on that first night? 4,425

1,259 + 2,067 + 1,099 = 4,425

3. Pretend that Peter and Helga could each carry 25 bars of gold on their sleds. They made 35 trips down to the fiord with their loads. How many bars did they move? 1,750

50 × 35 = 1,750

4. The children saw many small groups of soldiers marching. In one group they counted 53 soldiers. In another group, they counted 69 soldiers. In each of three groups, they counted 77. How many soldiers did they see? 353

53 + 69 = 122
77 x 3 = 231
122 + 231 = 353

Page 109

Whacky Waldo's Snow Show

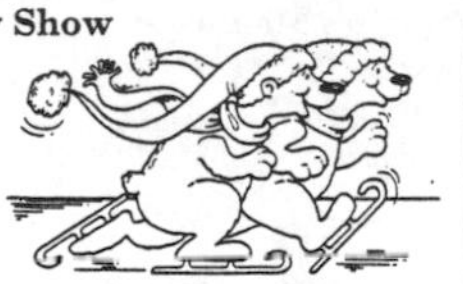

Wacky Waldo's Snow Show is an exciting and fantastic sight. Waldo has trained whales and bears to skate together on the ice. There is a hockey game between a team of sharks and a pack of wolves. Elephants ride sleds down steep hills. Horses and buffaloes ski swiftly down mountains.

1. Wacky Waldo has 4 ice-skating whales. He has 4 times as many bears who ice skate. How many bears can ice skate? 4x4=16

2. Waldo's Snow Show has 4 shows on Thursday, but it has 6 times as many shows on Saturday. How many shows are there on Saturday? 4x6=24

3. The Sharks' hockey team has 3 white sharks. It has 6 times as many tiger sharks. How many tiger sharks does it have? 3x6=18

4. The Wolves' hockey team has 4 gray wolves. It has 8 times as many red wolves. How many red wolves does it have? 4x8=32

5. Waldo taught 6 buffaloes to ski. He was able to teach 5 times as many horses to ski. How many horses did he teach? 6x5=30

6. Buff, a skiing buffalo, took 7 nasty spills when he was learning to ski. His friend Harry Horse fell down 8 times as often. How many times did Harry fall? 7x8=56

Page 110

Molly Mugwumps

Molly Mugwumps is the toughest kid in school. She picks fights with kindergarteners and spends more time in the office than the principal does.

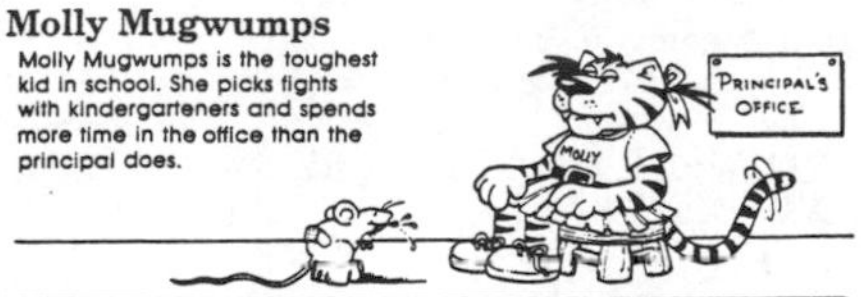

PRINCIPAL'S OFFICE

1. Molly is the toughest football player in her school. She ran for 23 yards on one play and went 3 times as far on the next play. How far did she run the second time? 23x3=69

2. Molly keeps a rock collection. She has 31 rocks in one sack. She has 7 times as many under her bed. How many rocks are under her bed? 31x7=217

3. Molly had 42 marbles when she came to school. She went home with 4 times as many. How many did she go home with? 42x4=168

4. Molly stuffed 21 sticks of gum in her mouth in the morning. In the afternoon, she crammed 9 times as many sticks into her mouth. How many sticks did she have in the afternoon? 21x9=189

5. Molly got 51 problems wrong in math last week. This week, she missed 8 times as many. How many did she miss this week? 51x8=408

6. Molly was sent to the office 21 days last year. This year, she was sent 7 times as often. How many days did she go this year? 21x7=147

Page 111

Snowball Bash

Help Pete climb down this mound of giant snowballs!

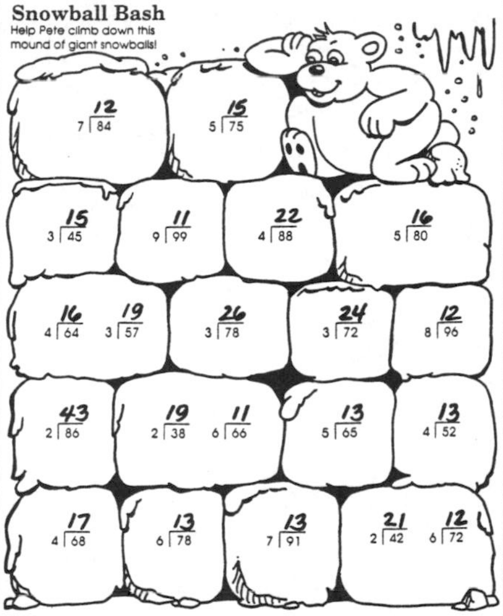

12 7|84
15 5|75
15 3|45
11 9|99
22 4|88
16 5|80
16 4|64
19 3|57
26 3|78
24 3|72
12 8|96
43 2|86
19 2|38
11 6|66
13 5|65
13 4|52
17 4|68
13 6|78
13 7|91
21 2|42
12 6|72

Page 112

Scaling the Heights

Work the problems. To find the path to the top, the answers should match the problem number. Color the path.

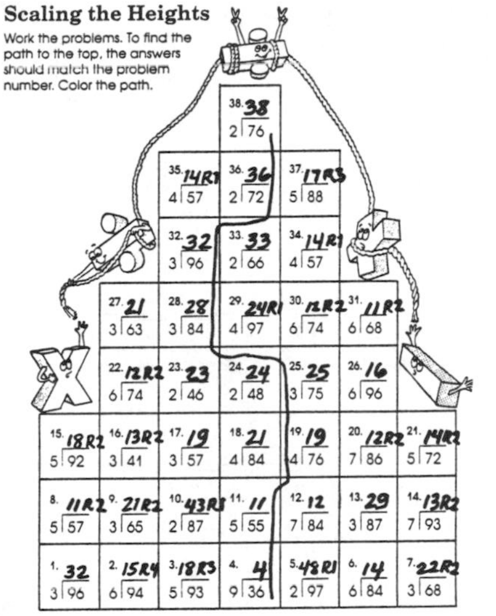

38. 38 2|76
35. 14R1 4|57
36. 36 2|72
37. 17R3 5|88
32. 32 3|96
33. 33 2|66
34. 14R1 4|57
27. 21 3|63
28. 28 3|84
29. 24R1 4|97
30. 12R2 6|74
31. 11R2 6|68
22. 12R2 6|74
23. 23 2|46
24. 24 2|48
25. 25 3|75
26. 16 6|96
15. 18R2 5|92
16. 13R2 3|41
17. 19 3|57
18. 21 4|84
19. 19 4|76
20. 12R2 7|86
21. 14R2 5|72
8. 11R2 5|57
9. 21R2 3|65
10. 43R1 2|87
11. 11 5|55
12. 12 7|84
13. 29 3|87
14. 13R2 7|93
1. 32 3|96
2. 15R4 6|94
3. 18R3 5|93
4. 4 9|36
5. 48R1 2|97
6. 14 6|84
7. 22R2 3|68

Page 113

Geometric Division!

Solve the division problems below and color each shape according to the matching problem and quotient (b = blue, r = red, y = yellow, g = green and p = purple).

Name seven shapes that are in the design.

1. circle
2. parallelogram
3. arch
4. trapezoid
5. triangle
6. rectangle
7. quadrilateral

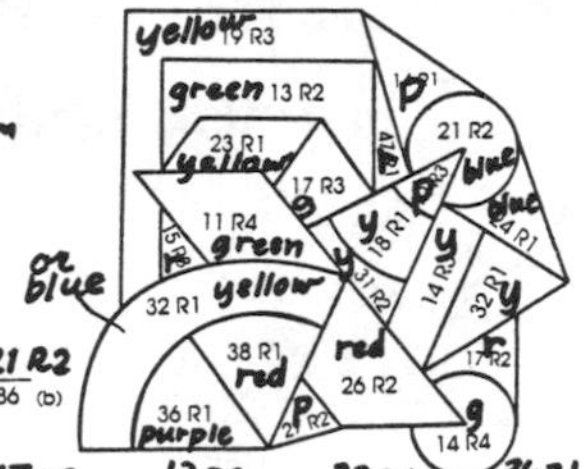

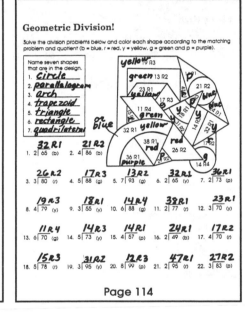

1. 2|65 (b) 32 R1
2. 4|86 (b) 21 R2
3. 3|80 (r) 26 R2
4. 5|88 (g) 17 R3
5. 7|93 (g) 13 R2
6. 2|65 (y) 32 R1
7. 2|73 (p) 36 R1
8. 4|79 (y) 19 R3
9. 3|55 (y) 18 R1
10. 6|88 (g) 14 R4
11. 2|77 (r) 38 R1
12. 3|70 (y) 23 R1
13. 6|70 (g) 11 R4
14. 5|73 (y) 14 R3
15. 4|57 (p) 14 R1
16. 2|49 (b) 24 R1
17. 4|70 (r) 17 R2
18. 5|78 (r) 15 R3
19. 3|95 (y) 31 R2
20. 8|99 (p) 12 R3
21. 2|95 (r) 47 R1
22. 3|83 (p) 27 R2

Page 114

On-Stage Division

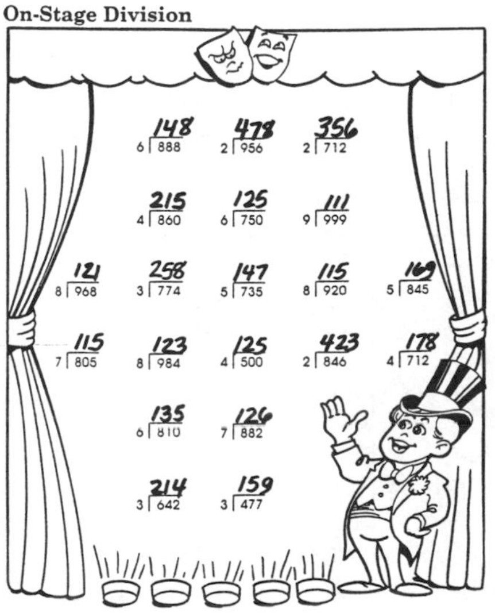

148 6|888
478 2|956
356 2|712
215 4|860
125 6|750
111 9|999
121 8|968
258 3|774
147 5|735
115 8|920
169 5|845
115 7|805
123 8|984
125 4|500
423 2|846
178 4|712
135 6|810
126 7|882
214 3|642
159 3|477

Page 115

Puzzling Problems

Solve the following problems. Write the answers in the puzzle.
Hint: Remainders (R) take up their own box.

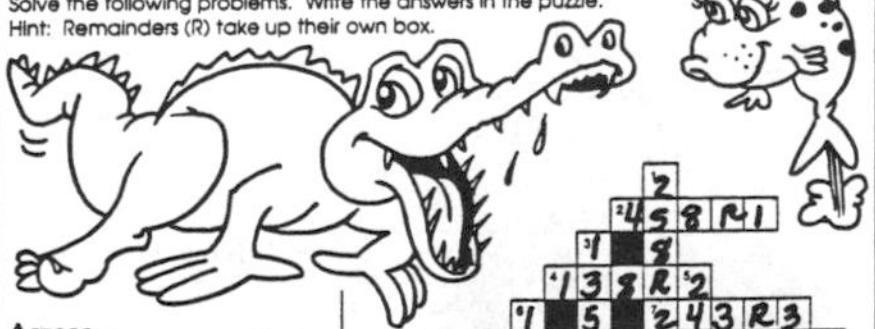

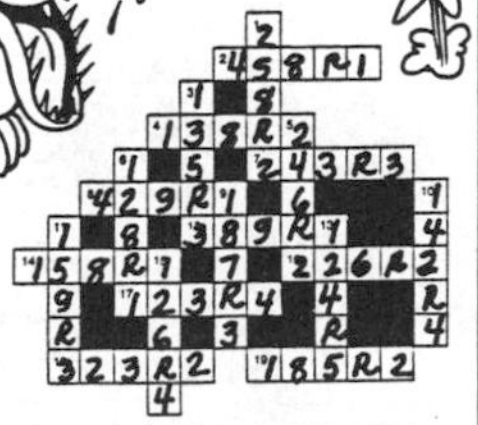

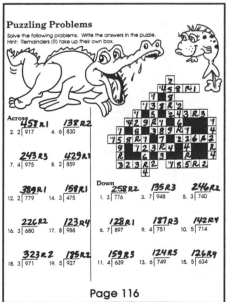

Across

2. 2|917 458 R1
4. 6|830 138 R2
7. 4|975 243 R3
8. 2|859 429 R1
12. 2|779 389 R1
14. 3|475 158 R1
16. 3|680 226 R2
17. 8|988 123 R4
18. 3|971 323 R2
19. 5|927 185 R2

Down

1. 3|776 258 R2
3. 7|948 135 R3
5. 3|740 246 R2
6. 7|897 128 R1
9. 4|751 187 R3
10. 5|714 142 R4
11. 4|639 159 R3
13. 6|749 124 R5
15. 5|634 126 R4

Page 116

Division Checklist

Work the problems. Draw a line from the division problem to the matching checking problem.

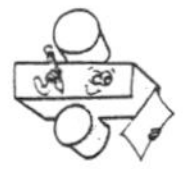

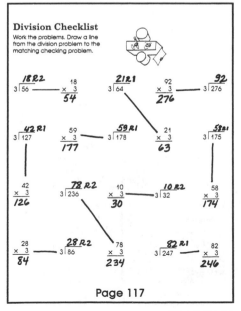

18 R2 3|56	18 × 3 = 54	21 R1 3|64	92 × 3 = 276	92 3|276
42 R1 3|127	59 × 3 = 177	59 R1 3|178	21 × 3 = 63	58 R1 3|175
42 × 3 = 126	78 R2 3|236	10 × 3 = 30	10 R2 3|32	58 × 3 = 174
28 × 3 = 84	28 R2 3|86	78 × 3 = 234	82 R1 3|247	82 × 3 = 246

Page 117

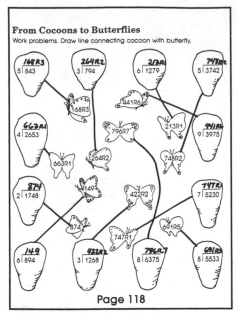

From Cocoons to Butterflies
Work problems. Draw line connecting cocoon with butterfly.

168 R3 — 5)843
264 R2 — 3)794
212 R1 — 6)1279
748 R2 — 5)3742
663 R1 — 4)2653
441 R6 — 9)3975
874 — 2)1748
747 R — 7)5230
149 — 6)894
422 R2 — 3)1268
796 R7 — 8)6375
691 R3 — 8)5533

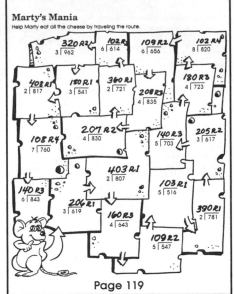

Marty's Mania
Help Marty eat all the cheese by traveling the route.

320 R2 — 3)962
102 R2 — 6)614
109 R2 — 6)656
102 R4 — 8)820
408 R1 — 2)817
180 R1 — 3)541
360 R1 — 2)721
180 R3 — 4)723
208 R3 — 4)835
108 R4 — 7)760
207 R2 — 4)830
140 R3 — 5)703
205 R2 — 3)617
140 R3 — 6)843
403 R1 — 2)807
103 R1 — 5)516
206 R1 — 3)619
160 R3 — 4)643
109 R2 — 5)547
390 R1 — 2)781

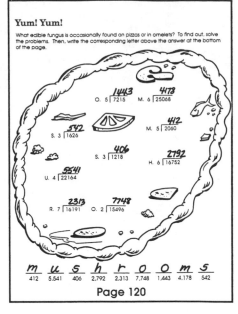

Yum! Yum!
What edible fungus is occasionally found on pizzas or in omelets? To find out, solve the problems. Then, write the corresponding letter above the answer at the bottom of the page.

1443 — O. 5)7215
4178 — M. 6)25068
542 — S. 3)1626
412 — M. 5)2060
406 — S. 3)1218
2792 — H. 6)16752
5541 — U. 4)22164
2313 — R. 7)16191
7748 — O. 2)15496

m u s h r o o m s
412 5,541 406 2,792 2,313 7,748 1,443 4,178 542

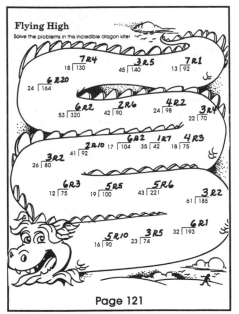

Flying High
Solve the problems in this incredible dragon kite!

7 R4 — 18)130
3 R5 — 45)140
7 R1 — 13)92
6 R20 — 24)164
6 R2 — 53)320
2 R6 — 42)90
4 R2 — 24)98
3 R4 — 22)70
2 R10 — 41)92
6 R2 — 17)104
1 R7 — 35)42
4 R3 — 18)75
3 R2 — 26)80
6 R3 — 12)75
5 R5 — 19)100
5 R6 — 43)221
3 R2 — 61)185
5 R10 — 16)90
3 R5 — 23)74
6 R1 — 32)193

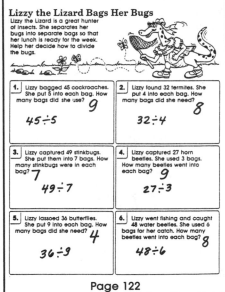

Lizzy the Lizard Bags Her Bugs
Lizzy the Lizard is a great hunter of insects. She separates her bugs into separate bags so that her lunch is ready for the week. Help her decide how to divide the bugs.

1. Lizzy bagged 45 cockroaches. She put 5 into each bag. How many bags did she use? **9**
45÷5

2. Lizzy found 32 termites. She put 4 into each bag. How many bags did she need? **8**
32÷4

3. Lizzy captured 49 stinkbugs. She put them into 7 bags. How many stinkbugs were in each bag? **7**
49÷7

4. Lizzy captured 27 horn beetles. She used 3 bags. How many beetles went into each bag? **9**
27÷3

5. Lizzy lassoed 36 butterflies. She put 9 into each bag. How many bags did she need? **4**
36÷9

6. Lizzy went fishing and caught 48 water beetles. She used 6 bags for her catch. How many beetles went into each bag? **8**
48÷6

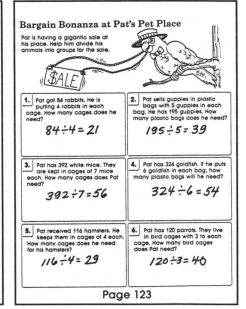

Bargain Bonanza at Pat's Pet Place
Pat is having a gigantic sale at his place. Help him divide his animals into groups for the sale.

1. Pat got 84 rabbits. He is putting 4 rabbits in each cage. How many cages does he need?
84÷4 = 21

2. Pat sells guppies in plastic bags with 5 guppies in each bag. He has 195 guppies. How many plastic bags does he need?
195÷5 = 39

3. Pat has 392 white mice. They are kept in cages of 7 mice each. How many cages does Pat need?
392÷7 = 56

4. Pat has 324 goldfish. If he puts 6 goldfish in each bag, how many plastic bags will he need?
324÷6 = 54

5. Pat received 116 hamsters. He keeps them in cages of 4 each. How many cages does he need for his hamsters?
116÷4 = 29

6. Pat has 120 parrots. They live in bird cages with 3 to each cage. How many bird cages does Pat need?
120÷3 = 40

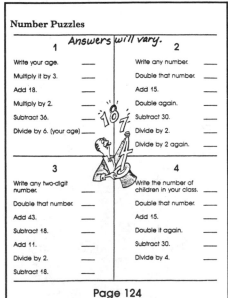

Number Puzzles

Answers will vary.

1
Write your age. ___
Multiply it by 3. ___
Add 18. ___
Multiply by 2. ___
Subtract 36. ___
Divide by 6. (your age) ___

2
Write any number. ___
Double that number. ___
Add 15. ___
Double again. ___
Subtract 30. ___
Divide by 2. ___
Divide by 2 again. ___

3
Write any two-digit number. ___
Double that number. ___
Add 43. ___
Subtract 18. ___
Add 11. ___
Divide by 2. ___
Subtract 18. ___

4
Write the number of children in your class. ___
Double that number. ___
Add 15. ___
Double it again. ___
Subtract 30. ___
Divide by 4. ___

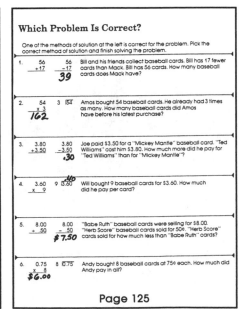

Which Problem Is Correct?
One of the methods of solution at the left is correct for the problem. Pick the correct method of solution and finish solving the problem.

1. 56 +17 | 56 -17 = **39** | Bill and his friends collect baseball cards. Bill has 17 fewer cards than Mack. Bill has 56 cards. How many baseball cards does Mack have?

2. 54 x 3 = **162** | 3)54 | Amos bought 54 baseball cards. He already had 3 times as many. How many baseball cards did Amos have before his latest purchase?

3. 3.80 +3.50 | 3.80 -3.50 = **.30** | Joe paid $3.50 for a "Mickey Mantle" baseball card. "Ted Williams" cost him $3.80. How much more did he pay for "Ted Williams" than for "Mickey Mantle"?

4. 3.60 x 9 | 9)3.60 = **.40** | Will bought 9 baseball cards for $3.60. How much did he pay per card?

5. 8.00 +.50 | 8.00 -.50 = **$7.50** | "Babe Ruth" baseball cards were selling for $8.00. "Herb Score" baseball cards sold for 50¢. "Herb Score" cards sold for how much less than "Babe Ruth" cards?

6. 0.75 x 8 = **$6.00** | 8)0.75 | Andy bought 8 baseball cards at 75¢ each. How much did Andy pay in all?

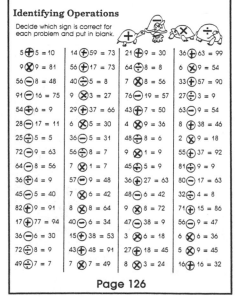

Identifying Operations
Decide which sign is correct for each problem and put in blank.

5 + 5 = 10	14 + 59 = 73	21 + 9 = 30	36 + 63 = 99
9 × 9 = 81	56 + 17 = 73	64 ÷ 8 = 8	6 × 9 = 54
56 − 8 = 48	40 ÷ 5 = 8	7 × 8 = 56	33 + 57 = 90
91 − 16 = 75	9 × 3 = 27	76 − 19 = 57	27 ÷ 3 = 9
54 ÷ 6 = 9	29 + 37 = 66	43 + 7 = 50	63 − 9 = 54
28 − 17 = 11	6 × 5 = 30	4 × 9 = 36	8 + 38 = 46
25 ÷ 5 = 5	36 − 5 = 31	48 ÷ 8 = 6	2 × 9 = 18
72 ÷ 9 = 63	56 ÷ 8 = 7	9 × 1 = 9	55 + 37 = 92
64 − 8 = 56	7 × 1 = 7	45 + 5 = 9	81 + 9 = 9
36 ÷ 4 = 9	57 − 9 = 48	36 + 27 = 63	80 − 17 = 63
45 ÷ 5 = 40	9 × 6 = 42	48 − 6 = 42	32 ÷ 4 = 8
82 + 9 = 91	8 × 8 = 64	9 × 8 = 72	71 + 15 = 86
17 + 77 = 94	40 − 6 = 34	47 − 38 = 9	56 − 9 = 47
36 − 6 = 30	15 + 38 = 53	3 × 6 = 18	6 × 6 = 36
72 ÷ 8 = 9	43 + 48 = 91	27 + 18 = 45	5 × 9 = 45
49 ÷ 7 = 7	7 × 7 = 49	8 × 3 = 24	16 + 16 = 32

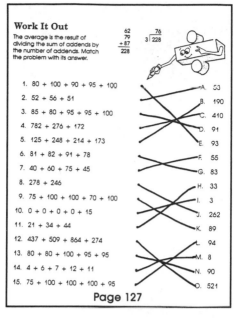

Work It Out

The average is the result of dividing the sum of addends by the number of addends. Match the problem with its answer.

$$\begin{array}{r} 62 \\ 79 \\ 87 \\ + 87 \\ \hline 228 \end{array} \qquad 3\overline{)228} = 76$$

1. 80 + 100 + 90 + 95 + 100
2. 52 + 56 + 51
3. 85 + 80 + 95 + 95 + 100
4. 782 + 276 + 172
5. 125 + 248 + 214 + 173
6. 81 + 82 + 91 + 78
7. 40 + 60 + 75 + 45
8. 278 + 246
9. 75 + 100 + 100 + 70 + 100
10. 0 + 0 + 0 + 0 + 15
11. 21 + 34 + 44
12. 437 + 509 + 864 + 274
13. 80 + 80 + 100 + 95 + 95
14. 4 + 6 + 7 + 12 + 11
15. 75 + 100 + 100 + 100 + 95

A. 53
B. 190
C. 410
D. 91
E. 93
F. 55
G. 83
H. 33
I. 3
J. 262
K. 89
L. 94
M. 8
N. 90
O. 521

Page 127

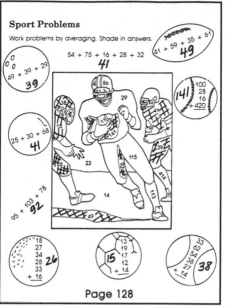

Sport Problems

Work problems by averaging. Shade in answers.

54 + 75 + 16 + 28 + 32 = 41

41 + 59 + 35 + 61 = 49

49 + 39 + 29 = 39

25 + 30 + 68 = 41

100 + 28 + 16 + 420 = 141

18 + 19 + 34 + 28 + 33 + 16 = 26

13 + 15 + 17 + 12 + 14 = 15

33 + 52 + 54 + 27 + 14 = 38

95 + 103 + 78 = 92

Page 128

What Fraction Am I?

Identify the fraction for each shaded section.

A. 4/13
B. 3/6   H. 1/3
C. 2/7   I. 2/5
D. 4/3   J. 2/8
E. 4/8   K. 5/16
F. 1/2   L. 1/4
G. 1/4   M. 7/27

Page 129

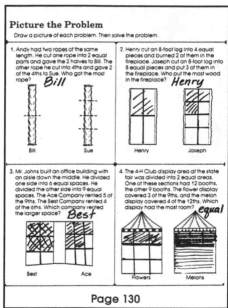

Picture the Problem

Draw a picture of each problem. Then solve the problem.

1. Andy had two ropes of the same length. He cut one rope into 2 equal parts and gave the 2 halves to Bill. The other rope he cut into 4ths and gave 2 of the 4ths to Sue. Who got the most rope? **Bill**

   Bill   Sue

2. Henry cut an 8-foot log into 4 equal pieces and burned 2 of them in the fireplace. Joseph cut an 8-foot log into 8 equal pieces and put 3 of them in the fireplace. Who put the most wood in the fireplace? **Henry**

   Henry   Joseph

3. Mr. Johns built an office building with an aisle down the middle. He divided one side into 6 equal spaces. He divided the other side into 9 equal spaces. The Ace Company rented 5 of the 9ths. The Best Company rented 4 of the 6ths. Which company rented the larger space? **Best**

   Best   Ace

4. The 4-H Club display area at the state fair was divided into 2 equal areas. One of these sections had 12 booths, the other 9 booths. The flower display covered 3 of the 9ths, and the melon display covered 4 of the 12ths. Which display had the most room? **equal**

   Flowers   Melons

Page 130

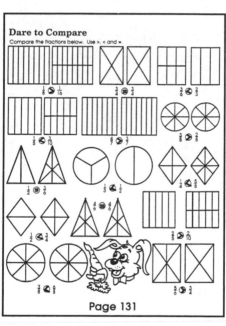

Dare to Compare

Compare the fractions below. Use >, < and =.

Page 131

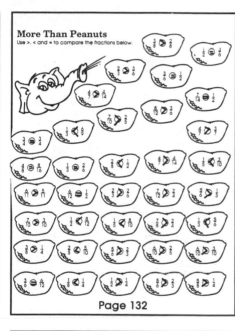

More Than Peanuts

Use >, < and = to compare the fractions below.

Page 132

Match the Fractions

Under each bar, write a fraction for the shaded part. Then, match each fraction on the left with its equivalent fraction on the right.

1. 3/6 _d_
2. 3/3 _f_
3. 6/10 _b_
4. 10/12 _g_
5. 2/8 _h_
6. 3/6 _d_
7. 3/10 _a_
8. 1/5 _c_

a. 4/5
b. 3/5
c. 3/10
d. 1/3
e. 1/2
f. 4/6
g. 5/6
h. 1/4

Page 133

Oh, My!

Draw the correct mouths on the animals by finding the whole number for each fraction.

10/2 = 5   16/4 = 4   18/2 = 9   21/7 = 12/2 = 2

16/2 = 8   40/7 = 7   16/16 = 1   12/12 =   2

8   12   5

6   1   3   7   2

Page 134

Reduce the Fat Grams

Help this reducing machine function properly! Reduce each fraction.

5/25 = 1/5   8/16 = 1/2   12/18 = 2/3   10/25 = 2/5   12/30 = 2/5   3/30 = 1/10

6/30 = 1/5   12/20 = 3/5   3/18 = 1/6   3/9 = 1/3   8/26 = 2/13   4/28 = 1/7

7/21 = 1/3   16/20 = 4/5   2/10 = 1/5   3/27 = 1/9   5/60 = 1/12

21/35 = 3/5   3/12 = 1/4   24/40 = 3/5   8/24 = 1/3

16/40 = 2/5   9/36 = 1/4   15/25 = 3/5   7/35 = 1/5

Page 135

303

Daily Learning Drills Grade 4

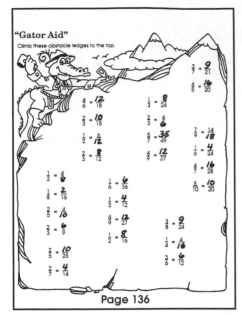

"Gator Aid"

Climb these obstacle ledges to the top.

$\frac{3}{7} = \frac{9}{21}$

$\frac{4}{5} = \frac{16}{20}$

$\frac{4}{6} = \frac{12}{18}$ $\frac{1}{3} = \frac{8}{24}$

$\frac{2}{3} = \frac{10}{15}$ $\frac{2}{3} = \frac{4}{6}$ $\frac{7}{9} = \frac{14}{18}$

$\frac{1}{2} = \frac{6}{12}$ $\frac{5}{7} = \frac{35}{49}$ $\frac{1}{6} = \frac{4}{24}$

$\frac{4}{6} = \frac{8}{12}$ $\frac{4}{9} = \frac{12}{27}$ $\frac{4}{7} = \frac{16}{28}$

$\frac{1}{2} = \frac{4}{8}$ $\frac{1}{6} = \frac{6}{36}$ $\frac{5}{10} = \frac{10}{20}$

$\frac{1}{8} = \frac{2}{16}$ $\frac{1}{3} = \frac{4}{12}$

$\frac{2}{5} = \frac{4}{10}$ $\frac{4}{9} = \frac{12}{27}$ $\frac{3}{8} = \frac{9}{24}$

$\frac{2}{3} = \frac{6}{9}$ $\frac{1}{2} = \frac{8}{16}$

$\frac{2}{5} = \frac{10}{25}$ $\frac{3}{6} = \frac{6}{12}$

$\frac{2}{7} = \frac{4}{14}$

Page 136

Figure It Out

Work problems. Connect the dots in order of answers.

1. $3\frac{3}{4} = \frac{15}{4}$
2. $\frac{9}{2} = 4\frac{1}{2}$
3. $\frac{30}{11} = 2\frac{8}{11}$
4. $8\frac{1}{2} = \frac{17}{2}$
5. $\frac{10}{4} = 4\frac{1}{4}$
6. $4\frac{3}{8} = \frac{35}{8}$
7. $4\frac{1}{5} = \frac{21}{5}$
8. $\frac{11}{3} = 3\frac{2}{3}$
9. $\frac{13}{7} = 1\frac{6}{7}$
10. $3\frac{5}{6} = \frac{23}{6}$
11. $1\frac{5}{6} = \frac{11}{6}$
12. $\frac{13}{5} = 2\frac{3}{5}$
13. $4\frac{1}{3} = \frac{13}{3}$
14. $\frac{9}{7} = 1\frac{2}{7}$
15. $2\frac{2}{5} = \frac{12}{5}$
16. $6\frac{2}{5} = \frac{32}{5}$
17. $1\frac{1}{9} = \frac{10}{9}$
18. $\frac{13}{8} = 1\frac{5}{8}$
19. $1\frac{2}{5} = \frac{7}{5}$
20. $1\frac{1}{8} = \frac{9}{8}$

Page 137

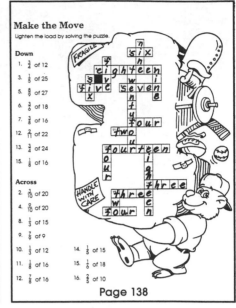

Make the Move

Lighten the load by solving the puzzle.

Down
1. $\frac{1}{2}$ of 12
3. $\frac{1}{5}$ of 25
5. $\frac{2}{9}$ of 27
6. $\frac{1}{3}$ of 18
7. $\frac{3}{8}$ of 16
12. $\frac{2}{11}$ of 22
13. $\frac{1}{2}$ of 24
15. $\frac{1}{8}$ of 16

Across
2. $\frac{3}{10}$ of 20
4. $\frac{9}{10}$ of 20
8. $\frac{1}{3}$ of 15
9. $\frac{7}{9}$ of 9
10. $\frac{1}{3}$ of 12
11. $\frac{1}{8}$ of 16
12. $\frac{7}{8}$ of 16
14. $\frac{1}{3}$ of 15
15. $\frac{1}{6}$ of 18
16. $\frac{2}{5}$ of 10

Page 138

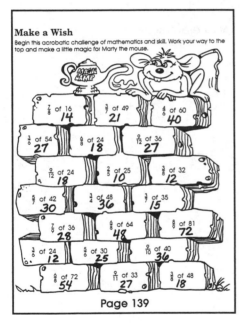

Make a Wish

Begin this acrobatic challenge of mathematics and skill. Work your way to the top and make a little magic for Marty the mouse.

$\frac{7}{8}$ of 16 = **14**	$\frac{3}{7}$ of 49 = **21**	$\frac{2}{3}$ of 60 = **40**
$\frac{1}{2}$ of 54 = **27**	$\frac{3}{4}$ of 24 = **18**	$\frac{3}{4}$ of 36 = **27**
$\frac{9}{12}$ of 24 = **18**	$\frac{2}{5}$ of 25 = **10**	$\frac{3}{8}$ of 32 = **12**
$\frac{5}{7}$ of 42 = **30**	$\frac{3}{4}$ of 48 = **36**	$\frac{3}{7}$ of 35 = **15**
$\frac{7}{9}$ of 36 = **28**	$\frac{3}{4}$ of 64 = **48**	$\frac{8}{9}$ of 81 = **72**
$\frac{1}{2}$ of 24 = **12**	$\frac{5}{6}$ of 30 = **25**	$\frac{9}{10}$ of 40 = **36**
$\frac{3}{4}$ of 72 = **54**	$\frac{9}{11}$ of 33 = **27**	$\frac{3}{8}$ of 48 = **18**

Page 139

The Ultimate Adding Machine

Find the sum for each problem. Reduce to lowest terms.

$\frac{7}{9} + \frac{1}{9} = \frac{8}{9}$ $\frac{4}{12} + \frac{3}{12} = \frac{7}{12}$ $\frac{3}{6} + \frac{2}{6} = \frac{5}{6}$ $\frac{1}{9} + \frac{3}{9} = \frac{4}{9}$

$\frac{4}{10} + \frac{2}{10} = \frac{3}{5}$ $\frac{3}{6} + \frac{2}{6} = \frac{5}{6}$ $\frac{5}{9} + \frac{3}{9} = \frac{8}{9}$ $\frac{2}{5} + \frac{1}{5} = \frac{3}{5}$

$\frac{6}{11} + \frac{5}{11} = \frac{10}{11}$ $\frac{3}{7} + \frac{2}{7} = \frac{5}{7}$ $\frac{4}{8} + \frac{1}{8} = \frac{5}{8}$ $\frac{4}{12} + \frac{1}{12} = \frac{5}{12}$

$\frac{5}{8} + \frac{2}{8} = \frac{7}{8}$ $\frac{4}{12} + \frac{4}{12} = \frac{5}{6}$

$\frac{5}{8} + \frac{1}{8} = \frac{3}{4}$

$\frac{2}{5} + \frac{2}{5} = \frac{4}{5}$ $\frac{1}{9} + \frac{2}{9} = \frac{1}{3}$

$\frac{7}{10} + \frac{2}{10} = \frac{9}{10}$ $\frac{4}{6} + \frac{1}{6} = \frac{5}{6}$

WOW!

Page 140

Bubble Math

Reduce each sum to a whole number or a mixed number in lowest terms.

Page 141

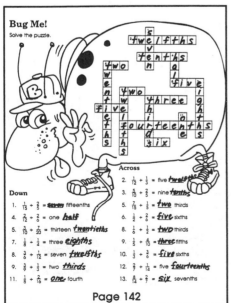

Bug Me!

Solve the puzzle.

Across
2. $\frac{1}{12} + \frac{1}{3}$ = five *twelfths*
3. $\frac{3}{10} + \frac{3}{5}$ = nine *tenths*
5. $\frac{7}{15} + \frac{1}{5}$ = *two* thirds
6. $\frac{1}{2} + \frac{1}{3}$ = *five* sixths
9. $\frac{1}{3} + \frac{4}{15}$ = *three* fifths
10. $\frac{1}{3} + \frac{3}{6}$ = *five* sixths
12. $\frac{2}{7} + \frac{3}{14}$ = five *fourteenths*
13. $\frac{4}{14} + \frac{2}{7}$ = *six* sevenths

Down
1. $\frac{1}{15} + \frac{2}{5}$ = ~~seven~~ fifteenths
4. $\frac{2}{12} + \frac{2}{6}$ = one *half*
5. $\frac{2}{5} + \frac{1}{4}$ = thirteen *twentieths*
7. $\frac{1}{4} + \frac{1}{8}$ = three *eighths*
8. $\frac{3}{4} + \frac{1}{12}$ = seven *twelfths*
9. $\frac{3}{6} + \frac{1}{3}$ = two *thirds*
11. $\frac{1}{8} + \frac{2}{16}$ = *one* fourth

Page 142

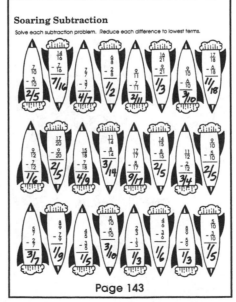

Soaring Subtraction

Solve each subtraction problem. Reduce each difference to lowest terms.

Row 1:
$\frac{14}{16} - \frac{6}{16} = \frac{2}{5}$ $\frac{7}{10} - \frac{1}{10} = \frac{7}{16}$ $\frac{7}{14} - \frac{4}{14} = \frac{1}{2}$ $\frac{12}{21} - \frac{9}{21} = \frac{1}{3}$ $\frac{14}{18} - \frac{3}{18} = \frac{11}{18}$

Row 2:
$\frac{6}{12} - \frac{2}{12} = \frac{1}{6}$ $\frac{17}{20} - \frac{9}{20} = \frac{2}{5}$ $\frac{15}{14} - \frac{7}{14} = \frac{4}{9}$ $\frac{14}{17} - \frac{5}{17} = \frac{3}{14}$ $\frac{9}{10} - \frac{5}{10} = \frac{2}{5}$

Row 3:
$\frac{5}{14} - \frac{2}{14} = \frac{3}{7}$ $\frac{6}{12} - \frac{4}{12} = \frac{1}{9}$ $\frac{5}{10} - \frac{2}{10} = \frac{1}{5}$ $\frac{5}{12} - \frac{1}{12} = \frac{1}{10}$ $\frac{6}{10} - \frac{4}{10} = \frac{1}{3}$

Page 143

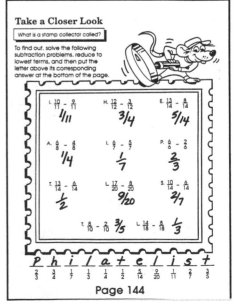

Take a Closer Look

What is a stamp collector called?

To find out, solve the following subtraction problems, reduce to lowest terms, and then put the letter above its corresponding answer at the bottom of the page.

I. $\frac{10}{11} - \frac{9}{11}$ = $\frac{1}{11}$
H. $\frac{12}{12} - \frac{3}{12}$ = $\frac{3}{4}$
E. $\frac{13}{14} - \frac{8}{14}$ = $\frac{5}{14}$

A. $\frac{6}{8} - \frac{4}{8}$ = $\frac{1}{4}$
L. $\frac{6}{7} - \frac{5}{7}$ = $\frac{1}{7}$
P. $\frac{6}{6} - \frac{2}{6}$ = $\frac{2}{3}$

T. $\frac{13}{14} - \frac{6}{14}$ = $\frac{1}{2}$
L. $\frac{17}{20} - \frac{8}{20}$ = $\frac{9}{20}$
S. $\frac{10}{14} - \frac{4}{14}$ = $\frac{2}{7}$

T. $\frac{8}{10} - \frac{2}{10}$ = $\frac{3}{5}$
L. $\frac{14}{18} - \frac{8}{18}$ = $\frac{1}{3}$

$\underset{\frac{2}{3}}{P} \ \underset{\frac{1}{11}}{h} \ \underset{\frac{1}{7}}{i} \ \underset{\frac{1}{4}}{l} \ \underset{\frac{5}{14}}{a} \ \underset{\frac{1}{2}}{t} \ \underset{\frac{5}{14}}{e} \ \underset{\frac{1}{3}}{l} \ \underset{\frac{1}{11}}{i} \ \underset{\frac{2}{7}}{s} \ \underset{\frac{3}{5}}{t}$

Page 144

Numeral Nibblers
Finish these number sentences.

$\frac{15}{16}$	−	$\frac{1}{2}$	=	$\frac{7}{16}$
−		−		−
$\frac{3}{4}$	−	$\frac{10}{16}$	=	$\frac{1}{8}$
=		=		=
$\frac{3}{16}$	−	$\frac{1}{8}$	=	$\frac{1}{16}$

$\frac{2}{3}$	−	$\frac{2}{12}$	=	$\frac{1}{2}$		$\frac{1}{48}$
−		−				−
$\frac{9}{24}$	−	$\frac{21}{24}$		$\frac{5}{6}$	=	$\frac{1}{24}$
=		=				=
$\frac{4}{9}$		$\frac{3}{4}$	−	$\frac{7}{12}$	=	$\frac{1}{6}$
$\frac{1}{8}$		$\frac{1}{4}$				

Page 145

Figuring Distance
Find the perimeter of each figure.

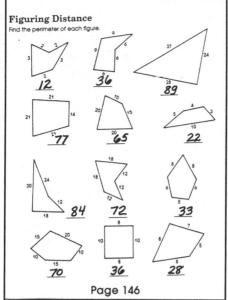

12   36   89
77   65   22
84   72   33
70   36   28

Page 146

Quilt Math
Find the perimeter and area of each quilt.

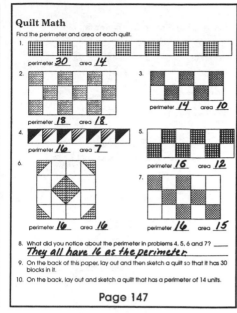

1. perimeter **30**   area **14**
2. perimeter **18**   area **18**
3. perimeter **14**   area **10**
4. perimeter **16**   area **7**
5. perimeter **16**   area **12**
6. perimeter **16**   area **16**
7. perimeter **16**   area **15**

8. What did you notice about the perimeter in problems 4, 5, 6 and 7? ____
   They all have 16 as the perimeter
9. On the back of this paper, lay out and then sketch a quilt so that it has 30 blocks in it.
10. On the back, lay out and sketch a quilt that has a perimeter of 14 units.

Page 147

Suzy Spider, Interior Decorator
Suzy Spider is decorating her house. She is a very clever decorator, but she needs your help figuring out the area and perimeter.

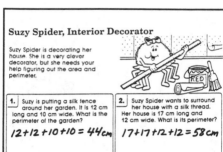

1. Suzy is putting a silk fence around her garden. It is 12 cm long and 10 cm wide. What is the perimeter of the garden?
   $12 + 12 + 10 + 10 = 44\,cm$

2. Suzy Spider wants to surround her house with a silk thread. Her house is 17 cm long and 12 cm wide. What is its perimeter?
   $17 + 17 + 12 + 12 = 58\,cm$

3. Suzy wants to carpet her living room. It is 5 cm long and 4 cm wide. How much carpet should she buy for her living room?
   $5\,cm \times 4\,cm = 20\,sq.cm$

4. Suzy wants to put wallpaper on a kitchen wall. The wall is 7 cm tall and 4 cm wide. What is its area?
   $7\,cm \times 4\,cm = 28\,sq.cm$

5. Suzy has decided to hang a silk thread all the way around her porch. The porch is 4 cm long and 3 cm wide. How long should the thread be?
   $4 + 4 + 3 + 3 = 14\,cm$

6. Suzy's bedroom is 6 cm long and 5 cm wide. How much carpet should she buy for it?
   $6\,cm \times 5\,cm = 30\,sq.cm$

Page 148

Turn Up the Volume
The volume is the measure of the inside of a space figure. Find the volume. Count the boxes.

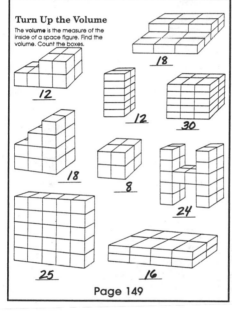

12   18
12   30
18   8
24
25   16

Page 149

Krab E. Krabby
Krab E. Krabby carries a yardstick with him everywhere he goes, and he measures everything that he can.

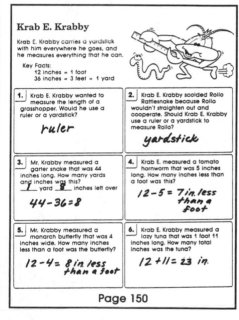

Key Facts:
12 inches = 1 foot
36 inches = 3 feet = 1 yard

1. Krab E. Krabby wanted to measure the length of a grasshopper. Would he use a ruler or a yardstick?
   ruler

2. Krab E. Krabby scolded Rollo Rattlesnake because Rollo wouldn't straighten out and cooperate. Should Krab E. Krabby use a ruler or a yardstick to measure Rollo?
   yardstick

3. Mr. Krabby measured a garter snake that was 44 inches long. How many yards and inches was this?
   1 yard **8** inches left over
   $44 - 36 = 8$

4. Krab E. measured a tomato hornworm that was 5 inches long. How many inches less than a foot was this?
   $12 - 5 = 7$ in. less than a foot

5. Mr. Krabby measured a monarch butterfly that was 4 inches wide. How many inches less than a foot was the butterfly?
   $12 - 4 = 8$ in. less than a foot

6. Krab E. Krabby measured a lazy tuna that was 1 foot 11 inches long. How many total inches was the tuna?
   $12 + 11 = 23$ in.

Page 150

Animal Math
The chart below lists some of the body statistics of 15 endangered animals. Use these measurements to solve the problems below the chart.

Animal	Height	Weight	Length
Mountain gorilla	6 feet	450 pounds	
Brown hyena	25 inches	70 pounds	3 feet **7**
Black rhinoceros	5.5 feet	4000 pounds	12 feet **1**
Cheetah	2.5 feet	100 pounds	5 feet **4**
Leopard	2 feet	150 pounds	4.5 feet **5**
Spectacled bear	2.5 feet	300 pounds	5 feet **4**
Giant armadillo		100 pounds	4 feet **6**
Vicuna	3 feet	100 pounds	
Central American tapir	3.5 feet	500 pounds	8 feet **2**
Black-footed ferret		1.5 pounds	20 inches **8**
Siberian tiger	38 inches	600 pounds	6 feet **3**
Orangutan	4.5 feet	200 pounds	
Giant panda		300 pounds	6 feet **3**
Polar Bear		1600 pounds	8 feet **2**
Yak	5.5 feet	1200 pounds	

Problems to solve:
1. What is the total height of a mountain gorilla, a vicuna and a yak? **14 ft.**
2. What is the total weight of a leopard, a cheetah and a polar bear? **1850 lb**
3. What is the total weight of a giant panda and a giant armadillo? **400 lb**
4. Add the lengths of a black rhinoceros, a spectacled bear and a Siberian tiger. **23 ft.**
5. Add the heights of two leopards, three yaks and four orangutans. **38.5 ft.**
6. Subtract the height of a vicuna from the height of a cheetah. **0**
7. Multiply the height of a Central American tapir by the height of a mountain gorilla. **21'**
8. Add the heights of a brown hyena and a Siberian tiger. **5'3"**
9. Add the weights of all the animals. **9671½ lbs**
10. For the animals whose lengths are given, arrange the lengths of the animals from longest to shortest on another sheet of paper. **See above.**

Page 151

It Suits Me to a Tee!
How many centimeters from the tee to the flag? Stay on "course"!

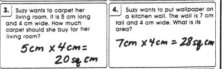

Example   12 cm

7 cm
9 cm
14 cm
16 cm
5 cm
10 cm
15 cm
6 cm

Page 152

Digging for Lost Treasure
While vacationing on Octopus Island in the Caribbean Sea, you discover an old treasure map in a bottle on the beach. Using a metric ruler, follow the directions below by plotting your movements to the location of the buried treasure using vertical and horizontal lines. Mark the spot on the map where you locate the treasure. You will be rewarded if you are correct!
1. From the starting point, go 8 centimeters east.
2. Go 6 centimeters north.
3. Go 9 centimeters east.
4. Go 3 centimeters south.
5. Go 7 centimeters west.
6. Go 5 centimeters north.
7. Go 7.5 centimeters west.
8. Go 2 centimeters north.
9. Go 9.5 centimeters east.
10. Go 10 centimeters south. Dig for treasure!

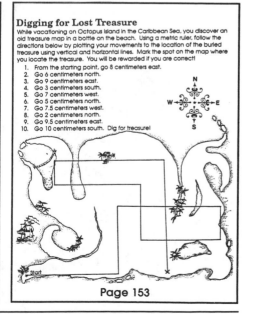

Page 153

Daily Learning Drills Grade 4

Discovering Metric Equivalents

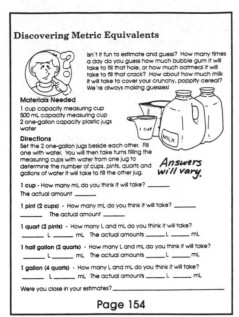

Isn't it fun to estimate and guess? How many times a day do you guess how much bubble gum it will take to fill that hole, or how much oatmeal it will take to fill that crack? How about how much milk it will take to cover your crunchy, poppity cereal? We're always making guesses!

Materials Needed
1 cup capacity measuring cup
500 mL capacity measuring cup
2 one-gallon capacity plastic jugs
water

Directions
Set the 2 one-gallon jugs beside each other. Fill one with water. You will then take turns filling the measuring cups with water from one jug to determine the number of cups, pints, quarts and gallons of water it will take to fill the other jug.

Answers will vary.

1 cup - How many mL do you think it will take? _____
The actual amount _____

1 pint (2 cups) - How many mL do you think it will take? _____
The actual amount _____

1 quart (2 pints) - How many L and mL do you think it will take?
_____ L _____ mL The actual amounts _____ L _____ mL

1 half gallon (2 quarts) - How many L and mL do you think it will take?
_____ L _____ mL The actual amounts _____ L _____ mL

1 gallon (4 quarts) - How many L and mL do you think it will take?
_____ mL The actual amounts _____ L _____ mL

Were you close in your estimates? _____

Page 154

Gliding Graphics

Draw the lines as directed from point to point for each graph.

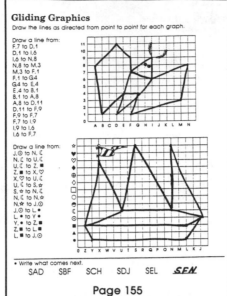

Draw a line from:
F,7 to D,1
D,1 to I,6
I,6 to N,8
N,8 to M,3
M,3 to F,1
F,1 to G,4
G,4 to E,4
E,4 to B,1
B,1 to A,8
A,8 to D,11
D,11 to F,9
F,9 to F,7
F,7 to I,9
I,9 to I,6
I,6 to F,7

Draw a line from:
J,☉ to N,◖
N,◖ to U,◖
U,◖ to Z,■
Z,■ to X,♡
X,♡ to U,◖
U,◖ to S,☆
N,◖ to N,✦
N,✦ to N,☆
N,☆ to J,☉
J,☉ to L,♦
L,♦ to Y,●
Y,● to Z,■
Z,■ to L,■
L,■ to J,☉

• Write what comes next.

SAD SBF SCH SDJ SEL *SFN*

Page 155

School Statistics

Read each graph and do as directed.

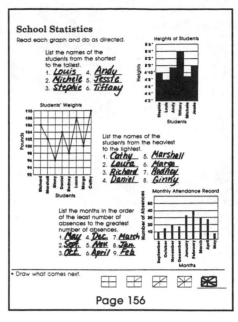

List the names of the students from the shortest to the tallest.
1. *Louis*   4. *Andy*
2. *Michele* 5. *Jessie*
3. *Stephie* 6. *Tiffany*

List the names of the students from the heaviest to the lightest.
1. *Cathy*   5. *Marshell*
2. *Laura*   6. *Margo*
3. *Richard*   7. *Rodney*
4. *Daniel*   8. *Ginny*

List the months in the order of the least number of absences to the greatest number of absences.
1. *May*   4. *Dec*   7. *March*
2. *Sept* 5. *Nov*   8. *Jan*
3. *Oct*   6. *April* 9. *Feb*

• Draw what comes next.

Page 156

It's About Time!

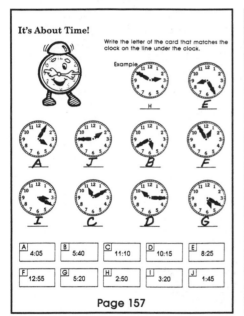

Write the letter of the card that matches the clock on the line under the clock.

Example

A	B	C	D	E
4:05	5:40	11:10	10:15	8:25

F	G	H	I	J
12:55	5:20	2:50	3:20	1:45

Page 157

Father Time Teasers

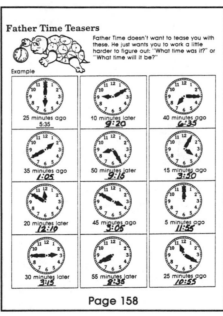

Father Time doesn't want to tease you with these. He just wants you to work a little harder to figure out: "What time was it?" or "What time will it be?"

Example

25 minutes ago *5:35*
10 minutes later *9:20*
40 minutes ago *6:35*

35 minutes ago *1:05*
50 minutes later *9:15*
15 minutes ago *3:50*

20 minutes later *12:10*
45 minutes ago *5:05*
5 minutes ago *11:55*

30 minutes later *3:15*
55 minutes later *8:35*
25 minutes ago *10:55*

Page 158

Time "Tables"

"Set" these tables by drawing the hands on these clocks.

Example

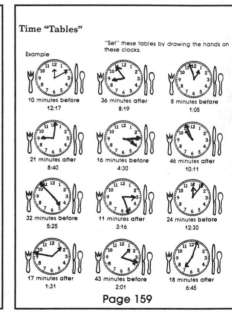

10 minutes before 12:17
36 minutes after 8:19
8 minutes before 1:05

21 minutes after 8:40
16 minutes before 4:30
46 minutes after 10:11

32 minutes before 5:25
11 minutes after 3:16
24 minutes before 12:30

17 minutes after 1:31
43 minutes before 2:01
18 minutes after 6:45

Page 159

Time Problems

Draw the hands on the clocks to show the starting time and the ending time. Then write the answer to the problem.

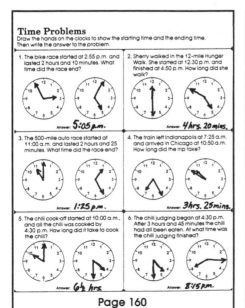

1. The bike race started at 2:55 p.m. and lasted 2 hours and 10 minutes. What time did the race end?
Answer: *5:05 p.m.*

2. Sherry walked in the 12-mile Hunger Walk. She started at 12:30 p.m. and finished at 4:50 p.m. How long did she walk?
Answer: *4 hrs. 20 mins.*

3. The 500-mile auto race started at 11:00 a.m. and lasted 2 hours and 25 minutes. What time did the race end?
Answer: *1:25 p.m.*

4. The train left Indianapolis at 7:25 a.m. and arrived in Chicago at 10:50 a.m. How long did the trip take?
Answer: *3 hrs. 25 mins.*

5. The chili cook-off started at 10:00 a.m., and all the chili was cooked by 4:30 p.m. How long did it take to cook the chili?
Answer: *6½ hrs*

6. The chili judging began at 4:30 p.m. After 3 hours and 45 minutes the chili had all been eaten. At what time was the chili judging finished?
Answer: *8:15 p.m.*

Page 160

Super Savers!

Adding money means you're saving money! Keep saving. It adds up. Here are a few success stories. Add 'em up!

Sam's Account
$8.03
.84
+ 5.47
$14.34

Debbie's Account
$45.32
2.41
+ 34.28
82.01

Sarah's Account
$85.42
12.58
+ 2.21
100.21

Roberto's Account
$41.46
8.89
+ ___
50.35

Cheryl's Account
$54.26
3.04
+ .25
57.55

Alex's Account
$ 4.06
81.23
+ 2.84
88.13

Eva's Account
$89.42
3.06
+ .94
93.42

Bill's Account
$62.41
3.84
+ 64.21
130.46

Monica's Account
$20.04
3.42
+ 25.81
49.27

David's Account
$56.04
2.81
+ .94
59.79

Tom's Account
$ 8.05
21.21
+ .98
30.24

Andy's Account
$ .47
31.24
+ 2.38
34.09

Earl's Account
$50.42
3.84
+ .98
55.24

Mark's Account
$21.46
20.00
+ 5.58
47.04

Michele's Account
$ .55
30.24
+ 3.49
34.28

Katelyn's Account
$ .42
.59
+ 3.42
4.43

Kimberly's Account
$ 5.42
40.64
+ 3.89
49.95

Gwen's Account
$60.42
3.84
+ 21.25
85.51

Whose account is the largest? *Bill's*
Whose is the smallest? *Katelyn's*
Whose is closest to $50? *Kimberly's*

Page 161

Match the $ale

Which item did each of the kids purchase? Calculate the amount. Write the purchase price in each blank.

Jessica:
$17.43
- 8.29
$9.14

Tammy:
$43.21
- 8.35
$34.86

Heather:
$10.06
- 8.42
$1.64

Mark:
$52.46
- 38.29
$14.17

Eva:
$65.04
- 28.10
$36.94

Roger:
$3.45
- .89
$2.56

Monica:
$6.99
- 3.43
$3.56

Katelyn:
$9.06
- 3.82
$5.24

David:
$15.25
- 8.43
$6.82

Curt:
$63.45
- 17.29
$46.16

Michele:
$32.45
- 18.95
$13.50

Carolyn:
$18.46
- 3.97
$14.49

Gwen:
$19.24
- 12.86
$6.38

Thomas:
$9.43
- 3.84
$5.59

$8.35
$28.10
$3.43
$18.95
$8.43
$3.84
$3.82
$12.86
$3.97
.89
$17.29
$8.29
$8.42
$38.29

Page 162

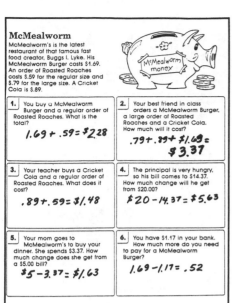

McMealworm

McMealworm's is the latest restaurant of that famous fast food creator, Buggs I. Lyke. His McMealworm Burger costs $1.69. An order of Roasted Roaches costs $.59 for the regular size and $.79 for the large size. A Cricket Cola is $.89.

1. You buy a McMealworm Burger and a regular order of Roasted Roaches. What is the total?

$1.69 + .59 = \$2.28$

2. Your best friend in class orders a McMealworm Burger, a large order of Roasted Roaches and a Cricket Cola. How much will it cost?

$.79 + .89 + 1.69 = \$3.37$

3. Your teacher buys a Cricket Cola and a regular order of Roasted Roaches. What does it cost?

$.89 + .59 = \$1.48$

4. The principal is very hungry, so his bill comes to $14.37. How much change will he get from $20.00?

$\$20 - 14.37 = \$5.63$

5. Your mom goes to McMealworm to buy your dinner. She spends $3.37. How much change does she get from a $5.00 bill?

$\$5 - 3.37 = \$1.63$

6. You have $1.17 in your bank. How much more do you need to pay for a McMealworm Burger?

$1.69 - 1.17 = .52$

Page 163

One-Stop Shopping

Stash McCash is shopping! Find the total cost of the items. Then find how much change Stash should receive.

$3.36 $.94 $.27 $2.68 $4.25
$3.99 $.88 $1.54 $3.15 $1.49
$3.61 $.77 $1.27 $2.49 $2.55

Example

Stash has $5.00 Buys	Stash has $8.50 Buys	Stash has $7.04 Buys	Stash has $9.00 Buys
.88 .77 +1.54 3.19	1.27 3.99 +2.68 7.94	1.49 3.15 +.27 4.91	3.15 3.61 +.88 7.64
5.00 −3.19 1.81 Change	8.50 −7.94 .56 Change	7.04 −4.91 2.13 Change	9.00 −7.64 1.36 Change

Stash has $10.95 Buys	Stash has $10.00 Buys	Stash has $9.24 Buys	Stash has $8.09 Buys
3.36 2.49 +4.25 10.10	2.55 3.61 +.94 7.10	4.25 1.27 1.54 7.06	2.49 2.68 +.94 6.11
10.95 −10.10 .85 Change	10.00 −7.10 2.90 Change	9.24 −7.06 2.18 Change	8.09 −6.11 1.98 Change

Page 164

Shifty Sam's Shop

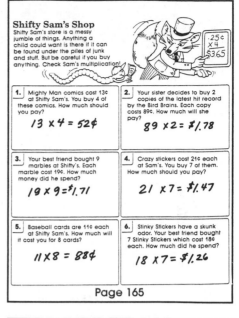

Shifty Sam's store is a messy jumble of things. Anything a child could want is there if it can be found under the piles of junk and stuff. But be careful if you buy anything. Check Sam's multiplication!

1. Mighty Man comics cost 13¢ at Shifty Sam's. You buy 4 of these comics. How much should you pay?

$13 \times 4 = 52¢$

2. Your sister decides to buy 2 copies of the latest hit record by the Bird Brains. Each copy costs 89¢. How much will she pay?

$89 \times 2 = \$1.78$

3. Your best friend bought 9 marbles at Shifty's. Each marble costs 19¢. How much money did he spend?

$19 \times 9 = \$1.71$

4. Crazy stickers cost 21¢ each at Sam's. You buy 7 of them. How much should you pay?

$21 \times 7 = \$1.47$

5. Baseball cards are 11¢ each at Shifty Sam's. How much will it cost you for 8 cards?

$11 \times 8 = 88¢$

6. Stinky Stickers have a skunk odor. Your best friend bought 7 Stinky Stickers which cost 18¢ each. How much did he spend?

$18 \times 7 = \$1.26$

Page 165

What a Great Catch!

This is "fishy" business! Use your money "sense" to solve these problems.

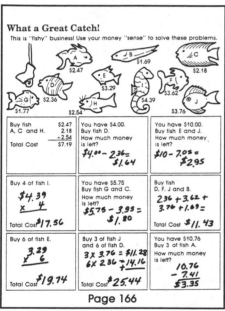

A $2.47 B $1.69 C $2.18
D (E) $3.29 F (I) $3.62
G $2.36 $4.39
$1.77 H $2.54

Buy fish A, C and H. Total Cost	You have $4.00. Buy fish D. How much money is left?	You have $10.00. Buy fish E and J. How much money is left?
2.47 2.18 +2.54 $7.19	$4.00 − 2.36 = $1.64	$10 − 7.05 = $2.95
Buy 4 of fish I. Total Cost $17.56	You have $5.75. Buy fish G and C. How much money is left?	Buy fish D, F, J and B. Total Cost $11.43
$4.39 × 4 = $17.56	$5.75 − 3.95 = $1.80	2.36 + 3.62 + 3.76 + 1.69 = $11.43
Buy 6 of fish E. Total Cost $19.74	Buy 3 of fish J and 6 of fish D. Total Cost $25.44	Buy 3 of fish A. How much money is left?
3.29 × 6 = $19.74	3 × 3.76 = $11.28 6 × 2.36 = +14.16 $25.44	$10.76 − 7.41 = $3.35

Page 166

Money Math

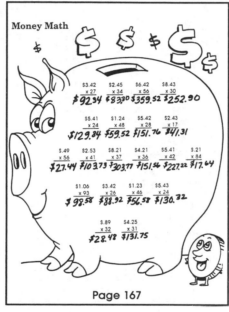

$3.42 $2.45 $6.42 $8.43
×27 ×34 ×56 ×30
$92.34 $83.30 $359.52 $252.90

$5.41 $1.24 $5.42 $2.43
×24 ×48 ×28 ×17
$129.84 $59.52 $151.76 $41.31

$.49 $2.53 $8.21 $4.21 $5.41 $.21
×56 ×41 ×37 ×36 ×42 ×84
$27.44 $103.73 $303.77 $151.56 $227.22 $17.64

$1.06 $3.42 $1.23 $5.43
×93 ×26 ×46 ×24
$98.58 $88.92 $56.58 $130.32

$.89 $4.25
×32 ×31
$28.48 $131.75

Page 167

Sam Sillicook's Doughnut Shoppe

Sam Sillicook believes that you should put a little jelly in your belly. He has invented the Super Duper Jelly Doughnuts that are so full of jelly, they leak. His Twisted Circles are drenched in sugar. He has also invented the Banana Cream Doughnut and Jam-jammed Cream Puffs.

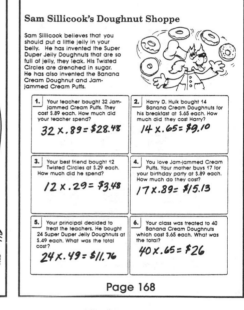

1. Your teacher bought 32 Jam-jammed Cream Puffs. They cost $.89 each. How much did your teacher spend?

$32 \times .89 = \$28.48$

2. Harry D. Hulk bought 14 Banana Cream Doughnuts for his breakfast at $.65 each. How much did they cost Harry?

$14 \times .65 = \$9.10$

3. Your best friend bought 12 Twisted Circles at $.29 each. How much did he spend?

$12 \times .29 = \$3.48$

4. You love Jam-jammed Cream Puffs. Your mother buys 17 for your birthday party at $.89 each. How much do they cost?

$17 \times .89 = \$15.13$

5. Your principal decided to treat the teachers. He bought 24 Super Duper Jelly Doughnuts at $.49 each. What was the total cost?

$24 \times .49 = \$11.76$

6. Your class was treated to 40 Banana Cream Doughnuts which cost $.65 each. What was the total?

$40 \times .65 = \$26$

Page 168

Perplexing Problems

Heather and Gwen went to the water park. How much did each of them pay? Total: $9.68	On Saturday, James, Gary, Ted and Paul went to the zoo. What was their individual cost to get in? Total: $8.72
$4.84	$2.18

Mark, David, Curt and Sam rented a motorized skateboard for 1 hour. What was the cost for each of them — split equally 4 ways? Total: $7.36 $1.84	Five students pitched in to buy Mr. Jokestopper a birthday gift. How much did each of them contribute? Total: $9.60 $1.92	All 6 members of the volleyball team received a special shirt for being in the final game. What was the amount of each shirt? Total: $8.16 $1.36

Mary, Cheryl and Betty went to the skating rink. What was their individual cost? Total: $7.44 $2.48	Carol, Katelyn and Kimberly bought lunch at their favorite salad shop. What did each of them pay for lunch? Total: $8.52 $2.84	Debbie, Sarah, Michele and Kelly earned $6.56 altogether for collecting cans. How much did each of them earn individually? Total: $6.56 $1.64

Five friends went to the Hamburger Hot Spot Cafe for lunch. They all ordered the special. What did each pay? Total: $7.45 $1.49	Lee and Ricardo purchased an awesome model rocket together. What was the cost for each of them? Total: $9.52 $4.76	The total fee for Erik, Bill and Steve to enter the science museum was $8.76. What amount did each of them pay? Total: $8.76 $2.92

Page 169

Too Much Information

Underline the distractor and solve the problems.

1. All 20 of the students from Sandy's class went to the movies. Tickets cost $1.50 each. Drinks cost 55¢ each. How much altogether did the students spend on tickets?

$20 \times \$1.50 = \$30$

2. Of the students, 11 were girls and 9 were boys. At $1.50 per ticket, how much did the boys' tickets cost altogether?

$9 \times \$1.50 = \$13.50$

3. While 5 students had ice cream, 12 others had candy. Ice cream cost 75¢ per cup. How much did the students spend on ice cream?

$5 \times 75¢ = \$3.75$

4. 7 of the 20 students did not like the movie. 3 of the 20 students had seen the movie before. How many students had not seen the movie before?

$20 - 3 = 17$

5. Mary paid 55¢ for an orange drink and 65¢ for a candy bar. Sarah paid 45¢ for popcorn. How much did Mary's refreshments cost her?

$55¢ + 65¢ = \$1.20$

6. 6 of the students spent a total of $16.50 for refreshments and $9.00 for their tickets. How much did each spend for refreshments?

$\$16.50 \div 6 = \$2.75$

7. 10 of the students went back to see the movie again the next day. Each student spent $1.50 for a ticket, 45¢ for popcorn and 55¢ for a soft drink. How much did each student pay?

$\$1.50 + .45 + .55 = \$2.50$

Page 170

Get the Point

When you add or subtract decimals, remember to "include the point."

Add	Subtract
3.6 +3.3 6.9	6.8 −2.6 4.2

4.2 +5.2 9.4	6.4 +1.4 7.8	3.1 +7.8 10.9	4.7 +3.2 7.9	4.9 +2.0 6.9	3.4 +1.2 4.6
5.9 −3.2 2.7	6.7 −5.6 1.1	7.8 −2.5 5.3	5.8 −3.3 2.5	3.9 −1.5 2.4	5.8 −2.2 3.6
.23 +.25 .48	.43 +.16 .59	.26 +.42 .68	.64 +.15 .79	.68 +.31 .99	.26 +.31 .57
.87 −.42 .45	.98 −.35 .63	.79 −.15 .64	.87 −.67 .20	.83 −.12 .71	.96 −.12 .84
3.13 +2.26 5.39	4.72 +1.15 5.87	6.87 +2.11 8.98	4.98 −2.32 2.66	5.97 −2.54 3.43	5.89 −1.35 4.54
4.86 −1.76 3.10	5.86 −3.83 2.03	6.98 −1.45 5.53	6.73 +1.15 7.88	4.27 +5.52 9.79	3.46 +2.31 5.77

Page 171

Doing Decimals

DECIMAL POINT—A dot placed between the ones place and the tenths place

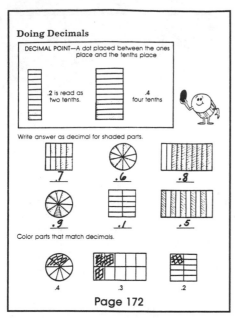

.2 is read as two tenths

.4 four tenths

Write answer as decimal for shaded parts.

.7   .6   .8

.9   .1   .5

Color parts that match decimals.

.4   .3   .2

Page 172

Animal Trivia

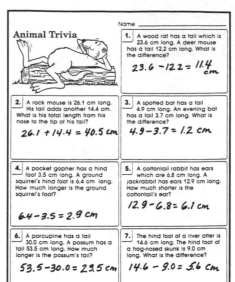

1. A wood rat has a tail which is 23.6 cm long. A deer mouse has a tail 12.2 cm long. What is the difference?

$23.6 - 12.2 = 11.4$ cm

2. A rock mouse is 26.1 cm long. His tail adds another 14.4 cm. What is his total length from his nose to the tip of his tail?

$26.1 + 14.4 = 40.5$ cm

3. A spotted bat has a tail 4.9 cm long. An evening bat has a tail 3.7 cm long. What is the difference?

$4.9 - 3.7 = 1.2$ cm

4. A pocket gopher has a hind foot 3.5 cm long. A ground squirrel's hind foot is 6.4 cm long. How much longer is the ground squirrel's foot?

$6.4 - 3.5 = 2.9$ cm

5. A cottontail rabbit has ears which are 6.8 cm long. A jackrabbit has ears 12.9 cm long. How much shorter is the cottontail's ear?

$12.9 - 6.8 = 6.1$ cm

6. A porcupine has a tail 30.0 cm long. A possum has a tail 53.5 cm long. How much longer is the possum's tail?

$53.5 - 30.0 = 23.5$ cm

7. The hind foot of a river otter is 14.6 cm long. The hind foot of a hog-nosed skunk is 9.0 cm long. What is the difference?

$14.6 - 9.0 = 5.6$ cm

Page 173

Living History Books

You can learn a lot about a tree by reading its special calendar of rings. Every year a tree grows a new layer of wood. This makes the tree trunk get fatter and fatter. The new layer makes a ring.

You can see the rings on a freshly cut tree stump. When the growing season is wet, the tree grows a lot and the rings are wide. When the season is dry, the tree grows very little. Then the rings are narrow.

This tree was planted in 1973. Use the picture clues to color the rings of the tree stump. Where will the very first ring be?

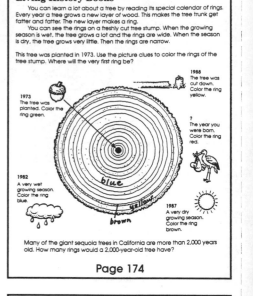

1988 The tree was cut down. Color the ring yellow.

1973 The tree was planted. Color the ring green.

? The year you were born. Color the ring red.

1982 A very wet growing season. Color the ring blue.

blue   yellow

1987 A very dry growing season. Color the ring brown.

brown

Many of the giant sequoia trees in California are more than 2,000 years old. How many rings would a 2,000-year-old tree have?

Page 174

Jogging Geraniums

You will probably never see a flower running down the sidewalk, but you might see one climbing a fence. Most plants are rooted in one place, but they still move.

Roots, stems, leaves, and even flowers move in different ways. The leaves grow toward the light. Roots will grow toward water. Even gravity will make a plant grow straight up in the air, away from the center of the earth.

Look at the three plants below. Tell what made the plants "move" or grow the way they did.

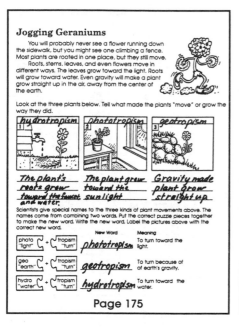

hydrotropism   phototropism   geotropism

The plant's roots grew toward the faucet and water.

The plant grew toward the sunlight.

Gravity made plant grow straight up.

Scientists give special names to the three kinds of plant movements above. The names come from combining two words. Put the correct puzzle pieces together to make the new word. Write the new word. Label the pictures above with the correct new word.

			New Word	Meaning
photo "light"	+	tropism "turn"	phototropism	To turn toward the light.
geo "earth"	+	tropism "turn"	geotropism	To turn because of of earth's gravity.
hydro "water"	+	tropism "turn"	hydrotropism	To turn toward the water.

Page 175

Cruising Coconuts

"Look at this coconut!" Amy called to Matt as they walked along the beach. Safe inside its thick husk, the coconut had floated across the water. Once it washed up on shore, the green leaves sprouted from this large seed.

Seeds travel in many ways. Below are five ways that seeds travel. Tell how each seed travels.

Answers may vary.
Seeds are carried by people and planted.

Seeds are carried by water.

Seeds are carried by attaching themselves to clothing.

Seeds are carried by wind.

Seeds are carried by animals.

Fun Fact
Blast Off
The seed pod of the "touch-me-not" swells as it gets ripe. Finally the seed pod bursts and launches seeds in all directions.

Page 176

Corny Medicine

Use the words from the Word Bank to complete the puzzle. Cross out each word in the Word Bank as you use it. The remaining words in the Word Bank will help you answer the "Corny Medicine" riddle.

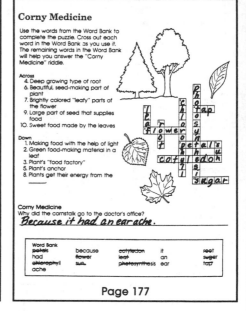

Across
4. Deep growing type of root
6. Beautiful, seed-making part of plant
7. Brightly colored "leafy" parts of the flower
9. Large part of seed that supplies food
10. Sweet food made by the leaves

Down
1. Making food with the help of light
2. Green food-making material in a leaf
3. Plant's "food factory"
5. Plant's anchor
8. Plants get their energy from the

Corny Medicine
Why did the cornstalk go to the doctor's office?
Because it had an ear ache.

Word Bank				
~~petals~~	because	~~cotyledon~~	it	~~root~~
had	flower	leaf	an	sugar
~~chlorophyll~~	sun	photosynthesis	ear	tap
ache				

Page 177

Guess What?

Use the following hints and the Word Bank to decide what insect each riddle describes.

1. I have stout, spiny forelegs.
   I eat insects, including some of my own kind.
   I camouflage well in my surroundings.
   My forelegs make me appear to be praying.
   What am I? **praying mantis**

2. I have clear wings.
   My body is quite round.
   The males of my species make long, shrill sounds in summer.
   Some of us take 17 years to develop.
   What am I? **cicada**

3. I have two pairs of long, thin wings.
   I eat mosquitoes and other small insects.
   I live near lakes, ponds, streams and rivers.
   My abdomen is very long . . . as long as a darning needle.
   What am I? **dragonfly**

4. I am a type of beetle.
   My young are often called glowworms.
   My abdomen produces light.
   What am I? **lightning bug**

5. I like warm, damp and dark places and come out at night.
   Humans hate me.
   I am a destructive household pest.
   I am closely related to grasshoppers and crickets.
   What am I? **cockroach**

Word Bank			
lightning bug	cicada	dragonfly	termite
mosquito	ladybug	aphid	praying mantis
bumblebee	cockroach		

Challenge: Research an insect. Draw a detailed picture and write a report about it.

Page 178

Going Places

Looking at a bird's feet can tell you a lot about how they are used. Look at the bird's feet below. Unscramble the bird's name. Write the bird's name by the best sentence. Can you match the pictures with the names?

duck "My webbed feet are great for swimming."

woodpecker "My feet are great for walking up trees."

heron "I use my feet with long toes to wade in the water and mud."

hawk "I use my strong, powerful feet to catch small animals."

kawh — hawk (ckud)
noreh — heron (reckwoodep)
duck — woodpecker

Can the shape of a bird's bill tell you anything about what it eats? Look closely at the bills below. Unscramble the bird's name. Write the bird's name by the best sentence. Can you match the pictures with the names?

woodpecker "I pound holes in wood to find insects."

hummingbird "I use my long bill to get nectar from flowers."

cardinal "I use my strong bill to crack open seeds."

hawk "I use my sharp bill to tear the flesh of animals."

heron "I stab at small fish with my sharp bill."

pelican "I scoop up large mouthfuls of water and fish."

noreh — heron (bummingbird)
reckwoodep — woodpecker (kawh)
hummingbird (panicel) — hawk
pelican — cardinal

Page 179

Family Ties

Unscramble the names of the mom, pop, and baby of these animal families. The coordinates in front of each scrambled name tell where to write it on the chart.

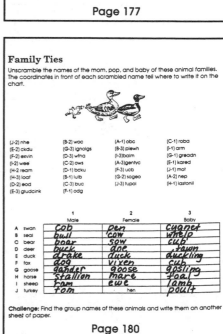

(J-2) nhe	(B-2) woc	(A-1) obc	(C-1) roba
(E-2) ckdu	(G-3) ignolgs	(B-3) plewh	(I-1) arm
(F-2) eervin	(D-3) wfna	(I-3)baim	(G-1) greadn
(I-2) wee	(C-2) ows	(A-3)gentvc	(E-1) kared
(H-2) ream	(D-1) bcku	(F-3) ucb	(J-1) mot
(H-3) loaf	(B-1) lulb	(G-2) sogeo	(A-2) nep
(D-2) eod	(C-3) buc	(J-3) tupoi	(H-1) lastonil
(E-3) gludcink	(F-1) odg		

		1	2	3
		Male	Female	Baby
A	swan	cob	pen	cygnet
B	seal	bull	cow	whelp
C	bear	boar	sow	cub
D	deer	buck	doe	fawn
E	duck	drake	duck	duckling
F	fox	dog	vixen	cub
G	goose	gander	goose	gosling
H	horse	stallion	mare	foal
I	sheep	ram	ewe	lamb
J	turkey	tom	hen	poult

Challenge: Find the group names of these animals and write them on another sheet of paper.

Page 180

Adopt an Animal

The seas of the world are filled with an amazing variety of life. Starfish, crabs, flying fish, angelfish, worms, turtles, sharks and whales all make their home underwater. The shape, color and size of most sea animals depend on their lifestyle and where they live in the seas. Select a sea animal and become an expert on it. Research your animal and complete the profile below. *Answers will vary.*

Common Name _____

Scientific Name _____

Description	Picture
weight:	
length:	
body shape:	
tail shape:	
color:	
unusual characteristics:	

Behaviors

Description of Habitat: _____

Food and Feeding Habits: _____

Migration (if applicable): _____

Page 181

Food Chains

All living things in the seas depend on each other for food. The food chain begins with sea plants called phytoplankton. A huge variety of tiny animals called zooplankton, feed on the phytoplankton. These animals include shrimp, copepods, and jellyfish. Some of the most common fish—herring, anchovies, and sprats—feed on zooplankton. These fish are eaten by others, such as tuna and mackerel, which in turn are eaten by the superpredators, such as sharks and dolphins. This pattern of eating is called a food chain.

Use the diagram to answer the following questions on another piece of paper.

Answers will vary.

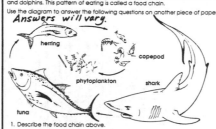

1. Describe the food chain above.
2. If there was a decrease in the copepod population, what would happen to the herring population? Why? *It would decrease. Not enough food.*
3. What would happen to the phytoplankton population? Why? *Increase. Less predators.*
4. If the tuna population became endangered, what would the result be? *Chain would be disrupted.*
5. What does it mean when we say, "The death of one species in the food chain upsets the rest of the chain"? *All are dependent on each other.*
6. An example of a land food chain might be fly-spider-bird-cat. Give an other example of a land food chain.
7. Draw another sea food chain. Explain and give an example for each step.

Page 182

Polluting Our Seas

The seas provide us with many resources that we need to survive and to keep our industries going. Fish, shellfish, seaweeds, and minerals are just a few of the seas' resources. How long these will last depends on if and how badly we continue to pollute the seas.

For hundreds of years, people have been throwing garbage into the seas. Every day, billions of tons of waste, such as poisonous chemicals, radioactive waste, and plastics, are dumped into the seas. One of the worst sources of pollution is an oil spill. This results when tankers collide with each other or crash into rocks. There are thousands of oil spills every year. Most are small and are not reported, but some are huge. The biggest was in February, 1991, when oil was spilled into the Persian Gulf. It is thought that more than 1.2 million tons of oil spilled into the sea. It was more than 20 times bigger than the *Exxon Valdez* oil spill in 1989 off the coast of Alaska.

The seas cannot continue to be polluted without endangering the sea life. As the world population increases, people will be looking more to the seas to find products and resources.

Pretend you are a reporter. Use the headline below to write an article about pollution of the seas. Research to find interesting facts to back up your story. *Articles will vary.*

Save Our Seas

Page 183

Animal Comparisons

A Venn diagram is a great way to compare things. Use the one below to compare two animals of the seas. Fill in the circle below the dolphin with characteristics common only to this animal. Fill in the circle below the shark with characteristics common only to the shark. Where the circles overlap, fill in characteristics both animals share. Write a story about your findings on another piece of paper.

Answers will vary.

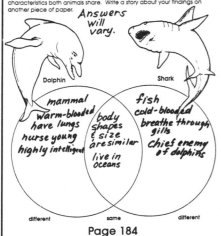

Dolphin — mammal, warm-blooded, have lungs, nurse young, highly intelligent

body shapes & size are similar, live in oceans

Shark — fish, cold-blooded, breathe through gills, chief enemy of dolphins

different — same — different

Page 184

Danger Ahead!

You will never see a dodo bird or a saber-tooth tiger. These animals are gone forever. They are extinct.

The animals on this page are not extinct, but they are in danger of becoming extinct. They are endangered. There may not be enough of them to reproduce. They are endangered because of the way people live.

There are many reasons why some animals are endangered. The signs on this page give clues to three main reasons.

Look at the signs. What do you think the three reasons are? Write them below.

1. *Loss of habitat - trees cut down.*
2. *Hunting. Animals are killed by man though hunting of some animals is sometimes necessary.*
3. *Pollution destroys habitats and also introduces poisons.*

Unscramble the names of these endangered animals.

bald eagle   green turtle   blue whale   timber wolf

• There are more than 100 endangered animals in North America. Find the name of one that lives near your area. Make a poster to help people become aware of this animal and the danger it is in.

Page 185

Threatened and Endangered Animals

Many of the earth's animals are threatened or extinct. Use the names of the animals to build a puzzle. Only use the bold-faced words.
Hint: Build off **rhinoceros**.

Word Box			
brown hyena	Darwin's **rhea**	red **wolf**	black-footed **ferret**
Spanish **lynx**	**Philippine eagle**	**gavial**	ring-tailed lemur
giant **panda**	blue whale	numbat	resplendent **quetzal**
Arabian **oryx**	Grevy's **zebra**	**kakapo**	Galapagos **penguin**
Indian **python**	wild **yak**	**dugong**	

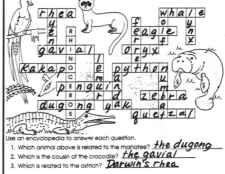

Use an encyclopedia to answer each question.
1. Which animal above is related to the manatee? *the dugong*
2. Which is the cousin of the crocodile? *the gavial*
3. Which is related to the ostrich? *Darwin's rhea*

Page 186

Animal Magic

Read Column A. Choose an answer from Column B. Write the number of the answer in the Magic Square. The first one has been done for you.

Column A		Column B
A.	grizzly bear	1. large bear of the American grasslands
B.	koala	2. lives on dry grasslands of South Africa
C.	peregrine falcon	3. the most valuable reptile in the world
D.	California condor	4. largest soaring bird of North America
E.	black-footed ferret	5. the tallest American bird
F.	cheetah	6. the fastest animal on land
G.	orangutan	7. the only great ape outside Africa
H.	giant panda	8. large aquatic sealike animal
I.	Florida manatee	9. large black and white mammal of China
J.	kit fox	10. small, fast mammal; nocturnal predator
K.	blue whale	11. largest animal in the world
L.	whooping crane	12. member of the weasel family
M.	red wolf	13. has interbred with coyotes in some areas
N.	green sea turtle	14. also called a duck hawk; size of a crow
O.	brown hyena	15. eats leaves of the eucalyptus tree
P.	jaguar	16. known as *el tigre* in Spanish

A 1	B 15	C 14	D 4
E 12	F 6	G 7	H 9
I 8	J 10	K 11	L 5
M 13	N 3	O 2	P 16

Add the numbers across, down and diagonally. What answer do you get? *34*

Why do you think this is called a magic square? _____

Page 187

Bald Eagle Puzzler

Read each statement about the bald eagle. If the statement is false, darken the letter in the circle to the left of that statement. The letters not darkened spell out the name of the chemical that affected the bald eagle's food supply.

- (P) Due to federal protection, the bald eagle population is increasing.
- ● It is legal to shoot this bird today.
- (E) This bird has keen eyesight and strong wings.
- ● The wingspan of this bird is about 3 feet.
- ● The nest of a bald eagle is made of mud and rocks.
- (S) This bird eats mainly fish.
- ● This bird likes to eat only berries and seeds.
- (T) The bald eagle is found only in North America.
- ● Only four bald eagles exist today in the United States.
- ● An injured bald eagle may be kept as a pet.
- (I) Chemical poisons in the bald eagle's food caused its eggs to crack before incubation could be completed.
- (C) The nest of a bald eagle is built high on a cliff or in a tree.
- (I) This bird is the national symbol of the United States.
- ● The bald eagle is noted for its bright orange head.
- (D) The bald eagle has a hooked beak.
- (E) The nest of a bald eagle is called an aerie.

What is the type of chemical? *pesticide*

Page 188

Nippers, Rippers, and Grinders

1.   2.   3.

Scientists tell us that some of the dinosaurs were meat-eaters and others were plant-eaters. But how do the scientists know? By looking at the teeth of certain dinosaur fossils, scientists can tell what those dinosaurs ate. Meat-eaters had sharp, saw-edged teeth (figure 1), for cutting and ripping flesh. Plant-eating dinosaurs had either peg-like teeth (figure 2), for nipping plants, or flat grinding teeth (figure 3), to munch tough twigs or leaves.

1. Match the dinosaur to its teeth by writing its name in the space provided.
2. Circle either "M" for meat-eater or "P" for plant-eater.

		Meat-eater or Plant-eater
Tyrannosaurus (tie-ran-o-SAWR-us)	*Hypsilophodon*	Ⓜ P
Parasaurolophus (par-uh-sawr-uh-LOW-fus)	*Monoclonius*	M Ⓟ
Monoclonius (man-no-KLONE-ee-us)	*Tyrannosaurus*	Ⓜ P
Hypsilophodon (HIP-sil-ahf-oh-don)	*Parasaurolophus*	M Ⓟ
Triceratops (try-SAIR-uh-tops)	*Triceratops*	M Ⓟ

Fantastic Fact

The Tyrannosaurus, whose name means "king of the tyrant lizards," was the largest meat-eater. It weighed over 8 tons and was over 15 meters long. Its teeth were over 15 cm long and had edges like a steak knife.

Page 189

Daily Learning Drills Grade 4

Dinosaur Defense

How did the plant-eating dinosaurs protect themselves from the attacks of the fierce meat-eating dinosaurs? One way was to travel in groups. But they also had other ways to defend themselves. For example, some had horns and some could run very fast.

• Look at the plant-eating dinosaurs below. Find the features of their bodies that gave them protection from their enemies. Explain in the space provided.

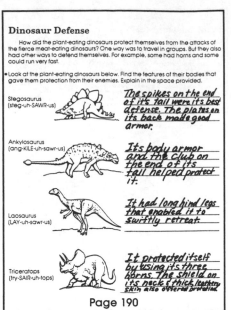

Stegosaurus (steg-uh-SAWR-us)

The spikes on the end of its tail were its best defense. The plates on its back made good armor.

Ankylosaurus (ang-KILE-uh-sawr-us)

Its body armor and the club on the end of its tail helped protect it.

Laosaurus (LAY-uh-sawr-us)

It had long hind legs that enabled it to swiftly retreat.

Triceratops (try-SAIR-uh-tops)

It protected itself by using its three horns. The shield on its neck & thick leathery skin also offered protection.

Page 190

Dino-Find

Find the hidden words in the puzzle below. The words may be written forward, backward, up, down or diagonally. Circle the words. When you have located and circled all the words, write the remaining letters at the bottom of the page to spell out a message.

ALLOSAURUS	BIRD HIP	FOSSIL	PLANT-EATER
APATOSAURUS	COELURUS	JURASSIC	PLATED
ARMORED	DINOSAUR	MEAT-EATER	SAUROPOD
ARCHAEOPTERYX	DIPLODOCUS	PALEONTOLOGIST	STEGOSAURUS

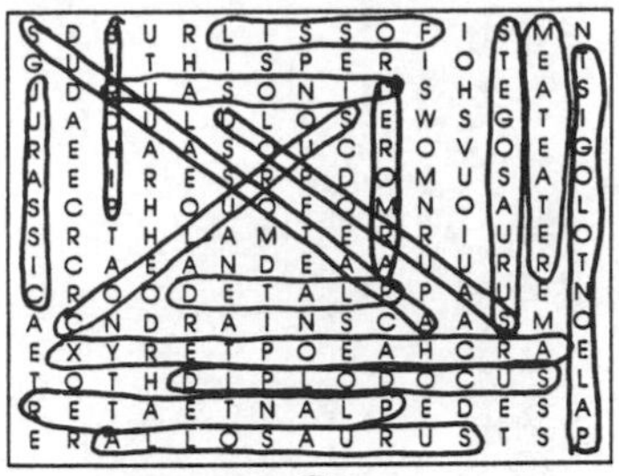

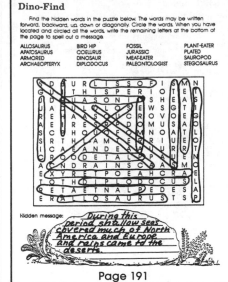

Hidden message:

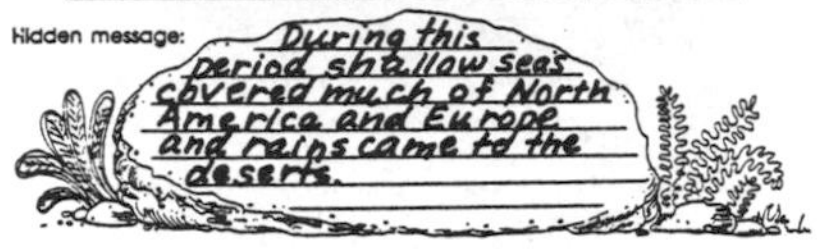
During this period shallow seas covered much of North America and Europe and rains came to the deserts.

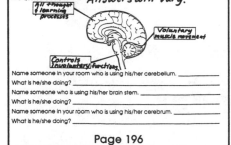

Page 191

Body Building Blocks

Just as some houses are built with bricks, your body is built with cells. Your body is made up of about 500 trillion **cells**.

Cells differ in **size** and **shape**, but they all have a few things in common. All cells have a nucleus. The **nucleus** is the center of the cell. It controls the cell's activities. Cells can **divide** and become two cells exactly like the original cell.

Your body has many kinds of cells. Each kind has a special job. **Muscle** cells help you move. Nerve cells carry messages between your brain and other parts of your body. Blood cells carry **oxygen** to other cells in your body.

Complete each sentence using the words in bold from above.

The *nucleus* controls the cell's activities.

Cells differ in *size* and *shape*

One cell can *divide* into two cells.

Muscle cells help you move.

Blood cells carry *oxygen* to other cells in your body.

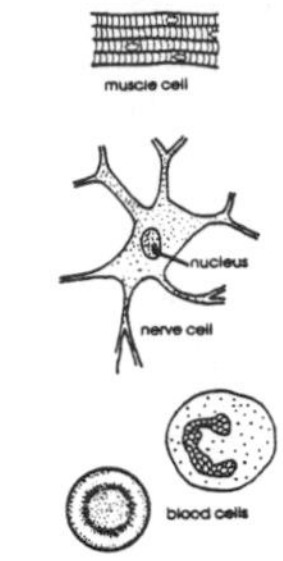
muscle cell
nucleus
nerve cell
blood cells

Unscramble the numbered letters above to discover this amazing fact.

You began life as a *single* cell!

Fun Facts

People and most animals are made of billions or even trillions of cells. But some animals are made of only one cell. To find out more about these animals, look up "protozoans" in your library.

Page 192

Bone Up on Your Bones!

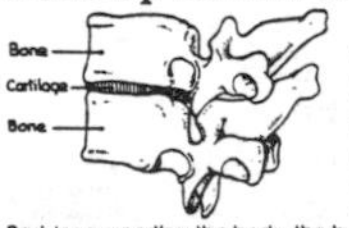
Bone
Cartilage
Bone

When you were born, your skeleton was made of soft bones called cartilage. As you grew, most of that cartilage turned into bone. However, all people still have some cartilage in their bodies. Our noses and our ears are cartilage, and there are pads of cartilage between sections of our backbone that act as cushions.

Besides supporting the body, the bones also serve other important purposes. They are storage houses for important minerals like calcium and phosphorous and the center of the bone, called bone marrow, produces new blood cells for our bodies. Try the experiment below to discover more about bones.

Materials Needed

soup bones from a butcher (Shin bones are ideal. Have him/her saw it in half for you.)

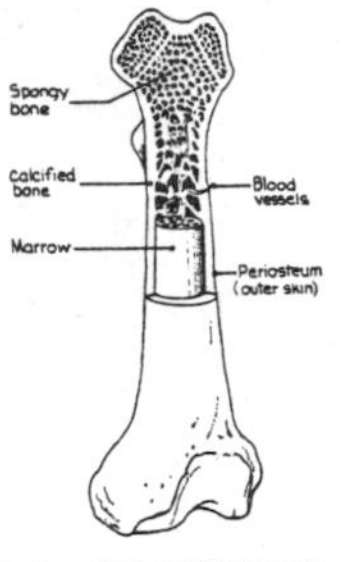
Spongy bone
Calcified bone
Blood vessels
Marrow
Periosteum (outer skin)

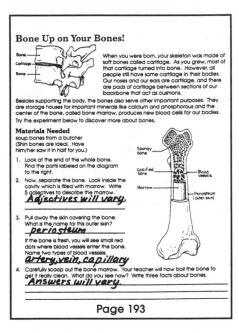

1. Look at the end of the whole bone. Find the parts labeled on the diagram to the right.
2. Now, separate the bone. Look inside the cavity which is filled with marrow. Write 5 adjectives to describe the marrow. *Adjectives will vary.*
3. Pull away the skin covering the bone. What is the name for this outer skin? *periosteum*

   If the bone is fresh, you will see small red dots where blood vessels enter the bone. Name two types of blood vessels. *artery, vein, capillary*
4. Carefully scoop out the bone marrow. Your teacher will now boil the bone to get it really clean. What do you see now? Write three facts about bones. *Answers will vary.*

Page 193

A Heart-y Puzzle for You

Use the clues to fill in the crossword puzzle about the heart.

Word Box

aorta	artery	atrium	capillary	cardiovascular
heart	vein	valves	ventricle	heartbeat

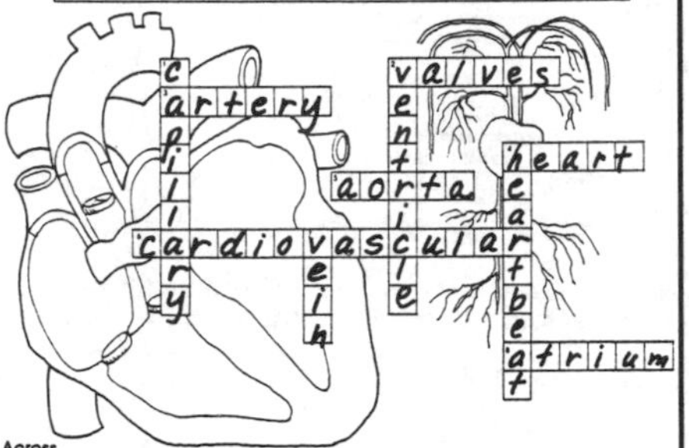
valves
artery
heart
aorta
cardiovascular
atrium
capillary
ventricle
heartbeat
vein

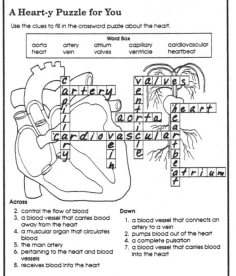

Across

2. control the flow of blood
3. a blood vessel that carries blood away from the heart
4. a muscular organ that circulates blood
5. the main artery
6. pertaining to the heart and blood vessels
8. receives blood into the heart

Down

1. a blood vessel that connects an artery to a vein
2. pumps blood out of the heart
4. a complete pulsation
7. a blood vessel that carries blood into the heart

Page 194

I Can Feel My Heartbeat

Each time your heart pumps the blood through veins and arteries, you can feel it! It's called a pulse. You can feel your pulse in two places where the arteries are close to your skin. Gently, place two fingers on the inside of your wrist or on your neck next to your windpipe. Silently count the pulses and complete the chart below.

*Teacher should time and direct each part. Time for 6 seconds, then multiply by 10.

Pulse Rate	Sitting	Walking Around Room for 1 Minute	Wait 2 Minutes, Then Standing	After 25 Jumping Jacks	Wait 1 Minute, Then Lying Down	After Jogging in Place for 2 Minutes	After Resting for 5 Minutes
in 6 sconds	*Answers*	*will*	*vary.*				
in 1 minute							

You should have found that your heart beats faster when you are active. That's because your body uses more oxygen when it exercises, and the blood must circulate faster to get more oxygen! Now, in a group of four, compare pulse rates and find the average for your group (using the 1 minute rate).

Pulse Rate	Sitting	After Walking	After Standing	After Jumping	After Lying Down	After Jogging	After Resting
You							
Person #2							
Person #3							
Person #4							
Total							
÷ 4 to find average							

Page 195

Our Busy Brains

Your body's central nervous system includes your brain, spinal cord, and nerves that transmit information. It is responsible for receiving information from your senses, analyzing this information, and deciding how your body should respond. Once it has decided, it sends instructions triggering the required actions.

The central nervous system makes some simple decisions about your body's actions within the spinal cord. These are called spinal reflexes and include actions like pulling your hand away from a hot object. For the most part, however, the majority of decisions involve the brain.

Your brain, which weighs about three pounds, controls almost all of the activities in your body. It is made up of three major parts—the cerebrum, the cerebellum, and the brain stem. The cerebrum is divided into two hemispheres which are responsible for all thought and learning processes. The cerebellum is also divided into two parts, and they control all voluntary muscle movement. The brain stem, which is about the size of your thumb, takes care of all involuntary functions. Look around your classroom. Everyone's brain is telling him/her to do things. Fill in the jobs of each part of the brain and then answer the questions below. *Answers will vary.*

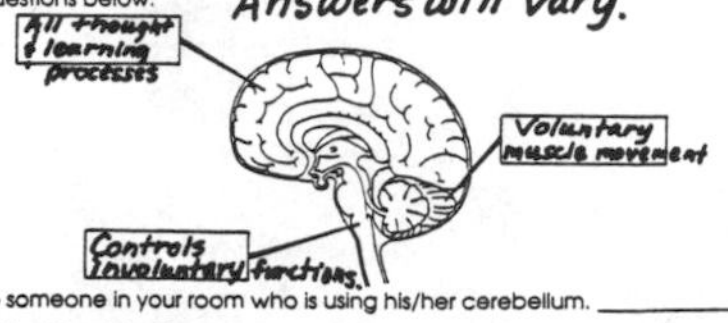
All thought learning processes
Voluntary muscle movement
Controls involuntary functions

Name someone in your room who is using his/her cerebellum. ________

What is he/she doing? ________

Name someone who is using his/her brain stem. ________

What is he/she doing? ________

Name someone in your room who is using his/her cerebrum. ________

What is he/she doing? ________

Page 196

Find Your Brain Dominance

The two sides of the cerebellum work to control all voluntary movements. These include walking, running, writing and all other movements that we consciously want to do. One side of the cerebellum is usually dominant, or depended upon more heavily. The side that is dominant depends on the person. The left side of the brain controls the right side of your body and vice versa. That means that if a person writes with his/her right hand, he/she is probably left-brain dominant. Answer these questions to find your dominance.

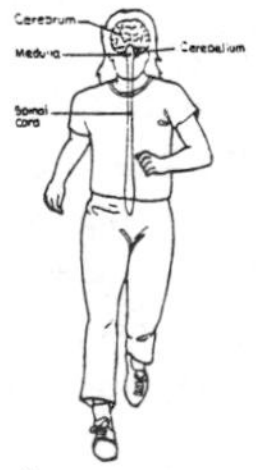
Cerebrum
Cerebellum

Try This:	Right	Left
Clasp your hands together. Which is on top?		
Pick up a pencil to write. Which hand do you use?		
Take 3 steps. Which foot did your start with?		
Try to do the splits. Which leg is in front?		
Hold your arms. Which arm is on top?		
Blink your eye. Which one did you wink?		
Pick up a fork. Which hand do you eat with?		
Hop 5 times on one foot. Which foot did you use?		
Look through a camera, telescope or microscope. Which eye did you use?		

Answers will vary.

How many times did you use your right? ______

How many times did you use your left? ______

Which side of your brain is probably more dominant? ______

(Be careful . . . they're opposite.)

*Make a class graph showing dominant sides.

Page 197

Your Pizza's Path

The digestive system is the group of organs that work together to gain fuel from the foods we eat and discard the unwanted waste. This system breaks down food into simple substances your body's cells can use. It then absorbs these substances into the bloodstream and any leftover waste matter is eliminated.

When you eat pizza (or any food), each bite you take goes through a path in the human body called the alimentary canal, or the digestive tract. This canal consists of the mouth, esophagus, stomach, and small and large intestines. It is in this path that foods are broken down, vitamins are saved and poisons are discarded. Study the path below.

Bite of pizza

1. Teeth tear and grind food moistened by saliva.
2. Esophagus carries food to stomach.
3. Stomach mixes food with acid to further break it down.

vitamins minerals:

4. Pancreas makes food small enough to mix with blood stream.
5. Liver cleanses food and mixes it with blood.
6. Broken down food is sent into bloodstream and taken to rest of body.

fats poisons:

7. Small intestine further breaks down food.
8. Large intestine - water and minerals are absorbed.
9. bladder and rectum - food is passed as waste
10. Gall bladder stores bile produced by liver and sends it to small intestine.

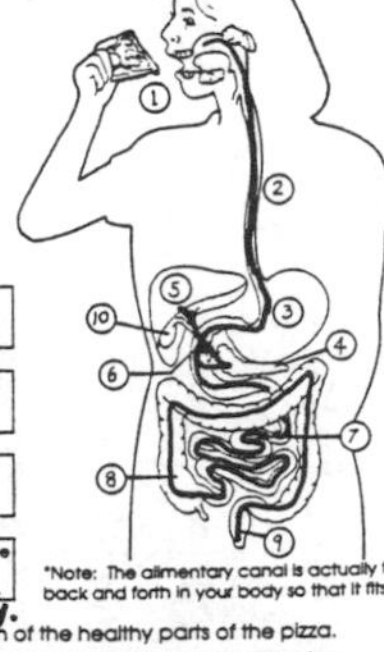

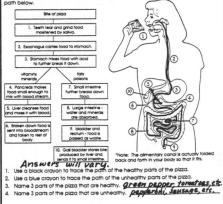

*Note: The alimentary canal is actually folded back and forth in your body so that it fits.

Answers will vary.

1. Use a black crayon to trace the path of the healthy parts of the pizza.
2. Use a blue crayon to trace the path of the unhealthy parts of the pizza.
3. Name 3 parts of the pizza that are healthy. *green pepper, tomatoes, etc.*
4. Name 3 parts of the pizza that are unhealthy. *pepperoni, sausage, etc.*

Page 198

Oh, Yes, I See Now!

One of the most sensitive nerves in your body is the optic nerve. It connects your eyes to your brain. The optic nerve receives messages from other nerves that surround your eyes in the retina. As light is caught in the pupils of your eyes, it is sent to the retina, then to the optic nerve, and at last to the brain. Try this experiment to watch your pupils change!

Answers will vary.

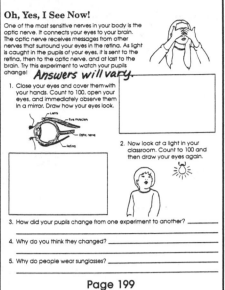

1. Close your eyes and cover them with your hands. Count to 100, open your eyes, and immediately observe them in a mirror. Draw how your eyes look.

2. Now look at a light in your classroom. Count to 100 and then draw your eyes again.

3. How did your pupils change from one experiment to another? _____

4. Why do you think they changed? _____

5. Why do people wear sunglasses? _____

Page 199

Energy Savers

Fats give you twice as much energy as protein or carbohydrates. Your body uses fats to save energy for future use. The fats we eat come from animals in the form of meat, eggs, milk, and much more. We also get fats from some plants like beans, peanuts, and corn. But not all plants give us fats in our diet.

Look at the pictures.
Circle the foods which are rich in fat.
Then list them on the chart.

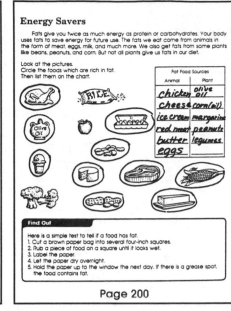

Fat Food Sources	
Animal	Plant
chicken	olive oil
cheese	corn (oil)
ice cream	margarine
red meat	peanuts
butter	legumes
eggs	

Find Out

Here is a simple test to tell if a food has fat.
1. Cut a brown paper bag into several four-inch squares.
2. Rub a piece of food on a square until it looks wet.
3. Label the paper.
4. Let the paper dry overnight.
5. Hold the paper up to the window the next day. If there is a grease spot, the food contains fat.

Page 200

You Are What You Eat!

Having a nutritious diet helps your body fight diseases. Write the foods from the Word Bank in their correct category(s). Use references if necessary.

Word Bank				
tomatoes	bread	eggs	milk	potatoes
oranges	sugar	fish	cereal	green beans
chicken	margarine	cheese	noodles	rice
butter	apples	red meat		

Carbohydrates
bread, green beans, sugar, potatoes, oranges, cereal, noodles, apples, tomatoes, rice

Proteins
red meat, cheese, fish, milk, eggs, bread, chicken, rice, noodles, cereal

Fats
butter, milk, margarine, cheese, eggs

Minerals
red meat, milk, chicken, fish, potatoes, oranges

Below is a list of the food groups. Write what you ate yesterday in each group. Did you get enough servings of each? *Answers will vary.*

Milk Group (3 servings a day) _____

Fruit & Vegetable Group (1 serving a day) _____

Grain Group (4 servings a day) _____

Meat-Egg-Nut-Bean Group (2 servings a day) _____

Page 201

What's in a Label?

Labels give us all kinds of information about the foods we eat. The ingredients of a food are listed in a special order. The ingredient with the largest amount is listed first, the one with the next largest amount is listed second, and so on.

Complete the "Breakfast Table Label Survey" using information from the label on this page.

Breakfast Table Label Survey

1. What does R.D.A. mean? *Recommended Daily Allowances*
2. Calories per serving with milk *190*
3. Calories per serving without milk *110*
4. Calories per ½ cup serving of milk *80*
5. Protein per serving with milk *8%*
6. Protein per serving without milk *2%*
7. Protein in ½ cup serving of milk *6%*
8. Percentage U.S. R.D.A. of Vitamin C *less than 2%*
9. First ingredient *Corn Flour*
10. Is sugar a listed ingredient? *yes*
    If yes, in what place is it listed? *second*
11. Were any vitamins added? *yes*
12. What preservative was added? *BHA*

Find Out: What food product has this ingredient label? "Carbonated water, sugar, corn sweetener, natural flavorings, caramel color, phosphoric acid, caffeine."

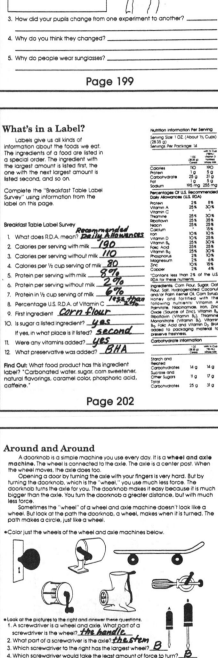

Page 202

I'm Tired

Do you feel tired after raking the lawn? You feel tired then because work takes a lot of energy. **Energy** is the ability to do work.

There are many forms of energy. Food contains **chemical energy**. Your television uses **electrical energy**. The furnace in your house gives you **heat energy**. The moving parts of your bicycle have another form of energy called **mechanical energy**. Anything that moves has mechanical energy.

Energy can be changed from one form to another. Your radio changes electrical energy into sound energy. Your parents' car may change chemical energy into heat energy and the heat energy into mechanical energy.

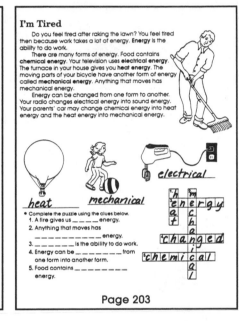

heat   mechanical   electrical

• Complete the puzzle using the clues below.
1. A fire gives us _ _ _ _ energy.
2. Anything that moves has _ _ _ _ _ _ _ _ _ _ energy.
3. _ _ _ _ _ _ is the ability to do work.
4. Energy can be _ _ _ _ _ _ _ from one form to another.
5. Food contains _ _ _ _ _ _ _ _ energy.

Crossword answers: energy, heat, changed, chemical, mechanical

Page 203

Energy in Motion

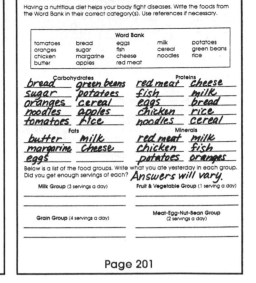

"Mom, how can I knock down more pins?" Matt asked. "You are bowling straight enough, Matt. Try rolling the ball faster, or try using a heavier ball," his mom replied.

The bowling ball is doing work by knocking over the pins. The ball has kinetic energy.

If the ball had more kinetic energy, it could do more work and knock down more pins. If you increase the mass of the ball or its speed, you would increase its kinetic energy.

Just before Matt rolled the ball, he was standing still and not moving. Matt's body had stored energy that would turn into kinetic energy once he started swinging the ball. This stored energy is called **potential energy**.

• Write P next to the pictures that show potential energy and K next to the pictures that show kinetic energy.

P   P   K   K P

• Look back at the picture of Matt getting ready to bowl.
1. At what point will the ball have the most potential energy? *A*
2. At what point will the ball have the most kinetic energy? *B*
3. At what point will the ball have the least kinetic energy? *A*
4. At what point will the ball have the least potential energy? *B*

Challenge: A roller-coaster car with people in it will travel much faster than an empty car. Why?

Page 204

Around and Around

A doorknob is a simple machine you use every day. It is a **wheel and axle machine**. The wheel is connected to the axle. The axle is a center post. When the wheel moves, the axle does too.

Opening a door by turning the axle with your fingers is very hard. But by turning the doorknob, which is the "wheel," you use much less force. The doorknob turns the axle for you. The doorknob makes it easy because it is much bigger than the axle. You turn the doorknob a greater distance, but with much less force.

Sometimes the "wheel" of a wheel and axle machine doesn't look like a wheel. But look at the path the doorknob, a wheel, makes when it is turned. The path makes a circle, just like a wheel.

• Color just the wheel and axle machines below.

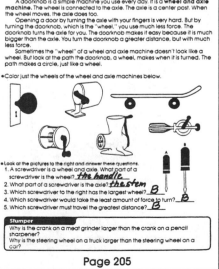

• Look at the pictures to the right and answer these questions.
1. A screwdriver is a wheel and axle. What part of a screwdriver is the wheel? *the handle*
2. What part of a screwdriver is the axle? *the stem*
3. Which screwdriver in the right has the largest wheel? *B*
4. Which screwdriver would take the least amount of force to turn? *B*
5. Which screwdriver must travel the greatest distance? *B*

Stumper
Why is the crank on a meat grinder larger than the crank on a pencil sharpener?
Why is the steering wheel on a truck larger than the steering wheel on a car?

Page 205

Levers

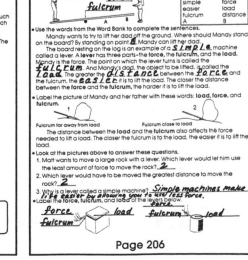

load   force   fulcrum
A   B

Word Bank	
simple	force
easier	load
fulcrum	distance
A	B

• Use the words from the Word Bank to complete the sentences.
Mandy wants to try to lift her dad off the ground. Where should Mandy stand on the board? By standing on point *B*, Mandy can lift her dad.
The board resting on the log is an example of a *simple* machine called a lever. A lever has three parts, the *force*, the *fulcrum*, and the *load*. Mandy is the force. The point on which the lever turns is called the *fulcrum*. And Mandy's dad, the object to be lifted, is called the *load*. The greater the *distance* between the *force* and the fulcrum, the *easier* it is to lift the load. The shorter the distance between the *force* and the *fulcrum*, the harder it is to lift the load.

• Label the picture of Mandy and her father with these words: **load, force,** and **fulcrum.**

1   2

Fulcrum far away from load   Fulcrum close to load

The distance between the **load** and the **fulcrum** also affects the force needed to lift a load. The closer the fulcrum is to the load, the easier it is to lift the load.

• Look at the pictures above to answer these questions.
1. Matt wants to move a large rock with a lever. Which lever would let him use the least amount of force to move the rock? *2*
2. Which lever would have to move the greatest distance to move the rock? *2*
3. Why is a lever called a simple machine? *Simple machines make life easier by allowing you to use less force.*
• Label the force, fulcrum, and load of the levers below.

force   load   fulcrum   load
fulcrum   force

Page 206

Dancing Parsley

Investigate

Run a comb through your hair 30 times. Go only one way. Hold the comb next to some parsley flakes. What happened? *they "danced"*

Run the comb through your hair 30 times again. Hold it next to some shredded tissue. What happened? *moved toward comb*

Rub the comb 30 times against the hairs on your arm, or a woolen sweater or on a shiny shirt or blouse. Rub only one way. Hold the comb next to the parsley flakes. Did the comb pick them up? *yes*
Hold the comb next to the shredded tissue. Did the comb pick up the tissue? *yes*

Results may vary.

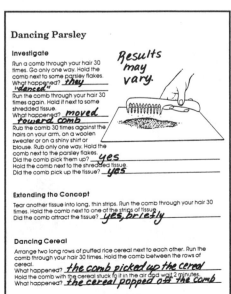

Extending the Concept

Tear another tissue into long, thin strips. Run the comb through your hair 30 times. Hold the comb next to one of the strips of tissue. Did the comb attract the tissue? *yes, briefly*

Dancing Cereal

Arrange two long rows of puffed rice cereal next to each other. Run the comb through your hair 30 times. Hold the comb between the rows of cereal. What happened? *the comb picked up the cereal*
Hold the comb with the cereal stuck to it in the air about 2 minutes. What happened? *the cereal popped off the comb*

Page 207

Charge It!

Have you ever scuffed your feet as you walked across the carpet and then brought your finger close to someone's nose? Zap! Did the person jump? The spark you made was **static electricity.**

Static electricity is made when objects gain or lose tiny bits of electricity called **electrical charges.** The charges are either positive or negative.

Objects that have electrical charges act like magnets, attracting or repelling each other. If two objects have **like charges** (the same kind of charges), they will repel each other. If two objects have **unlike charges** (different charges), the objects will attract each other.

Find out more about static electricity by unscrambling the word(s) in each sentence.

1. Flashes of (ghtlining) *lightning* in the sky are caused by static electricity in the clouds.
2. Electrical charges are either (ospivite) *positive* or (givnatee) *negative*
3. Small units of electricity are called (srgache) *charges*.
4. Two objects with unlike charges will (arcttat) *attract* each other.
5. Sometimes electric charges jump between objects with (unkile) *unlike* charges. This is what happens when lightning flashes in the sky.

Look at the pictures below to see how static electricity affects objects.
1. Name the two objects that are interacting in each picture.
2. Tell whether the two objects have **like charges** or **unlike charges.**

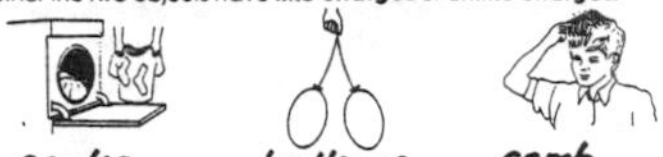

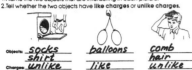

Objects:	*socks*	*balloons*	*comb*
	shirt		*hair*
Charges:	*unlike*	*like*	*unlike*

Something Special: Hold this paper against a wall and rub it with 50 quick strokes with the side of your pencil. Take your hand away. Presto! The paper stays on the wall because of the static electricity you have made.

Page 208

Power Paths

A **circuit** is a path along which electricity travels. It travels in a loop around the circuit. In the circuit pictured below, the electricity travels through the wire, battery, switch, and bulb. The electricity must have a source. What is the source in this circuit? You're right if you said the battery.

If the wire in the circuit were cut, there would be a **gap**. The electricity wouldn't be able to flow across the gap. Then the bulb would not light. This is an example of an **open circuit**. If there were no gaps, the bulb would light. This is an example of a **closed circuit**.

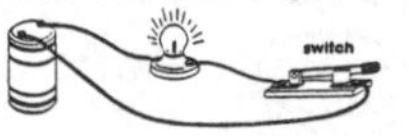

1. Draw in the wire to the battery, switch, and bulb to make a closed circuit.

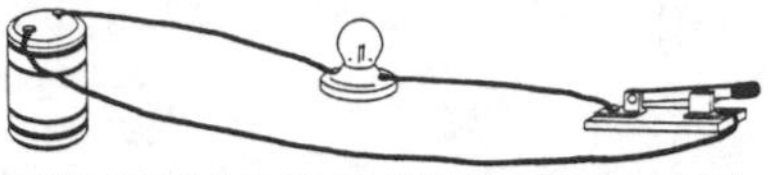

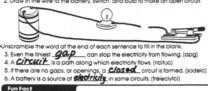

2. Draw in the wire to the battery, switch, and bulb to make an open circuit.

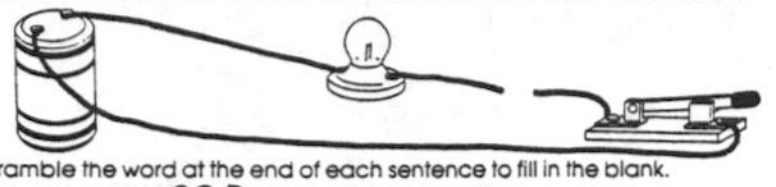

• Unscramble the word at the end of each sentence to fill in the blank.

3. Even the tiniest *gap* can stop the electricity from flowing. (apg)
4. A *circuit* is a path along which electricity flows. (ricituc)
5. If there are no gaps, or openings, a *closed* circuit is formed. (sodelc)
6. A battery is a source of *electricity* in some circuits. (treleciytci)

Fun Fact

If all of the circuits in a small personal computer were made out of wire and metal switches, the computer would fill the average classroom. Today these circuits are found in tiny chips called microchips.

Page 209

Fill the Gap

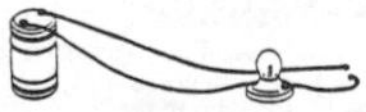

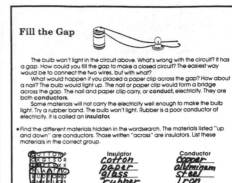

The bulb won't light in the circuit above. What's wrong with the circuit? It has a gap. How could you fill the gap to make a closed circuit? The easiest way would be to connect the two wires, but with what?

What would happen if you placed a paper clip across the gap? How about a nail? The bulb would light up. The nail or paper clip would form a bridge across the gap. The nail and paper clip carry, or **conduct,** electricity. They are both **conductors.**

Some materials will not carry the electricity well enough to make the bulb light. Try a rubber band. The bulb won't light. Rubber is a poor conductor of electricity. It is called an **insulator.**

• Find the different materials hidden in the wordsearch. The materials listed "up and down" are conductors. Those written "across" are insulators. List these materials in the correct group.

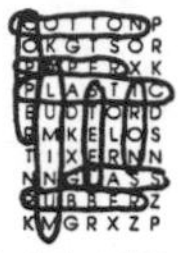

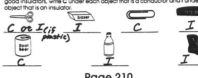

Insulator	Conductor
cotton	*copper*
paper	*aluminum*
glass	*steel*
rubber	*Iron*
plastic	

• Now that you know which materials make good conductors and which make good insulators, write **C** under each object that is a conductor and **I** under each object that is an insulator.

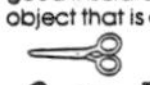
C or I (is plastic)

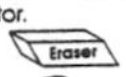

I

C

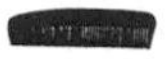
I

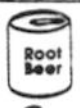

C

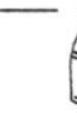
I

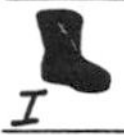
I

Page 210

Series or Parallel?

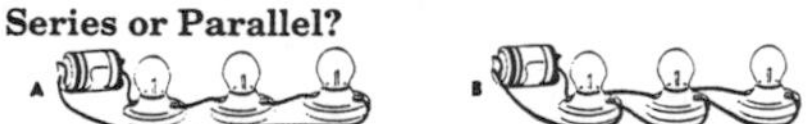

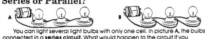

You can light several light bulbs with only one cell. In picture **A**, the bulbs are connected in a **series circuit.** What would happen to the circuit if you unscrewed one bulb? All the lights would go out. In picture **B,** the bulbs are connected in a **parallel circuit.** What would happen if you unscrewed a light bulb in a parallel circuit? The other lights would still burn.

Dry cells can also be connected in series and parallel circuits. However, cells are usually connected in series. A series of cells increases the amount of power that flows in a circuit. A series of cells will make a light bulb burn brighter.

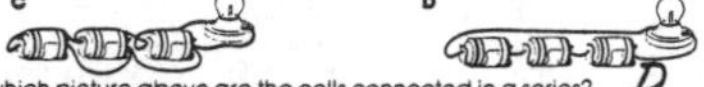

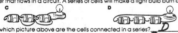

1. In which picture above are the cells connected in a series? *D*
2. In which picture above will the bulb light more brightly? *D*
3. When one light burned out on Sally's Christmas tree, the rest of the lights went out, too. In what kind of circuit were the bulbs connected? *series*
4. Do you think the electric lights in your house are connected in a series circuit or a parallel circuit? *parallel* Why? *If one light burns out, the others will still light.*
5. How are the batteries connected in the flashlight below? In a series or parallel? *series*
6. Some flashlights have four or five cells. How would the brightness of the light from this kind of flashlight compare with one that only has one or two cells? *The light would be much brighter.*

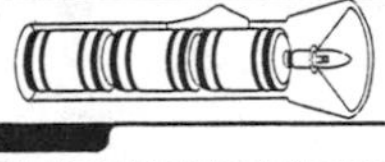

Fun Fact

A single dry cell is often called a battery, but it really isn't a battery. A battery is two or more cells connected together. You can buy batteries that look like a single cell, but they are really two or more cells connected together and put inside one case.

Page 211

Powered Up

Where does the electricity that is in your house come from? It all begins at a large **power plant.** The power plant has a large **turbine generator.** High pressure steam spins the turbines and the generator that is attached to the turbine shaft. As the generator spins, it produces hundreds of megawatts of electricity.

• Below is a picture of a power plant where electricity is generated. Label each part using the terms found in the Power Bank below.

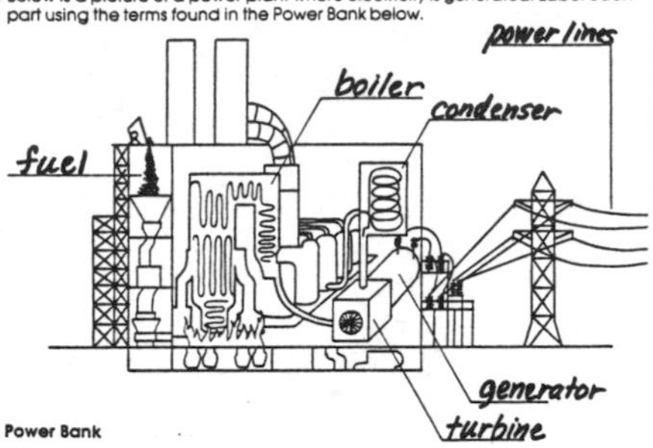

Power Bank

Fuel – Fuel, such as coal, enters the power plant.
Boiler – The burning fuel heats water in the boiler, making high pressure steam.
Turbine – High pressure steam spins the blades of the turbine up to 3,000 times a minute.
Condenser – Steam is cooled in the condenser and is turned back into water. The water is sent back to the boiler.
Generator – The generator attached to the turbine turns, producing hundreds of megawatts of electricity.
Power Lines – Electricity is sent to your home through wires.

Page 212

Portable Power

Steve and Lenny really enjoyed listening to the radio while they fished. Radios need electricity to work. Where did Steve's radio get its power? From a **dry cell battery,** of course. Dry cells are sources of portable power.

Most portable radios use dry cells. A dry cell makes electricity by changing chemical energy into electrical energy. Chemicals in the dry cell act on each other and make **electrons** flow. The flow of electrons is called **electricity.**

• Use the words from the Word Bank to label the parts of the dry cell. You can use your science book to help, but first try to figure out each part by yourself.

Word Bank
chemical paste
carbon rod
zinc case
terminal

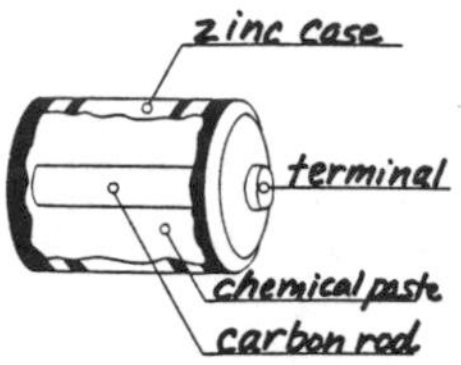

Portable Power Inventory

List the appliances, tools, or toys in your house that are powered with dry cells.

flashlight
radio
smoke detector
watch
train set
toy robot

Answers will vary.

Find Out

Before batteries were invented, scientists did all their experiments with static electricity. Find out who made the first battery and when it was made.

Page 213

Magnetic Attraction

Try to pick up each of these objects with your magnet. Circle the ones which it picks up. *If metal.*

(scissors) eraser ruler pencil crayon
(paper clip) (thumbtack) toothpick pen

A magnet will only pick up an object made of *metal*.

Investigate

List all the objects you can find which your magnet picks up or is attracted to.

1. *Answers will*
2. *vary.*
3. ____
4. ____
5. ____
6. ____
7. ____
8. ____
9. ____
10. ____

Is the magnet attracted to any non-metal object? *no*

Extending the Concept

Hold a piece of tagboard between the magnet and each object you listed in the "Investigate" section. List each one the magnet is still attracted to.

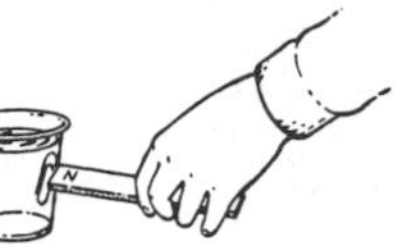

Place each of the objects the magnet is still attracted to in a cup of water.
Hold the magnet against the outside of the cup.

Which items was the magnet still able to attract? ____

What other materials can a magnet attract objects through, besides tagboard and water? *index cards, similar materials*

Page 214

Working with Electromagnets

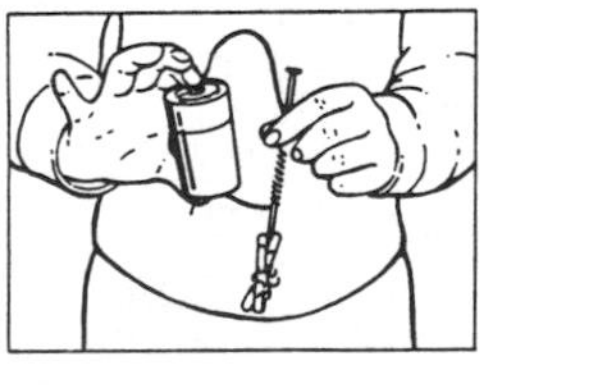

Investigate *Answers will vary.*

1. Strip 1 inch of insulation from each end of a 2-foot-long piece of thin wire.
2. Wrap the wire around a nail 30 times, leaving most of the extra wire dangling at one end.
3. Touch one bare end of the wire to the top of the battery.
4. Touch the other bare end of the wire to the bottom of the battery.
5. Hold the nail near some paper clips.
   How many paper clips did the electromagnet pick up? ____

Making the Electromagnet Stronger

Wrap the wire around the nail 30 more times.
How many paper clips will the electromagnet pick up now? ____
Tape two batteries together with the top of one battery touching the bottom of the other.
How many paper clips will the electromagnet pick up now? ____
Wrap as many coils around the nail as you can.
How many paper clips can you pick up now? ____
Name two ways to make an electromagnet stronger. *Wrap the wire around several more times and use extra batteries.*

Page 215

Weight and Gravity

Making a Scale

1. Use a hole punch or scissors to punch two holes at the top of a clear plastic cup. Make the holes exactly opposite each other.
2. Cut a piece of fish line 6 inches long. Tie one end to one hole and the other end to the opposite hole.
3. Tape a ruler to the top of your desk so one end hangs over the edge. Then tape a piece of tagboard to the side of the desk.
4. Wrap a rubber band around the fish line and loop it inside itself. Now hang the rubber band from the ruler. The cup should hang in front of the tagboard.

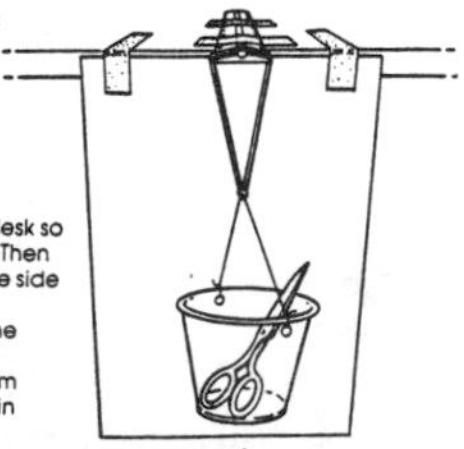

Comparing Weights *Answers will vary.*

To weigh an object, place it in the cup. The heavier the object, the lower the cup will sag. To record its weight, put a mark on the tagboard even with the bottom of the cup and write the name of the object next to the mark.

Weigh these objects. Then number them from lightest to heaviest.

____scissors ____water ____pencil ____coin
____stone ____crayon box ____eraser ____magnifying glass

Extending the Concept

Why is gravity important to man? *It keeps objects from floating off the earth.*

What would happen if there were no gravity? *We would be weightless; earth would be barren.*

Page 216

Great Gravity Changes

The gravity that pulls on the moon is ⅙ as strong as the pull on Earth. This means that you could jump up and stay in the air six times longer than you can now! Work with a partner to find the measurements below. Record them and then multiply them by six to see how different life would be on the moon.

Activity/Object	Measurement on Earth	Measurement on Moon (Earth x 6)
Distance you can jump with running start (in inches)	Answers will	
Height you can jump (in inches)	vary.	
Distance you can throw a ball (in feet)		
Distance you can kick a ball (in feet)		
Number of books you can pick up at one time		

The gravitational pull on the sun is 28 times stronger than that on Earth. This means that everything would weigh 28 times more if it were on the sun. Below are several objects. Use a scale to find their approximate weight on the sun by multiplying them by 28. To find their weight on the moon, divide their Earth-weight by 6 because the gravitational pull of the moon is that much less than Earth's.

Object	Weight on Earth	Weight on Sun (Earth x 28)	Weight on Moon (Earth ÷ 6)
your math book			
your book bag (full)			
yourself			
(object of your choice)			
(object of your choice)			
(object of your choice)			

Page 217

A Lo-o-o-ong Trip

What is the longest trip you have ever taken? Was it 100 km? 500 km? Maybe it was more than 1,000 km. You probably didn't know it, but last year you traveled 1 billion kilometers.

The Earth travels in a path around the sun called its **orbit**. Earth's orbit is almost 1 billion kilometers. It takes 1 year, or 365 days, for the Earth to orbit or **revolve** around the sun.

Look at the picture of Earth's orbit. It is not a perfect circle. It is a special shape called an **ellipse.**

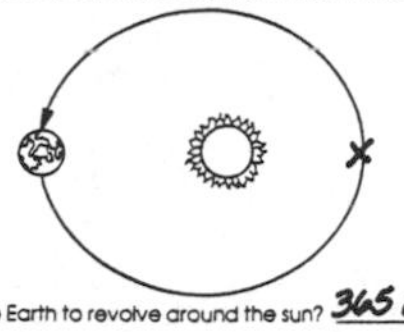

1. How long does it take for the Earth to revolve around the sun? 365 days
2. How many times has the Earth revolved around the sun since you were born? Answers will vary.
3. How many kilometers has the Earth traveled in orbit since you were born? Age x 1 billion km
4. Put an "X" on Earth's orbit to show where it will be in six months.

Experiment

You can draw an ellipse. Place two straight pins about 8 cm apart in a piece of cardboard. Tie the ends of a 25 cm piece of string to the pins. Place your pencil inside the string. Keeping the string tight, draw an ellipse.

Make four different ellipses by changing the length of the string and the distance between the pins. How do the ellipses change?

Fun Fact

Hold on tight. The Earth travels at a speed of 100,000 km per hour in its orbital path around the sun.

Page 218

"Lift-off"

"3-2-1, lift-off!" With a mighty roar, the Saturn V **rocket leaves the launch pad.**

Riding high on top of the Saturn V in the **Command Module** are the three Apollo astronauts. Below their Command Module is a Lunar Landing Module that will land two of the astronauts on the moon's surface.

Below this, the Saturn V has three parts, or **stages.** It takes a lot of power to escape the Earth's pull, called **gravity.** The spacecraft must reach a speed of almost 40,000 km per hour. The bottom, or first stage, is the largest. After each stage uses up its **fuel,** it drops off and the next stage starts. Each stage has its own fuel and **oxygen.** The fuels need oxygen in order to burn.

The astronauts are now on their 3-day journey to the moon.

Color each Saturn V section a different color. Color the key to match each section.

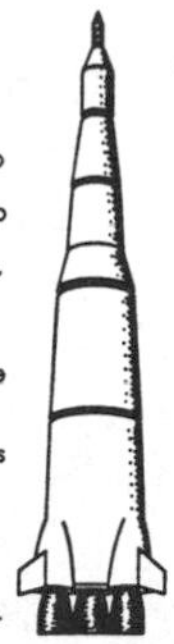

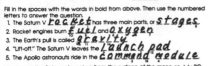

Apollo Mission Saturn V

Color Key
- Command Module
- Lunar Landing Module
- 3rd Stage
- 2nd Stage
- 1st Stage

Fill in the spaces with the words in bold from above. Then use the numbered letters to answer the question.

1. The Saturn V rocket has three main parts, or stages.
2. Rocket engines burn fuel and oxygen.
3. The Earth's pull is called gravity.
4. "Lift-off." The Saturn V leaves the launch pad.
5. The Apollo astronauts ride in the command module.

What were the first words spoken from the surface of the moon on July 20, 1969?

"That's one small step for man, one giant leap for mankind."

Neil Armstrong, Apollo II Commander

Page 219

"Live Via Satellite"

"This program is brought to you live via satellite from halfway around the world." Satellites are very helpful in sending TV messages from one side of the world to the other. But this is only one of the special jobs that satellites can do.

Most satellites are placed into orbit around the Earth by riding on top of giant rockets. Only recently have some satellites been carried into orbit by a space shuttle. While orbiting the Earth, the giant doors of the shuttle are opened, and the satellite is pushed into orbit.

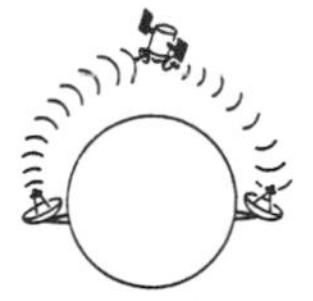

This satellite relays TV signals from halfway around the world.

Satellites send information about many things. Use the code to find the different kinds of messages and information satellites send.

television, telephone, floods, forest fires, weather, pollution, pictures of space, moving animals

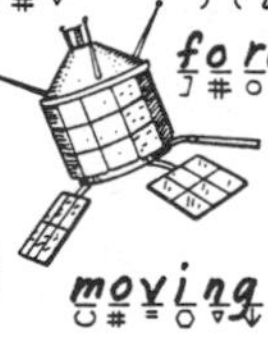

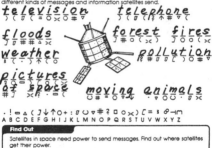

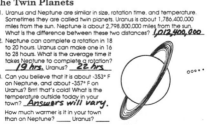

A B C D E F G H I J K L M N O P Q R S T U V W X Y Z

Find Out

Satellites in space need power to send messages. Find out where satellites get their power.

Page 220

Just Imagine . . .

Earth is a very special planet because it is the only planet known to have life. Only Earth has the necessities to support life—water, air, moderate temperatures, and suitable air pressure. Earth is about 92,960,000 miles from the sun and is 7,926 miles in diameter. Its highest recorded temperature was 136° F in Libya and the lowest was -127° F in Antarctica.

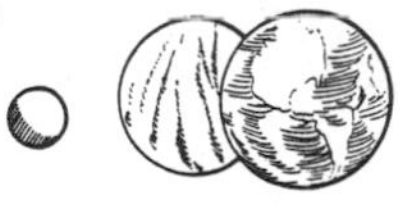

Venus is known as Earth's "twin" because the two planets are so similar in size. At about 67,230,000 miles from the sun, Venus is 7,521 miles in diameter. Venus is the brightest planet in the sky, as seen from Earth, and is brighter even than the stars. The temperature on the surface of this planet is about 850° F.

Mercury is the planet closest to the sun. It is about 35,980,000 miles from the sun and is 3,031 miles in diameter. The temperature on this planet ranges from -315° F to 648° F.

Pretend you were going to Venus or Mercury for spring break. Make a list of the things you would bring (you may have to invent them in order to survive) and draw a picture of the vehicle that would take you there. Write about your experiences on another sheet of paper.

Things I Need to Take	Vehicle
Answers will vary.	

Page 221

The Large Planets

Jupiter is the largest planet in the solar system. The diameter at its equator is about 88,836 miles. It was named after the king of the Roman gods and is the fifth closest planet to the sun at about 483,600,000 miles away. This large planet also spins faster than any other. It makes a complete rotation in about 9 hours and 55 minutes.

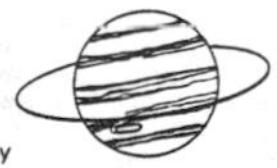

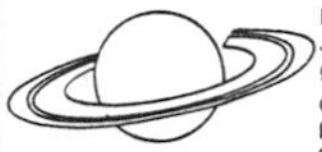

The surface of Jupiter cannot be seen from Earth because of the layers of dense clouds surrounding it. Jupiter has no solid surface but is made of liquid and gases that are held together by gravity.

One characteristic unique to Jupiter is the Great Red Spot that is about 25,000 miles long and about 20,000 miles wide. Astronomers believe the spot to be a swirling, hurricane-like mass of gas.

Saturn, the second largest planet, is well known for its seven thin, flat rings encircling it. Its diameter is about 74,898 miles at the equator. It was named for the Roman god of agriculture. Saturn is the sixth planet closest to the sun and is about 888,200,000 miles away from it. Like Jupiter, Saturn travels around the sun in an oval-shaped (elliptical) orbit, and it takes the planet about 10 hours and 39 minutes to make one rotation.

Scientists believe Saturn is a giant ball of gas that also has no solid surface. Like Jupiter, they believe it too may have an inner core of rocky material. Whereas Saturn claims 23 satellites, Jupiter has only 16 known satellites.

Fill in the chart below to compare Jupiter and Saturn. Make two of your own categories.

Categories	Jupiter	Saturn
1. diameter	88,836 miles	74,898 miles
2. origin of name	king of the Roman gods	Roman god of agriculture
3. distance from sun	483,600,000 miles	888,200,000 miles
4. rotations	one in 9 hrs. 55 mins	10 hrs. 39 mins
5. surface	liquid and gases	giant ball of gas
6. unique characteristics	Great Red Spot	7 thin, flat rings
7.		
8.		

Page 222

The Twin Planets

1. Uranus and Neptune are similar in size, rotation time, and temperature. Sometimes they are called twin planets. Uranus is about 1,786,400,000 miles from the sun. Neptune is about 2,798,800,000 miles from the sun. What is the difference between these two distances? 1,012,400,000
2. Neptune can complete a rotation in 18 to 20 hours. Uranus can make one in 16 to 28 hours. What is the average time it takes Neptune to complete a rotation? 19 hrs. Uranus? 22 hrs
3. Can you believe that it is about -353° F on Neptune, and about -357° F on Uranus? Brrr! that's cold! What is the temperature outside today in your town? Answers will vary. How much warmer is it in your town than on Neptune? ____ Uranus? ____

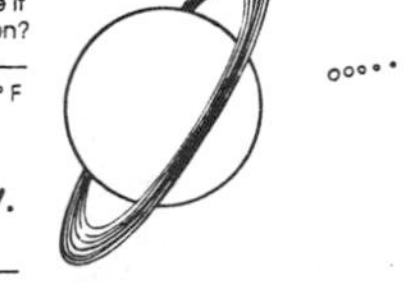

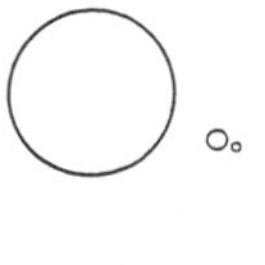

4. Uranus has at least five small satellites moving around it. Their names are Miranda, Ariel, Umbriel, Tatania and Oberon. They are 75, 217, 155, 310 and 280 miles in diameter respectively. What is the average diameter of Uranus' satellites? 207.4
5. Neptune was first seen in 1846 by Johanna G. Galle. Uranus was first discovered by Sir William Herschel in 1781. How many years ago was Neptune discovered? Will vary. Uranus? ____ About how many years later was Uranus discovered than Neptune? 65

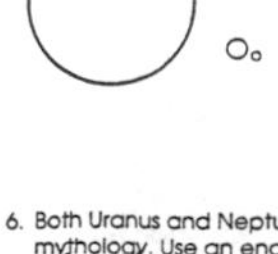

6. Both Uranus and Neptune have names taken from Greek and Roman mythology. Use an encyclopedia to find their names and their origins. Neptune was named for Neptune, the Roman sea god. Uranus was named for the first god of the sky.

Page 223

Pluto and Planet X

Pluto, 1,430 miles in diameter, is the smallest planet. It is also the farthest planet from the sun at 3,666,200,000 miles away. However, this is not always true! Pluto's orbit forms a long, thin oval shape that crosses the path of Neptune's orbit every 248 years. So, for about 200 Earth-years, Pluto is actually closer to the sun than Neptune! It is closer now and won't return to its outer position until 1999. Try this art project:

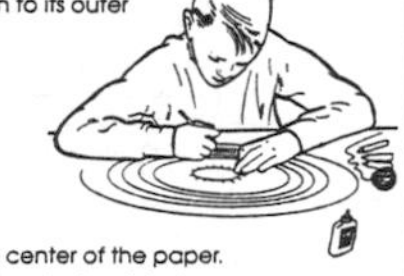

Materials Needed

construction paper
crayons or chalk
glue
yarn (various colors)
pencil

Directions

1. Use a crayon to draw the sun in the center of the paper.
2. Use your pencil to draw the orbit of each planet, being careful to cross Pluto's with Neptune's.
3. Color the planets along the orbits.
4. Trace the orbits in glue, then lay yarn on top.

*Only Pluto's and Neptune's orbits should cross.

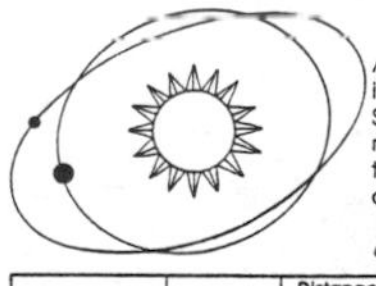

Although there are only nine known planets, it is possible that another exists beyond Pluto. Some people refer to it as Planet X. Write a name for it below and use information about the other planets to estimate and create answers in the chart.

Answers will vary.

Planet Name	Diameter	Distance from Sun	Revolution	Rotation	Satellites	Symbol

Page 224

Keeping the Order

Nine planets orbit the sun. These planets are arranged in order according to their distance from the sun. Do you know which planet is closest and which is farthest from the sun?

Number the planets in order below with number one being the planet closest to the sun. Use the mean (average) distances in miles to help you.

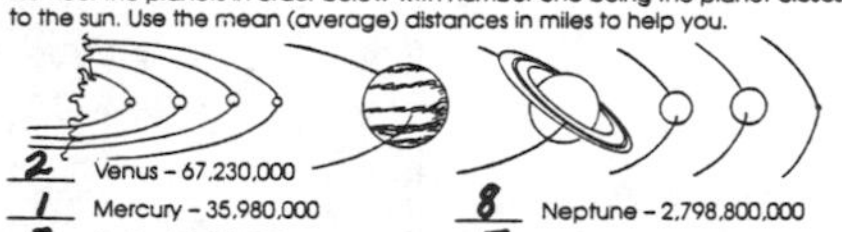

2 Venus – 67,230,000	8 Neptune – 2,798,800,000
1 Mercury – 35,980,000	7 Uranus – 1,786,400,000
3 Earth – 92,960,000	5 Jupiter – 483,600,000
9 Pluto – 3,666,200,000	6 Saturn – 888,200,000
4 Mars – 141,000,000	

To help you remember the order of the planets, write a sentence. Use the first letter of each planet, in order from the planet closest to the sun to the one farthest from it, to write words to make a sentence. **Note:** To help you get started, write the planets in order on the lines below and then write down some words on each line that begin with the first letter of that planet.

Mercury-
Venus-
Earth-
Mars-
Jupiter-
Saturn-
Uranus-
Neptune-
Pluto-

Your sentence: Sentences will vary.

Page 225

Star Search

On a clear dark night, you can look up in the sky and see about 2,000 stars without the help of a telescope. But unless you know which stars form constellations, all you will be seeing are stars. Carefully poke holes in the *Constellation Patterns* sheet using a sharp pencil. Then tonight, when it is dark, hold a flashlight behind the paper to make the constellations appear.

Below are star charts to further help you recognize the constellations. To use the charts, turn them until the present month is at the bottom. Depending on your latitude and the time of night, you should be able to see most of the constellations in the middle and upper part of the chart.

Answers will vary.

1. Using the *Constellation Patterns* sheet to help you, label as many of the constellations in the chart as you can.
2. Which constellations should you be able to see tonight? _____

3. When it is dark, go outside to look for constellations.
4. Which ones do you actually see?

_____
_____

5. On the back of this paper, draw the night sky you see. Put a small X in the center. This should be the point in the sky directly above you.

Page 226

Constellation Patterns

See pages 226 (*Star Search*) and 228 (*Class Constellation*) for directions.

The Big Dipper	Cygnus the Swan	Hercules the Hero
Orion the Hunter	Leo the Lion	Sagittarius the Archer
Draco the Dragon	Scorpius the Scorpion	Pegasus the Winged Horse
Taurus the Bull	Gemini the Twins	Virgo the Virgin
Canis Major the Dog	Andromeda the Chained Lady	Cassiopeia the Queen

Page 227

Class Constellation

Thousands of years ago, people believed that there were many gods in the heavens above. They believed that the gods made the sun rise, the weather change, the oceans move, and even made people fall in love! The people made up stories (myths) about the gods and their great powers. Many of the characters in these myths can be found in the shapes of the stars. These "star pictures" are called constellations. There are 88 constellations in the sky, but not all of them can be seen from one location. Some are only visible in the Southern Hemisphere while others can only be seen in the Northern Hemisphere. Some are also best observed only in certain seasons. Look at some of the constellations on page 227, *Constellation Patterns*. Pick one or create your own and write a myth about it. Follow the directions below.

1. On a lined sheet of 8 ½" x 11" paper, write your name, the title of your myth, and the myth.
2. Glue the paper on the right side of a 12" x 18" piece of black construction paper.
3. In the box below, design your constellation using star stickers.
4. Connect the stars to show your constellation and add details.
5. Cut out and glue your constellation on the left side of the construction paper.

Myths and constellations will vary.

Page 228

Read My Mind

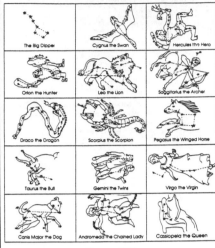

Pretend you have been contacted by NASA to serve as an astronaut on a secret mission. Because of its secrecy, NASA cannot give you your destination. Instead, you must figure it out using the clues below. After each clue, check the possible answers. Your destination will soon be evident.

Destination Clues	Mercury	Venus	Earth	Mars	Jupiter	Saturn	Uranus	Neptune	Pluto
It is part of our Solar System.	✓	✓	✓	✓	✓	✓	✓	✓	✓
It is a bright object in the sky.	✓	✓	✓						
It is less than 2,000,000,000 miles from the sun.	✓	✓	✓	✓	✓	✓			
It orbits the sun.	✓	✓	✓	✓	✓	✓	✓	✓	✓
It has less than 15 known satellites.	✓	✓	✓	✓				✓	✓
There is weather here.	✓	✓	✓	✓	✓	✓	✓	✓	
It rotates in the opposite direction of Earth.		✓							
It is the hottest planet.		✓							
Its years are longer than its days.		✓							
It is called "Earth's twin."		✓							
It is closest to Earth.		✓							

Secret Mission Destination is *Venus*

I know this because _____

Page 229

Space Snowballs

Planets and moons are not the only objects in our solar system that travel in orbits. Comets also orbit the sun.

A **comet** is like a giant dirty snowball from 1 to 5 kilometers wide. It is made of frozen gases, dust, ice, and rocks.

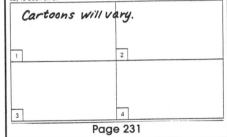

As the comet gets closer to the sun, the frozen gases melt and evaporate. Dust particles float in the air. The dust forms a cloud called a **coma.** The "wind" from the sun blows the coma away from the sun. The blowing coma forms the comet's tail.

There are more than 800 known comets. Halley's Comet is the most famous. It appears about every 76 years. The year 1985 was the last scheduled appearance in this century. When will it appear next?

Find the words from the Word Bank in the wordsearch. When you are finished, write down the letters that are not circled. Start at the top of the puzzle and go from left to right.

Word Bank	
dust	orbit
Halley	tail
coma	ice
snowball	sky
melt	shining
solar system	

Planets have orbits like circles. Comets have orbits shaped like a football.

Page 230

Amazing Asteroids

Asteroids are extremely small planets that revolve around the sun. They are also called minor planets or planetoids. These small planets travel mainly between the orbits of Mars and Jupiter. There are thousands of them, and new ones are constantly being discovered.

Many asteroids are made of dark, rocky material, have irregular shapes and range widely in size. Ceres, the largest and first-known asteroid, is about 600 miles in diameter. Eros, another asteroid, is only about 9/10 of a mile in diameter.

Because the asteroids' orbits change slowly due to the gravitational attraction of Jupiter and other large planets, asteroids sometimes collide with each other. Fragments from these collisions can cause other collisions. Any resulting small fragments that reach the surface of Earth are called meteorites.

Try your hand at personification. Personification means giving an inanimate (non-living) object human qualities. Draw a cartoon below of two asteroids colliding with each other. Give the asteroids names and write what they might say to each other.

Cartoons will vary.

1	2
3	4

Page 231

Star Light, Star Bright

Lay on your back. Gaze up into the night sky. Which star is the brightest? On a clear night you can see hundreds of stars—some are bright and others are dim.

Why are some stars brighter than others? Let's try to find out by looking at the picture on this page.

1. Look at the two streetlights in the picture. Which streetlight appears the brightest? *the closest*
   Why? *Because it is closest. The light looks larger and brighter.*
2. Look at the bicycle and the truck. Which headlights appear the brightest? *the truck's*
   Why? *They are larger*
3. Some stars appear brighter than others for the same reasons as those stated above. What are the two reasons?
   a. *They are larger.*
   b. *They are closer to Earth.*

Color Me Hot

Stars differ not only in brightness but also in color. As a star gets hotter, its color changes.

Refer to the chart to color these stars.

Star Color	
Temperature	Color
20,000° C	Blue
10,500° C	White
5,500° C	Yellow
3,000° C	Red

 blue
Spica
20,000°C

 white
Sirius
10,500°C

 yellow
Sun
5,500°C

 red
Betelgeuse
3,000°C

Page 232

Pass the Profiles

How much do your classmates know about you? Give copies of this sheet to a few other students. Tell them to fill out the information about you. Fill in the blanks that they cannot complete.

Answers will vary.

Full name: _____
How my name was chosen: _____
Address: _____
Other places I have lived: _____
Parents' names: _____
Parents' occupations: _____
Brothers' and sisters' names: _____
Pets (kinds and names/ present or past): _____
Kinds of clothes I like: _____
Fun things I like to do: _____
Favorite foods: _____
Favorite songs: _____
Favorite videos and TV shows: _____
Someday I'd like to be: _____
I'm really good at: _____
My favorite expression is: _____
States I've visited: _____
My hero or heroine: _____
Some of my closest friends: _____
What I like to do with friends: _____
Someday I'd like to try to: _____
My birthday is: _____
My favorite restaurant is: _____
Things at school I'm good at: _____

Page 233

List Bliss!

Making lists helped Harvey cope. Try some lists of your own. Each school day for one month, make a list from one of the titles given below. Keep your lists together in a special notebook or binder. You'll be surprised how well you get to know yourself in one month! Check off each list as you've used it. Make up new list titles if you run out.

Lists will vary.

1. Big Events in My Life
2. Things That Worry Me
3. Projects I've Liked in School
4. Things I Like about Me
5. Bad Things That Have Happened to Me
6. Things I Like to Make
7. My Favorite Things To Do
8. Jobs I'd Like To Do When I'm Older.
9. Gifts I Got That I Didn't Want
10. Sad Moments I Remember
11. Places I've Visited
12. Songs I've Always Liked
13. Important People in My Life.
14. Months and Dates Special to Me
15. Foods I Just Don't Like
16. Games That I Play Well
17. Books I've Enjoyed
18. Things I Wish For
19. Animals I'd Like to Have
20. Things That Make Me Happy

Page 234

It's a Shame!

With which children are you most likely to sympathize? Rate these characteristics from the greatest to the least with number 1 drawing the greatest amount of sympathy.

Answers will vary.

Characteristics	Rating
no father at home	—
teacher's pet	—
poor eating habits	—
overweight	—
cries easily	—
death in the family	—
rich	—
little self-control	—
poor health	—
ignorance	—
bad reputation	—
very thin	—
poor	—
adults have high expectations of	—
uncoordinated	—
little adult guidance	—

Should you be more sympathetic with some people? Write a contract in which you make a promise you can keep.

Sympathy Contract

I, _____ (your name), do hereby promise to be more understanding and sympathetic to those who _____. I hope to show consideration by _____

_____ (signature)   _____ (date)

Give this contract to a trustworthy friend or adult who will help you to be more caring.

Page 235

Emily Post Says . . .

Emily Post's book *Etiquette*, published in 1922, established behavior guidelines for all sorts of situations. She believed good manners were based on common sense and feelings for others. She kept up with the changing times and wrote ten editions of her book during her lifetime. People still refer to it when they have a question about proper behavior in social situations. Post also gave advice in a newspaper column and on the radio.

Write a column and give advice for the following situations.

1. Jane wants to have a party. There are ten boys and twelve girls in her class. She wants to invite everyone in the class except two of the girls. She also wants to ask her neighbors Emily and Bridgette, but her Mom says she can only have fifteen guests including herself. Who should she ask? How should they be asked? Answer these questions and give reasons for your answers.
   Answers will vary.

2. Tim is one of the lucky invited guests, but he knows his best friend, Tom, was not asked. What should Tim tell Tom when Tom asks him to spend the night on the night the party is being given? Why?

3. Michael was pleased because he got one of the leading roles in the school play, but Joe was very disappointed because he did not get a part. What can Michael do to not hurt Joe further and perhaps help ease his disappointment?

Personality Plus Write a question you have concerning the polite thing to do in a certain situation. Put your question in a box with the questions of your classmates. The questions may be discussed in a small group or as a class.

Page 236

Me and My Shadow

Addie can hardly wait to have a friend. Tilla becomes that friend even though the two are different in many ways. In the chart below, compare yourself to one of your friends. You may wish to compare such things as hair color, eye color, family size, hobbies, favorite songs, and so on.

Charts will vary.

Myself	My friend	Alike or different?

Page 237

Families

One of the things people all over the world have in common is the need to give and receive love. Love is given when you help, talk, listen and share with another person. Family members are often the ones who do these things to show love for each other.

1. List ways your family cares for you. *Answers will vary.*

2. What do you do to show your family you care?

3. Do you have specific chores to do at home daily or weekly? If yes, what are they?

4. Does your parents giving you chores to do show that they care about you? Why or why not?

5. List things a family member has taught you.

6. List things you have taught or could teach a member of your family.

7. List ways a family member helps you deal with a variety of emotions.

8. Members of a family often take on certain roles within the family structure. Which member of your family is usually the disciplinarian?

9. It is often said that a parent's love for a child is unconditional. What do you think unconditional love is?

10. On the back of this page, write two positive statements about each member of your family. Share these with the person on a day when he/she needs cheering up.

Page 238

It's All in the Family!   *Page will vary.*

Write the names of family members with whom you live. _____

Write the names of the members of your immediate family. _____

Write the names of your extended family on the correct lines in the diagram below. Fill in the names of your immediate family in the box.

great-grandparents

grandparents

mother _____	_____ father
you and your sisters and/or brothers	

aunts and uncles   aunts and uncles

cousins   cousins

Page 239

Uniforms

People on all continents wear some type of covering on their bodies. Originally, clothing was used merely to protect a person from climatic conditions. Today, the clothes a person wears tell something about his/her lifestyle or status in society. While many businesses allow people to wear their own clothes to work, others require workers to wear a uniform. Why do you think people in some jobs must wear uniforms? *to identify them as someone of a certain profession, to eliminate confusion, etc. Answers will vary.*

List several jobs that require workers to wear uniforms. *hospital staff, police officers, military, some factory workers, maids, airline workers*

Cut out pictures of people wearing uniforms from old catalogs, magazines, or newspapers. Glue the pictures on a piece of construction paper or posterboard to make a collage of uniforms.

Pretend that you are the president or CEO of your own company. Decide what your company will sell or produce. In the space below, show examples of the uniforms you would require workers to wear: 1) clerical; 2) executive officers; 3) assembly line; 4) maintenance.

Pictures will vary.

Should you, as president of the company, have to wear a uniform? Why, or why not?

Page 240

Places to Live

Shelters provide a place in which people can live and keep their possessions. Early man took shelter in places provided by nature, such as a cave, hollow or hole in the ground. One of the first shelters devised by humans is still in use today — the tent. As man improved his tools and learned to farm, permanent homes were built. Today, people throughout the world live in a wide variety of homes. List as many different types of shelter as you can think of on the lines below. *Answers will vary.*

Condominiums, apartments, tents, houses, cabins, hotel, mobile home, houseboat, treehouse

Make a list of the different types of shelter the students in your class occupy. Use the information to complete the graph below.

Types of Housing

	1 2 3 4 5 6 7 8 9 10 11 12 13 14 15 16 17 18 19 20 21 22 23 24 25 26 27 28 29 30
House	
Apartment	
Mobile Home	
Condominium	
Houseboat	
Cabin	
Other	

Use the list of homes above to complete this next activity. Some types of shelter are better suited to hot climates. Others are designed for cold climates. Write the name of each type of home under the correct heading. Some may be suitable for both types of climate.

HOT CLIMATES	COLD CLIMATES	BOTH CLIMATES
tents houseboat		apartments mobile homes houses, condos

Page 241

Picture Your Life in Time

Though you have only lived a short time, many significant events have happened in your life and in the world around you. Record some of these events on this page and the next.

Write the year you were born on the first line under YEAR. Write every year thereafter up to the current year. Before each year, the age you were during that year is written in parentheses. On the first line after each year, use a blue pen to write something significant you did that year. (You may have to ask a family member to help you with this.) On the second and third lines, use a red pen to write an important event that happened in the world during that year. (You may refer to an almanac or another reference.) Try to find a coin minted during each year of your life. Tape it in the circle to the right of the corresponding year.

Answers will vary.

AGE	YEAR
(0-1)	
(1-2)	
(2-3)	
(3-4)	

Page 242

Picture Your Life in Time (cont.)

Answers will vary.

(4-5)	
(5-6)	
(6-7)	
(7-8)	
(8-9)	
(9-10)	
(10-11)	

Page 243

Daily Learning Drills Grade 4

Customs and Traditions

1. List several special days or occasions you observe, such as holidays or birthdays. *Answers will vary.*

2. Pick one of the above that you celebrate with your family. Write a paragraph on the back of this page about what you and your family did to celebrate this special event the last time it occurred. Was the celebration the same as it always has been or were there some differences? Write what was the same and what was different.

   Same _____   Different _____

3. Write the name of a holiday that you observed in the past year. _____
   With whom did you observe it? _____
   What did you do to celebrate? _____
   Name three things associated with the holiday that are a traditional part of its celebration. _____

4. List some traditions you and/or your family have. _____

5. What custom do you carry on today that you would like to see changed or dropped? _____
   Why? _____

6. What custom do you intend to carry on when you have a family? _____

7. What customs observed by the general population do you no longer see a need for and why? _____

8. What would you like to see become a custom and why? _____

Page 244

U.S. Patriotic Holidays

Memorial Day	Flag Day	Columbus Day	Presidents' Day
Bill of Rights Day	Labor Day	Veterans Day	Independence Day

Use the list of holidays above to write each holiday in the appropriate blank in each sentence or paragraph below.

1. *Presidents Day*, on the third Monday in February, honors two United States Presidents, George Washington and Abraham Lincoln, born in the month.

2. *Memorial Day* originally was celebrated May 30 and honored the war dead of the Civil War. It now is observed on the last Monday in May and is dedicated to the memory of all war dead. It is also known as Decoration Day because graves of service people are often decorated.

3. *Bill of Rights Day*, December 15, honors the date in 1791 on which Congress made them law. They are the first ten amendments of the U.S. Constitution.

4. *Columbus Day*, on the second Monday in October, commemorates the discovery of America by honoring the man who sailed near its shores in 1492.

5. *Flag Day* commemorates the act of Congress on June 14, 1777, that adopted America's stars and stripes as the country's official banner.

6. *Labor Day*, observed the first Monday in September in all states, honors America's backbone, its workers.

7. *Independence Day* on July 4, perhaps the most patriotic of all America's holidays, is celebrated in all states. It observes the adoption of the Declaration of Independence.

8. *Veterans Day* was once called Armistice Day. It began in 1926 to commemorate the signing of the armistice that ended World War I in 1918. In 1954, the holiday's name was changed to honor all men and women who have served their country in the armed services.

Select one of the above holidays. Then, on another sheet of paper, do one of the following:
- Design a stamp to honor its observance.
- Write a poem about the holiday.
- Draw a mural of a parade honoring that holiday.

Page 245

An Interview
Interviews will vary.

Person interviewed _____   Date of interview _____

1. Were you my age about 20, 30, 40, 50, 60, 70 or 80 years ago? _____
2. Where did you live when you were my age? _____
   If not here, how long ago did you move here? _____
3. How has the community changed? _____
4. What time did you get up when you were my age? _____
   What was your morning schedule? _____
5. What did you do after school? _____
6. What was your bedtime when you were my age? _____
7. What sort of things did you eat when you were my age? _____
8. What toys did you have? What were your favorites? _____
9. What chores did you have, if any? _____
10. Did you get an allowance? ____ How much was it? ____
    Did you earn any money when you were my age? ____ Doing what? ____
    About what did you make in an hour? ____
11. How did you spend your money? _____
12. What was your most favorite thing to do during "free time"? _____
    Tell about it. _____
13. What games did you play? _____
14. What did you study at school? _____

Page 246

An Interview (cont.)
Interviews will vary.

15. How did you get to school? _____
16. What was school like? What did you have that was the same? Different? (i.e. physical education, cafeteria, etc.) _____
17. Do you remember any rhymes or songs? Name one. _____
18. Did you ever get in trouble? ____ Tell about one time. _____
    What happened to you when you got in trouble? _____
19. What was the best thing that ever happened to you? _____
    What was the worst? _____
20. What were some of your family customs or traditions (i.e.: birthdays, holidays, games, jokes, etc)? _____
21. What are some of the biggest changes you have seen during your lifetime? _____

Write additional questions or information given that was not asked for below or on another sheet of paper.

Page 247

Other Ways to Communicate

For those people who are hearing impaired, vocal communication is not possible. People who cannot hear use sign language. Even those who can hear but do not speak the same language often use a modified form of sign language. You will often see visitors in a foreign land trying to sign to be understood.

Using the alphabet to the right, learn to sign your name, your hometown and the name of your school. Try to have a conversation with a friend using only sign language.

Braille is a system of printing and writing for the blind. It was developed by Louis Braille, a blind Frenchman, in the 1820's. Braille uses raised dots on a page. A blind person reads dots by touching with his/her fingertips. The Braille symbols are large and thick, so they can be felt easily.

Using the alphabet below, write a paragraph about your favorite hobby. After you finish, answer these questions.

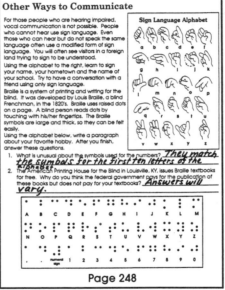
Sign Language Alphabet

1. What is unusual about the symbols used for the numbers? *They match the symbols for the first ten letters of the alphabet.*
2. The American Printing House for the Blind in Louisville, KY, issues Braille textbooks for free. Why do you think the federal government pays for the publication of these books but does not pay for your textbooks? *Answers will vary.*

Page 248

Got the Message?

Hieroglyphics is a form of writing used by the ancient Egyptians in which picture symbols represented ideas and sounds. It was the Rosetta Stone, a decree carved on stone with hieroglyphics, that gave the world the key to understanding this writing when it was found in 1799.

Use the hieroglyphics below to write a secret message to your friend. Have him/her decipher your message and write a response to it in hieroglyphics. Then, write your message and his/her response in English. **Note:** There were no vowels in hieroglyphics. Use capital vowels to represent a vowel sound. Note also that there were many variations of this type of writing.

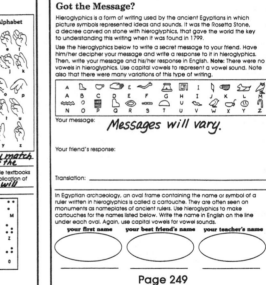

Your message: *Messages will vary.*

Your friend's response: _____

Translation: _____

In Egyptian archaeology, an oval frame containing the name or symbol of a ruler written in hieroglyphics is called a cartouche. They are often seen on monuments as nameplates of ancient rulers. Write hieroglyphics to make cartouches for the names listed below. Write the name in English on the line under each oval. Again, use capital vowels for vowel sounds.

your first name	your best friend's name	your teacher's name
(oval)	(oval)	(oval)

Page 249

Community Needs

Mother Teresa of Calcutta has dedicated her life to helping "the poorest of the poor." Mother Teresa and the members of her congregation, the Missionaries of Charity, aid poor, sick, and abandoned children and adults around the world.

Think about your community. List three of its social problems or needs.
Answers will vary.

Tell how you think each problem might be solved. Include what you might do to help in each solution.

_____

Follow the Leader Find out about an organization in your community that works to solve some of the problems you listed above. How do they work to solve the problem? Is there any way you can get involved? Share your information with the class.

Page 250

Community Workers

Ask several men and women in your community what their occupations are (e.g., doctor, farmer, maintenance worker). Record their answers, without names, on another sheet of paper.

When you have completed your survey, plot the two bar graphs below. If you have too many different responses, you may want to group them by categories, such as Medical, Sales, Government, and Service.

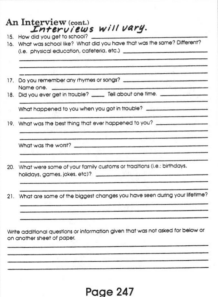
Answers will vary.

Men / Women (bar graphs)
Kind of Work

Answer these questions to draw some conclusions from your graphs.
What kinds of jobs do most of the community's population have? _____
Are most workers skilled or non-skilled? _____
Are there differences between jobs held by men and women? _____
What types of workers are needed in the community? _____
What else have you observed? _____

Page 251

What Kind of Community?

Read the definitions of three different types of communities below.

Rural Community country; large amount of open space; rustic; agriculture predominates	**Urban Community** big city or town; often at least 50,000 people; crowded with buildings and people; business center	**Suburban Community** largely residential; often near a large city; often incorporated separately

Read the sentences on this page and page 253. Underline only the sentences that describe your community. Then, answer this: In what kind of a community do you live? *Answers will vary.*

1. All that can be seen from a rooftop is land criss-crossed by dirt roads and fences.
2. Neighbors may sometimes wake neighbors if they mow their lawns too early in the morning.
3. There is a feeling of open space, and yet there are shopping malls, supermarkets, schools, etc.
4. The sounds of elevated trains and honking horns are heard almost twenty-four hours a day.
5. Many families who work in the city live here because it is quieter, and the commute to the city every day is not too long.
6. During the summer, neighborhood children set up lemonade stands, and families have picnics and barbecues in their back yards.
7. Homes are very close together. Many are stacked one on top of one another in buildings called apartments.
8. Streets and sidewalks are crowded with workers going to and from work and shoppers looking in store front windows.
9. Many people work at farming.
10. Mailboxes are often very far from the houses.
11. Neighbors are often miles apart.
12. It is on the outskirts of a city.

Page 252

What Kind of Community? (cont.)

13. Residents of the community seldom see one another, so a community gathering is a real social event.
14. Hotels provide a place for visitors to stay who come for meetings at the convention center.
15. The population is over 50,000.
16. The high school's students come from several outlying communities and must ride the bus because distances are great.
17. Nights are quiet except for the occasional sound of an animal.
18. Children play in parks rather than in back yards.
19. There is a feeling of country with the conveniences of a city.

Write two or three paragraphs about your community on the lines below. Ideas to include: its population, contact with neighbors, and availability of services.

Paragraphs will vary.

Page 253

Waste Materials

Next to each picture on this page and the next, write one or two sentences about what is pictured that is harmful for the environment. Tell why or how it is harmful. Then, write ways to correct the problem.

Answers will vary.
Plastic drink holders are thrown into lakes and other wildlife get caught and often die.

Solutions will also vary.

Garbage continues to increase so that landfills are over-flowing. More space is needed to hold the garbage.

Noise pollution (loud stereos, etc.) invade others' space and result in stress and/or animosity.

Page 254

Waste Materials (cont.)

Forests are stripped of trees are cut down and animals lose more habitat.

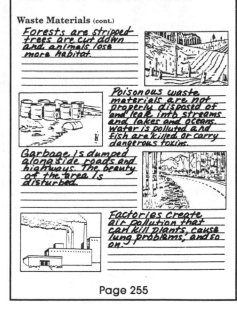

Poisonous waste materials are not properly disposed of and leak into streams and lakes and oceans. Water is polluted and fish are killed, or carry dangerous toxins.

Garbage is dumped alongside roads and highways. The beauty of the area is disturbed.

Factories create air pollution that can kill plants, cause lung problems, and so on.

Page 255

Money Sources

Ask four people of different ages how they get their money. When they answer yes to a category, check the line in front of it. A person may answer yes to more than one category. Many of the categories may not apply and therefore will not be checked. If the category is "other," write the source.

Answers will vary.

Ask someone between 8-11 years old: How do you get your money?
___ allowance ___ gifts ___ full-time job ___ part-time job
___ interest ___ dividends ___ borrowed ___ pension
___ other: _____

Ask someone between 15-18 years of age: How do you get your money?
___ allowance ___ gifts ___ full-time job ___ part-time job
___ interest ___ dividends ___ borrowed ___ pension
___ other: _____

Ask someone between 35-45 years of age: How do you get your money?
___ allowance ___ gifts ___ full-time job ___ part-time job
___ interest ___ dividends ___ borrowed ___ pension
___ other: _____

Ask someone over 65 years of age: How do you get your money?
___ allowance ___ gifts ___ full-time job ___ part-time job
___ interest ___ dividends ___ borrowed ___ pension
___ other: _____

Compare findings with other class members. Tally where people's money comes from in the different age groups. If desired, make a bar graph for each group.

	8-11	15-18	35-45	65 or over
allowance				
gifts				
full-time job				
part-time job				
interest				
dividends				
borrowed				
pension				
other				

Page 256

Where Money Goes

Ask four people of different ages on what they spend their money. When they answer yes to a category, put a check mark on the line in front of it. A person may answer yes to more than one, or some of the categories may not apply and therefore will not get checked. If the category is "other," write how that money is spent.

Answers will vary.

Ask someone between 8-11 years old: On what do you spend your money?
___ rent/mortgage ___ clothing ___ food ___ utilities
___ transportation ___ vacation ___ taxes ___ savings
___ entertainment ___ insurance ___ dates ___ school
___ investments ___ presents ___ treats ___ supplies
___ medical/doctors ___ eating out ___ sports ___ hobbies
___ other: _____

Ask someone between 15-18 years of age: On what do you spend your money?
___ rent/mortgage ___ clothing ___ food ___ utilities
___ transportation ___ vacation ___ taxes ___ savings
___ entertainment ___ insurance ___ dates ___ school
___ investments ___ presents ___ treats ___ supplies
___ medical/doctors ___ eating out ___ sports ___ hobbies
___ other: _____

Ask someone between 35-45 years of age: On what do you spend your money?
___ rent/mortgage ___ clothing ___ food ___ utilities
___ transportation ___ vacation ___ taxes ___ savings
___ entertainment ___ insurance ___ dates ___ school
___ investments ___ presents ___ treats ___ supplies
___ medical/doctors ___ eating out ___ sports ___ hobbies
___ other: _____

Ask someone over 65 years of age: On what do you spend your money?
___ rent/mortgage ___ clothing ___ food ___ utilities
___ transportation ___ vacation ___ taxes ___ savings
___ entertainment ___ insurance ___ dates ___ school
___ investments ___ presents ___ treats ___ supplies
___ medical/doctors ___ eating out ___ sports ___ hobbies
___ other: _____

Compare class findings. On another page, tally how the age groups spend money.

Page 257

Needs for Your "Full Circle"

We all have **physical, intellectual, emotional** and **social** needs to live a happy and healthy life. Read each statement from the text and decide which need is being met. Write it on the blank.

1. Mattie finished the test before anyone else and turned her paper over on her desk. She reached inside for a book. *intellectual*
2. Matt had dinner started when Mattie got home—salad and leftover spaghetti. *physical*
3. Mr. Ashby had outdone himself this weekend. His homework assignments included math, spelling, a social studies essay, a book report, and vocabulary words. He was determined to make his fifth graders work. *intellectual*
4. "But Mattie, I do love you," said Mrs. Benson with tears in her eyes. *emotional*
5. When the telephone rang in the living room, Matt called to his sister. It was Toni. *social*
6. Humming softly, Mattie sat up, reached in her back pocket and un-wrapped her favorite photograph. She had decided to carry it with her today, and her father's strength seemed to reach out and hold her. *emotional*
7. Mattie started dinner—chili, rice, and salad. *physical*
8. "Oh, Toni, this sounds like a lot of maybes. I'm going to Stern's on Saturday and stopping in to see Mrs. Stamps. I wanted you to come with me." *social*

Page 258

Do You Speak My Language?

It is estimated that there are about 3,000 spoken languages in use today by the people of the world. This is not a precise figure because linguists disagree as to what constitutes a spoken language and what constitutes a dialect. A dialect is usually considered to be a variation within a language.

Language influences all aspects of a culture, including social behavior. If people can understand each other, human society tends to function smoothly. If people are not able to understand one another, society often grinds to a halt.

To the right are the most widely spoken languages in the world and the percent of the world's population that speaks each one. Use the list to complete the graph below.

Language	
German	1.5
French	1.5
Japanese	2.0
Portuguese	2.0
Arabic	2.0
Spanish	3.0
Russian	3.5
Hindi	4.5
English	6.0
Mandarin	20.0

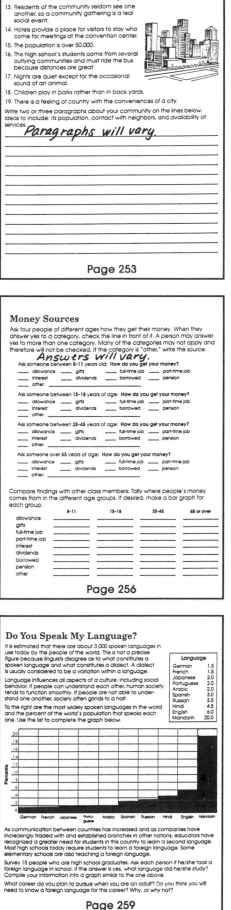

As communication between countries has increased and as companies have increasingly traded with and established branches in other nations, educators have recognized a greater need for students in this country to learn a second language. Most high schools today require students to learn a foreign language. Some elementary schools are also teaching a foreign language.

Survey 15 people who are high school graduates. Ask each person if he/she took a foreign language in school. If the answer is yes, what language did he/she study? Compile your information into a graph similar to the one above.

What career do you plan to pursue when you are an adult? Do you think you will need to know a foreign language for this career? Why, or why not?

Page 259

Where Is Wheat Grown?

Wheat grows best in dry temperate regions. The ideal climate includes a cool, moist spring, a warm dry harvest period and an annual rainfall of 9 to 30 inches. There are nine areas of the world which provide a wheat-growing climate.

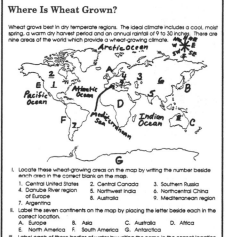

I. Locate these wheat-growing areas on the map by writing the number beside each area in the correct blank on the map.
1. Central United States
2. Central Canada
3. Southern Russia
4. Danube River region of Europe
5. Northwest India
6. Northcentral China
7. Argentina
8. Australia
9. Mediterranean region

II. Label the seven continents on the map by placing the letter beside each in the correct location.
A. Europe B. Asia C. Australia D. Africa
E. North America F. South America G. Antarctica

III. Label each of these bodies of water by writing the name in the correct location on the map: Mediterranean Sea, Pacific Ocean, Atlantic Ocean, Indian Ocean, Arctic Ocean.

IV. On the map, draw a compass rose which shows all cardinal and intermediate directions.

Page 260

The Beginning of Rome

The earliest Roman settlers were mostly shepherds. Their settlements, mainly in the Roman hills, eventually joined to form the city of Rome. It is believed Romulus and Remus were the legendary founders of Rome, but no one knows for sure if they really existed. However, their story exemplifies strength, a quality admired by ancient Romans. There are several versions of the Romulus and Remus legend. Read the one below. Follow the directions after the story.

Romulus and Remus were twin sons of the war god, Mars. They were set adrift in a basket on the Tiber River by a wicked uncle who hoped they would die. But they survived. A she-wolf heard their cries and rescued them. She nursed them until they grew to be young boys. Then, Faustulus, a shepherd, adopted them. Along with his wife, he raised them as if they were his own. When Romulus and Remus became young men, they set out to found a city. The brothers argued about where their city should be located. Then, supposedly, Romulus killed Remus, named Rome after himself, and became Rome's first king.

1. List the things in the story that symbolize or are examples of strength. *Answers will vary; might include Mars, the war god; she-wolf; king*
2. Name places in the story that are real. *Tiber River, Rome*
3. Do you think this is a true story? Give reasons for your opinion. *Answers will vary.*
4. Write a pretend story about the founders of your city/town. *Stories will vary*

Page 261

Two Great Statues

Two of the Seven Wonders of the World are statues. Both of them were in Greece: The Statue of Zeus at Olympia and The Colossus of Rhodes, near the harbor of the island in the Aegean Sea.

The statue of Zeus was made by the Greek sculptor Phidias around 435 B.C. It was dedicated to Zeus, the king of gods. It showed Zeus seated on his throne and was forty feet tall. Zeus' robe and ornaments were made out of gold and his flesh was made of ivory. In his right hand, he held a figure of his messenger, Nike. In his left hand, he held a scepter with an eagle.

Imagine a conversation the statue of Zeus might have had with an athlete at an Olympic Game. Choose an athlete and write the conversation below.

Conversations will vary.

The Colossus of Rhodes, a bronze statue of the sun god, Helios, stood about 120 feet tall. It took the Greek sculptor Chares about twelve years to complete it in the early 200's B.C. The statue did not stand very long as it was destroyed in an earthquake around 224 B.C. It lay in ruins until 653 A.D. when its remains were sold as scrap metal. Imagine what the Colossus of Rhodes would tell you if it could talk. Write about a conversation between you and it below.

Conversations will vary.

Page 262

Comparing Civilizations

A Venn diagram is a great way to compare things. Use the one below to compare two leaders, gods, or civilizations of Ancient Greece or Rome. Write the names of the two things you are comparing on the lines provided. Fill in the unshared portion of each circle with characteristics common only to the subject. In the overlapped portion, write down characteristics the two subjects share. Then, write a story about your findings on the lines below.

subject name _____   subject name _____

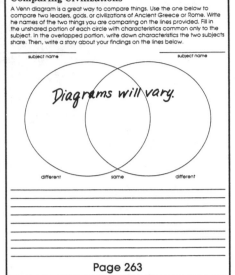

Diagrams will vary.

different   same   different

Page 263

How!

How many of these Indian names can you identify as state names? Write the name of the state for each Indian name. Then draw the matching symbol of that state on the United States map where it belongs.

★ Ute	*Utah*	◁ Dakotas	*North Dakota / South Dakota*
Emissourita	*Missouri*	Alakshak	*Alaska*
Wishdonsing	*Wisconsin*	Arizonac	*Arizona*
Mishigamaw	*Michigan*	Minisota	*Minnesota*
Massaadchauset	*Massachusetts*	Iliniiwek	*Illinois*
▲ Misisipi	*Mississippi*	Arkansaw	*Arkansas*
Oheo	*Ohio*	Alibamu	*Alabama*
Idaho	*Idaho*	Tanasi	*Tennessee*

Page 264

Decision-Making Map

As the United States government began forcing the Sioux off their land, the Sioux fought to keep it. They took great care of the land and believed that it belonged to them. The white settlers believed that they were smarter and more deserving of the land. The battles between the two sides resulted in the death of many men, women, and children. Was there a better way they could have used to solve the problem? Find the best solution by working with a partner to complete the chart below.

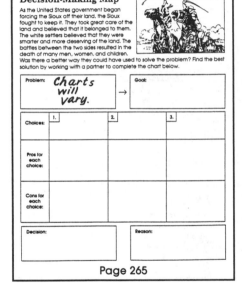

Problem:	*Charts will vary.*	→	Goal:	
Choices:	1.	2.	3.	
Pros for each choice:				
Cons for each choice:				
Decision:		Reason:		

Page 265

Welcome to the Union

* 39 & 40 could be reversed.

The fifty United States are listed below alphabetically. The date each one entered the Union is given after it. On the line to the left of each state, write the number that tells in what order the state joined the Union.

22 Alabama	Dec. 14, 1819	41 Montana	Nov. 8, 1889
49 Alaska	Jan. 3, 1959	37 Nebraska	Mar. 1, 1867
48 Arizona	Feb. 14, 1912	36 Nevada	Oct. 31, 1864
25 Arkansas	June 15, 1836	9 New Hampshire	June 21, 1788
31 California	Sept. 9, 1850	3 New Jersey	Dec. 18, 1787
38 Colorado	Aug. 1, 1876	47 New Mexico	Jan. 6, 1912
5 Connecticut	Jan. 9, 1788	11 New York	July 26, 1788
1 Delaware	Dec. 7, 1787	12 North Carolina	Nov. 21, 1789
27 Florida	Mar. 3, 1845	39 North Dakota	Nov. 2, 1889
4 Georgia	Jan. 2, 1788	17 Ohio	Mar. 1, 1803
50 Hawaii	Aug. 21, 1959	46 Oklahoma	Nov. 16, 1907
43 Idaho	July 3, 1890	33 Oregon	Feb. 14, 1859
21 Illinois	Dec. 3, 1818	2 Pennsylvania	Dec. 12, 1787
19 Indiana	Dec. 11, 1816	13 Rhode Island	May 29, 1790
29 Iowa	Dec. 28, 1846	8 South Carolina	May 23, 1788
34 Kansas	Jan. 29, 1861	40 South Dakota	Nov. 2, 1889
15 Kentucky	June 1, 1792	16 Tennessee	June 1, 1796
18 Louisiana	Apr. 30, 1812	28 Texas	Dec. 29, 1845
23 Maine	Mar. 15, 1820	45 Utah	Jan. 4, 1896
7 Maryland	Apr. 28, 1788	14 Vermont	Mar. 4, 1791
6 Massachusetts	Feb. 6, 1788	10 Virginia	June 25, 1788
26 Michigan	Jan. 26, 1837	42 Washington	Nov. 11, 1889
32 Minnesota	May 11, 1858	35 West Virginia	June 20, 1863
20 Mississippi	Dec. 10, 1817	30 Wisconsin	May 29, 1848
24 Missouri	Aug. 10, 1821	44 Wyoming	July 10, 1890

• Draw what comes next. △ ◇ ▽ ◇ ◈ **◆**

Page 266

Figure Out Freedom

In 1861, 19 states declared themselves "Free States." People in these states were opposed to slavery. Unscramble each name to find out which states were considered "Free."

EIMNA — *Maine*
EWN SEERJY — *New Jersey*
TREOVMN — *Vermont*
WNE ROYK — *New York*
LFIINAAORC — *California*
WIOA — *Iowa*
EGROON — *Oregon*
NESNOMITA — *Minnesota*
IICHAGMN — *Michigan*
DAANIIN — *Indiana*
SILLIONI — *Illinois*
SASKNA — *Kansas*
CHASETSUTSMAS — *Massachusetts*
NOSSCIIWN — *Wisconsin*
HIOO — *Ohio*
CCUTTCIENON — *Connecticut*
HODER SLANDI — *Rhode Island*
VANPIASENYNL — *Pennsylvania*
WNE SHEPRAMIH — *New Hampshire*

Page 267

Topical Titles

Pick the best title for each paragraph. Be certain to capitalize the first, last and all important words in each title. You will not use all choices listed.

the gregorian calendar	schools in england
george washington's birthday	lieutenant colonel george washington
the french and indian war	mount vernon

1. *Lieutenant Colonel George Washington*

In 1754, the Governor of Virginia made George Washington a lieutenant colonel and sent him and his troops into the Ohio River Valley to claim the land for Britain. Although the French and their Indian allies fought hard to keep this land, when the war ended in 1763, Britain was the victor.

2. *Mount Vernon*

Augustine Washington had three farms. When his son, Lawrence, returned home from school in England, Augustine asked him to manage one of the plantations for him. Lawrence later renamed his plantation "Mount Vernon" in honor of his hero, Admiral Edward Vernon, and both he and George loved living there.

3. *George Washington's Birthday*

George Washington was actually born on February 11. But in 1752, the British adopted a new calendar, and this changed his birthday to February 22. George, however, always considered February 11 to be his date of birth and preferred to celebrate his birthday on that date.

A NOW...ADD The picture at the top of this page shows Mount Rushmore, a national memorial that has the largest figures of any statue in the entire world. If you were going to design such a memorial, which four faces would you choose to include? Then draw a picture of what your memorial would look like.

Page 268

Personality Profiles

All the fourth graders are doing reports on famous Americans. Jackie has gathered lots of information on John Adams. Now all she has to do is put it together. Help her out by numbering the events below in chronological order.

3 After teaching school for awhile, Adams studied law. He began practicing in 1758.

7 Adams was elected by the people of Braintree to help write what became the Massachusetts Constitution of 1780.

1 John Adams was born in Braintree, Massachusetts, on October 30, 1735.

2 When Adams was about 20, he was graduated from Harvard College. He was one of the best students in the class.

6 In 1778, Congress sent Adams to Paris to help Benjamin Franklin and Arthur Lee strengthen American ties with the French.

10 Adams died on July 4, 1826. He lived longer than any other U.S. President.

8 In 1789, Adams was named Vice-President under George Washington.

5 Adams was chosen as one of the four Massachusetts delegates to the First Continental Congress in 1774.

4 In 1764, Adams married Abigail Smith. Their eldest son, John Quincy, became our 6th President.

9 John Adams became our 2nd President in 1797. He was the first President to live in the White House.

•SOMETHING EXTRA•
Cut the above facts apart. Glue each of them on a piece of paper. Illustrate each page. Combine the pages to make a book.

Page 269

What a Trip!

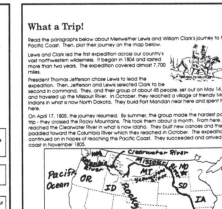

Read the paragraphs below about Meriwether Lewis and William Clark's journey to the Pacific Coast. Then, plot their journey on the map below.

Lewis and Clark led the first expedition across our country's vast northwestern wilderness. It began in 1804 and lasted more than two years. The expedition covered almost 7,700 miles.

President Thomas Jefferson chose Lewis to lead the expedition. Then, Jefferson and Lewis selected Clark to be second in command. They, and their group of about 45 people, set out on May 14, 1804, and traveled up the Missouri River. In October, they reached a village of friendly Mandan Indians in what is now North Dakota. They built Fort Mandan near here and spent the winter here.

On April 17, 1805, the journey resumed. By summer, the group made the hardest part of the trip - they crossed the Rocky Mountains. This took them about a month. From here, they reached the Clearwater River in what is now Idaho. They built new canoes and then paddled toward the Columbia River which they reached in October. The expedition continued on in hopes of reaching the Pacific Coast. They succeeded and arrived at the coast in November 1805.

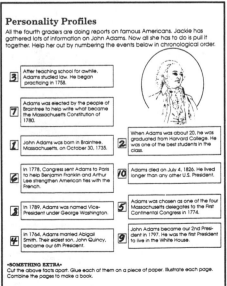

1. Label the areas that are now states through which Lewis and Clark journeyed.
2. Label the rivers on which the expedition traveled.
3. Label the Rocky Mountains.
4. Label the Pacific Ocean.
5. Put a star where the group met the Mandan Indians.

Personality Plus Pretend you are a news reporter and you get to interview Lewis and Clark about their journey. Write the questions you would ask and their responses.

Page 270

Down with Slavery

Rewrite the sentences in the paragraph below in the correct order.

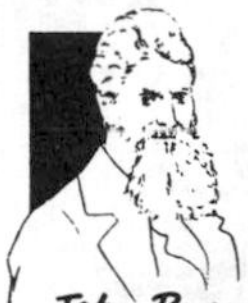

John Brown

Brown was tried for and convicted of treason. He rented a farm near Harper's Ferry, Virginia from which he led an armed group of eighteen men. They seized the town and the United States Arsenal there. John Brown spent much of his adult life opposing slavery, but he is best remembered for his final act in 1859. He was hanged in Charleston, South Carolina. Within twenty-four hours the raid was over. Brown's forces were either killed or captured by the United States Marines led by Robert E. Lee.

John Brown spent much of his adult life opposing slavery, but he is best remembered for his final act in 1859. He rented a farm near Harper's Ferry Virginia, from which he led an armed group of eighteen men. They seized the town and the United States Arsenal there. Within twenty-four hours the raid was over. Brown's forces were either killed or captured by the United States Marines led by Robert E. Lee. Brown was tried for and convicted of treason. He was hanged in Charlestown, South Carolina.

- Nat Turner is another black man who was important in American history. What did he do?

Nat Turner led the most famous slave revolt in United States' history in 1831.

Page 271

Nuts About Nuts!

A famous American was responsible for the recognition of the peanut as a crop. This brilliant and creative person was George Washington Carver. Carver's research lead to the development of over 300 products made with peanuts!

To find out the influence of peanuts on our lives, complete the activities below.

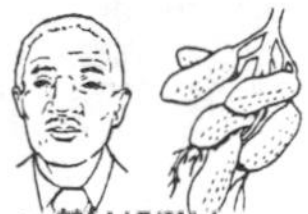

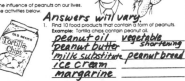

Answers will vary.

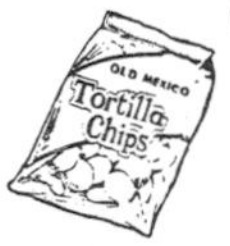

OLD MEXICO
Tortilla Chips

1. Find 10 food products that contain a form of peanuts. **Example:** Tortilla chips contain peanut oil.

peanut oil, vegetable shortening, peanut butter, milk substitute, peanut bread, ice cream, margarine

2. List 4 non-edible items that contain a form of peanuts. **Example:** A derivative of peanuts is used to make plastic.

face powder, paint, printers ink, soap, shampoo, shaving creams

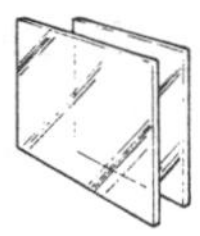

3. Write your favorite recipe below that contains a form of peanuts. Share it with the class.

Recipes will vary.

Personality Plus Find another person who you think contributed something important to our society. Write what he/she contributed and why you think it was important. Share it with your class.

Page 272

A Point of View

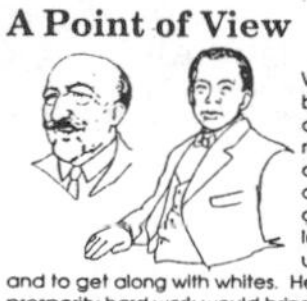

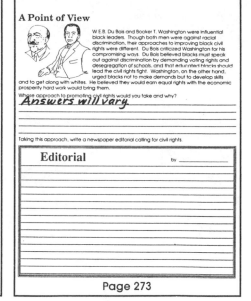

W.E.B. Du Bois and Booker T. Washington were influential black leaders. Though both men were against racial discrimination, their approaches to improving black civil rights were different. Du Bois criticized Washington for his compromising ways. Du Bois believed blacks must speak out against discrimination by demanding voting rights and desegregation of schools, and that educated blacks should lead the civil rights fight. Washington, on the other hand, urged blacks not to make demands but to develop skills and to get along with whites. He believed they would earn equal rights with the economic prosperity hard work would bring them.

Whose approach to promoting civil rights would you take and why?

Answers will vary.

Taking this approach, write a newspaper editorial calling for civil rights.

Editorial by ____________

Page 273

One Great Inventor

Rewrite the set of sentences in the correct order. Use the proper paragraph form.

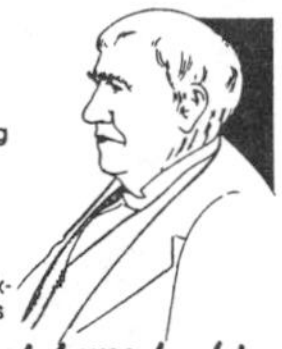

Thomas Edison

1. By the time he was twelve years old, he was selling newspapers to finance his experiments.
2. He sold the firm his patents and used the money from this sale to set himself up as a freelance inventor.
3. Thomas Edison was taught at home by his mother.
4. At the age of twenty-one, while working for a stock-ticker firm, Thomas patented various improvements on the stock ticker.

Thomas Edison was taught at home by his mother. By the time he was twelve years old, he was selling newspapers to finance his experiments. At the age of twenty-one, while working for a stock-ticker firm, Thomas patented various improvements on the stock ticker. He sold the firm his patents and used the money from this sale to set himself up as a freelance inventor.

- What other inventions are Thomas Edison noted for?

Edison invented the electric light and the phonograph and improved many other inventions.

- Name one other inventor. Tell what he invented and when.

Answers will vary.

- Draw what comes next.

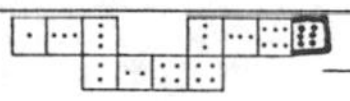

Page 274

Inventions in Time

Use the time line to help decide whether each statement is true or false.

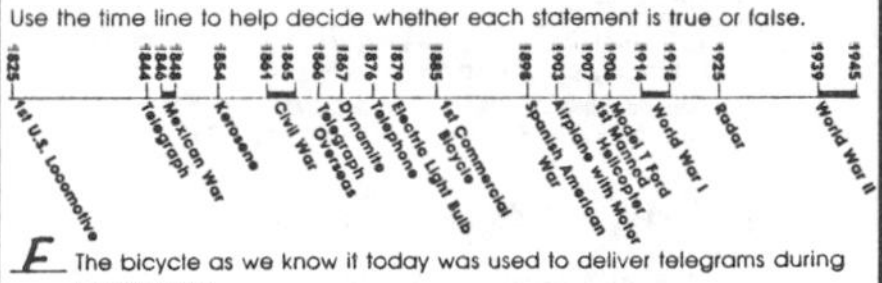

1825 1st U.S. Locomotive
1844 Telegraph
1846–1848 Mexican War
1854 Kerosene
1861–1865 Civil War
1866 Telegraph Overseas
1867 Dynamite
1876 Telephone
1879 Electric Light Bulb
1885 1st Commercial Bicycle
1898 Spanish American War
1903 Airplane with Motor
1907 1st Manned Helicopter
1908 Model T Ford
1914–1918 World War I
1925 Radar
1939–1945 World War II

F The bicycle as we know it today was used to deliver telegrams during the Civil War.

F The helicopter was used during the Spanish American War.

T People in New York could talk to people in California on the telephone during the first World War.

F Dynamite could have been used during the Civil War by the Union Army.

T Kerosene was used before the Civil War.

F In 1865 Andrew Johnson was notified by telephone that Lincoln had been shot.

F The Spanish American War was the second major war that the United States was involved in since 1840.

T When Lincoln studied law in the 1830's he sat by the fire at night in order to have light to read by.

T Planes were used in combat during World War II.

F Trains were not used until 1878.

F America fought in five wars in ninety-nine of the years shown above.

T A telegram could be sent between New York and England after the Civil War.

T World War I ended four years after it began.

T The airplane was invented before the helicopter.

T The Model T was used before World War I.

- Draw what comes next.

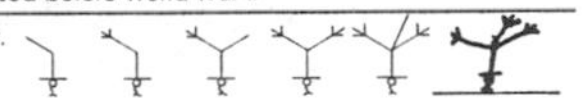

Page 275

Visiting Chile

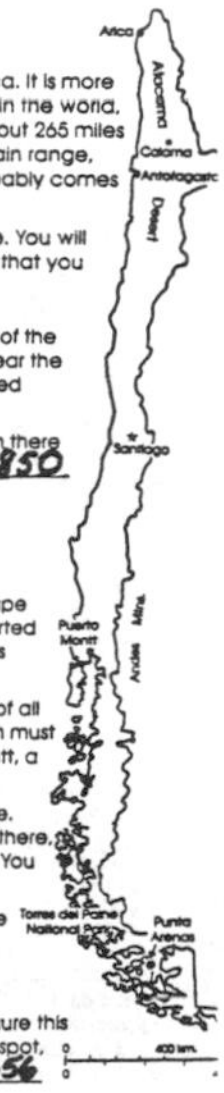

Arica
Atacama
Calama
Antofagasta
Desert
Santiago
Puerto Montt
Andes Mtns.
Torres del Paine National Park
Punta Arenas
0
400 km.

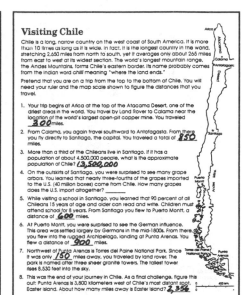

Chile is a long, narrow country on the west coast of South America. It is more than 10 times as long as it is wide. In fact, it is the longest country in the world, stretching 2,650 miles from north to south, yet it averages only about 265 miles from east to west at its widest section. The world's longest mountain range, the Andes Mountains, forms Chile's eastern border. Its name probably comes from the indian word *chilli* meaning "where the land ends."

Pretend that you are on a trip from the top to the bottom of Chile. You will need your ruler and the map scale shown to figure the distances that you travel.

1. Your trip begins at Arica at the top of the Atacama Desert, one of the driest areas in the world. You travel by Land Rover to Calama near the location of the world's largest open-pit copper mine. You traveled 300 miles.
2. From Calama, you again travel southward to Antofagasta. From there you fly directly to Santiago, the capital. You traveled a total of 850 miles.
3. More than a third of the Chileans live in Santiago. If it has a population of about 4,500,000 people, what is the approximate population of Chile? 13,500,000
4. On the outskirts of Santiago, you were surprised to see many grape arbors. You learned that nearly three-fourths of the grapes imported to the U.S. (40 million boxes) come from Chile. How many grapes does the U.S. import altogether? ______
5. While visiting a school in Santiago, you learned that 90 percent of all Chileans 15 years of age and older can read and write. Children must attend school for 8 years. From Santiago you flew to Puerto Montt, a distance of 600 miles.
6. At Puerto Montt, you were surprised to see the German influence. This area was settled largely by Germans in the mid-1800s. From there, you flew into the rugged Archipelago, landing at Punta Arenas. You flew a distance of 900 miles.
7. Northwest of Punta Arenas is Torres del Paine National Park. Since it was only 150 miles away, you traveled by land rover. The park is named after three sheer granite towers. The tallest tower rises 8,530 feet into the sky.
8. This was the end of your journey in Chile. As a final challenge, figure this out: Punta Arenas is 3,800 kilometers west of Chile's most distant spot, Easter Island. About how many miles away is Easter Island? 2,356

Page 276

Rich Coast

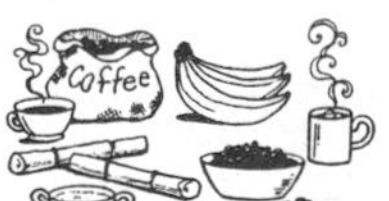

Coffee
SUGAR

Costa Rica is located between Nicaragua and Panama in Central America. Christopher Columbus was the first European to see and explore the region on his second voyage in 1502. He and the Spaniards who came after him called it *Costa Rica*, "rich coast." Costa Rica's fertile soil is its chief natural resource. Coffee, bananas, sugar, chocolate, and meat are its leading exports.

Costa Rica is a small, mountainous region. Its coasts have some of the best beaches north of the equator. San José, established in 1737, is the capital and the country's environmental, artistic, educational, and cultural center.

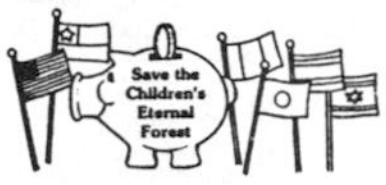

Save the Children's Eternal Forest

Significant sights include Barva Volcano in Braulio Carrillo National Park, Barra de Matina Beach, site of a leatherback turtle sanctuary, and Bosque Eterno de los Niños, the Children's Eternal Forest. This rain forest has been preserved due to the efforts of school-children around the world who donated time and money.

Choose 10 words from the information above. Write the words on the lines below and then incorporate them into a wordsearch on the Costa Rican flag. Then, lightly color the flag as follows: the top and bottom stripe blue, the center stripe red. Leave the other two stripes white.

Words will vary.

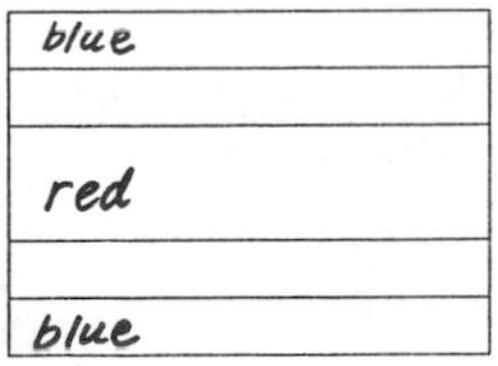

blue
red
blue

Page 277

The Great Sphinx

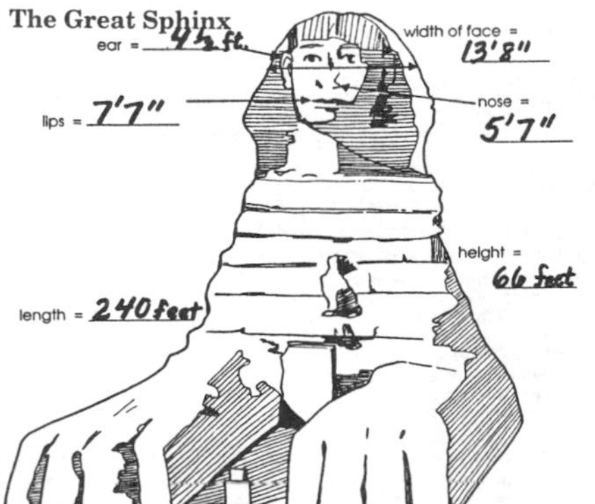

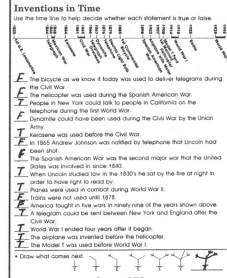

ear = 4½ ft.
width of face = 13'8"
lips = 7'7"
nose = 5'7"
height = 66 feet
length = 240 feet

Probably the most incredible sight a visitor would see in Egypt is the Great Sphinx. The Great Sphinx has the head of a man and the body of a lion. No one knows for sure which king built the Great Sphinx. Most historians say that this sphinx has the facial features of the Egyptian king, Khafre, and that he had it built.

Convert these measurements from inches to feet. Label the Great Sphinx with the new measurements.

height = 792 inches
width of face = 164 inches
length = 2,880 inches

ear = 54 inches
nose = 67 inches
lips = 91 inches

Page 278

Tour de France

The Tour de France is a 2,000-mile bicycle race that winds around France for over three weeks in July. The route changes from year to year. The map of France below shows the principal cities through which more than 100 professional bicyclists might travel. Pretend you are a rider striving for the yellow jersey. Follow the directions below.

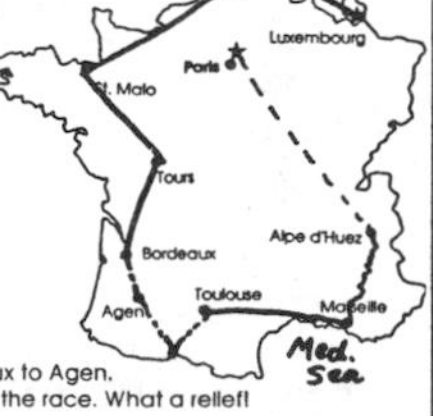

Luxembourg
Paris
St. Malo
Tours
Bordeaux
Alpe d'Huez
Agen
Toulouse
Marseille
Med. Sea

1. You live in Luxembourg. You and your bicycle fly from Luxembourg across Belgium to Lille on July 1st. Draw a solid red line from Luxembourg to Lille. You begin the race here.
2. Next travel to St. Malo. Draw a solid blue line from Lille to St. Malo.
3. Continue on to Tours. Draw a red line from St. Malo to Tours.
4. From Tours, you travel to Bordeaux. Draw a solid red line from Tours to Bordeaux.
5. Draw a blue dotted line from Bordeaux to Agen. This takes you about halfway through the race. What a relief!
6. From Agen, you ride your bicycle down to the border of Spain and back up to Toulouse. Continue your blue dotted line.
7. From Toulouse, you go east to Marseille on the Mediterranean Sea. Draw your route in red and label the sea.
8. Draw a wiggly red line from Marseille through the French Alps to Alpe d'Huez.
9. Your climb to Alpe d'Huez is nine miles long and has 21 hairpin turns. Thousands of spectators are watching you. On the back of your paper, draw what you look like when you reach the top.
10. From there you cycle to just a few miles outside of Paris. Draw a blue dotted line to that point.
11. You are first to cross the finish line! Draw and decorate your yellow T-shirt on construction paper.

Page 279

A Tale of Two Families

A September, 1991, issue of *National Geographic* told a story of the lives of two families who live only 30 miles apart, yet whose lives are worlds apart. The Hapide family, in what was West Germany, live a modest, but comfortable life. The article pictured Eva celebrating her eleventh birthday with friends in the finished basement of their house. Her mother has time for sewing, batik, and a class in jazz dancing. Sometimes Eva's father will pick up chicken, butter, milk, and vegetables as he returns from work at a printing company.

In contrast, the Rabe family in East Germany has few frills in life though Gunther, the father, has his own electrical business. The teenaged son of the family was depicted cutting kindling for the coal furnace that heats their home. For them, raising pigs and chickens and growing a garden is a necessity. Under Communism, they had their jobs, a home and food but they could not speak or travel freely. Time will tell if democracy serves to lessen the gap between these two families.

Let's learn to write a diamante poem. There are seven lines in this type of poem.

- Line 1 is made up of one noun that tells the subject of the poem.
- Line 2 has 2 adjectives describing that noun.
- Line 3 has 3 verbs ending in "ing" that tell what the subject does.
- Next, think of a word that is opposite of or contrasts to line 1. This is line 7.
- Line 6 has 2 adjectives that describe line 7.
- Line 5 usually has 3 verbs ending in "ing" that tell what the word in line 7 does.
- Line 4 has 4 words relating to lines 1 and 7. These are usually nouns.

1	Farms
2	Quiet, Spacious
3	Plowing, Planting, Pruning
4	Tractors, Barns, Cars, Planes
5	Waiting, Walking, Working
6	Noisy, Crowded
7	Cities

Poems will vary.

In the box to the left, practice writing a diamante poem about Germany. Think of the two nouns first. You could use East and West, Communism and Democracy, or Germany and the U.S. Or, you could be creative and come up with your own pair of nouns! After refining your poem, copy and illustrate it on another sheet of paper.

Page 280

Journey to Japan

Use colored pencils to label the map according to the instructions below.

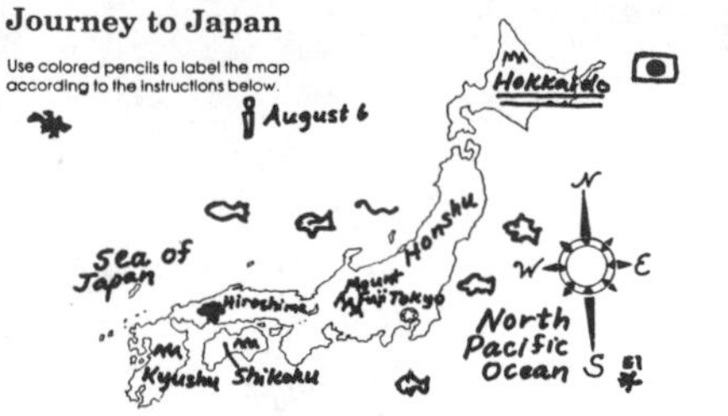

August 6
Hokkaido
Honshu
Sea of Japan
Hiroshima
Mount Fuji
Tokyo
Kyushu
Shikoku
North Pacific Ocean
N
W
E
S

1. Label the islands of Japan from north to south in this order.
   Hokkaido Honshu Shikoku Kyushu
2. Draw brown mountains on all the islands, but not on the east coast of Honshu.
3. Trace the ✪ red and label Tokyo as the capital of Japan.
4. Color the mushroom atom bomb cloud black. Label the city Hiroshima.
5. Label the water to the northwest of Japan "Sea of Japan" in blue.
6. Label the water to the east of the islands "North Pacific Ocean" in green letters.
7. Place a golden crane in the northwest corner of the map.
8. Draw two orange lines under the Japanese island that has the most vowels.
9. Japan's flag is a white rectangle with a large red circle in the center. Draw it in the northeast corner of the map.
10. Japan's highest mountain, an inactive volcano, is Mount Fuji. Label and draw it on Honshu.
11. Japan is one of the world's greatest fishing countries. Draw and color six different kinds of fish surrounding the islands.
12. Draw 日本, the symbol for Japan, in the southeast corner of the map.
13. Light a candle for Sadako. Draw a lit candle anywhere on the map. Write the date of Japan's Peace Day, August 6, by the candle.

Page 281

Visiting New Zealand

Laura took a trip to a location deep in the South Pacific—New Zealand. Nearly a thousand miles away from its neighbors, Australia and New Caldonia, New Zealand is a land of incredible beauty. Long ago, Rudyard Kipling sang of it as "loneliest, loveliest, exquisite, apart . . . the Happy Isles!" North Island is the site of the largest city, Auckland. It is a modern, cosmopolitan area with hints of the emerald isles in its subtropical climate. South Island, with its snowy, glacier-hung alps and remote deer, sheep and cattle stations, is the site of Wellington, the nation's capital.

Thousands of Pacific islanders have been coming to Auckland in recent years—Samoans, Tongans and Fijians to name a few. Combined with the native Maori, the first inhabitants of the area, they are making Auckland into one of the largest Polynesian cities in the world. By the year 2000, every third or fourth New Zealander will have a Polynesian ancestor.

About the size of Colorado, New Zealand is nearly equidistant from the South Pole and the equator. Nowhere are you ever more than 80 miles from the sea. The fishermen harvest and export rock lobsters, blue cod, abalone and grouper. Salmon farming is a new, growing industry. The farms are actually out in the open sea with pens on either sides of causeways.

New Zealand offers a free education to all students up to the age of 19. If students live too far away to ride the bus, they receive instruction from the Correspondence School in Wellington. The school mails lessons to the students who then send their homework back.

Fill in the blanks below.

A. Write the names of New Zealand's nearest neighbors. Australia, New Caldonia

B. From the above paragraph, copy words or group of words meaning the same as the following:
1. snow-covered mountains (paragraph 1) glacier-hung alps
2. ranches (paragraph 1) sheep and cattle stations
3. urban (paragraph 1) cosmopolitan
4. people who occupy a land (paragraph 2) inhabitants
5. older relative (paragraph 2) ancestor
6. same distance (paragraph 3) equidistant
7. schooling (paragraph 4) instruction, education

C. From the list on the right, choose the correct meanings of the words on the left which are in the story.
1. incredible unbelievable — green
2. emerald green — raised roads
3. location site — unbelievable
4. causeways raised roads — site

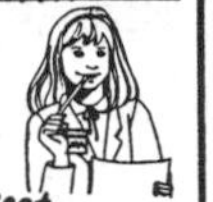

D. Find the words in the story that are the opposite of the words below.
1. sow harvest
2. import export
3. ugliest loveliest
4. teachers students

Page 282

The South American Rainforests

Pretend you just spent a great summer vacation visiting the rainforest in South America. You know you covered a lot of ground and you want to find out just how many miles you traveled. Chart your trip and the miles you covered using a ruler and the map below. Hint: Pretend each centimeter equals 250 miles.

1. You started off your South American rainforest adventure at the basin of the Amazon River. There you saw a jaguar taking a drink. Up in the trees, you see a three-toed sloth casually munching on green leaves. It was hard to leave, but you had to fly westward to Ecuador east of the Andes Mountains. You traveled about 1,250 miles.
2. The Andes Mountains were beautiful! From there, you flew into Guyana and were surrounded to the west, east, and north by rainforests filled with sound and color. A noisy red-green macaw and a spider monkey watched you from their perches in the canopy. Off in the bush, you were sure you heard a hunting coati. What a great place Guyana was! You traveled about 1,000 miles.

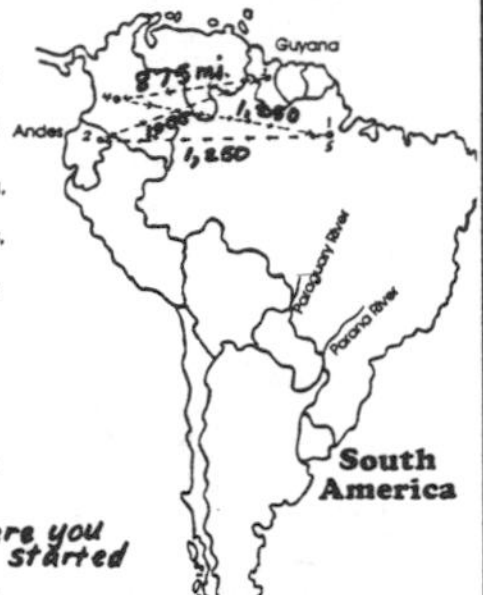

Guyana
875 mi.
Andes
1,000
1,250
Paraguay River
Parana River
South America

3. Leaving this part of South America, you flew to the smaller strips of rainforest to the west of the Andes, in Colombia. As you continued observing and photographing the animals, you realized that any animal caught unaware on the forest floor by another animal could become this animal's next meal. While you were thinking about this, you saw butterflies searching for blossoms and a red-eyed tree frog waiting for insects. Your next stop took you back to point 1 . or: where you started
4. Add three more stops in your trip. You could even venture to one of the rainforests in another land. Use maps to help you!

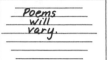

Page 283

Americans All!

People from many different countries have come to live in the United States. They have brought with them the rich heritage and culture of their native lands.

Build a puzzle with the names of twenty-one countries from which people have emigrated to America. The letters given in the puzzle will help you.

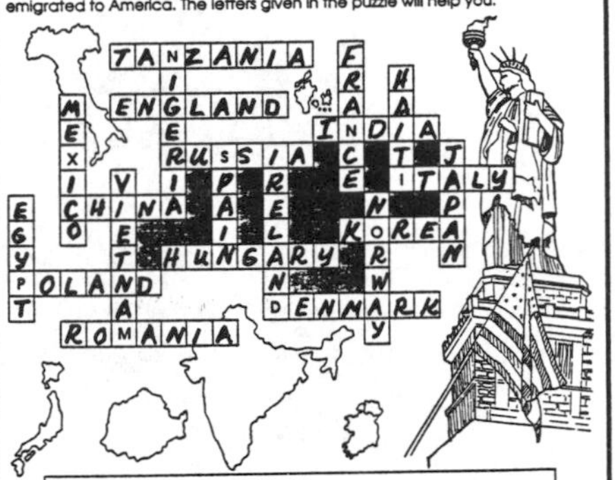

TANZANIA
ENGLAND
INDIA
RUSSIA
ITALY
CHINA
KOREA
HUNGARY
POLAND
DENMARK
ROMANIA

Word Box

China	Egypt	Haiti	India	Italy
Japan	Korea	Spain	France	Mexico
Norway	Poland	Russia	Denmark	England
Ireland	Nigeria	Romania	Vietnam	Tanzania
Hungary				

Page 284

What Happened?

Have you ever thought about how many events occur during a person's life? Below you will learn what was happening during the lives of some famous Americans. Shade in the events, listed at the bottom of the graph, that occurred during each person's lifetime.

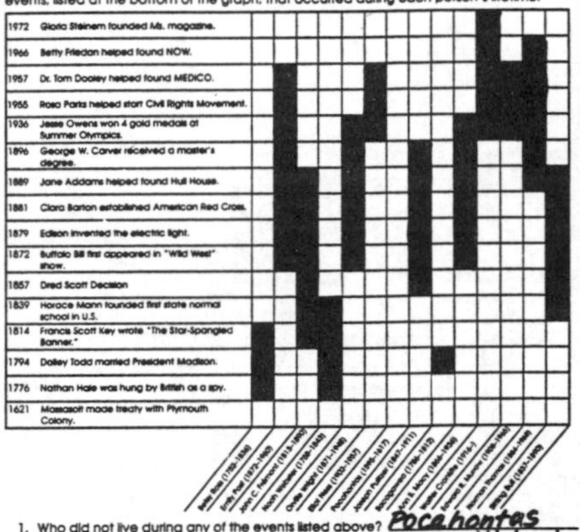

1972 Gloria Steinem founded Ms. magazine.
1966 Betty Friedan helped found NOW.
1957 Dr. Tom Dooley helped found MEDICO.
1955 Rosa Parks helped start Civil Rights Movement.
1936 Jesse Owens won 4 gold medals at Summer Olympics.
1896 George W. Carver received a master's degree.
1889 Jane Addams helped found Hull House.
1881 Clara Barton established American Red Cross.
1879 Edison invented the electric light.
1872 Buffalo Bill first appeared in "Wild West" show.
1857 Dred Scott Decision
1839 Horace Mann founded first state normal school in U.S.
1814 Francis Scott Key wrote "The Star-Spangled Banner."
1794 Dolley Todd married President Madison.
1776 Nathan Hale was hung by British as a spy.
1621 Massasoit made treaty with Plymouth Colony.

1. Who did not live during any of the events listed above? Pocahontas
2. During which event were none of the personalities alive? Massasoit's treaty
3. What is NOW? the National Organization of Women
4. Of which of the events listed above would you have liked to have been a part? Why? Answers will vary.

Personality Plus Make a list of 10 important events that have occurred during your lifetime. Share them with the class.

Page 285

Where Did They Come From?

Our country has been shaped by great minds from many states. Use the clues and the Word Bank to discover from which states many American personalities came. Label the map with the appropriate states' names or abbreviations.

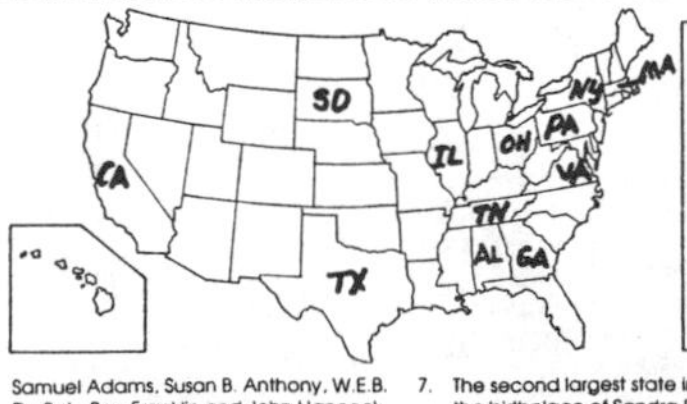

SD
NY
MA
CA
IL
OH
PA
VA
TN
AL
GA
TX

Word Bank
Massachusetts
Pennsylvania
New York
Texas
Illinois
California
South Dakota
Tennessee
Ohio
Georgia
Virginia
Alabama

1. Samuel Adams, Susan B. Anthony, W.E.B. Du Bois, Ben Franklin and John Hancock once lived in this state which is now home to Harvard, Martha's Vineyard and the Freedom Trail. Massachusetts
2. This Land of Infinite Variety is mainly a farm state and was once home to Hubert Humphrey. South Dakota
3. One of four states officially known as a commonwealth, this Keystone State is where Daniel Boone and George Marshall were born. Pennsylvania
4. William Tecumseh Sherman and Ulysses S. Grant once called this Buckeye State home. Ohio
5. Niagara Falls graces this Empire State in which John Jay, John Rockefeller, Elizabeth Cady Stanton and Geraldine Ferraro were born. New York
6. Martin Luther King, Jr. once called this Goober State home. Georgia
7. The second largest state in the U.S., it was the birthplace of Sandra Day O'Connor, Chester Nimitz and Dwight D. Eisenhower. Texas
8. Known as the Mother of Presidents, this state was also home at one time to Booker T. Washington, Robert E. Lee, Henry Clay, Patrick Henry, Sam Houston, Thomas "Stonewall" Jackson and John Marshall. Virginia
9. President Abraham Lincoln lived much of his life in this state as did William Jennings Bryan. Illinois
10. Jesse Owens and George Wallace were born in this Heart of Dixie. Alabama
11. The site of the famous gold rush, George S. Patton, Jr., and Earl Warren were both born in this Golden State. California
12. Indians once roamed this Volunteer State where Sam Rayburn and Dave Farragut were born. Tennessee

Personality Plus Make a list of some people from your state who you think are famous Americans in history. Tell what they have done.

Page 286

Treasure Hunt in the Rainforest

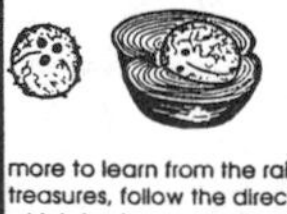

Tribes living in the rainforest use as many of its treasures as they can for meals, shelter, clothes, medicines, tools and cosmetics. Your home is filled with rainforest products too. Many fruits and nuts and even the domestic chicken originated from the rainforest. And scientists believe that there is much more to learn from the rainforest. To learn more about some of the rainforest's treasures, follow the directions below. You will need another sheet of paper on which to draw your discoveries. Maps will vary.

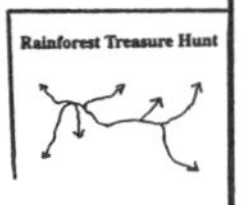

Rainforest Treasure Hunt

1. Title the top of your map, Rainforest Treasure Hunt.
2. Draw a compass rose in the top left corner.
3. In the southwest corner of your paper, draw an orange and black frog. This is an arrow-poison frog. These tiny rainforest frogs produce a strong poison. This poison is extracted and used on the tips of blowpipe darts when hunting big game.
4. Travel northeast to the center of your paper. There is an Amazonian tree that produces a sap very similar to diesel. It can be used as fuel by trucks. Draw a tree with a gas hose coming from it.
5. Heading southeast, you discover plants and animals from which medicines originate. Draw a picture of medicine bottles in this corner.
6. Move up to the northeast corner to see the insects that provide an alternative to expensive pesticides. Three types of wasps were successfully introduced in Florida to control pests that were damaging citrus tree crops. Draw three wasps in this corner.

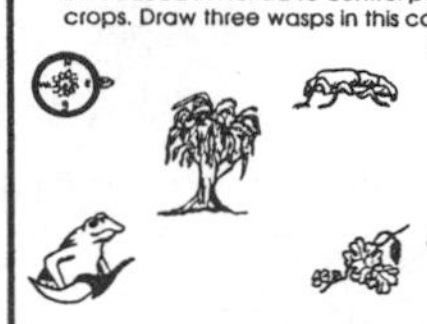

7. Traveling west, you stop to listen to a scientist estimating that there are at least 1,500 potential new fruits and vegetables growing in the rainforest. Draw a picture of a fruit or vegetable you discovered. Be sure to name it.
8. Return home and discuss with your parents the interesting facts you learned on your treasure hunt.

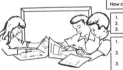

Page 287

Problems in the Rainforest

In many countries, slash-and-burn agriculture is one of the leading causes of tropical deforestation. Slash-and-burn farmers clear rainforest land to grow their crops. During the first few years, the crops do well, but after the land has been cultivated for a while, the soil becomes worn out and the plot is abandoned. The rains wash away the topsoil and the land becomes difficult to cultivate. What can you do to help the rainforests?

Before solving a problem, it is often helpful to go through it in steps. For example, read the steps below to learn how you can try to help solve the slash-and-burn problem.

1. Restate the problem into a question.
2. State the facts you know about the problem.
3. Brainstorm possible ways to help solve the problem. Remember, in brainstorming, all the ideas you have are written down, even if you aren't sure they will work.

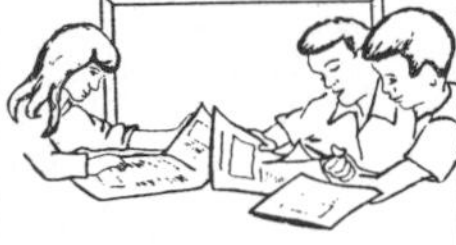

How can we stop slash-and-burn agriculture?

1. Many trees are cut down.
2. The soil is only fertile for a short while.
3. The land is abandoned.

1. Remove the trees with aerial cables instead of heavy logging equipment.
2. Allow only certain areas to be cut down one at a time.
3. Research to learn more about how rainforests can regenerate.

How can we stop deforestation?

1. Native peoples are forced to move or relocate.
2. The people suffer from diseases brought by "outsiders."

Answers will vary.

Read the following problem and fill in your ideas in the graphic organizer to the left. Share your ideas with the class.

Deforestation has a direct impact on tribes native to the rainforest. In many cases, these people are forced to move or relocate through government programs. The people also suffer from diseases brought by "outsiders."

1. Restate the problem into a question.
2. State the facts you know about the problem.
3. Brainstorm possible ways to help solve the problem.

Page 288

Name _____

At the Library

To alphabetize means to arrange things in alphabetical order. The following words are alphabetized: *xylophone, yacht, zipper.*

Connie is clumsy. She keeps tipping things over at the library. Help her put the magazines, books, and videos back on the shelf in alphabetical order. Number them to show which comes first, second, and so on.

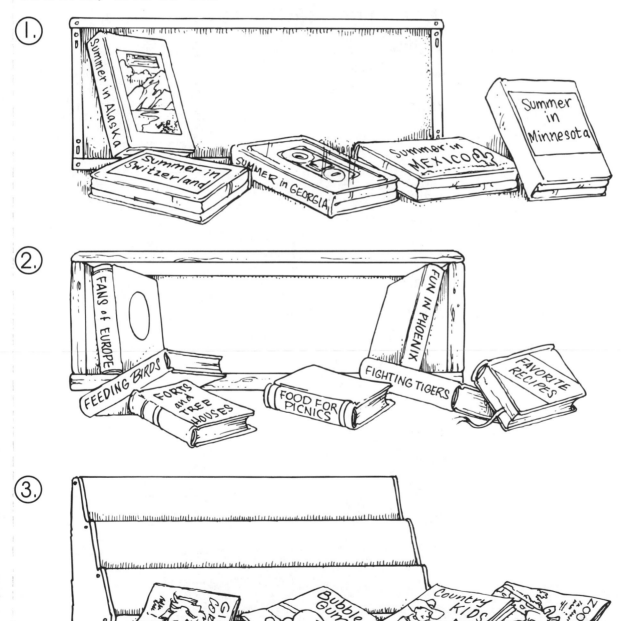

1.

2.

3.

Name _____

Get it Together!

Compound words are two separate words combined to form a new word. *Flowerpot* is a compound word made up of the words *flower* and *pot*. Choose one word from the first column and one word from the second to form a compound word that makes sense. How many compound words can you make? Words can be used more than once.

Beginnings	Endings	
get	meal	_____
gold	time	_____
grass	paper	_____
green	light	_____
head	balls	_____
home	man	_____
house	house	_____
ice	guard	_____
oat	slide	_____
key	hole	_____
land	board	_____
life	away	_____
light	box	_____
mail	work	_____
meat	boat	_____
moon	hopper	_____
news	fish	_____
night		_____

Name _____

Community Food Share

The **complete subject** is all the words in a sentence that tell whom or what the sentence is about.

The **simple subject** is the one main word that tells whom or what the sentence is about.

Read each sentence. Underline the complete subject. Write the simple subject on the line.

children	The children in our class wanted to do a service project.
We	We voted on different ideas.
project	The project I thought of got the most votes.

1. We chose to hold a food drive at our school to help the Community Food Share program.

2. That program gives away food to people who need it.

3. One group of kids made posters about the food drive to hang all over school.

4. Another group spoke about the food drive at a school assembly.

5. The group I was in wrote a note to send home to families.

6. Kids in all the different classes brought in cans and boxes of food from home.

7. Our class sorted all the food.

8. Our parents helped deliver the food we collected.

9. We took a field trip to the Community Food Share building.

10. The people at Community Food Share showed us where they store the food.

11. They were thankful for all that our class and school did.

12. Our class felt great that we had made a difference in our community!

Name _____

Give It a Name

A noun that names any person, place, or thing is called a **common noun**.
A noun that names a special person, place, or thing is called a **proper noun**.
A proper noun begins with a capital letter.

Write two proper nouns for each common noun given.
Example: *river—Mississippi River, Rio Grande*

school	state	girl	boy
restaurant	author	lake	street
president	month	day	athlete
store	pet	country	planet

Name _____

Travel the World

Read this story Patrick wrote.
Circle the **verbs** that are incorrect.
Write the correct verb on the line.

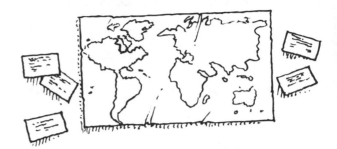

made

1. _____

2. _____

3. _____

4. _____

5. _____

6. _____

7. _____

8. _____

9. _____

10. _____

11. _____

12. _____

13. _____

14. _____

15. _____

Last week my friends and I (make) a geography game called "Travel the World." It were for a social studies project at school.

First we finded a large map of the world. Our map showed each of the continents in a different color.

Then we thinked of game ideas. I told our group about a game I seen at the store once. Megan had the best idea. She say the purpose of the game should be to visit every continent. We choosed her idea.

Ben and I writed cards for the game. The cards told the players which continent to go to. For example, one card sayed this: *Go to the continent where the Nile River is found.* Theo thought our cards might be too hard for some kids. So we add the name of the continent on each card also. Megan and Theo maked score sheets. The score sheets haved check-off boxes next to each continent name.

We played the game to test it. I keeped picking cards that sent me to South America or Europe. I never did get a card for Asia. Ben winned our practice game.

Finally we turn in our project. Our teacher liked it. He letted us teach the class how to play it that day.

Name _____

Past, Present, and Future
Facts About Verbs

The present tense of a verb states an action that is happening now or that happens regularly: *I like jeans. I wear them every day.*

The past tense of a verb states an action that happened in the past: *I liked jeans last year.*

The future tense of a verb states an action that will take place. The future tense is made by using the helping verbs *will* or *shall* before the main verb: *I will be home tomorrow.*

Underline the verbs in the story below. Then fill in the table with the past, present, and future verbs from the story. The first two verbs are done for you.

The Levi Strauss Story

Levi Strauss invented blue jeans. That's why people call them Levi's. Strauss first made work pants out of canvas for California goldminers. Later, he used sturdy cotton denim that he dyed blue, using dye made from the indigo plant. By the 1860s, farmers, miners, and cowboys throughout the American West wore blue jeans.

Today, people all over the world wear jeans. Levi Strauss Company was the official outfitter for the 1984 Olympics. The company designed the uniforms for the U.S. Team. They also created one-of-a-kind jeans for each gold medal winner. The jeans had buttons and rivets made with 22-karat gold.

Jeans come in a variety of different colors and styles. The most popular color, though, is still blue. Do you think jeans will be popular when you are a grandparent?

Present Tense	Past Tense	Future Tense
call	invented	

Name _____

Smart, Smarter, Smartest

Adjectives that compare two things usually end in **er**.
Adjectives that compare three or more things usually end in **est**.
If the adjective is a long word, **more** or **most** is used with it instead.

A dog is smart.
A monkey is smarter than a dog.
A chimpanzee is one of the smartest animals of all.

*Marine animals with backbones are more intelligent
than those without.*
A dolphin may be the most intelligent marine animal of all.

Fill in the missing adjectives in this chart. Use the last three lines to write your own examples.

Adjective	Adjective that compares two	Adjective that compares three or more
shiny	shinier	shiniest
graceful	more graceful	most graceful
	quieter	
cautious		most cautious
tall		
		brightest
beautiful		
	stronger	
		most spirited
late	later	
funny		
		nicest
	more generous	

Name _____

How Does . . . ?

An **adverb** is a word that describes a verb. Some adverbs tell how something is done. They often end in *ly*. *Quickly, carefully, silently,* and *happily* are examples of adverbs.

Look at the picture. Think about how the animals are moving. Write two adverbs for each. Do not repeat adverbs.

How does an eagle fly?

powerfully

_____

How does a bear cub climb?

_____

_____

How does a deer run?

_____

_____

How does a rabbit hop?

_____

_____

How does a turtle move?

_____

_____

How does a frog swim?

_____

_____

Name _____

Prefix Rainbow

A **prefix** is a word part added to the beginning of a word that changes the word's meaning. On each band of the rainbow, write words from the Word Bank that can be used with each prefix.

Word Bank		
open	frost	used
build	part	screw
appear	write	sign
pack	order	tie
press	known	read

Daily Learning Drills Grade 4

Name _____

Word Builders

Suffixes are word parts that help you build new words. When you add a suffix to the end of a root word, you make a new word. Examples of the suffix *-ish* used with root words are: *reddish, girlish, Spanish*. Notice that the hyphen is not in the word.

Complete each word below using the following suffixes. Then write a new sentence using the word you made.

   -ful   -er   -ish   -proof   -ist   -less

1. Someone who acts silly like a clown may be called clown _____.

   _____

2. The amount of sugar that fills a cup is called a cup _____.

   _____

3. A medicine bottle cap that is hard to remove is called child _____.

   _____

4. Someone who sings is called a sing _____ .

   _____

5. A person who studies science is called a scient _____.

   _____

6. A telephone without a cord is cord _____.

   _____

Dictionaries include suffix entries. Look up one of the suffixes above in the dictionary to see what it says.

Name _____

Analogies

An **analogy** is a way to compare things using the relationships the words share. The sentence below is an example of an analogy.

An <u>apple</u> is to <u>fruit</u> as <u>broccoli</u> is to <u>vegetable</u>.

An easier way to write an analogy looks like this:

apple:fruit::broccoli:vegetable

Complete the analogies below. Then draw the objects to illustrate each analogy.

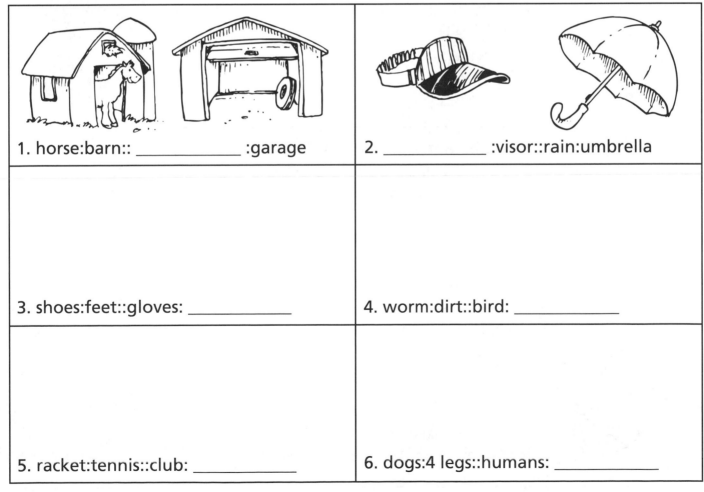

1. horse:barn:: _____ :garage

2. _____ :visor::rain:umbrella

3. shoes:feet::gloves: _____

4. worm:dirt::bird: _____

5. racket:tennis::club: _____

6. dogs:4 legs::humans: _____

Daily Learning Drills Grade 4

Name _____

Knew York or New York?

Homophones are words that sound alike but have different spellings and meanings.

Fill in the circle next to the correct homophone for each sentence.

1. My family is planning a trip to ____ York State. ◯ Knew ◯ New	2. We each get to pick ____ place to visit. ◯ one ◯ won	3. My mom ____ to go see the Statue of Liberty. ◯ once ◯ wants	4. It stands ____ New York Harbor. ◯ in ◯ inn
5. My dad wants ____ visit the Guggenheim Museum. ◯ to ◯ two	6. ____ a famous building designed by Frank Lloyd Wright. ◯ Its ◯ It's	7. Of course, the museum has lots of great art, ____. ◯ to ◯ too	
8. My sister has ____ books about Harriet Tubman. ◯ read ◯ red	9. She wants to go ____ Harriet Tubman's home in Auburn. ◯ sea ◯ see	10. And me, ____ do I want to go? ◯ wear ◯ where	11. I thought it over ____ a long time. ◯ for ◯ four
	12. I ____ like to see Niagara Falls. ◯ wood ◯ would	13. It is on the ____ between New York and Canada. ◯ boarder ◯ border	14. I ____ this will be a wonderful vacation. ◯ know ◯ no

Name _____

A Meaning of Its Own

An **idiom** is a phrase, or group of words, that has a special meaning. The meaning is different from what the words usually mean. An example of an idiom is *to call it a day*. This means to stop activity for the day. In a dictionary, this idiom would appear near the end of the definition for *day*.

Circle the most important word in each idiom below. Look up the circled word in your dictionary and see if you can find the idiom. Then make up a sentence using the idiom.

1. by heart: _____

2. give out: _____

3. on the fence: _____

4. at bat: _____

5. getting on my nerves: _____

6. walk on air: _____

7. out of the blue: _____

8. run across: _____

9. make believe: _____

Look for examples of idioms in the books you read. Write your favorite one here. Then draw a picture of what the idiom seems to mean.

_____

Daily Learning Drills Grade 4

Name _____

Poetry Diamonds

Creating poetry diamonds is a fun way to play with words and write poetry that sparkles. The formula below is a simple way to make your own diamond-shaped poem. Choose a topic that interests you, such as animals, nature, holidays, or even a city or country.

Poetry Diamond Formula
Line 1: Noun 1
Line 2: 2 words describing the noun
Line 3: 3 words ending in -ed or -ing
Line 4: 4 words describing the noun
Line 5: 3 words ending in -ed or -ing
Line 6: 2 words describing the noun
Line 7: Noun 2

Example:

Puppy
clumsy, cute
jumping, running, biting
sweet, joyous, friendly, loyal
barking, fetching, playing
graceful, strong
Dog

Now try a diamond poem of your own!

_____

_____

_____

_____

_____

_____

_____

Name _____

Creative Comparisons

Similes are comparisons in which the words *like* or *as* are used:

> The sun is like a hot oven.

Metaphors are comparisons in which *like* or *as* are not used:

> The sun is a hot oven.

Choose two objects. Write a simile and a metaphor for each.
Then draw a picture to illustrate each comparison.

1.	2.

Simile:_____   Simile:_____

_____   _____

_____   _____

Metaphor:_____   Metaphor:_____

_____   _____

_____   _____

    Daily Learning Drills Grade 4

Name _____

Friend from Outer Space

Pretend you have encountered an alien from a distant planet. The extraterrestrial has just landed on Earth and you are the first person he or she—or it!—has met. Write a story on a separate piece of paper. Include the title, setting, and characters in your story. Use the tips below to help you get started.

Title: This tells readers something about the story. It might grab readers' interest and make them curious and eager to read more. Some well-known story titles for young readers are: *Island of the Blue Dolphins; The Lion, the Witch and the Wardrobe;* and *Green Eggs and Ham.*

Setting: This is the surroundings or environment of the story. The setting can provide exciting action. It could be a boat, the roof of a tall building, the school playground, or anywhere you dream up!

Characters: The characters are the people in your story. They can be real people you know or imaginary people that you make up, like your new alien friend. Characters can also be animals or ghosts.

Here are some questions to think about to help you write your story:

- *What is your new alien friend's name?*
- *What does the alien look like?*
- *Does the alien appear to be afraid of you?*
- *Are you afraid of the alien?*
- *Why has the alien come to Earth?*
- *What would you like to show the alien about your home planet? Your favorite toys, a pet, a sister, or a brother?*

Name _____

Dear Character

Think of a good book you've read recently. Use this page to write a friendly letter to your favorite book character. Tell the character why you admire him or her. Describe what you might have done in one of the same situations. Invite the character to do something with you, or give him or her some good advice! Follow the instructions to the left for using correct letter form.

Date:

_____

Salutation:

_____

Body of letter:

_____

_____

_____

_____

_____

_____

Closing:

_____

Your Name:

_____

Name _____

What's Your Prediction?

Choose a book and read the first chapter. Then start using this chart. (Use another piece of paper if you need to.) Before you read each chapter, write what you think will happen. After you finish the chapter, write what actually happened. See how close your predictions are. Do they get better as you read the book?

Chapter	What I predict will happen:	What actually happened:
Chapter 2		
Chapter 3		
Chapter 4		
Chapter 5		
Chapter 6		

Name _____

Wild Ride!

If you want a super ride this summer, try a roller coaster. If you want a really wild ride, head for *Superman: The Escape* at the Great Adventure amusement park in Valencia, California. When it opened in 1997, the ride set a new record in roller-coaster speed.

The cars, which hold 15 people, don't need to head downhill to reach their top speed. They zoom to 100 miles per hour along a level track in just seven seconds. Then the cars begin their upward climb. After climbing as high as a 42-story building, the cars return down the same track, only they're traveling backward!

Like all roller-coaster cars, the cars of *Superman: The Escape* have magnets attached to their undersides. Small electric motors create the energy to propel these magnets along the track. But the cars make less contact with the rails than other rides do. This means the wheels and the track create less friction, causing the cars to move along the track more freely. Less friction means the cars can travel faster. No wonder this ride is called *Superman: The Escape*!

Refer to the story to answer these questions:

1. What kind of record did *Superman: The Escape* set?

_____

2. Where is the Superman roller coaster located?

_____

3. How many people can ride in one of the roller-coaster cars?

_____

4. How long does it take for *Superman: The Escape* to reach 100 miles per hour?

_____

5. Explain friction.

_____

Daily Learning Drills Grade 4

Name _____

Rhyme Time Riddles

Answer the questions below by writing two words that rhyme.

Example:

What do you call an obese feline? _____ fat cat _____

1. What do you call a wet pooch? _____

2. What do you call a sick large ocean mammal? _____

3. What do you call a mallard with its feet caught in the mud? _____

4. What do you call an ill young chicken? _____

5. What do you call a ridiculous male goat? _____

6. What do you call a seat for a rabbit? _____

7. What do you call a clever detective? _____

8. What do you call a clever prank? _____

9. What do you call a noisy mob of people? _____

10. What do you call a dwelling for a rodent? _____

Here's how you can create your own rhyming riddles.

1. Write a list of word pairs that rhyme. Choose one rhyming pair. It will be your riddle answer. Example: *funny bunny*
2. Next, create your riddle question. Make a list of words that have the same meaning as each word in your rhyming answer. These are called *synonyms.* They do not have to rhyme. The synonyms become part of your riddle question.

    Examples: *What do you call a . . .*
    comical   rabbit?
    silly   hare?

3. Pick one word from each column and make up your riddle question.
    Example: What do you call a silly rabbit? Answer: a funny bunny!

Name _____

What's the Big Idea?

Understanding the similarity between items is an important part of reading and thinking. Below you will find groups of four words. Each group has something in common. Give each group of items a name on the line next to it. Then make up a few of your own and see if your friends or family can guess The Big Idea!

1. lion, tiger, panther, leopard _____

2. quarter, dime, nickel, penny _____

3. cake, pie, ice cream, brownies _____

4. sister, brother, father, mother _____

5. white, wheat, rye, pumpernickel _____

6. pig, cow, chicken, goat _____

7. orange, lemon, lime, grapefruit _____

8. Earth, Venus, Mars, Uranus _____

9. blue, green, yellow, red _____

10. tulip, rose, daisy, violet _____

11. Ford, Washington, Lincoln, Clinton _____

12. Alaska, Colorado, Iowa, Kansas _____

13. zebra, giraffe, elephant, lion _____

14. June, July, August, September _____

Daily Learning Drills Grade 4

Name _____

Creating Your Own Numbers

Write a numeral from 0 to 9 in each box below. Then spell out the number you wrote, using words. The first one is done for you.

ten thousands	thousands	hundreds	tens	ones
7	0	3	4	9

1. Seventy thousand three hundred forty-nine _____

hundreds	tens	ones

2. _____

thousands	hundreds	tens	ones

3. _____

ten thousands	thousands	hundreds	tens	ones

4. _____

Name _____

Round and Round

In each number below, circle the number that tells you if the
number should round up or stay the same. Round each number.

A. **10**

85⑥ _____

47 _____

293 _____

64 _____

327 _____

B. **100**

467 _____

821 _____

299 _____

1,371 _____

5,614 _____

C. **1,000**

5,764 _____

8,213 _____

9,621 _____

2,473 _____

1,121 _____

D. Round to the nearest thousand. Color the balls when the numbers round up.

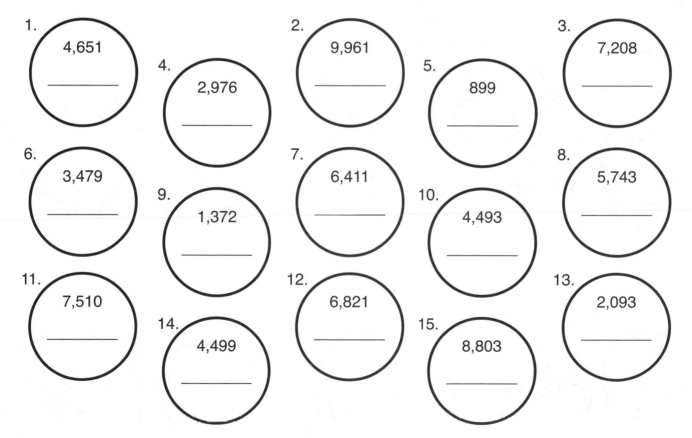

1. 4,651 _____

4. 2,976 _____

2. 9,961 _____

5. 899 _____

3. 7,208 _____

6. 3,479 _____

9. 1,372 _____

7. 6,411 _____

10. 4,493 _____

8. 5,743 _____

11. 7,510 _____

14. 4,499 _____

12. 6,821 _____

15. 8,803 _____

13. 2,093 _____

E. Answers for tens need to end in _____ zero(s).

Those for the nearest hundred end in _____ zero(s).

Answers to the nearest thousand end in _____ zero(s).

Daily Learning Drills Grade 4

MATH REVIEW

Name _____

Adding Balloons

Add to find the sum. Color the balloon for each problem you worked correctly.

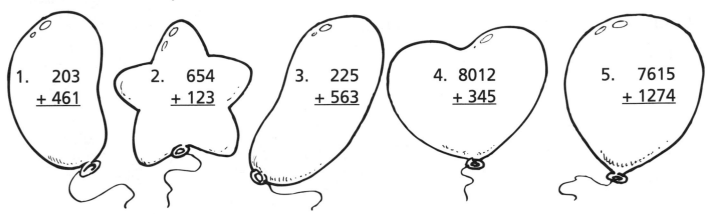

1. 203
  + 461

2. 654
  + 123

3. 225
  + 563

4. 8012
  + 345

5. 7615
  + 1274

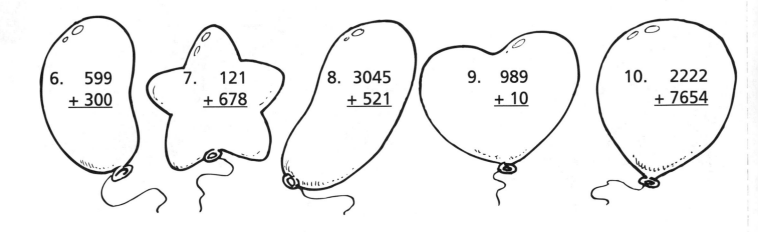

6. 599
  + 300

7. 121
  + 678

8. 3045
  + 521

9. 989
  + 10

10. 2222
  + 7654

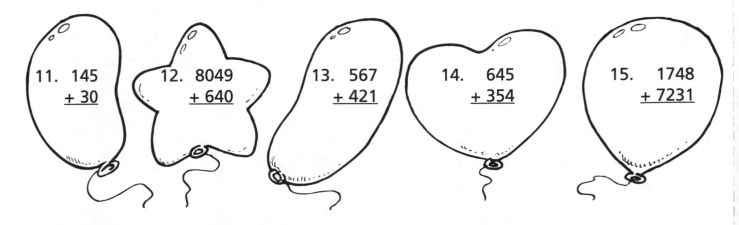

11. 145
  + 30

12. 8049
  + 640

13. 567
  + 421

14. 645
  + 354

15. 1748
  + 7231

Name _____

Add It Up!

Color the sums.

red = 1,400–7,900   green = 8,000–16,000   yellow = over 16,000   blue = under 1,400

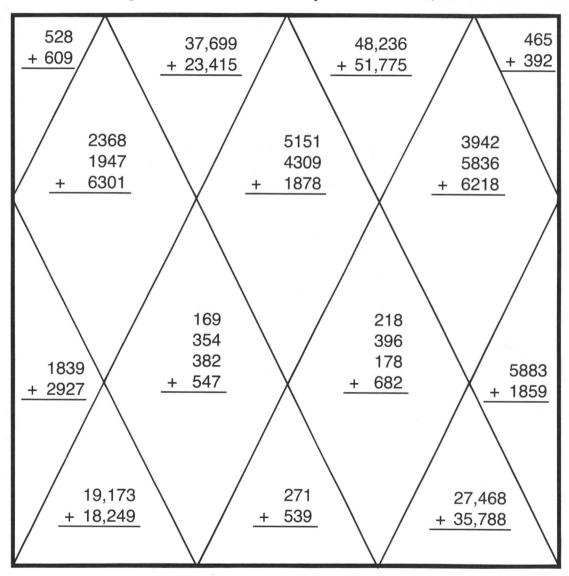

Solve.

1. Julie and her dad drove across the country on vacation. They drove 349 miles, 276 miles, and 362 miles in three days. How many miles did they drive in all?

   _____

2. Our postman delivers mail five days each week. He delivered 249 pieces of mail on Monday. On the other days, he delivered 782 letters and 381 magazines. How many pieces of mail did he deliver in that one week?

   _____

Name _____

Zeros Are Important

Subtract. Add to check your answers.

1.
```
    207        64
  - 143    + 143
    64       207
```

2.
```
    100
  -  64    + _____
```

3.
```
    602
  - 314    + _____
```

4.
```
  5,007
 - 2,106   + _____
```

5.
```
  4,109
 - 1,174   + _____
```

6.
```
  3,000
 - 2,674   + _____
```

7.
```
  9,008
 - 3,962   + _____
```

8.
```
  12,003
 - 10,666  + _____
```

9.
```
  70,405
 - 21,510  + _____
```

largest

Write the problems below in column form and subtract.

Write the answers in correct order from smallest to largest.

1. 560 − 392 = _____

2. 4,300 − 571 = _____

3. 5,000 − 297 = _____

4. 640 − 399 = _____

5. 7,040 − 2,607 = _____

6. 1,007 − 352 = _____

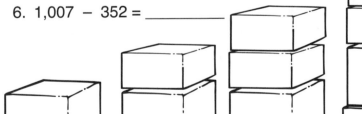
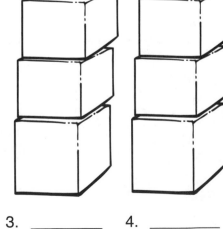
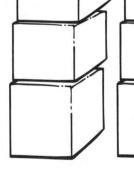
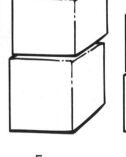
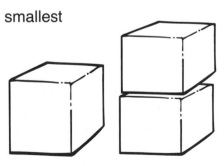
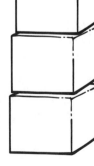

smallest

1. _____   2. _____   3. _____   4. _____   5. _____   6. _____

Name _____

Chipmunk Multiplication

Help this chipmunk put away acorns for the winter by multiplying. Color the acorn for each problem you worked correctly.

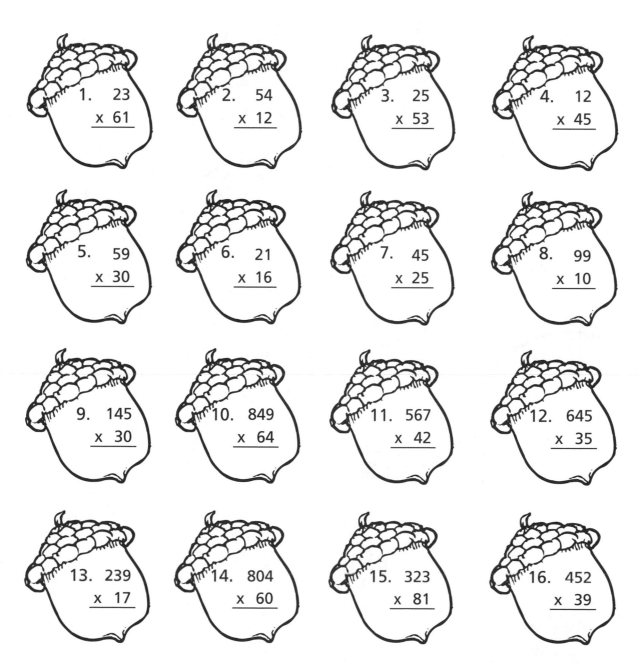

1. 23
  x 61

2. 54
  x 12

3. 25
  x 53

4. 12
  x 45

5. 59
  x 30

6. 21
  x 16

7. 45
  x 25

8. 99
  x 10

9. 145
  x 30

10. 849
  x 64

11. 567
  x 42

12. 645
  x 35

13. 239
  x 17

14. 804
  x 60

15. 323
  x 81

16. 452
  x 39

Daily Learning Drills Grade 4

Name _____

Up, Up, and Away

Multiply. Put the letters of the answers on the lines below to find out a secret message.

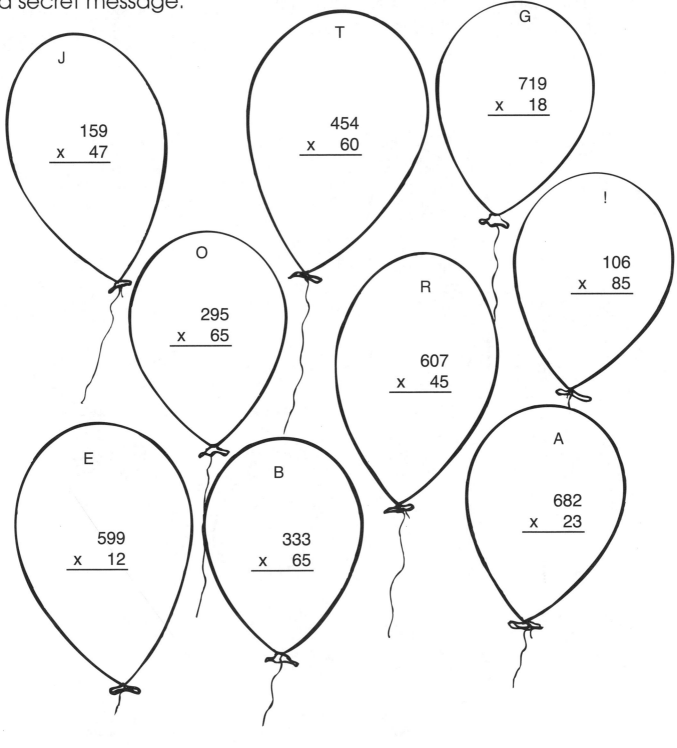

J
159
x 47

T
454
x 60

G
719
x 18

!
106
x 85

O
295
x 65

R
607
x 45

E
599
x 12

B
333
x 65

A
682
x 23

| 12,942 | 27,315 | 7,188 | 15,686 | 27,240 | | 7,473 | 19,175 | 21,645 | 9,010 |

Name _____

Doggie Trouble

Help the dog get to his bone by connecting the correctly-done division problems to make a path.

85 R17 23) 1972	30 R29 32) 989	14 R27 43) 629	232 R3 30) 6963	107 R4 65) 6959
104 R8 15) 1508	31 R4 22) 687	31 R12 19) 582	78 R6 87) 6933	155 R11 52) 8071
255 R15 31) 8013	14 R15 42) 6231	20 R18 26) 541	54 R9 18) 819	31 R3 26) 809
52 R27 60) 3207	158 R31 39) 6193	36 R11 27) 983	115 R8 71) 8203	58 R3 17) 989
		18 R26 81) 1484	44 R7 44) 1943	63 R9 28) 1773

MATH REVIEW

Name _____

Wacky City

Here are some math word problems about Wacky City. Wacky City is a town not too far from your town where people are just a little bit different. Use multiplication or division to find the answer to each problem below.

1. On Saturdays, the people of Wacky City eat nothing but bananas all day long. If there are 3,500 people in Wacky City, and they each eat seven bananas on Saturdays, how many bananas would they eat on that day?

   _____

2. The mayor of Wacky City gives visitors a pet frog when they come to town. If 75 visitors come to Wacky City every day, how may frogs would the mayor need to give away each year? _____

3. In Wacky City, a rainbow appears in the sky once a week. How many rainbows would appear over a 15-year period? _____

4. Wacky City citizens spent $23,569 in 20 years to take their teddy bears on picnics. How much did they spend each year, on the average, for teddy bear picnics?

   _____

5. Children in Wacky City get a free ride on a carousel whenever they want. If there were 25,000 free rides last year, and 250 children took rides, how many rides did each child have? _____

6. The people in Wacky City always march in a parade when it rains. If there were 1,235 parades in the last 15 years, how many days did it rain each year, on average? _____

Name _____

Circle Time

Below are problems in addition, subtraction, multiplication, and division. Note which operation to use and circle the sign. Then work the problems.

1.   235
    + 61

2.   504
    x 12

3.   725
    − 53

4. 45 ÷ 12

5.   590
    x 30

6. 3000 ÷ 21

7.   4145
    + 265

8.   1980
    − 810

9.   1450
    − 837

10.   8490
    + 264

11. 704 ÷ 56

12.   642
    x 75

13. 50 ÷ 14

14.   8764
    x 6

15.   5601
    − 427

16.   6405
    + 309

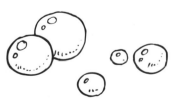

MATH REVIEW

Name _____

Operation Butterfly

Complete each equation with the sign that shows the correct mathematical operation. Then color the butterfly using the Color Key below. For example, for the number 1 on the butterfly, look at problem number 1. A plus sign was used, meaning the operation was addition. Color that section purple.

1. $20 \_\_ 20 = 40$

2. $20 \_\_ 2 = 40$

3. $40 \_\_ 20 = 20$

4. $8 \_\_ 9 = 72$

5. $64 \_\_ 8 = 8$

6. $234 \_\_ 34 = 200$

7. $818 \_\_ 81 = 899$

8. $50 \_\_ 20 = 30$

9. $49 \_\_ 7 = 42$

10. $49 \_\_ 7 = 7$

11. $250 \_\_ 100 = 150$

12. $100 \_\_ 300 = 400$

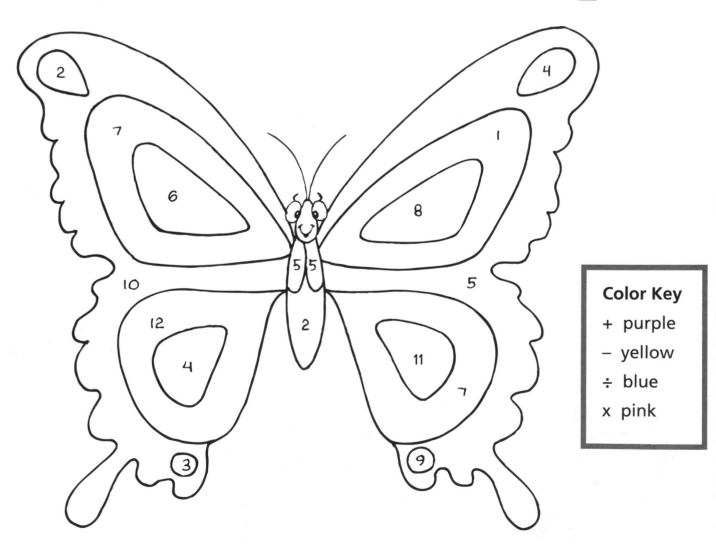

Color Key

+ purple

− yellow

÷ blue

x pink

Name _____

Let's Compare

Use >, <, or = to compare the fractions below.

A.
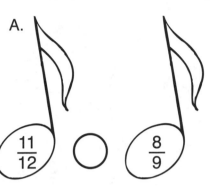
$\frac{11}{12}$ ◯ $\frac{8}{9}$

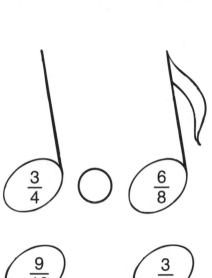
$\frac{3}{4}$ ◯ $\frac{6}{8}$

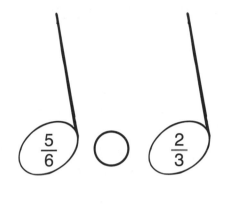
$\frac{5}{6}$ ◯ $\frac{2}{3}$

B.
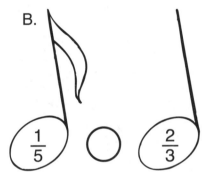
$\frac{1}{5}$ ◯ $\frac{2}{3}$

$\frac{9}{10}$ ◯ $\frac{3}{4}$

$\frac{2}{5}$ ◯ $\frac{10}{11}$

C.
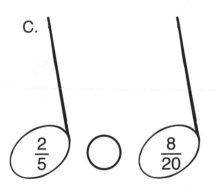
$\frac{2}{5}$ ◯ $\frac{8}{20}$

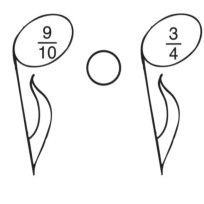
$\frac{1}{4}$ ◯ $\frac{3}{8}$

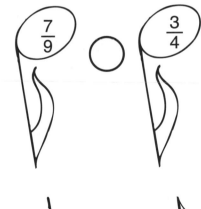
$\frac{7}{9}$ ◯ $\frac{3}{4}$

D.
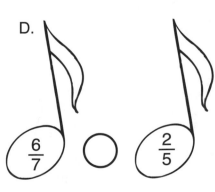
$\frac{6}{7}$ ◯ $\frac{2}{5}$

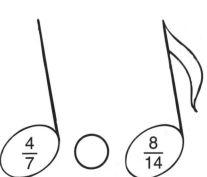
$\frac{4}{7}$ ◯ $\frac{8}{14}$

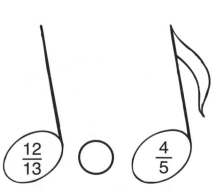
$\frac{12}{13}$ ◯ $\frac{4}{5}$

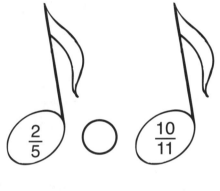
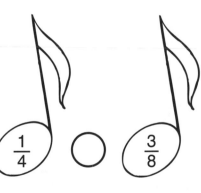

Daily Learning Drills Grade 4

MATH REVIEW

Name _____

Bubble Fun

Change each improper fraction to a mixed number, or change each mixed number to an improper fraction.

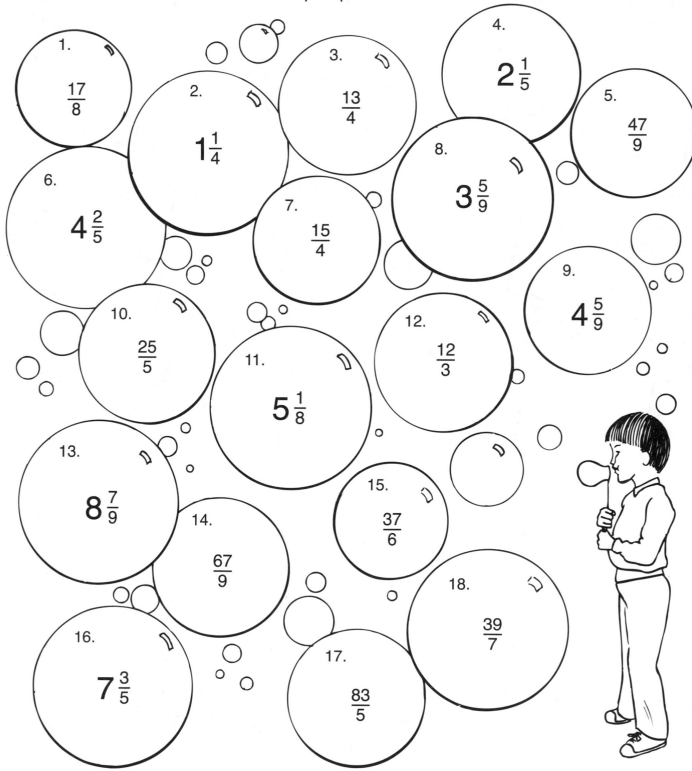

1. $\dfrac{17}{8}$

2. $1\dfrac{1}{4}$

3. $\dfrac{13}{4}$

4. $2\dfrac{1}{5}$

5. $\dfrac{47}{9}$

6. $4\dfrac{2}{5}$

7. $\dfrac{15}{4}$

8. $3\dfrac{5}{9}$

9. $4\dfrac{5}{9}$

10. $\dfrac{25}{5}$

11. $5\dfrac{1}{8}$

12. $\dfrac{12}{3}$

13. $8\dfrac{7}{9}$

14. $\dfrac{67}{9}$

15. $\dfrac{37}{6}$

16. $7\dfrac{3}{5}$

17. $\dfrac{83}{5}$

18. $\dfrac{39}{7}$

Name _____

Adding and Subtracting

Fractions can be added or subtracted if the denominators are the same.

Example: $\frac{1}{4} + \frac{2}{4} = \frac{3}{4}$

Add the fractions below.

1. $\frac{1}{5} + \frac{3}{5} =$ _____

2. $\frac{3}{7} + \frac{5}{7} =$ _____

3. $\frac{6}{10} + \frac{9}{10} =$ _____

4. $\frac{1}{3} + \frac{1}{3} =$ _____

5. $\frac{3}{9} + \frac{2}{9} =$ _____

6. $\frac{3}{8} + \frac{6}{8} =$ _____

7. $\frac{3}{6} + \frac{2}{6} =$ _____

8. $\frac{4}{12} + \frac{5}{12} =$ _____

9. $\frac{1}{2} + \frac{1}{2} =$ _____

Subtract these fractions.

10. $\frac{4}{4} - \frac{2}{4} =$ _____

11. $\frac{6}{7} - \frac{5}{7} =$ _____

12. $\frac{10}{11} - \frac{9}{11} =$ _____

13. $\frac{4}{3} - \frac{2}{3} =$ _____

14. $\frac{5}{6} - \frac{2}{6} =$ _____

15. $\frac{8}{8} - \frac{6}{8} =$ _____

16. $\frac{3}{4} - \frac{1}{4} =$ _____

17. $\frac{3}{5} - \frac{2}{5} =$ _____

18. $\frac{5}{8} - \frac{5}{8} =$ _____

To add or subtract mixed numbers, add or subtract fractions first, then whole numbers. Add and subtract the mixed numbers below.

19. $\begin{array}{r} 1\frac{2}{6} \\ + 3\frac{3}{6} \\ \hline \end{array}$

20. $\begin{array}{r} 4\frac{1}{10} \\ + 4\frac{8}{10} \\ \hline \end{array}$

21. $\begin{array}{r} 7\frac{2}{5} \\ + \frac{2}{5} \\ \hline \end{array}$

22. $\begin{array}{r} 7\frac{2}{4} \\ - 3\frac{1}{4} \\ \hline \end{array}$

23. $\begin{array}{r} 4\frac{5}{9} \\ - 4\frac{4}{9} \\ \hline \end{array}$

24. $\begin{array}{r} 47\frac{2}{5} \\ - \frac{2}{5} \\ \hline \end{array}$

MATH REVIEW

Name _____

Fraction Fun

Before adding two fractions, both fractions must have the same denominator. Use the number lines to rewrite the fractions. Then add.

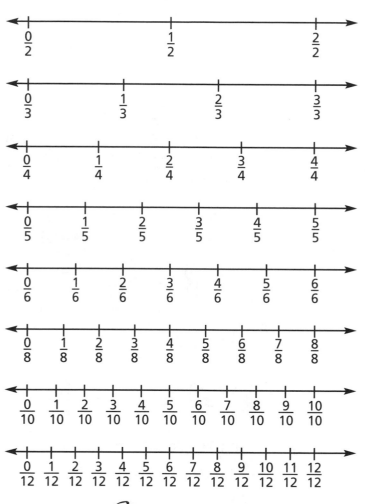

1. $\dfrac{1}{4} + \dfrac{5}{8} =$ _____

2. $\dfrac{1}{2} + \dfrac{3}{10} =$ _____

3. $\dfrac{1}{3} + \dfrac{1}{6} =$ _____

4. $\dfrac{1}{2} + \dfrac{3}{12} =$ _____

5. $\dfrac{1}{2} + \dfrac{5}{6} =$ _____

6. $\dfrac{1}{2} + \dfrac{3}{4} =$ _____

7. $\dfrac{2}{5} + \dfrac{3}{10} =$ _____

8. $\dfrac{9}{10} + \dfrac{3}{5} =$ _____

9. $\dfrac{3}{4} + \dfrac{7}{8} =$ _____

10. $\dfrac{7}{10} + \dfrac{3}{5} =$ _____

11. $\dfrac{2}{3} + \dfrac{1}{6} =$ _____

12. $\dfrac{1}{10} + \dfrac{1}{5} =$ _____

13. $\dfrac{3}{12} + \dfrac{2}{3} =$ _____

14. $\dfrac{2}{4} + \dfrac{7}{8} =$ _____

15. $\dfrac{1}{4} + \dfrac{8}{12} =$ _____

16. $\dfrac{1}{8} + \dfrac{3}{4} =$ _____

17. $\dfrac{7}{12} + \dfrac{2}{6} =$ _____

Name _____

Analyzing Area

Area tells the number of square units in a figure. Find the area of each figure below.

1.  _____ sq. units

2. 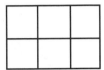 _____ sq. units

3. 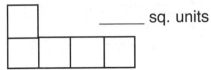 _____ sq. units

4. 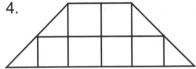 _____ sq. units

5. 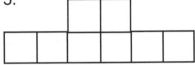 _____ sq. units

The area can be found by multiplying the length times the width: A = lw.

6.
6 ft.
4 ft.
_____ x _____ = _____ ft.^{2}

7.
5 ft.
_____ x _____ = _____ ft.^{2}

Find the areas below.

8. 4 ft.
A = _____

9. 3 ft.
12 ft.
A = _____

A = _____

10. 10 ft.
9 ft.
A = _____

11. 6 ft.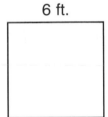
A = _____

12. 15 ft.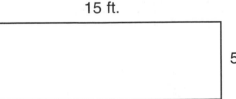
5 ft.
A = _____

13.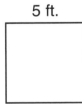
11 ft.
A = _____
2 ft.

14. 9 ft.
A = _____

Daily Learning Drills Grade 4

MATH REVIEW

Name _____

Very Important Volume

Volume is the number of cubic units that will fit inside a space figure. Build each figure below using linking cubes. Tell the number of cubes used.

1.
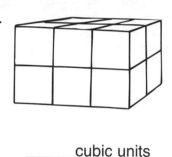

3.
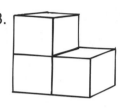 _____ cubic units

2.
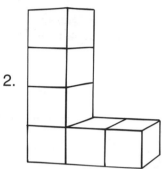

_____ cubic units

_____ cubic units

Volume can be found by multiplying the length times the width times the height: V = lwh.

Find the volume of each figure below.

5.
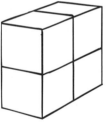

4.
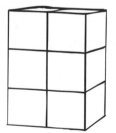

_____ x _____ x _____ = _____ cu. units

_____ x _____ x _____ = _____ cu. units

6.
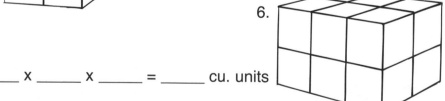

9.
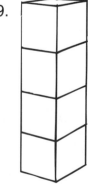

_____ x _____ x _____ = _____ cu. units

7.

8.

_____ x _____ x _____ = _____ cu. units

_____ x _____ x

_____ = _____

cu. units

_____ x _____ x _____ = _____ cu. units

Name _____

What Makes the Most Sense?

Draw a line from each object to the unit that best measures it. Remember that small and medium objects are measured in millimeters and centimeters. Bigger objects are measured in decimeters or meters.

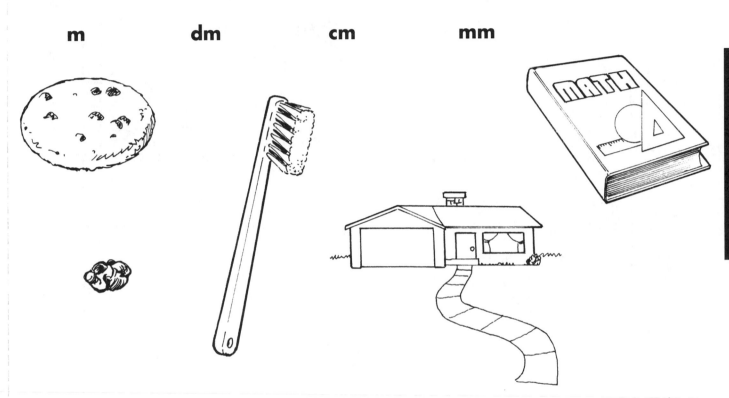

m　　　　**dm**　　　　**cm**　　　　**mm**

In the chart below, list three items that would best be measured with each unit.

METER	DECIMETER	CENTIMETER	MILLIMETER
1.	1.	1.	1.
2.	2.	2.	2.
3.	3.	3.	3.

More Measurement Fun!

Measure three objects from your house. Measure one in cm, one in mm, and one in m.

Name _____

How Hot Is It?

Temperature is measured in degrees Celsius or Fahrenheit.

Temperatures

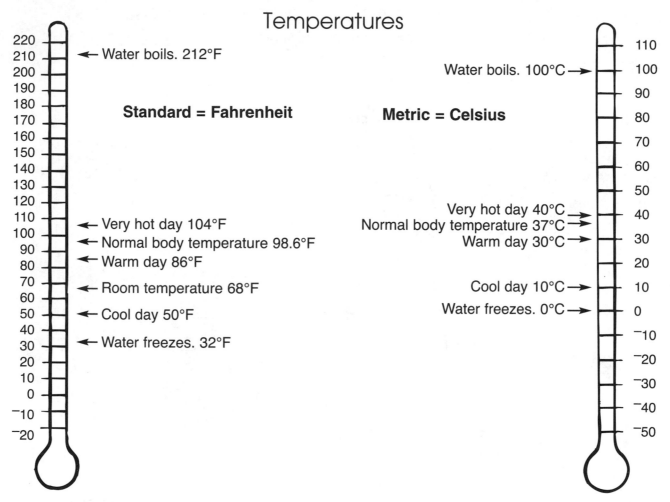

220	
210	← Water boils. 212°F
200	
190	
180	
170	**Standard = Fahrenheit**

Metric = Celsius

Water boils. 100°C →

Very hot day 40°C →
Normal body temperature 37°C →
Warm day 30°C →

Cool day 10°C →
Water freezes. 0°C →

← Very hot day 104°F
← Normal body temperature 98.6°F
← Warm day 86°F
← Room temperature 68°F
← Cool day 50°F
← Water freezes. 32°F

Use the thermometers to show the temperatures below in Celsius and Fahrenheit.

	degrees Fahrenheit	degrees Celsius
Water boils.		
Normal body temperature		
A very hot day		
A warm day		
A cool day		
Water freezes.		

Name _____

T-shirt Count

Jan grouped her 12 t-shirts according to these colors: red, blue, green, and yellow. Read the clues and figure out how many t-shirts Jan has of each color. Write your answers on the chart.

Clues:

◆ There are twice as many blue t-shirts as there are red t-shirts.

◆ There is the same number of green t-shirts and yellow t-shirts.

◆ There is 1 more blue t-shirt than there are green t-shirts.

◆ There are 2 red t-shirts.

t-shirt Color	Number of t-shirts
red	
blue	
green	
yellow	

Now use the information from your chart to create a circle graph. First color the key so that the rectangles match their colors. Then color each section of the circle to show how many t-shirts Jan has of each color.

Jan's t-shirts

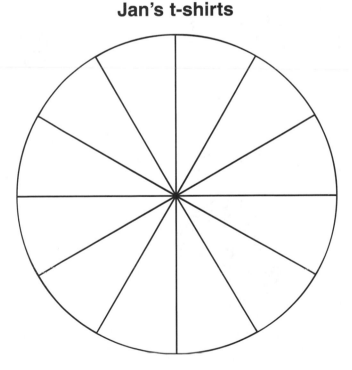

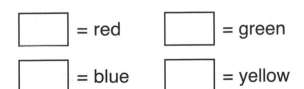

☐ = red ☐ = green

☐ = blue ☐ = yellow

Name _____

Is Willy Late?

Below are clocks that show the schedule Willy has to keep throughout the school day. Above the clocks in each square is the time Willy actually did each activity. Tell whether Willy was late by writing yes or no.

1. He gets up at 7:15 a.m.  Is Willy late? <u>no</u>	2. He catches a bus at 8:05 a.m.  Is Willy late?____	3. He starts school at 8:40 a.m.  Is Willy late?____
4. He gets to gym at 10:45 a.m.  Is Willy late?____	5. He has lunch at 12:10 p.m.  Is Willy late?____	6. He catches a bus at 3:20 p.m.  Is Willy late?____
7. He has dinner at 5:00 p.m.  Is Willy late?____	8. He does his homework at 7:05 p.m.  Is Willy late?____	9. He's in bed at 9:30 p.m.  Is Willy late?____

Name _____

What Time Is It?

Look at the clock and
circle the correct time.

1.

12:45   6:20   5:15

2.

1:20   4:00   2:25

3.

8:15   9:45   7:30

4.

9:45   12:00   3:15

5.

1:10   6:40   8:50

6.

11:00   11:05   11:10

7.

2:25   10:35   3:35

8.

4:05   5:35   9:15

9.

7:55   8:00   8:05

MATH REVIEW

Name _____

Sport Shopping

Fill in and total the receipts. Be careful! Sometimes the amount is more than one.

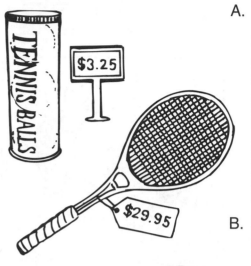

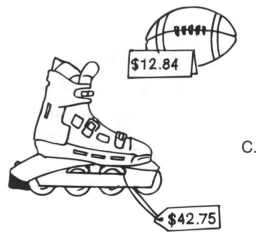

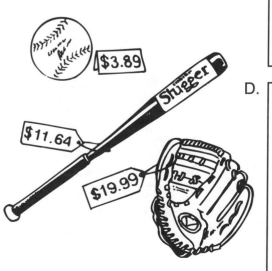

A.

Jeff's Sporting Goods		Date _____	
Amount	Item	Price per item	Total
2	baseballs	_____	_____
1	bat	_____	_____
1	glove	_____	_____
		Grand Total	_____

B.

Jeff's Sporting Goods		Date _____	
Amount	Item	Price per item	Total
2	tennis rackets	_____	_____
3	cans tennis balls	_____	_____
		Grand Total	_____

C.

Jeff's Sporting Goods		Date _____	
Amount	Item	Price per item	Total
1 pair	in-line skates	_____	_____
2	cans tennis balls	_____	_____
		Grand Total	_____

D.

Jeff's Sporting Goods		Date _____	
Amount	Item	Price per item	Total
2	footballs	_____	_____
3	baseballs	_____	_____
4	cans tennis balls	_____	_____
		Grand Total	_____

Name _____

The Magic Ruler

It is easier to work with numbers that have only one whole digit (i.e., 1.345 not 1345). You can make numbers with more than two whole digits into smaller numbers by just moving the decimal point to the right or to the left and adjusting the prefix term (i.e., 34.5 m = 3.45 dkm). An easy way to move the decimal point is to use the "Magic Equivalent Ruler."

Here is how to use the magic ruler. Suppose you have a number of 1506.3 cm. Your objective is to have only one whole digit to the left of the decimal point. First, you need to move the decimal point in the number three places to the left to end up with 1.5063. Next, since you started with the prefix term of cm, you need to also move three boxes (on the ruler) to the left (the same amount you moved decimal places). You end up with dk. Therefore, your new number is 1.5063 dkm (1506.3 cm = 1.5063 dkm).

Magic Equivalent Ruler

kilo	hecto	deka	root	deci	centi	milli
1 000	100	10	1	0.1	0.01	0.001

Change the numbers below so that one whole digit is to the left of the decimal.

Examples: 130 cm = 1.3 m   0.023 dkm = 2.3 dm

1. 24 m _____

2. 2456 cm _____

3. 897 mm _____

4. 96 cm _____

5. 6780 dm _____

6. 956 m _____

7. 843 dm _____

8. 0.356 hm _____

9. 0.023 dkm _____

10. 0.467 m _____

11. 0.045 dm _____

12. 0.0098 dkm _____

13. 0.87 km _____

14. 0.00023 hm _____

15. 0.234 m _____

16. 0.0108 dkm _____

Name _____

Seeing Symmetry in Nature

Study each figure shown below. Place a check mark in the column that tells what kind of symmetry the figure has. Then draw a line that divides the figure into symmetrical pieces. If you think the figure shows more than one line of symmetry, show two ways it could be divided.

Shape

Lines of Symmetry

	1 Line	More than 1 line
1. 	☐	☐
2. 	☐	☐
3. 	☐	☐
4. 	☐	☐

Look for symmetry in the natural world around you. On another piece of paper, illustrate three examples of symmetrical figures you found. Draw one line of symmetry through each figure.

Name _____

Sharp Senses

Successful writers are good observers of
nature. They use their senses as they react
personally to experiences in the natural
world. How does the snow sound underfoot?
What does a warm summer rain smell like?
How does the surface of a flower petal feel?
A writer might use these observations later
when describing something in a story.

Go for a walk or sit quietly in a natural setting and observe. Then
record everything your senses tell you about the experience. Write
your observations in colorful detail so you will remember them.
Don't just record that you heard the sound of a waterfall. Instead,
describe the sound. Was the water rushing, trickling, or dripping?
Later, use some of the observations in your own writing.

My observation experience: _____

Sights: _____

_____

Sounds: _____

_____

Textures: _____

_____

Smells: _____

_____

Tastes: _____

_____

SCIENCE REVIEW

Name _____

Shunning the Sun

What can you do if you get too hot this summer? Maybe you'll rest in the shade, turn on a fan, or go swimming. But what do animals do to beat the summer heat? They do many of the same things.

Read the story for clues about how animals avoid getting overheated. Choose an animal to fill in each blank.

sidewinder rattlesnake   honeybee
elephant   dog

1.

   Some animals escape the heat by soaking in cool water. When temperatures get hot, this land giant takes a dip in the nearest water hole. The mud and water help this animal cool off and keep its skin from drying out. When the water isn't deep enough to cover its entire body, this clever mammal sucks in as much as a gallon and a half, then sprays itself with the water.

2. _____

   This creature cools off with the help of sweat glands on the tip of its nose and the pads of its feet. The best way for it to cool off is to hang out its tongue and pant. The air drawn in by the panting evaporates the moisture in the animal's mouth and cools its body. That makes its mouth dry, so on hot days this critter needs plenty of water to drink.

3. _____

   This desert creature has a special cooling technique. Other cold-blooded desert creatures may crawl into an empty burrow or slither under a rock to survive scorching days. But not this one. After it coils itself up, it uses its head like a shovel to toss sand over its body. The sand blanket becomes a shield for keeping cool.

4. _____

   This creature's task in the summertime is to keep its wax home from melting! On warm summer days, these insects fan their wings rapidly. If fanning doesn't work, some stay behind while others fly off to drink lots of water, which they spit onto the wax when they return. The fanning of all these insect wings makes a breeze that evaporates the water, cooling the hive.

Name _____

Flying Flickers

Read the story, then answer the questions below.

Fireflies

Have you ever seen tiny, flashing lights on dark summer nights? These blinking lights come from fireflies. These insects aren't really flies, though; they're beetles. As with all beetles, they have a front pair of wings that is hardened to protect the hind wings, which are used to fly.

A flashing light in the dark often carries a message, like the searchlight on top of a lighthouse. The firefly is sending a message, too. It is looking for a mate. Each species of firefly has its own special combination of flashes. The message is meant to attract a firefly of the same species. The male flashes a code first, then the female responds. She raises her tail and turns her body as she sends her code. This makes the light shine in many directions, so the male can find her.

A firefly gets its light from an organ at the rear of the abdomen. A special chemical in the organ is released. When the chemical mixes with oxygen, a glow is created. This special glow is not like a fire or a furnace, which gives off heat. The firefly's glow does create light, however. Some people have even made firefly lanterns by putting fireflies in jars.

1. What causes tiny flashing lights in the darkness on hot summer nights?

_____

2. What causes the firefly to glow?

_____

3. Why would it be easier to find a firefly at night than during the day?

_____

4. How does a female firefly attract a male firefly?

_____

5. How does the glow of fireflies help the species survive?

_____
_____

Name _____

Summer in the Deep Freeze

Read the selection below. Then make a 2-column chart on another piece of paper. In the first column, tell what happens to emperor penguins during the winter. In the second column, tell what happens to emperor penguins during the summer.

Emperor Penguins

You're thinking about swimming, playing outside, and having fun on your summer vacation, but it's not summer everywhere! It's winter in the Southern Hemisphere, and emperor penguin chicks are being born. While you're trying to cool off, emperor penguins are trying to stay warm!

Winter is a busy time for emperor penguins in Antarctica. After the female lays a single egg, the male takes over. He holds the egg on top of his feet. Rolls of fat on the male's belly cover the egg and keep it warm. The male penguin—and all the other male birds in the colony—now wait for more than nine weeks while the eggs get ready to hatch. During egg time, all the male penguins form huge huddles to help shelter one another from the icy wind.

In Antarctica, temperatures can drop to 75° F below zero (-60° C). Still, it's very important for emperor chicks to be born in the winter. Because they grow so large, these chicks need more time to mature than an Antarctic summer allows. When the female lays the eggs in June—the start of winter—the parents are there to care for the chick. There's time for the chicks to hatch, develop, and mature by January. That's when summer starts. In summer, chicks eat heartily and build up a layer of blubber so they will be able to survive on their own when winter arrives.

Name _____

Food Web

How do people fit into the food chain? Study the plants and animals shown below. Then draw lines and arrows to create a food web that shows the relationships among them. Arrows should point toward the plant or animal being eaten. More than one arrow can be included for each element of the food web. An example is drawn for you.

In the space below, use words or illustrations to create another example of a food web. Include different plants and animals than those shown above.

Name _____

Watch Those Bones!

Discover the effects of heat and vinegar on bones. An adult should be present during this activity.

Materials Needed:

2 chicken leg bones   source of heat (an alcohol burner or a Bunsen burner)

vinegar   tongs

jar with lid

1. Place one chicken leg bone in a jar.
2. Fill the jar with vinegar.
3. Let the bone soak for three to seven days.
4. Use the tongs to hold the unsoaked chicken bone directly over the flame for about two minutes.
5. Try to bend the heated bone. Record your observations.
6. Remove the bone from the vinegar. Try to bend it. Record your observations.

Write your observations on the lines.
   heated bone:

_____

_____

   bone soaked in vinegar:

_____

_____

What conclusions can you draw from this activity?
1. Heating the bone removed cartilage. How does cartilage help the skeletal system do its job?

_____

_____

2. The vinegar removed calcium from the bone. How does calcium help the skeletal system do its job?

_____

_____

Name _____

Target Your Heart

Choose an activity listed in the chart below. Perform the activity for 2 to 5 minutes. Then feel your pulse to determine the number of heartbeats per minute. Check the heart-rate chart to see if you are in your target range. Try the other activities to see how they affect your heart.

Age	Beats Per Minute
9	148–211
10	147–210
11	146–209
12	145–208

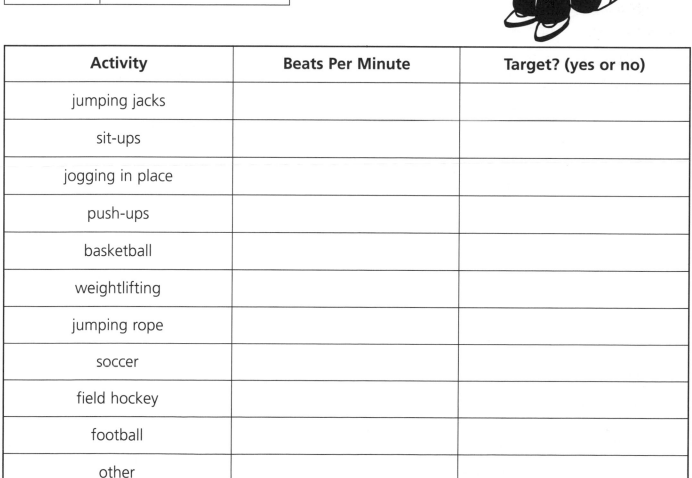

Activity	Beats Per Minute	Target? (yes or no)
jumping jacks		
sit-ups		
jogging in place		
push-ups		
basketball		
weightlifting		
jumping rope		
soccer		
field hockey		
football		
other		

SCIENCE REVIEW

Name _____

Where to Take Your Pulse

Learn the proper way to take a pulse and the various places it can be taken.

Materials Needed:

watch

paper

pencil

Write numbers on the diagram at the right to show the approximate locations of the seven pulse sites listed.

1. Carotid artery (neck)

2. Brachial artery (arm)

3. Radial artery (wrist)

4. Femoral artery (thigh)

5. Popliteal artery (behind knee)

6. Dorsalis Pedis (ankle)

7. Temporal artery (temples)

Taking Your Pulse:

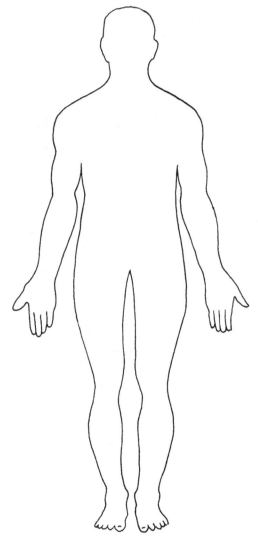

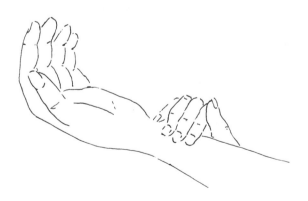

Name _____

1. Work with a partner. Position your first two fingers where you feel a strong pulse.
2. Press gently and count the beats for 15 seconds. Caution: Do not use your thumb, since there is a pulse site in your thumb. You do not want to take your own pulse instead of your partner's.
3. Multiply the number of beats by four to get the pulse rate for one minute. Record the information below.
4. Try to take your partner's pulse in three other locations. Record the results.

Observations

PULSE SITE	PULSE	STRENGTH
_____	_____	_____
_____	_____	_____
_____	_____	_____
_____	_____	_____

Conclusions

1. What similarities or differences in strength and number did you observe in the pulse readings?

_____

_____

_____

_____

_____

_____

2. What factors might cause differences in a person's pulse?

_____

_____

_____

_____

_____

_____

Name _____

Reaction Time

How fast do you react? Can you improve your reaction time? Work with a partner to find out. Take turns trying to catch a ruler between the fingers of one hand. You can measure your reaction time by seeing where you grab the ruler.

1. Stand facing your partner. Ask him or her to hold the ruler at the 1-inch mark, with 12 inches at the bottom. The top of the ruler should be even with the top of your head.

2. Keep your eyes on the ruler. As soon as your partner lets go of it, try to catch it between the fingers of one hand.

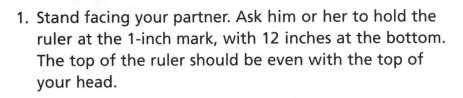

3. Look at the ruler to see which inch measurement is closest to the spot where your fingers grasped the ruler. Record that measurement on the graph at the bottom of the page. First find the inch measurement where you caught the ruler. (If you didn't catch it in time, use the line marked 0.) Trace that line down to the line labeled Trial #1. Make a large dot where the two lines meet.

4. Have your partner test you four more times. Use dots to record each measurement on the graph. When you are done, draw straight lines to connect the dots. If the lines head to the right, your reaction time has improved.

	0	1	2	3	4	5	6	7	8	9	10	11	12
Trial #5													
Trial #4													
Trial #3													
Trial #2													
Trial #1													

Name _____

Personal Fitness Goals

Make your own physical fitness goals in each of the fitness areas listed below. You can work on one of the example skills or on another skill of your choice. Many activities build more than one skill. For example, sit-ups build abdominal strength. Doing them faster builds speed. Doing them for a longer period of time builds endurance. Check the boxes as your goals are achieved.

Strength Goal: I will develop the amount of force my muscles can produce.
Strength skill examples: push-ups, pull-ups, sit-ups, leg lifts

By _____, I will _____ .
☐ **Goal achieved**

Endurance Goal: I will be able to do something for a longer period of time.
Endurance skill examples: running in place, jumping jacks, distance run

By _____, I will _____ .
☐ **Goal achieved**

Agility Goal: I will improve my ability to change direction and position quickly.
Agility skill examples: zig-zag run, obstacle run, jumping rope

By _____, I will _____ .
☐ **Goal achieved**

Flexibility Goal: I will improve my ability to bend, reach, twist, and turn.
Flexibility skill examples: toe touches, cartwheels

By _____, I will _____ .
☐ **Goal achieved**

Speed Goal: I will do something faster.
Speed skill examples: fifty-yard dash, sit-ups

By _____, I will _____ .
☐ **Goal achieved**

Coordination Goal: I will be able to work different muscles together efficiently.
Coordination skill examples: dribbling a basketball, batting

By _____, I will be able to _____ .
☐ **Goal achieved**

SCIENCE REVIEW

Name _____

Fat Floats

Compare the buoyancy of a fatty mass and a lean mass.

Materials Needed:

beaker

tablespoon of solid shortening

4-centimeter piece of carrot

slice of potato

water

a stirrer or plastic spoon

1. Fill the beaker two-thirds full of tap water.
2. Gently place the carrot in the beaker.
3. Draw a diagram below to record your observation.
4. Gently place the slice of potato in the beaker.
5. Draw a diagram below to record your observation.
6. Use the stirrer to gently slide the shortening into the beaker.
7. Draw a diagram below to record your observation.

Observations

CARROT   POTATO   SHORTENING

Conclusion

1. Based on the information gained in this experiment, who would float more easily—a person with a high proportion of body fat or a person with a low proportion of body fat?

_____

_____

_____

Name _____

Magnet Fun

Use the clues and the words in the Word Box to complete the puzzle.

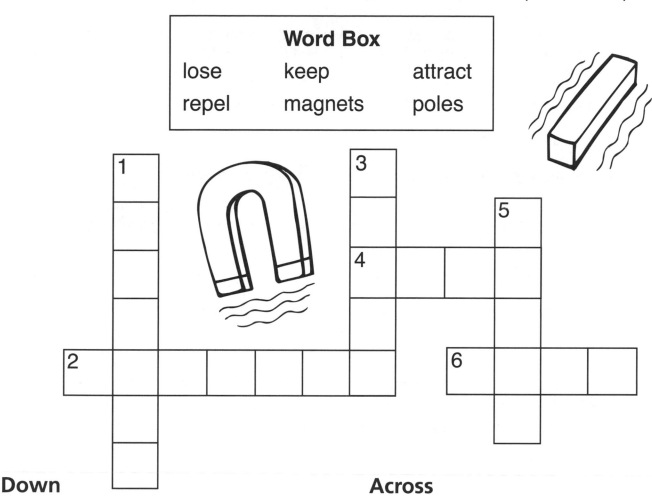

Word Box

lose	keep	attract
repel	magnets	poles

Down

Across

1. Opposite poles _____, or draw toward each other.

2. _____ are objects that can attract other objects.

3. Bar magnets have two _____, one on each end.

4. Temporary magnets _____ their magnetism.

5. Like poles push away from each other, or _____.

6. Permanent magnets _____ their magnetism.

Name _____

Cost of Electricity

Develop an awareness of the cost of running small appliances.

In order to calculate the cost of electrical energy, you need to know the wattage of the appliance that you are using (wattage), the length of time it is used (time), and the cost per kilowatt hour (cost p/k).

Use the following formula to determine the cost of running an appliance.

wattage x time = kilowatt hours

kilowatt hours x cost p/k = cost of the electricity to run the appliance

Example: You use a bedside lamp to read for 45 minutes each night before you go to bed. The bulb is a 25-watt bulb. How much does it cost to run the lamp for one week? Work with a cost/kilowatt of $0.000611.

25 watts x .75 hours = 18.75 kilowatt hours

18.75 kilowatt hours x $0.000611 = $0.01145625

$0.01145625 x 7 days = $0.08 cost for one week

Select five appliances that you or someone in your family uses. List them beside the numbers 1 to 5. Calculate the weekly cost for each item.

hair dryer	curling iron
TV	radio
toaster	electric iron
electric saw	electric drill
VCR/DVD	stereo

Show your calculations in the spaces to the right.

1. _____

wattage   _____

time   _____

cost per kilowatt hour   _____

cost of running the item   _____

Name _____

2. _____

    wattage   _____

    time   _____

    cost per kilowatt hour   _____

    cost of running the item   _____

3. _____

    wattage   _____

    time   _____

    cost per kilowatt hour   _____

    cost of running the item   _____

4. _____

    wattage   _____

    time   _____

    cost per kilowatt hour   _____

    cost of running the item   _____

5. _____

    wattage   _____

    time   _____

    cost per kilowatt hour   _____

    cost of running the item   _____

1. Which appliance costs the least to operate? _____

2. Which appliance costs the most to operate? _____

Name _____

Weight Is Not Mass!

Another word for the pull of gravity is weight. Weight changes according to how far away an object is from its source of gravity. The mass of an object does not change regardless of where in the universe that object is located. This is because mass is the amount of matter in the object. To understand weight and mass better, answer the questions below. Pretend you are on a spaceship to the moon.

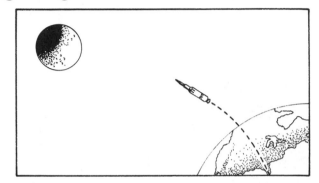

ON EARTH (Earth's pull of gravity)

   Your mass: _____ kg X 2.2 =   _____ lb

   Your weight: _____ kg X 9.8 m/s^2 =   _____ N

1/4 OF THE WAY TO THE MOON (Earth's lessening pull of gravity)

   Your mass: _____ kg X 2.2 =   _____ lb

   Your weight: _____ kg X 7.7 m/s^2 _____ N

1/2 OF THE WAY TO THE MOON (Earth's lessening pull of gravity)

   Your mass: _____ kg X 2.2 =   _____ lb

   Your weight: _____ kg X 5.6 m/s^2 =   _____ N

3/4 OF THE WAY TO THE MOON (Earth's lessening pull of gravity)

   Your mass: _____ kg X 2.2 =   _____ lb

   Your weight: _____ kg X 3.5 m/s^2 =   _____ N

ON THE MOON (Moon's pull of gravity)

   Your mass: _____ kg X 2.2 =   _____ lb

   Your weight: _____ kg X 1.6 m/s^2 =   _____ N

What value is changing in each of these sets of numbers? _____

More Measurement Fun!

Find the pull of gravity on other planets. Determine what your mass and weight would be if you were on that planet.

Name _____

Weather Wisdom

Why is weather important?

The following are sayings about weather. Write T, for *true*, if you think the saying has some basis in science. Write F, for *false*, if you think it has no basis in scientific fact.

_____ 1. An old timer says, "I can tell it's going to rain, my feet hurt."

_____ 2. When an old cat acts like a kitten, a storm is on the way.

_____ 3. Kill a snake and turn it on its belly for rain.

_____ 4. Frogs croak before a rain, but in the sun they stay quiet.

_____ 5. When bees stay close to the hive, rain is close by.

_____ 6. Red sky at night, sailor's delight—Red sky in morning, sailors take warning.

_____ 7. A tough apple means a hard winter is coming.

_____ 8. When the night has a fever, it cries in the morning.

Think about how weather affects you and complete the following.

Why do you think people want to predict the weather?

_____

_____

Give an example of when the weather might affect what you do.

_____

_____

When might the weather affect how you feel?

_____

_____

When do you talk about the weather?

_____

_____

Fill in the vowels **e** and **o** to spell the word for the science of weather.

M ___ T ___ ___ R ___ L ___ G Y

SCIENCE REVIEW

Name _____

The Red Planet

Mars is often called the red planet because of its brick-red color as seen in Earth's night sky. Sometimes giant dust storms cover the whole planet. When this happens, the Sun doesn't shine on the Martian surface for weeks.

Both Earth and Mars are made mostly of rock. Earth is the third planet from the Sun, and Mars is the fourth. Earth has one satellite, the Moon, in its orbit. Mars has two satellites. They are both shaped something like potatoes.

Although Mars is thought to be the second most livable planet in the solar system, there is almost no liquid water or breathable air on Mars. Thus, nothing from Earth could live there.

Name _____

The Red Planet

Use the facts to complete the Venn diagram. One fact will be shared by both circles.

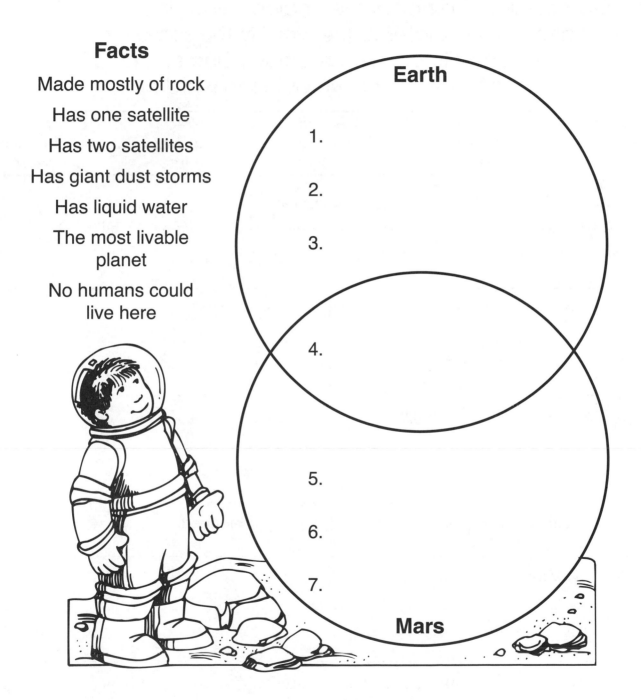

Facts

Made mostly of rock

Has one satellite

Has two satellites

Has giant dust storms

Has liquid water

The most livable planet

No humans could live here

Earth

1.

2.

3.

4.

5.

6.

7.

Mars

Daily Learning Drills Grade 4

Name _____

Science Analogies

Use your scientific knowledge to complete each of the analogies. Think about how the first two words are related to one another. Then read the second half of the analogy. Look in the word box and find a term that relates to the word in the same way. Then explain the relationship on the line below. One example is done for you. Hint: You won't use all the words in the word box.

kidney	ice	pound	acacia	toad
monkey	caterpillar	penicillin	quartz	dinosaur
lava	Earth	liter	Pluto	heart

Example: frog : tadpole as butterfly : _____caterpillar_____

   A frog develops from a tadpole. A butterfly develops from a caterpillar.

1. sedimentary : sandstone as metamorphic : _____

_____

2. rattlesnake : alligator as _____ : salamander

_____

3. panda : bamboo as giraffe : _____

_____

4. astrology : star as paleontology : _____

_____

5. lungs : respiration as _____ : circulation

_____

6. snake : cold-blooded as _____ : warm-blooded

_____

7. Mercury : Venus as Uranus : _____

_____

8. avalanche : snow as glacier : _____

_____

9. Curie : radium as Fleming : _____

_____

10. centimeter : inch as _____ : quart

_____

Name _____

Portrait Poetry

Who are you? There are many different ways to describe who we are. This is a special poem that helps you think about who you are right now. Here's the formula and an example. Try it. You'll like it!

Portrait Poetry

Line 1: your first name	Susan
Line 2: 4 descriptive traits	Caring, cheerful, creative, pretty
Line 3: sibling or friend of	Sister of Julie and David
Line 4: lover of	Music, jokes, learning, animals
Line 5: who feels	Sad when she's far from family
Line 6: who needs	Chocolate every day
Line 7: who gives	Encouragement, friendship, hugs
Line 8: who would like to see	Kindness to animals, no report cards, a money tree, a longer summer

Now try your own!

1. _____

2. _____

3. _____

4. _____

5. _____

6. _____

7. _____

8. _____

Write portrait poetry about your pet, a best friend, your parent, or a favorite relative. Save your poems and look at them a year from now. Do you think anything will change?

SOCIAL STUDIES REVIEW

Name _____

My "Blooming" Story

Finish the statements on the flower below. Write about something you do better now than you did at the beginning of the year. Explain what you did to become better, and how you feel about it now.

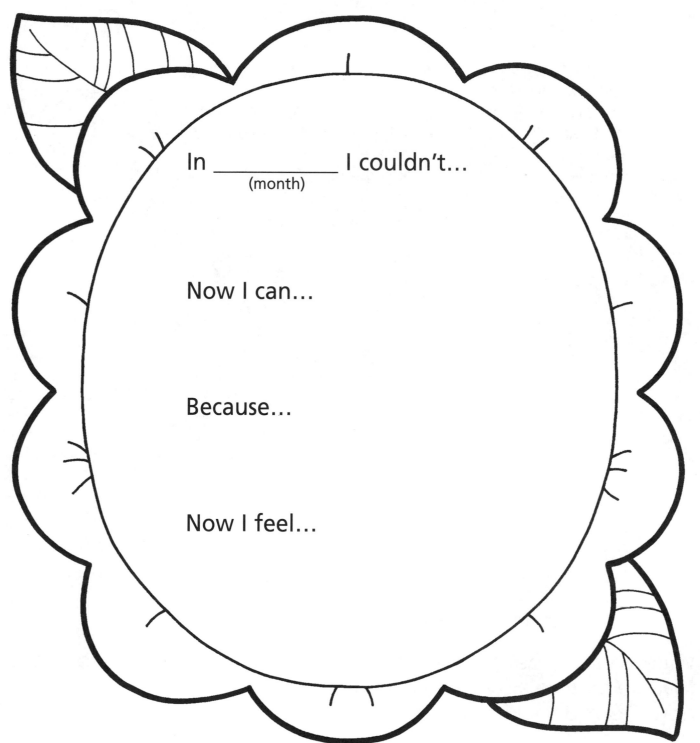

In _____ I couldn't...
(month)

Now I can...

Because...

Now I feel...

Name _____

Friendship Inventory

Think about friendships you have or would like to have. How do you choose your friends? How do you make new friends? How do you and your friends treat one another? How important are friends to you? Once you've given some thought to those questions, finish the sentences below. Remember, there are no right or wrong answers. Be ready to discuss your thoughts with your classmates.

1. I like to be friends with people who are: _____

_____

2. A fun thing to do with a friend is: _____

_____

3. If a friend hurts my feelings, I: _____

_____

4. If I make a friend angry, I feel: _____

_____

5. I think friends should never: _____

_____

6. I think friends should always: _____

_____

7. I make friends by: _____

_____

8. One thing I'd change about my friendships is: _____

_____

9. One of my best memories about a friend is: _____

_____

10. When a friend moves away, I: _____

_____

11. Something I'll do with a friend in the future is: _____

_____

Name _____

Happy Birthday, U.S.A.

Each year on the Fourth of July, the United States celebrates its birthday and the adoption of the Declaration of Independence. Solve this word search by looking for words associated with this holiday. Words can go down and across. Use the Word Bank for help.

Word Bank

sparklers

parades

red

fireworks

picnics

stars

white

independence

marching band

stripes

blue

celebration

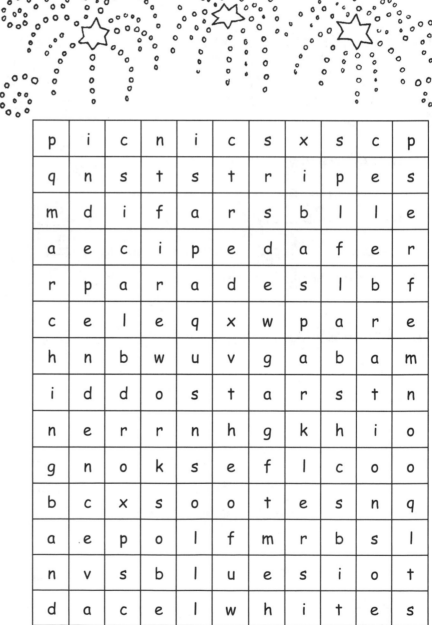

p	i	c	n	i	c	s	x	s	c	p
q	n	s	t	s	t	r	i	p	e	s
m	d	i	f	a	r	s	b	l	l	e
a	e	c	i	p	e	d	a	f	e	r
r	p	a	r	a	d	e	s	l	b	f
c	e	l	e	q	x	w	p	a	r	e
h	n	b	w	u	v	g	a	b	a	m
i	d	d	o	s	t	a	r	s	t	n
n	e	r	r	n	h	g	k	h	i	o
g	n	o	k	s	e	f	l	c	o	o
b	c	x	s	o	o	t	e	s	n	q
a	e	p	o	l	f	m	r	b	s	l
n	v	s	b	l	u	e	s	i	o	t
d	a	c	e	l	w	h	i	t	e	s

Name _____

Holiday Crossword

Use the clues to solve the crossword puzzle.

ACROSS

2. _____ Day remembers those who fought in wars.
5. July 4th celebrates America's _____.
6. The night before New Year's Day is New Year's _____.

DOWN

1. Bands and floats come down the street in a _____.
2. One Sunday in May we all honor our _____.
3. Labor day celebrates the hard _____ of America.
4. One Sunday in June we all honor our _____.
7. What you give your sweetheart on February 14th.

Name _____

Many Maps

Circle the words. They may go across, down, diagonally, or backward.

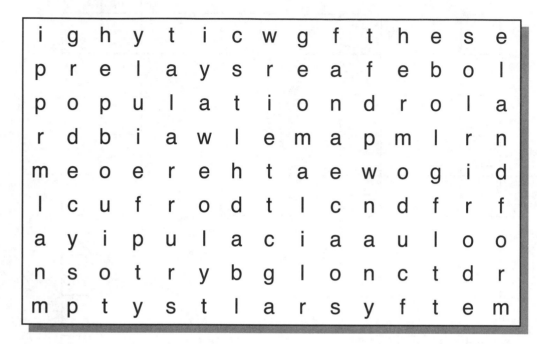

i	g	h	y	t	i	c	w	g	f	t	h	e	s	e
p	r	e	l	a	y	s	r	e	a	f	e	b	o	l
p	o	p	u	l	a	t	i	o	n	d	r	o	l	a
r	d	b	i	a	w	l	e	m	a	p	m	l	r	n
m	e	o	e	r	e	h	t	a	e	w	o	g	i	d
l	c	u	f	r	o	d	t	l	c	n	d	f	r	f
a	y	i	p	u	l	a	c	i	a	a	u	l	o	o
n	s	o	t	r	y	b	g	l	o	n	c	t	d	r
m	p	t	y	s	t	l	a	r	s	y	f	t	e	m

city
globe
landform
population
relief
road
weather

Write the words in the blanks.

1. A _____ map shows different types of roads, the distances from town to town, scenic routes, rest areas, and other things.

2. A _____ map shows streets, major buildings, parks, and other things.

3. A _____ map shows the shape and features of the land.

4. A _____ is a round model of earth.

5. A _____ map shows how many people live in a certain area.

6. A _____ map shows how high and low the land is.

7. A _____ map shows the weather of a certain area.

Name _____

The Tepee

The tepee was commonly used by the Plains Indians. A tepee is easy for one person to set up, take down, and move. This made it possible for Indians to roam over hundreds of miles as they searched for buffalo.

Tepees were set up on level ground. Wooden poles were arranged on the ground in the shape of a cone. Near the top, the poles were tied together. The tepees were then covered with buffalo hides. Openings were left at the tops so that fires could be lit inside and smoke could escape. The tents were attached to the ground with pegs. The fronts had slits for entrances. Inside, the tepees were covered with hide to help protect them from the weather.

SOCIAL STUDIES REVIEW

Daily Learning Drills Grade 4

Name _____

The Tepee (continued)

Complete the directions for building a tepee with words from the story on the previous page.

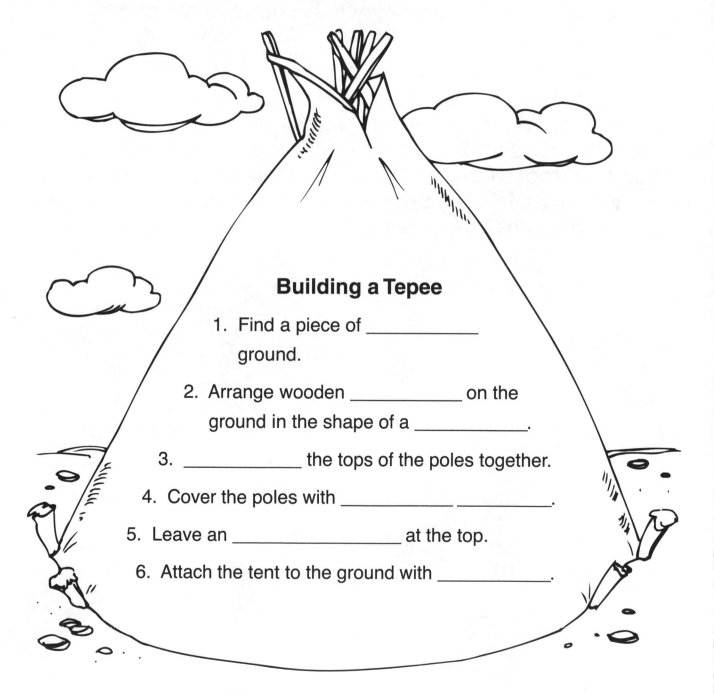

Building a Tepee

1. Find a piece of _____ ground.

2. Arrange wooden _____ on the ground in the shape of a _____.

3. _____ the tops of the poles together.

4. Cover the poles with _____ _____.

5. Leave an _____ at the top.

6. Attach the tent to the ground with _____.

George Washington Collage

Use this silhouette to create a collage about President George Washington.

Directions:

1. Cut out this silhouette, then cut another out of black construction paper.

2. Color, cut, and glue the pictures from the next page in a collage on the front of the silhouette. Glue the fact strips to the back.

3. Title the collage as shown, punch a hole in the top of the profile, and hang.

SOCIAL STUDIES REVIEW

Name _____

George Washington Collage

Color and cut out the elements below and glue them to the silhouette of George Washington.

Washington had false teeth made out of ivory.

Washington is called the "Father of Our Country."

Washington was born on February 22, 1732.

Washington worked as a surveyor when he was young.

Washington lead the colonial army during the Revolutionary War.

The Washington Monument stands in Washington, D.C.

Washington, D.C., the United States' capital, is named for George Washington.

SOCIAL STUDIES REVIEW

Name _____

Exploring for Explorers

What do you know about explorers of the past? Explore the encyclopedia, a biographical dictionary, your social studies text, and other references to fill in the missing information on the chart below.

Year	Explorer	Accomplishment	Nationality
1488	Bartolomeu Dias	Sailed around Africa's Cape of Good Hope	1.
1492	2.	First European to reach the West Indies	Italian; explored for Spain
1497	John Cabot	First European to reach Newfoundland	3.
1498	4.	Discovered a sea route to India	Portuguese
1513	Vasco Núñez de Balboa	5.	Spanish
1513	6.	First European to discover Florida	Spanish
1519	Hernán Cortés	7.	Spanish
1533	8.	Conquered Peru for Spain	Spanish
1541	Hernando de Soto	First European to discover the Mississippi River	9.
1603	Samuel de Champlain	Explored the Saint Lawrence River	10.
1610	Henry Hudson	11.	English
1673	12.	First to navigate length of the Mississippi River	French
1767	James Cook	13.	English
1804	Meriwether Lewis and William Clark	14.	American
1805	Charles Fraser	Explored Canada west of the Rocky Mountains	15.
1819	16.	First to find the Northwest Passage in Arctic	English
1842	John Fremont	Explored America west of the Rocky Mountains	17.
1856	David Livingstone	18.	Scottish
1909	Robert Peary	19.	American
1911	20.	Led first expedition to reach South Pole	Norwegian

Daily Learning Drills Grade 4

SOCIAL STUDIES REVIEW

Name _____

Jackie Robinson

Jackie Robinson was the first African American to play major league baseball. He began playing with the Brooklyn Dodgers in 1947. Because of the color of his skin, Robinson was ridiculed by fans and other players. However, he did not let their prejudices discourage him. Robinson worked very hard and was voted the Most Valuable Player in 1949. Robinson achieved another great honor in 1962 when he was inducted into the National Baseball Hall of Fame.

Name _____

Match the words in the box to the correct definition.

_____ 1. To use words or actions to make
         fun of a person or thing

_____ 2. To be important

_____ 3. Glory or recognition

_____ 4. To carry out successfully;
         accomplish

_____ 5. Hostility toward a particular group,
         such as a race or religion

_____ 6. To install into an office or
         position, especially with
         formal ceremonies

a. Honor
b. Ridicule
c. Prejudice
d. Valuable
e. Achieve
f. Induct

SOCIAL STUDIES REVIEW

Name _____

Playing Mancala

Learn how to play mancala, an African game for two players. Mancala is popular with adults and children. It's easy to learn, but thinking mathematically helps you play well!

What you will need:

1 12-compartment egg carton, lid removed

48 beans or counters—24 of one color; 24 of another color

2 small bowls

How to set things up:

Place the egg carton between you and your partner, with one of the small bowls at each end. Each player gets 24 beans or counters of one color and puts 4 beans in each of the compartments on his or her side.

How to play:

The six cups on your side of the egg carton are yours. The cups on the other side are your partner's. Use the small bowl at your right for beans you capture during the game.

1. The first player picks up all the beans in any one of the six cups on her side. Moving to the right, she drops one bean in each cup, going around the carton to the right until she runs out.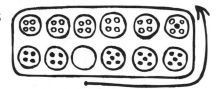

2. The second player picks up all the beans in one of his cups. Moving to the right, he drops one bean in each cup until he runs out.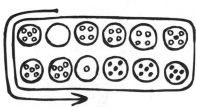

3. Take turns doing the same thing. If the last bean dropped by a player makes two or three beans in a cup on the opponent's side, the beans are "captured" and put into the player's small bowl. In addition, if the cup just before that one has only two or three beans, and is on the opponent's side, those beans are captured as well.

4. Keep going until one of you has no beans left on your side. You must pick up and drop a cupful of beans on each turn.

Mancala is easy, but it pays to think ahead. Try to figure out how to get two or three beans into one of the cups on your partner's side. And try not to leave any cups on your side with only one or two beans.

Name _____

Take Note!

If you can't travel to faraway lands, explore the places in books! Taking notes helps you remember facts.

The note card below shows one way to take notes. The topic is written on the top line. Questions are listed below it, and then the answers.

Go to the library and check out a nonfiction book about another country. Use a note card to take notes from the book.

Topic:	
Indonesia	
Write a question for each fact.	**Find and write facts or ideas.**
What type of land?	— dense tropical rain forests
What's the capital?	— Jakarta
How many active volcanoes?	— over 60 active volcanoes

SOCIAL STUDIES REVIEW

Review Answer Key

At the Library

To alphabetize means to arrange things in alphabetical order. The following words are alphabetized: *xylophone, yacht, zipper*.

Connie is clumsy. She keeps tipping things over at the library. Help her put the magazines, books, and videos back on the shelf in alphabetical order. Number them to show which comes first, second, and so on.

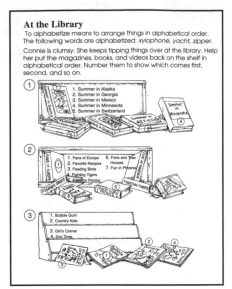

(1)
1. Summer in Alaska
2. Summer in Georgia
3. Summer in Mexico
4. Summer in Minnesota
5. Summer in Switzerland

(2)
1. Fans of Europe
2. Favorite Recipes
3. Feeding Birds
4. Fighting Tigers
5. Food for Picnics
6. Forts and Tree Houses
7. Fun in Phoenix

(3)
1. Bubble Gum
2. Country Kids
3. Girl's Corner
4. Zoo Time

321

Get it Together!

Compound words are two separate words combined to form a new word. *Flowerpot* is a compound word made up of the words *flower* and *pot*. Choose one word from the first column and one word from the second to form a compound word that makes sense. How many compound words can you make? Words can be used more than once.

Beginnings	Endings	
get	meal	getaway
gold	time	goldfish
grass	paper	grasshopper
green	light	greenhouse
head	balls	headlight
home	man	homework
house	house	houseboat
ice	guard	icebox
oat	slide	oatmeal
key	hole	keyhole or keyboard
land	board	landslide
life	away	lifegaurd
light	box	lighthouse
mail	work	mailman
meat	boat	meatballs
moon	hopper	moonlight
news	fish	newspaper
night		nighttime

322

Community Food Share

The **complete subject** is all the words in a sentence that tell whom or what the sentence is about.

The **simple subject** is the one main word that tells whom or what the sentence is about.

Read each sentence. Underline the complete subject. Write the simple subject on the line.

children	The children in our class wanted to do a service project.
We	We voted on different ideas.
project	The project I thought of got the most votes.
We	1. We chose to hold a food drive at our school to help the Community Food Share program.
program	2. That program gives away food to people who need it.
group	3. One group of kids made posters about the food drive to hang all over school.
group	4. Another group spoke about the food drive at a school assembly.
group	5. The group I was in wrote a note to send home to families.
Kids	6. Kids in all the different classes brought in cans and boxes of food from home.
class	7. Our class sorted all the food.
parents	8. Our parents helped deliver the food we collected.
We	9. We took a field trip to the Community Food Share building.
people	10. The people at Community Food Share showed us where they store the food.
They	11. They were thankful for all that our class and school did.
class	12. Our class felt great that we had made a difference in our community!

323

Give It a Name

A noun that names any person, place, or thing is called a **common noun**.
A noun that names a special person, place, or thing is called a **proper noun**.
A proper noun begins with a capital letter.

Write two proper nouns for each common noun given.
Example: *river—Mississippi River, Rio Grande*

school	state	girl	boy
Answers will vary.			
restaurant	author	lake	street
president	month	day	athlete
store	pet	country	planet

324

Travel the World

Read this story Patrick wrote. Circle the **verbs** that are incorrect. Write the correct verb on the line.

made	Last week my friends and I (make) a geography
1. was	game called "Travel the World." It (were) for a social studies project at school.
2. found	First we (finded) a large map of the world. Our map showed each of the continents in a different color.
3. thought	Then we (thinked) of game ideas. I told our group
4. saw	about a game I (seen) at the store once. Megan had the
5. said	best idea. She (say) the purpose of the game should be
6. chose	to visit every continent. We (choosed) her idea.
7. wrote	Ben and I (writed) cards for the game. The cards told the players which continent to go to. For example,
8. said	one card (sayed) this: Go to the continent where the Nile River is found. Theo thought our cards might be too
9. added	hard for some kids. So we (add) the name of the
10. made	continent on each card also. Megan and Theo (maked)
11. had	score sheets. The score sheets (haved) check-off boxes next to each continent name.
12. kept	We played the game to test it. I (keeped) picking
13. won	cards that sent me to South America or Europe. I never did get a card for Asia. Ben (winned) our practice game.
14. turned	Finally we (turn) in our project. Our teacher liked it.
15. let	He (letted) us teach the class how to play it that day.

325

Past, Present, and Future

Facts About Verbs

The present tense of a verb states an action that is happening now, or that happens regularly: *I like jeans. I wear them every day.*

The past tense of a verb states an action that happened in the past: *I liked jeans last year.*

The future tense of a verb states an action that will take place. The future tense is made by using the helping verbs *will* or *shall* before the main verb: *I will be home tomorrow.*

Underline the verbs in the story below. Then fill in the table with the past, present, and future verbs from the story. The first two verbs are done for you.

The Levi Strauss Story

Levi Strauss invented blue jeans. That's why people call them Levi's. Strauss first made work pants out of canvas for California goldminers. Later, he used sturdy cotton denim that he dyed blue, using dye made from the indigo plant. By the 1860s, farmers, miners, and cowboys throughout the American West wore blue jeans.

Today, people all over the world wear jeans. Levi Strauss Company was the official outfitter for the 1984 Olympics. The company designed the uniforms for the U.S. Team. They also created one-of-a-kind jeans for each gold medal winner. The jeans had buttons and rivets made with 22-karat gold.

Jeans come in a variety of different colors and styles. The most popular color, though, is still blue. Do you think jeans will be popular when you are a grandparent?

Present Tense	Past Tense	Future Tense
call	invented	will be
using	made	was
wear	used	designed
is	dyed	created
think	wore	had
	come	

326

Smart, Smarter, Smartest

Adjectives that compare two things usually end in **er**.
Adjectives that compare three or more things usually end in **est**.
If the adjective is a long word, **more** or **most** is used with it instead.

A dog is smart.
A monkey is smarter than a dog.
A chimpanzee is one of the smartest animals of all.
Marine animals with backbones are more intelligent than those without.
A dolphin may be the most intelligent marine animal of all.

Fill in the missing adjectives in this chart. Use the last three lines to write your own examples.

Adjective	Adjective that compares two	Adjective that compares three or more
shiny	shinier	shiniest
graceful	more graceful	most graceful
quiet	quieter	quietest
cautious	more cautious	most cautious
tall	taller	tallest
bright	brighter	brightest
beautiful	more beautiful	most beautiful
strong	stronger	strongest
spirited	more spirited	most spirited
late	later	latest
funny	funnier	funniest
nice	nicer	nicest
generous	more generous	most generous
Examples will vary.		

327

How Does . . .?

An **adverb** is a word that describes a verb. Some adverbs tell how something is done. They often end in *ly*. *Quickly, carefully, silently,* and *happily* are examples of adverbs.

Look at the picture. Think about how the animals are moving. Write two adverbs for each. Do not repeat adverbs.

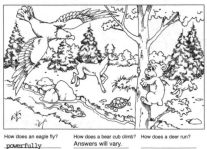

How does an eagle fly?
powerfully

How does a bear cub climb?
Answers will vary.

How does a deer run?

How does a rabbit hop?

How does a turtle move?

How does a frog swim?

328

Prefix Rainbow

A **prefix** is a word part added to the beginning of a word that changes the word's meaning. On each band of the rainbow, write words from the Word Bank that can be used with each prefix.

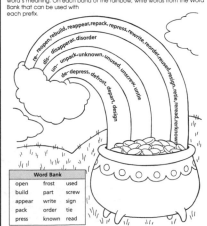

re- reopen, rebuild, reappear, repack, repress, rewrite, reorder, reused, resign, retie, reread, reknown

dis- disappear, disorder

un- unpack, unknown, unused, unscrew, untie

de- depress, defrost, depart, design

Word Bank		
open	frost	used
build	part	screw
appear	write	sign
pack	order	tie
press	known	read

329

Word Builders

Suffixes are word parts that help you build new words. When you add a suffix to the end of a root word, you make a new word. Examples of the suffix *-ish* used with root words are: *reddish, girlish, Spanish.* Notice that the hyphen is not in the word.

Complete each word below using the following suffixes. Then write a new sentence using the word you made.

-ful   -er   -ish   -proof   -ist   -less

1. Someone who acts silly like a clown may be called clown _-ish_ .
   Sentences will vary.

2. The amount of sugar that fills a cup is called a cup _-ful_ .

3. A medicine bottle cap that is hard to remove is called child _-proof_

4. Someone who sings is called a sing _-er_ .

5. A person who studies science is called a scient _-ist_ .

6. A telephone without a cord is cord _-less_ .

Dictionaries include suffix entries. Look up one of the suffixes above in the dictionary to see what it says.

red- dish

330

Analogies

An **analogy** is a way to compare things using the relationships the words share. The sentence below is an example of an analogy.

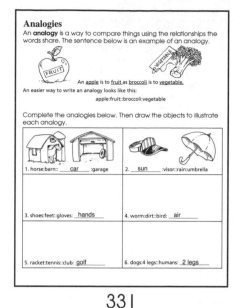

An <u>apple</u> is to <u>fruit</u> as <u>broccoli</u> is to <u>vegetable</u>.

An easier way to write an analogy looks like this:

apple:fruit::broccoli:vegetable

Complete the analogies below. Then draw the objects to illustrate each analogy.

1. horse:barn:: _car_ :garage	2. _sun_ :visor::rain:umbrella
3. shoes:feet::gloves: _hands_	4. worm:dirt::bird: _air_
5. racket:tennis::club: _golf_	6. dogs:4 legs::humans: _2 legs_

331

Knew York or New York?

Homophones are words that sound alike but have different spellings and meanings.

Fill in the circle next to the correct homophone for each sentence.

1. My family is planning a trip to ____ York State. ○ Knew ● New	2. We each get to pick ____ place to visit. ● one ○ won	3. My mom ____ to go see the Statue of Liberty. ○ once ● wants	4. It stands ____ New York Harbor. ● in ○ inn
5. My dad wants ____ visit the Guggenheim Museum. ● to ○ two	6. ____ a famous building designed by Frank Lloyd Wright. ○ Its ● It's	7. Of course, the museum has lots of great art, ____. ○ to ● too	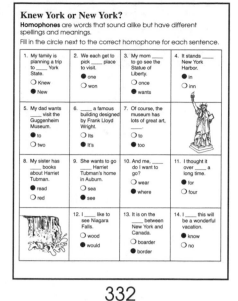
8. My sister has ____ books about Harriet Tubman. ● read ○ red	9. She wants to go ____ Harriet Tubman's home in Auburn. ○ sea ● see	10. And me, ____ do I want to go? ○ wear ● where	11. I thought it over ____ a long time. ● for ○ four
	12. I ____ like to see Niagara Falls. ○ wood ● would	13. It is on the ____ between New York and Canada. ○ boarder ● border	14. I ____ this will be a wonderful vacation. ● know ○ no

332

A Meaning of Its Own

An **idiom** is a phrase, or group of words, that has a special meaning. The meaning is different from what the words usually mean. An example of an idiom is *to call it a day.* This means to stop activity for the day. In a dictionary, this idiom would appear near the end of the definition for *day.*

Circle the most important word in each idiom below. Look up the circled word in your dictionary and see if you can find the idiom. Then make up a sentence using the idiom.

1. by (heart) _Sentences will vary._

2. (give) out: _____

3. on the (fence) _____

4. at (bat) _____

5. getting on my (nerves) _____

6. walk on (air) _____

7. out of the (blue) _____

8. run (across) _____

9. make (believe) _____

Look for examples of idioms in the books you read. Write your favorite one here. Then draw a picture of what the idiom seems to mean.

Idioms will vary.

333

Poetry Diamonds

Creating poetry diamonds is a fun way to play with words and write poetry that sparkles. The formula below is a simple way to make your own diamond-shaped poem. Choose a topic that interests you, such as animals, nature, holidays, or even a city or country.

Poetry Diamond Formula
Line 1: Noun 1
Line 2: 2 words describing the noun
Line 3: 3 words ending in -ed or -ing
Line 4: 4 words describing the noun
Line 5: 3 words ending in -ed or -ing
Line 6: 2 words describing the noun
Line 7: Noun 2

Example:

Puppy
clumsy, cute
jumping, running, biting
sweet, joyous, friendly, loyal
barking, fetching, playing
graceful, strong
Dog

Now try a diamond poem of your own!

Poems will vary.

_____
_____
_____
_____

334

Creative Comparisons

Similes are comparisons in which the words *like* or *as* are used:
   The sun is like a hot oven.

Metaphors are comparisons in which *like* or *as* are not used:
   The sun is a hot oven.

Choose two objects. Write a simile and a metaphor for each. Then draw a picture to illustrate each comparison.

Pictures will vary.

1.   2.

Simile: _Answers will vary._   Simile: _____

_____   _____

Metaphor: _____   Metaphor: _____

335

Dear Character

Think of a good book you've read recently. Use this page to write a friendly letter to your favorite book character. Tell the character why you admire him or her. Describe what you might have done in one of the same situations. Invite the character to do something with you, or give him or her some good advice! Follow the instructions to the left for using correct letter form.

Date:
_____

Salutation:
_____

Body of letter:
Letters will vary.
_____
_____
_____
_____
_____

Closing:
_____

Your Name:
_____

337

What's Your Prediction?

Choose a book and read the first chapter. Then start using this chart. (Use another piece of paper if you need to.) Before you read each chapter, write what you think will happen. After you finish the chapter, write what actually happened. See how close your predictions are. Do they get better as you read the book?

Chapter	What I predict will happen:	What actually happened:
Chapter 2	Answers will vary.	
Chapter 3		
Chapter 4		
Chapter 5		
Chapter 6		

338

Wild Ride!

If you want a super ride this summer, try a roller coaster. If you want a really wild ride, head for *Superman: The Escape* at the Great Adventure amusement park in Valencia, California. When it opened in 1997, the ride set a new record in roller-coaster speed.

The cars, which hold 15 people, don't need to head downhill to reach their top speed. They zoom to 100 miles per hour along a level track in just seven seconds. Then the cars begin their upward climb. After climbing as high as a 42-story building, the cars return down the same track, only they're traveling backward!

Like all roller-coaster cars, the cars of *Superman: The Escape* have magnets attached to their undersides. Small electric motors create the energy to propel these magnets along the track. But the cars make less contact with the rails than other rides do. This means the wheels and the track create less friction, causing the cars to move along the track more freely. Less friction means the cars can travel faster. No wonder this ride is called *Superman: The Escape!*

Refer to the story to answer these questions.

1. What kind of record did *Superman: The Escape* set?
   a speed record

2. Where is the Superman roller coaster located?
   Valencia, California

3. How many people can ride in one of the roller-coaster cars?
   15 people

4. How long does it take for *Superman: The Escape* to reach 100 miles per hour?
   7 seconds

5. Explain friction.
   Friction is the rubbing of one object or surface against another.

339

Daily Learning Drills Grade 4

Rhyme Time Riddles

Answer the questions below by writing two words that rhyme.

Example:
What do you call an obese feline? ___fat cat___

1. What do you call a wet pooch? __soggy doggy__
2. What do you call a sick large ocean mammal? __pale whale__
3. What do you call a mallard with its feet caught in the mud? __stuck duck__
4. What do you call an ill young chicken? __sick chick__
5. What do you call a ridiculous male goat? __silly billy__
6. What do you call a seat for a rabbit? __hare chair__
7. What do you call a clever detective? __super snooper__
8. What do you call a clever prank? __slick trick__
9. What do you call a noisy mob of people? __loud crowd__
10. What do you call a dwelling for a rodent? __mouse house__

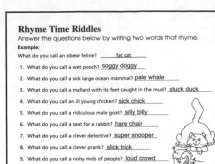

Here's how you can create your own rhyming riddles.

1. Write a list of word pairs that rhyme. Choose one rhyming pair. It will be your riddle answer. Example: *funny bunny*
2. Next, create your riddle question. Make a list of words that have the same meaning as each word in your rhyming answer. These are called *synonyms*. They do not have to rhyme. The synonyms become part of your riddle question.

   Examples: *What do you call a . . .*
   comical   rabbit?
   silly   hare?
3. Pick one word from each column and make up your riddle question.
   Example: What do you call a silly rabbit? Answer: a funny bunny!

340

What's the Big Idea?

Understanding the similarity between items is an important part of reading and thinking. Below you will find groups of four words. Each group has something in common. Give each group of items a name on the line next to it. Then make up a few of your own and see if your friends or family can guess The Big Idea!

1. lion, tiger, panther, leopard — animals in the cat family
2. quarter, dime, nickel, penny — U.S. coins
3. cake, pie, ice cream, brownies — desserts
4. sister, brother, father, mother — family members
5. white, wheat, rye, pumpernickel — breads
6. pig, cow, chicken, goat — farm animals
7. orange, lemon, lime, grapefruit — citrus fruits
8. Earth, Venus, Mars, Uranus — planets
9. blue, green, yellow, red — colors
10. tulip, rose, daisy, violet — flowers
11. Ford, Washington, Lincoln, Clinton — U.S. presidents
12. Alaska, Colorado, Iowa, Kansas — states
13. zebra, giraffe, elephant, lion — wild/zoo animals
14. June, July, August, September — summer months

341

Creating Your Own Numbers

Write a numeral from 0 to 9 in each box below. Then spell out the number you wrote, using words. The first one is done for you.

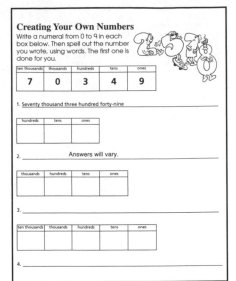

ten thousands	thousands	hundreds	tens	ones
7	0	3	4	9

1. Seventy thousand three hundred forty-nine

hundreds	tens	ones

2. _____ Answers will vary.

thousands	hundreds	tens	ones

3. _____

ten thousands	thousands	hundreds	tens	ones

4. _____

342

Round and Round

In each number below, circle the number that tells you if the number should round up or stay the same. Round each number.

A. 10
85(0) 860
4(0) 50
29(0) 290
6(0) 60
32(7) 330

B. 100
4(8) 500
8(4) 800
2(5) 300
1,3(7) 1,400
5,6(0) 5,600

C. 1,000
5,7(5)4 6,000
8,2(1)3 8,000
9,8(5)1 10,000
2,0(7)9 2,000
1,0(2)1 1,000

D. Round to the nearest thousand. Color the balls when the numbers round up.

1. 4,651 → 5,000
2. 9,961 → 10,000
3. 7,208 → 7,000
4. 2,976 → 3,000
5. 699 → 1,000
6. 3,479 → 3,000
7. 6,411 → 6,000
8. 5,743 → 6,000
9. 1,372 → 1,000
10. 4,493 → 4,000
11. 7,510 → 8,000
12. 6,821 → 7,000
13. 2,093 → 2,000
14. 4,499 → 4,000
15. 8,803 → 9,000

E. Answers for tens need to end in __one__ zero(s).
Those for the nearest hundred end in __two__ zero(s).
Answers to the nearest thousand end in __three__ zero(s).

343

Adding Balloons

Add to find the sum. Color the balloon for each problem you worked correctly.

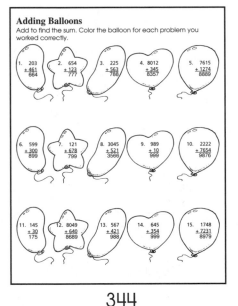

1. 203 + 461 = 664
2. 654 + 123 = 777
3. 225 + 563 = 788
4. 8012 + 345 = 8357
5. 7615 + 1274 = 8889
6. 599 + 300 = 899
7. 121 + 678 = 799
8. 3045 + 521 = 3566
9. 989 + 10 = 999
10. 2222 + 7654 = 9876
11. 145 + 30 = 175
12. 8049 + 640 = 8689
13. 567 + 421 = 988
14. 645 + 354 = 999
15. 1748 + 7231 = 8979

344

Add It Up!

Color the sums.

red = 1,400–7,900   green = 8,000–16,000   yellow = over 16,000   blue = under 1,400

528 + 609 = 1,137	37,699 + 23,415 = 61,114	48,236 + 51,775 = 100,011	465 + 392 = 857
2368 + 1947 + 6301 = 10,616	5151 + 4309 + 1878 = 11,338	3942 + 5836 + 6218 = 15,996	
1839 + 2927 = 4,766	169 + 354 + 382 + 547 = 1,452	218 + 396 + 178 + 682 = 1,474	5883 + 1859 = 7,742
19,173 + 18,249 = 37,422	271 + 539 = 810	27,468 + 35,788 = 63,256	

Solve.

1. Julie and her dad drove across the country on vacation. They drove 349 miles, 276 miles, and 362 miles in three days. How many miles did they drive in all?
   __987__

2. Our postman delivers mail five days each week. He delivered 249 pieces of mail on Monday. On the other days, he delivered 782 letters and 381 magazines. How many pieces of mail did he deliver in that one week?
   __1,412__

345

Zeros Are Important

Subtract. Add to check your answers.

1. 207 − 143 = 64 ; 64 + 143 = 207
2. 100 − 64 = 36 ; 36 + 64 = 100
3. 602 − 314 = 288 ; 288 + 314 = 602
4. 5,007 − 2,106 = 2,901 ; 2,901 + 2,106 = 5,007
5. 4,109 − 1,174 = 2,935 ; 2,935 + 1,174 = 4,109
6. 3,000 − 2,674 = 326 ; 326 + 2,674 = 3,000
7. 9,008 − 3,962 = 5,046 ; 5,046 + 3,962 = 9,008
8. 12,003 − 10,666 = 1,337 ; 1,337 + 10,666 = 12,003
9. 70,405 − 21,510 = 48,895 ; 48,895 + 21,510 = 70,405 (largest)

Write the problems below in column form and subtract. Write the answers in correct order from smallest to largest.

1. 560 − 392 = __168__
2. 4,300 − 571 = __3,729__
3. 5,000 − 297 = __4,703__
4. 640 − 399 = __241__
5. 7,040 − 2,607 = __4,433__
6. 1,007 − 352 = __655__

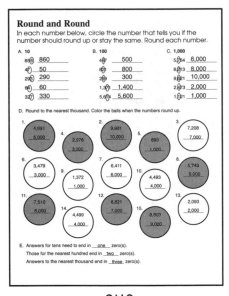

smallest
1. __168__   2. __241__   3. __655__   4. __3,729__   5. __4,433__   6. __4,703__

346

Chipmunk Multiplication

Help this chipmunk put away acorns for the winter by multiplying. Color the acorn for each problem you worked correctly.

1. 23 × 61 = 1403
2. 54 × 12 = 648
3. 25 × 53 = 1325
4. 12 × 45 = 540
5. 59 × 30 = 1770
6. 21 × 16 = 336
7. 45 × 25 = 1125
8. 99 × 10 = 990
9. 145 × 30 = 4350
10. 849 × 64 = 54,336
11. 567 × 42 = 23,814
12. 645 × 35 = 22,575
13. 239 × 17 = 4063
14. 804 × 60 = 48,240
15. 323 × 81 = 26,163
16. 452 × 39 = 17,628

347

Up, Up, and Away

Multiply. Put the letters of the answers on the lines below to find out a secret message.

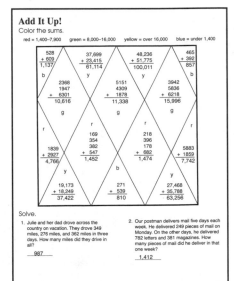

J. 159 × 47 = 7,473
T. 454 × 60 = 27,240
G. 719 × 18 = 12,942
O. 295 × 65 = 19,175
R. 607 × 45 = 27,315
I. 106 × 85 = 9,010
E. 599 × 12 = 7,188
B. 333 × 65 = 21,645
A. 682 × 23 = 15,686

G R E A T   J O B !
12,942 27,315 7,188 15,686 27,240   7,473 19,175 21,645 9,010

348

Doggie Trouble

Help the dog get to his bone by connecting the correctly-done division problems to make a path.

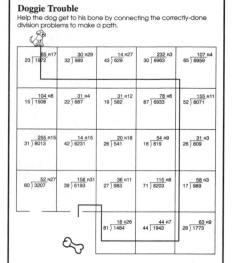

85 R17 $23\overline{)1972}$	30 R29 $32\overline{)989}$	14 R27 $43\overline{)629}$	232 R3 $30\overline{)6963}$	107 R4 $65\overline{)6959}$
104 R8 $15\overline{)1508}$	31 R4 $22\overline{)687}$	31 R12 $19\overline{)582}$	78 R6 $87\overline{)6933}$	155 R11 $52\overline{)8071}$
255 R15 $31\overline{)8013}$	14 R15 $42\overline{)6231}$	20 R18 $26\overline{)541}$	54 R9 $18\overline{)819}$	31 R3 $26\overline{)809}$
52 R27 $60\overline{)3207}$	158 R31 $39\overline{)6193}$	36 R11 $27\overline{)983}$	115 R8 $71\overline{)8203}$	58 R3 $17\overline{)989}$
		18 R26 $81\overline{)1484}$	44 R7 $44\overline{)1943}$	63 R9 $28\overline{)1773}$

349

Wacky City

Here are some math word problems about Wacky City. Wacky City is a town not too far from your town where people are just a little bit different. Use multiplication or division to find the answer to each problem below.

1. On Saturdays, the people of Wacky City eat nothing but bananas all day long. If there are 3,500 people in Wacky City, and they each eat seven bananas on Saturdays, how many bananas would they eat on that day? _____ 24,500

2. The mayor of Wacky City gives visitors a pet frog when they come to town. If 75 visitors come to Wacky City every day, how may frogs would the mayor need to give away each year? _____ 27,375

3. In Wacky City, a rainbow appears in the sky once a week. How many rainbows would appear over a 15-year period? _____ 780

4. Wacky City citizens spent $23,569 in 20 years to take their teddy bears on picnics. How much did they spend each year, on the average, for teddy bear picnics? _____ $1178.45

5. Children in Wacky City get a free ride on a carousel whenever they want. If there were 25,000 free rides last year, and 250 children took rides, how many rides did each child have? _____ 100

6. The people of Wacky City always march in a parade when it rains. If there were 1,235 parades in the last 15 years, how many days did it rain each year, on average? _____ 82

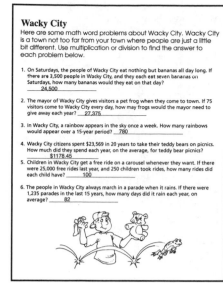

350

Circle Time

Below are problems in addition, subtraction, multiplication, and division. Note which operation to use and circle the sign. Then work the problems.

1. 235 $\oplus$ 61 = 296
2. 504 $\ominus$ 12 = 6048
3. 725 $\ominus$ 53 = 672
4. 45 $\oplus$ 12 = 3 R9

5. 590 $\times$ 30 = 17,700
6. 3000 $\oplus$ 21 = 142 R18
7. 4145 $\oplus$ 265 = 4410
8. 1980 $\ominus$ 810 = 1170

9. 1450 $\ominus$ 837 = 613
10. 8490 $\oplus$ 264 = 8754
11. 704 $\oplus$ 56 = 12 R32
12. 642 $\times$ 75 = 48,150

13. 50 $\oplus$ 14 = 3 R8
14. 8764 $\times$ 6 = 52,584
15. 5601 $\ominus$ 427 = 5174
16. 6405 $\oplus$ 309 = 6714

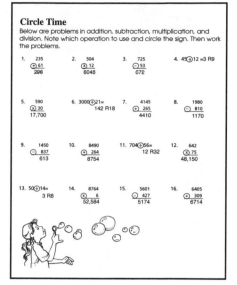

351

Operation Butterfly

Complete each equation with the sign that shows the correct mathematical operation. Then color the butterfly using the Color Key below. For example, for the number 1 on the butterfly, look at problem number 1. A plus sign was used, meaning the operation was addition. Color that section purple.

1. 20 + 20 = 40
2. 20 x 2 = 40
3. 40 – 20 = 20
4. 8 x 9 = 72
5. 64 ± 8 = 8
6. 234 – 34 = 200
7. 818 + 81 = 899
8. 50 – 20 = 30
9. 49 – 7 = 42
10. 49 ÷ 7 = 7
11. 250 – 100 = 150
12. 100 + 300 = 400

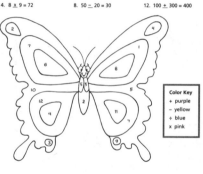

Color Key
+ purple
– yellow
÷ blue
x pink

352

Let's Compare

Use >, <, or = to compare the fractions below.

A. $\frac{11}{12}$ > $\frac{8}{9}$ $\frac{3}{4}$ = $\frac{6}{8}$ $\frac{5}{6}$ > $\frac{2}{3}$

B. $\frac{1}{5}$ < $\frac{2}{3}$ $\frac{9}{10}$ > $\frac{3}{4}$ $\frac{2}{5}$ < $\frac{9}{11}$

C. $\frac{2}{5}$ = $\frac{8}{20}$ $\frac{7}{9}$ > $\frac{3}{4}$

D. $\frac{6}{7}$ > $\frac{5}{6}$ $\frac{1}{4}$ < $\frac{2}{5}$ $\frac{12}{13}$ > $\frac{4}{5}$

$\frac{4}{7}$ = $\frac{8}{14}$

353

Bubble Fun

Change each improper fraction to a mixed number, or change each mixed number to an improper fraction.

1. $2\frac{1}{8}$ $\frac{17}{8}$
2. $3\frac{1}{4}$ $\frac{3}{5}$
3. $\frac{11}{5}$ $2\frac{1}{5}$
4. $5\frac{2}{9}$ $\frac{47}{9}$
5. $\frac{5}{4}$ $1\frac{1}{4}$
6. $\frac{22}{5}$ $4\frac{2}{5}$
7. $3\frac{3}{4}$ $\frac{15}{4}$
8. $\frac{32}{9}$ $3\frac{5}{9}$
9. $\frac{41}{9}$ $4\frac{5}{9}$
10. 5 $\frac{25}{5}$
11. $4\frac{1}{3}$ $\frac{13}{3}$
12. $\frac{79}{9}$ $8\frac{7}{9}$
13. $\frac{41}{8}$ $5\frac{1}{8}$
14. $6\frac{1}{6}$ $\frac{37}{6}$
15. $7\frac{4}{9}$ $\frac{67}{9}$
16. $\frac{38}{5}$ $7\frac{3}{5}$
17. $16\frac{3}{5}$ $\frac{83}{5}$
18. $5\frac{4}{7}$ $\frac{39}{7}$

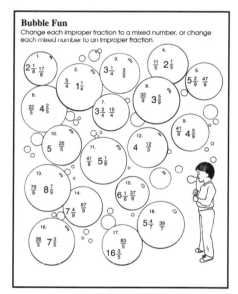

354

Adding and Subtracting

Fractions can be added or subtracted if the denominators are the same.

Example: $\frac{1}{4} + \frac{2}{4} = \frac{3}{4}$

Add the fractions below.

1. $\frac{1}{5} + \frac{3}{5} = \frac{4}{5}$
2. $\frac{3}{7} + \frac{5}{7} = \frac{8}{7}$
3. $\frac{6}{10} + \frac{9}{10} = \frac{15}{10}$
4. $\frac{1}{3} + \frac{1}{3} = \frac{2}{3}$
5. $\frac{3}{8} + \frac{2}{8} = \frac{5}{8}$
6. $\frac{6}{9} + \frac{3}{9} = \frac{9}{9}$
7. $\frac{3}{6} + \frac{2}{6} = \frac{5}{6}$
8. $\frac{4}{12} + \frac{5}{12} = \frac{9}{12}$
9. $\frac{1}{2} + \frac{1}{2} = \frac{2}{2}$

Subtract these fractions.

10. $\frac{4}{4} - \frac{2}{4} = \frac{2}{4}$
11. $\frac{8}{7} - \frac{5}{7} = \frac{1}{7}$
12. $\frac{10}{11} - \frac{9}{11} = \frac{1}{11}$
13. $\frac{4}{3} - \frac{2}{3} = \frac{2}{3}$
14. $\frac{5}{6} - \frac{2}{6} = \frac{3}{6}$
15. $\frac{8}{8} - \frac{6}{8} = \frac{2}{8}$
16. $\frac{3}{4} - \frac{1}{4} = \frac{2}{4}$
17. $\frac{7}{5} - \frac{2}{5} = \frac{5}{5}$
18. $\frac{8}{8} - \frac{5}{8} = \frac{0}{8}$

To add or subtract mixed numbers, add or subtract fractions first, then whole numbers. Add and subtract the mixed numbers below.

19. $5\frac{2}{6} + 3\frac{3}{6} = 4\frac{5}{6}$
20. $4\frac{1}{10} + \frac{8}{10} = 8\frac{9}{10}$
21. $7\frac{2}{5} + \frac{2}{5} = 7\frac{4}{5}$
22. $5\frac{2}{4} - 3\frac{1}{4} = 4\frac{1}{4}$
23. $5\frac{5}{9} - 4\frac{4}{9} = \frac{1}{9}$
24. $47\frac{2}{5} - \frac{2}{5} = 47$

355

Fraction Fun

Before adding two fractions, both fractions must have the same denominator. Use the number lines to rewrite the fractions. Then add.

1. $\frac{1}{4} + \frac{1}{2} = \frac{7}{8}$
2. $\frac{1}{2} + \frac{3}{10} = \frac{8}{10}$
3. $\frac{1}{3} + \frac{1}{6} = \frac{3}{6}$
4. $\frac{1}{2} + \frac{3}{12} = \frac{9}{12}$
5. $\frac{1}{2} + \frac{2}{6} = \frac{5}{6}$
6. $\frac{1}{2} + \frac{3}{4} = \frac{5}{4}$
7. $\frac{2}{5} + \frac{3}{10} = \frac{7}{10}$
8. $\frac{2}{5} + \frac{3}{10} = \frac{15}{10}$
9. $\frac{3}{4} + \frac{7}{8} = \frac{13}{8}$
10. $\frac{7}{10} + \frac{3}{5} = \frac{13}{10}$
11. $\frac{2}{3} + \frac{1}{6} = \frac{5}{6}$
12. $\frac{1}{10} + \frac{3}{5} = \frac{0}{10}$
13. $\frac{3}{12} + \frac{2}{3} = \frac{11}{12}$
14. $\frac{2}{4} + \frac{7}{8} = \frac{11}{8}$
15. $\frac{1}{4} + \frac{3}{12} = \frac{7}{12}$
16. $\frac{1}{8} + \frac{3}{4} = \frac{7}{8}$
17. $\frac{7}{12} + \frac{2}{3} = \frac{11}{12}$

356

Analyzing Area

Area tells the number of square units in a figure. Find the area of each figure below.

1. _____ 4 sq. units
2. _____ 6 sq. units
3. _____ 5 sq. units
4. _____ 8 sq. units
5. _____ 8 sq. units

The area can be found by multiplying the length times the width: A = lw.

6. 6 ft. x 4 ft. $6 \times 4 = 24$ ft.²
7. 5 ft. x 5 ft. $5 \times 5 = 25$ ft.²

Find the areas below.

8. 4 ft. A = 16 ft.²
9. 3 ft. A = 36 ft.²
10. 10 ft., 9 ft. A = 90 ft.²
11. 6 ft. A = 36 ft.²
12. 15 ft., 5 ft. A = 75 ft.²
13. 11 ft., 2 ft. A = 22 ft.²
14. 9 ft. A = 81 ft.²

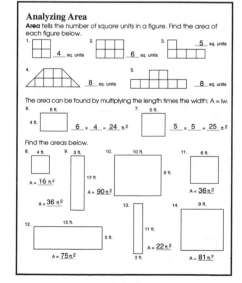

357

Daily Learning Drills Grade 4

Very Important Volume

Volume is the number of cubic units that will fit inside a space figure. Build each figure below using linking cubes. Tell the number of cubes used.

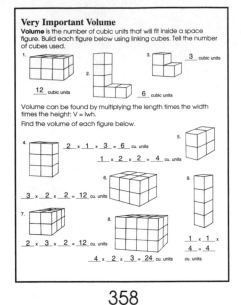

1. __12__ cubic units
2. __3__ cubic units
3. __6__ cubic units

Volume can be found by multiplying the length times the width times the height: V = lwh.

Find the volume of each figure below.

4. __2__ x __1__ x __3__ = __6__ cu. units
    __1__ x __2__ x __2__ = __4__ cu. units

5.

6. __3__ x __2__ x __2__ = __12__ cu. units

7. __2__ x __3__ x __2__ = __12__ cu. units

8.

9. __1__ x __1__ x __4__ = __4__ cu. units
    __4__ x __2__ x __3__ = __24__ cu. units

358

What Makes the Most Sense?

Draw a line from each object to the unit that best measures it. Remember that small and medium objects are measured in millimeters and centimeters. Bigger objects are measured in decimeters or meters.

m   dm   cm   mm

In the chart below, list three items that would best be measured with each unit.

METER	DECIMETER	CENTIMETER	MILLIMETER
1.	1.	1.	1.
2. Answers will vary.	2.	2.	2.
3.	3.	3.	3.

More Measurement Fun!

Measure three objects from your house. Measure one in cm, one in mm, and one in m.

359

How Hot Is It?

Temperature is measured in degrees Celsius or Fahrenheit.

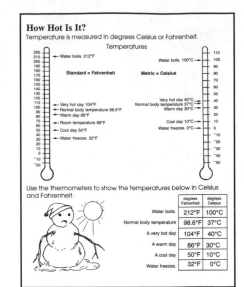

Temperatures

Water boils. 212°F   Water boils. 100°C

Standard = Fahrenheit   Metric = Celsius

Very hot day 104°F   Very hot day 40°C
Normal body temperature 98.6°F   Normal body temperature 37°C
Warm day 86°F   Warm day 30°C
Room temperature 68°F
Cool day 50°F   Cool day 10°C
Water freezes. 32°F   Water freezes. 0°C

Use the thermometers to show the temperatures below in Celsius and Fahrenheit.

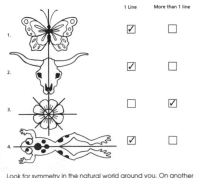

	degrees Fahrenheit	degrees Celsius
Water boils.	212°F	100°C
Normal body temperature	98.6°F	37°C
A very hot day	104°F	40°C
A warm day	86°F	30°C
A cool day	50°F	10°C
Water freezes.	32°F	0°C

360

T-shirt Count

Jan grouped her 12 t-shirts according to these colors: red, blue, green, and yellow. Read the clues and figure out how many t-shirts Jan has of each color. Write your answers on the chart.

Clues:

◆ There are twice as many blue t-shirts as there are red t-shirts.

◆ There is the same number of green t-shirts and yellow t-shirts.

◆ There is 1 more blue t-shirt than there are green t-shirts.

◆ There are 2 red t-shirts.

t-shirt Color	Number of t-shirts
red	2
blue	4
green	3
yellow	3

Now use the information from your chart to create a circle graph. First color the key so that the rectangles match their colors. Then color each section of the circle to show how many t-shirts Jan has of each color.

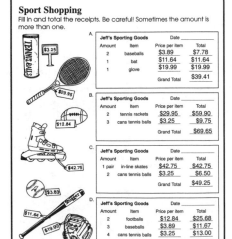

Jan's t-shirts

☐ = red   ☐ = green
☐ = blue   ☐ = yellow

361

Is Willy Late?

Below are clocks that show the schedule Willy has to keep throughout the school day. Above the clocks in each square is the time Willy actually did each activity. Tell whether Willy was late by writing yes or no.

1. He gets up at 7:15 a.m.
   Is Willy late? __no__

2. He catches a bus at 8:05 a.m.
   Is Willy late? __no__

3. He starts school at 8:40 a.m.
   Is Willy late? __no__

4. He gets to gym at 10:45 a.m.
   Is Willy late? __yes__

5. He has lunch at 12:10 p.m.
   Is Willy late? __no__

6. He catches a bus at 3:20 p.m.
   Is Willy late? __no__

7. He has dinner at 5:00 p.m.
   Is Willy late? __no__

8. He does his homework at 7:05 p.m.
   Is Willy late? __yes__

9. He's in bed at 9:30 p.m.
   Is Willy late? __no__

362

What Time Is It?

Look at the clock and circle the correct time.

1. (12:45) 6:20 5:15
2. 1:20 4:00 (2:25)
3. 8:15 (9:45) 7:30
4. 9:45 12:00 (3:15)
5. (1:10) 6:40 8:50
6. 11:00 (11:05) 11:10
7. (2:25) 10:35 3:35
8. 4:05 (5:35) 9:15
9. (7:55) 8:00 8:05

363

Sport Shopping

Fill in and total the receipts. Be careful! Sometimes the amount is more than one.

A. Jeff's Sporting Goods Date ____

Amount	Item	Price per item	Total
2	baseballs	$3.89	$7.78
1	bat	$11.64	$11.64
1	glove	$19.99	$19.99
		Grand Total	$39.41

B. Jeff's Sporting Goods Date ____

Amount	Item	Price per item	Total
2	tennis rackets	$29.95	$59.90
3	cans tennis balls	$3.25	$9.75
		Grand Total	$69.65

C. Jeff's Sporting Goods Date ____

Amount	Item	Price per item	Total
1 pair	in-line skates	$42.75	$42.75
2	cans tennis balls	$3.25	$6.50
		Grand Total	$49.25

D. Jeff's Sporting Goods Date ____

Amount	Item	Price per item	Total
2	footballs	$12.84	$25.68
3	baseballs	$3.89	$11.67
4	cans tennis balls	$3.25	$13.00
		Grand Total	$50.35

364

The Magic Ruler

It is easier to work with numbers that have only one whole digit (i.e., 1.345 not 1345). You can make numbers with more than two whole digits into smaller numbers by just moving the decimal point to the right or to the left and adjusting the prefix term (i.e., 34.5 m = 3.45 dkm). An easy way to move the decimal point is to use the "Magic Equivalent Ruler."

Here is how to use the magic ruler. Suppose you have a number of 1506.3 cm. Your objective is to have only one whole digit to the left of the decimal point. First, you need to move the decimal point in the number three places to the left to end up with 1.5063. Next, since you started with the prefix term of cm, you need to also move three boxes (on the ruler) to the left (the same amount you moved decimal places). You end up with dk. Therefore, your new number is 1.5063 dkm (1506.3 cm = 1.5063 dkm).

Magic Equivalent Ruler

kilo	hecto	deka	root	deci	centi	milli
1 000	100	10	1	0.1	0.01	0.001

Change the numbers below so that one whole digit is to the left of the decimal.

Examples: 130 cm = 1.3 m   0.023 dkm = 2.3 dm

1. 24 m   __2.4 dkm__
2. 2456 cm   __2.456 dkm__
3. 897 mm   __8.97 dm__
4. 96 cm   __9.6 dm__
5. 6780 dm   __6.780 hm__
6. 956 m   __9.56 hm__
7. 843 dm   __8.43 dkm__
8. 0.356 hm   __3.56 dkm__
9. 0.023 dkm   __2.3 dm__
10. 0.467 m   __4.67 dm__
11. 0.045 dm   __4.5 mm__
12. 0.0098 dkm __9.8 cm__
13. 0.87 km   __8.7 hm__
14. 0.000023 km __2.3 dm__
15. 0.234 m   __2.34 dm__
16. 0.0108 dm   __1.08 dm__

365

Seeing Symmetry in Nature

Study each figure shown below. Place a check mark in the column that tells what kind of symmetry the figure has. Then draw a line that divides the figure into symmetrical pieces. If you think the figure shows more than one line of symmetry, show two ways it could be divided.

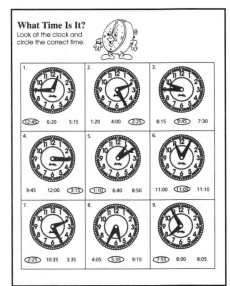

Shape	Lines of Symmetry	
	1 Line	More than 1 line
1.	☑	☐
2.	☑	☐
3.	☐	☑
4.	☑	☐

Look for symmetry in the natural world around you. On another piece of paper, illustrate three examples of symmetrical figures you found. Draw one line of symmetry through each figure.

366

Sharp Senses

Successful writers are good observers of nature. They use their senses as they react personally to experiences in the natural world. How does the snow sound underfoot? What does a warm summer rain smell like? How does the surface of a flower petal feel? A writer might use these observations later when describing something in a story.

Go for a walk or sit quietly in a natural setting and observe. Then record everything your senses tell you about the experience. Write your observations in colorful detail so you will remember them. Don't just record that you heard the sound of a waterfall. Instead, describe the sound. Was the water rushing, trickling, or dripping? Later, use some of the observations in your own writing.

My observation experience: _____

Sights: _____ Answers will vary. _____

Sounds: _____

Textures: _____

Smells: _____

Tastes: _____

367

Shunning the Sun

What can you do if you get too hot this summer? Maybe you'll rest in the shade, turn on a fan, or go swimming. But what do animals do to beat the summer heat? They do many of the same things.

Read the story for clues about how animals avoid getting overheated. Choose an animal to fill in each blank.

sidewinder rattlesnake   honeybee
elephant   dog

1. **elephant**

   Some animals escape the heat by soaking in cool water. When temperatures get hot, this land giant takes a dip in the nearest water hole. The mud and water help this animal cool off and keep its skin from drying out. When the water isn't deep enough to cover its entire body, this clever mammal sucks in as much as a gallon and a half, then sprays itself with the water.

2. **dog**

   This creature cools off with the help of sweat glands on the tip of its nose and the pads of its feet. The best way for it to cool off is to hang out its tongue and pant. The air drawn in by the panting evaporates the moisture in the animal's mouth and cools its body. That makes its mouth dry, so on hot days this critter needs plenty of water to drink.

3. **sidewinder rattlesnake**

   This desert creature has a special cooling technique. Other cold-blooded desert creatures may crawl into an empty burrow or slither under a rock to survive scorching days. But not this one. After it coils itself up, it uses its head like a shovel to toss sand over its body. The sand blanket becomes a shield for keeping cool.

4. **honeybee**

   This creature's task in the summertime is to keep its wax home from melting! On warm summer days, these insects fan their wings rapidly. If fanning doesn't work, some stay behind while others fly off to drink lots of water, which they spit onto the wax when they return. The fanning of all these insect wings makes a breeze that evaporates the water, cooling the hive.

368

Flying Flickers

Read the story, then answer the questions below.

Fireflies

Have you ever seen tiny, flashing lights on dark summer nights? These blinking lights come from fireflies. These insects aren't really flies, though; they're beetles. As with all beetles, they have a front pair of wings that is hardened to protect the hind wings, which are used to fly.

A flashing light in the dark often carries a message, like the searchlight on top of a lighthouse. The firefly is sending a message, too. It is looking for a mate. Each species of firefly has its own special combination of flashes. The message is meant to attract a firefly of the same species. The male flashes a code first, then the female responds. She raises her tail and turns her body as she sends her code. This makes the light shine in many directions, so the male can find her.

A firefly gets its light from an organ at the rear of the abdomen. A special chemical in the organ is released. When the chemical mixes with oxygen, a glow is created. This special glow is not like a fire or a furnace, which gives off heat. The firefly's glow does create light, however. Some people have even made firefly lanterns by putting fireflies in jars.

1. What causes tiny flashing lights in the darkness on hot summer nights?

   fireflies

2. What causes the firefly to glow?

   A special organ that mixes a chemical with oxygen makes a firefly glow.

3. Why would it be easier to find a firefly at night than during the day?

   They glow in the dark.

4. How does a female firefly attract a male firefly?

   The female sends a code.

5. How does the glow of fireflies help the species survive?

   It helps mates find eachother.

369

Food Web

How do people fit into the food chain? Study the plants and animals shown below. Then draw lines and arrows to create a food web that shows the relationships among them. Arrows should point toward the plant or animal being eaten. More than one arrow can be included for each element of the food web. An example is drawn for you.

In the space below, use words or illustrations to create another example of a food web. Include different plants and animals than those shown above.

Food webs will vary.

371

Watch Those Bones!

Discover the effects of heat and vinegar on bones. An adult should be present during this activity.

Materials Needed:
2 chicken leg bones   source of heat (an alcohol burner or a Bunsen burner)
vinegar   tongs
jar with lid

1. Place one chicken leg bone in a jar.
2. Fill the jar with vinegar.
3. Let the bone soak for three to seven days.
4. Use the tongs to hold the unsoaked chicken bone directly over the flame for about two minutes.
5. Try to bend the heated bone. Record your observations.
6. Remove the bone from the vinegar. Try to bend it. Record your observations.

Write your observations on the lines.
heated bone:
   Students should observe that the bones are brittle.

bone soaked in vinegar:
   Students should observe that the bones are flexible.

What conclusions can you draw from this activity?
1. Heating the bone removed cartilage. How does cartilage help the skeletal system do its job?
   Cartilage strengthens the skeleton.

2. The vinegar removed calcium from the bone. How does calcium help the skeletal system do its job?
   Calcium hardens the bones.

372

Target Your Heart

Choose an activity listed in the chart below. Perform the activity for 2 to 5 minutes. Then feel your pulse to determine the number of heartbeats per minute. Check the heart-rate chart to see if you are in your target range. Try the other activities to see how they affect your heart.

Age	Beats Per Minute
9	148–211
10	147–210
11	146–209
12	145–208

Activity	Beats Per Minute	Target? (yes or no)
jumping jacks		
sit-ups		
jogging in place		
push-ups		
basketball		
weightlifting		
jumping rope	Answers will vary.	
soccer		
field hockey		
football		
other		

373

---

1. Work with a partner. Position your first two fingers where you feel a strong pulse.
2. Press gently and count the beats for 15 seconds. Caution: Do not use your thumb, since there is a pulse site in your thumb. You do not want to take your own pulse instead of your partner's.
3. Multiply the number of beats by four to get the pulse rate for one minute. Record the information below.
4. Try to take your partner's pulse in three other locations. Record the results.

Observations

PULSE SITE	PULSE	STRENGTH

Conclusions
1. What similarities or differences in strength and number did you observe in the pulse readings?
   Students should observe that the pulse rate is the same at all sites.

2. What factors might cause differences in a person's pulse?
   Answers will vary.

375

Reaction Time

How fast do you react? Can you improve your reaction time? Work with a partner to find out. Take turns trying to catch a ruler between the fingers of one hand. You can measure your reaction time by seeing where you grab the ruler.

1. Stand facing your partner. Ask him or her to hold the ruler at the 1-inch mark, with 12 inches at the bottom. The top of the ruler should be even with the top of your head.

2. Keep your eyes on the ruler. As soon as your partner lets go of it, try to catch it between the fingers of one hand.

3. Look at the ruler to see which inch measurement is closest to the spot where your fingers grasped the ruler. Record that measurement on the graph at the bottom of the page. First find the inch measurement where you caught the ruler. (If you didn't catch it in time, use the line marked 0.) Trace that line down to the line labeled Trial #1. Make a large dot where the two lines meet.

4. Have your partner test you four more times. Use dots to record each measurement on the graph. When you are done, draw straight lines to connect the dots. If the lines head to the right, your reaction time has improved.

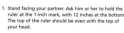
Students should find that reaction times improve.

	0	1	2	3	4	5	6	7	8	9	10	11	12
Trial #5													
Trial #4													
Trial #3													
Trial #2													
Trial #1													

376

Personal Fitness Goals

Make your own physical fitness goals in each of the fitness areas listed below. You can work on one of the example skills or on another skill of your choice. Many activities build more than one skill. For example, sit-ups build abdominal strength. Doing them faster builds speed. Doing them for a longer period of time builds endurance. Check the boxes as your goals are achieved.

Strength Goal: I will develop the amount of force my muscles can produce.
Strength skill examples: push-ups, pull-ups, sit-ups, leg lifts

By _____, I will _____ Answers will vary. _____
☐ Goal achieved

Endurance Goal: I will be able to do something for a longer period of time.
Endurance skill examples: running in place, jumping jacks, distance run

By _____, I will _____ .
☐ Goal achieved

Agility Goal: I will improve my ability to change direction and position quickly.
Agility skill examples: zig-zag run, obstacle run, jumping rope

By _____, I will _____ .
☐ Goal achieved

Flexibility Goal: I will improve my ability to bend, reach, twist, and turn.
Flexibility skill examples: toe touches, cartwheels

By _____, I will _____ .
☐ Goal achieved

Speed Goal: I will do something faster.
Speed skill examples: fifty-yard dash, sit-ups

By _____, I will _____ .
☐ Goal achieved

Coordination Goal: I will be able to work different muscles together efficiently.
Coordination skill examples: dribbling a basketball, batting

By _____, I will be able to _____ .
☐ Goal achieved

377

Fat Floats

Compare the buoyancy of a fatty mass and a lean mass.

Materials Needed:
beaker
tablespoon of solid shortening
4-centimeter piece of carrot
slice of potato
water
a stirrer or plastic spoon

1. Fill the beaker two-thirds full of tap water.
2. Gently place the carrot in the beaker.
3. Draw a diagram below to record your observation.
4. Gently place the slice of potato in the beaker.
5. Draw a diagram below to record your observation.
6. Use the stirrer to gently slide the shortening into the beaker.
7. Draw a diagram below to record your observation.

Observations

CARROT   POTATO   SHORTENING

Students should observe the shortening floating.

Conclusion
1. Based on the information gained in this experiment, who would float more easily—a person with a high proportion of body fat or a person with a low proportion of body fat?
   A person with a high proportion of body fat floats more easily than a person with a low proportion of body fat.

Magnet Fun

Use the clues and the words in the Word Box to complete the puzzle.

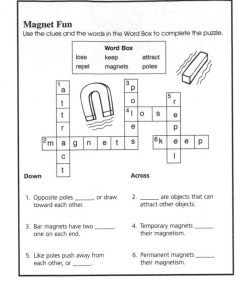

Word Box

lose	keep	attract
repel	magnets	poles

Crossword answers: attract, pole, lose, magnets, keep

Down

1. Opposite poles _____, or draw toward each other.
3. Bar magnets have two _____, one on each end.
5. Like poles push away from each other, or _____.

Across

2. _____ are objects that can attract other objects.
4. Temporary magnets _____ their magnetism.
6. Permanent magnets _____ their magnetism.

Cost of Electricity

Develop an awareness of the cost of running small appliances.

In order to calculate the cost of electrical energy, you need to know the wattage of the appliance that you are using (wattage), the length of time it is used (time), and the cost per kilowatt hour (cost p/k).

Use the following formula to determine the cost of running an appliance.

wattage x time = kilowatt hours

kilowatt hours x cost p/k = cost of the electricity to run the appliance

Example: You use a bedside lamp to read for 45 minutes each night before you go to bed. The bulb is a 25-watt bulb. How much does it cost to run the lamp for one week? Work with a cost/kilowatt of $0.000611.

25 watts x .75 hours = 18.75 kilowatt hours

18.75 kilowatt hours x $0.000611 = $0.01145625

$0.01145625 x 7 days = $0.08 cost for one week

Select five appliances that you or someone in your family uses. List them beside the numbers 1 to 5. Calculate the weekly cost for each item.

hair dryer	curling iron
TV	radio
toaster	electric iron
electric saw	electric drill
VCR/DVD	stereo

Show your calculations in the spaces to the right.

1. _____
   wattage _____
   time _____
   cost per kilowatt hour _____
   cost of running the item _____

Appliances and calculations will vary.

---

2. _____
   wattage _____
   time _____
   cost per kilowatt hour _____
   cost of running the item _____

3. _____
   wattage _____
   time _____
   cost per kilowatt hour _____
   cost of running the item _____

4. _____
   wattage _____
   time _____
   cost per kilowatt hour _____
   cost of running the item _____

Answers will vary.

5. _____
   wattage _____
   time _____
   cost per kilowatt hour _____
   cost of running the item _____

1. Which appliance costs the least to operate? _____
2. Which appliance costs the most to operate? _____

Weight Is Not Mass!

Another word for the pull of gravity is weight. Weight changes according to how far away an object is from its source of gravity. The mass of an object does not change regardless of where in the universe that object is located. This is because mass is the amount of matter in the object. To understand weight and mass better, answer the questions below. Pretend you are on a spaceship to the moon.

ON EARTH (Earth's pull of gravity)
Your mass: _____ kg X 2.2 = _____ lb
Your weight: _____ kg X 9.8 m/s² = _____ N

Answers will vary.

1/4 OF THE WAY TO THE MOON (Earth's lessening pull of gravity)
Your mass: _____ kg X 2.2 = _____ lb
Your weight: _____ kg X 7.7 m/s² = _____ N

1/2 OF THE WAY TO THE MOON (Earth's lessening pull of gravity)
Your mass: _____ kg X 2.2 = _____ lb
Your weight: _____ kg X 5.6 m/s² = _____ N

3/4 OF THE WAY TO THE MOON (Earth's lessening pull of gravity)
Your mass: _____ kg X 2.2 = _____ lb
Your weight: _____ kg X 3.5 m/s² = _____ N

ON THE MOON (Moon's pull of gravity)
Your mass: _____ kg X 2.2 = _____ lb
Your weight: _____ kg X 1.6 m/s² = _____ N

What value is changing in each of these sets of numbers? **weight**

More Measurement Fun!
Find the pull of gravity on other planets. Determine what your mass and weight would be if you were on that planet.

Weather Wisdom

Why is weather important?

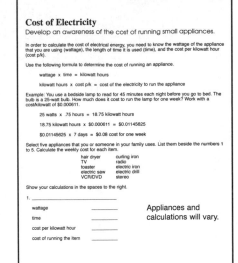

The following are sayings about weather. Write T, for true, if you think the saying has some basis in science. Write F, for false, if you think it has no basis in scientific fact.

- **T** 1. An old timer says, "I can tell it's going to rain, my feet hurt."
- **T** 2. When an old cat acts like a kitten, a storm is on the way.
- **F** 3. Kill a snake and turn it on its belly for rain.
- **T** 4. Frogs croak before a rain, but in the sun they stay quiet.
- **T** 5. When bees stay close to the hive, rain is close by.
- **T** 6. Red sky at night, sailor's delight—Red sky in morning, sailors take warning.
- **F** 7. A tough apple means a hard winter is coming.
- **T** 8. When the night has a fever, it cries in the morning.

Think about how weather affects you and complete the following.
Why do you think people want to predict the weather?
Answers will vary.

Give an example of when the weather might affect what you do.

When might the weather affect how you feel?

When do you talk about the weather?

Fill in the vowels e and o to spell the word for the science of weather.
M E T E O R O L O G Y

The Red Planet

Use the facts to complete the Venn diagram. One fact will be shared by both circles.

Facts
Made mostly of rock
Has one satellite
Has two satellites
Has giant dust storms
Has liquid water
The most livable planet
No humans could live here

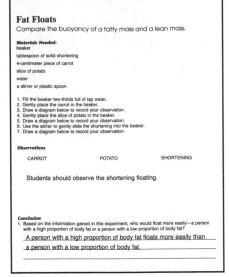

Earth
1. has one satellite
2. has liquid water
3. the most livable planet
4. made mostly of rock
5. has two satellites
6. has giant dust storms
7. no humans could live here

Mars

Science Analogies

Use your scientific knowledge to complete each of the analogies. Think about how the first two words are related to one another. Then read the second half of the analogy. Look in the word box and find a term that relates to the word in the same way. Then explain the relationship on the line below. One example is done for you. Hint: You won't use all the words in the word box.

kidney	ice	pound	acacia	toad
monkey	caterpillar	penicillin	quartz	dinosaur
lava	Earth	liter	Pluto	heart

Example: frog : tadpole as butterfly : ___caterpillar___
A frog develops from a tadpole. A butterfly develops from a caterpillar.

1. sedimentary : sandstone as metamorphic : ___quartz___
Sandstone is a kind of sedimentary raock. Quartz is a kind of metamorphic rock.

2. rattlesnake : alligator as ___toad___ : salamander
Rattlesnake and alligator belong to the same family. A toad and a salamander belong to the same family.

3. panda : bamboo as giraffe : ___acacia___
Pandas eat bamboo. Giraffes eat acaia.

4. astrology : star as paleontology : ___dinosaur___
Astrology is the study of stars, and paleontology is the study of dinosaurs.

5. lungs : respiration as ___heart___ : circulation
The lungs control respiration, and the heart controls cirulation.

6. snake : cold-blooded as ___monkey___ : warm-blooded
A snake is a cold-blooded animal. A monkey is a warm-blooded animal.

7. Mercury : Venus as Uranus : ___Pluto___
Mercury and Venus are inner planets. Uranus and Pluto are outer planets.

8. avalanche : snow as glacier : ___ice___
An avalanche is moving snow. A glacier is moving ice.

9. Curie : radium as Fleming : ___penicillin___
Curie discovered radium. Fleming discovered penicillin.

10. centimeter : inch as ___liter___ : quart
Centimeter and inch are metric and standard measurements for length. Liter and quarts are metric and standard measurements for volume.

Portrait Poetry

Who are you? There are many different ways to describe who we are. This is a special poem that helps you think about who you are right now. Here's the formula and an example. Try it. You'll like it!

Portrait Poetry

Line 1: your first name	Susan
Line 2: 4 descriptive traits	Caring, cheerful, creative, pretty
Line 3: sibling or friend of	Sister of Julie and David
Line 4: lover of	Music, jokes, learning, animals
Line 5: who feels	Sad when she's far from family
Line 6: who needs	Chocolate every day
Line 7: who gives	Encouragement, friendship, hugs
Line 8: who would like to see	Kindness to animals, no report cards, a money tree, a longer summer

Now try your own!

1. ___Poems will vary.___
2. _____
3. _____
4. _____
5. _____
6. _____
7. _____
8. _____

Write portrait poetry about your pet, a best friend, your parent, or a favorite relative. Save your poems and look at them a year from now. Do you think anything will change?

My "Blooming" Story

Finish the statements on the flower below. Write about something you do better now than you did at the beginning of the year. Explain what you did to become better, and how you feel about it now.

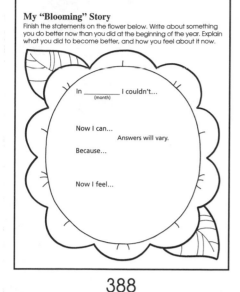

In _____ I couldn't...
(month)

Now I can...

Answers will vary.

Because...

Now I feel...

388

Friendship Inventory

Think about friendships you have or would like to have. How do you choose your friends? How do you make new friends? How do you and your friends treat one another? How important are friends to you? Once you've given some thought to those questions, finish the sentences below. Remember, there are no right or wrong answers. Be ready to discuss your thoughts with your classmates.

1. I like to be friends with people who are: ___Answers will vary.___

2. A fun thing to do with a friend is: _____

3. If a friend hurts my feelings, I: _____

4. If I make a friend angry, I feel: _____

5. I think friends should never: _____

6. I think friends should always: _____

7. I make friends by: _____

8. One thing I'd change about my friendships is: _____

9. One of my best memories about a friend is: _____

10. When a friend moves away, I: _____

11. Something I'll do with a friend in the future is: _____

389

Happy Birthday, U.S.A.

Each year on the Fourth of July, the United States celebrates its birthday and the adoption of the Declaration of Independence. Solve this word search by looking for words associated with this holiday. Words can go down and across. Use the Word Bank for help.

Word Bank
sparklers
parades
red
fireworks
picnics
stars
white
independence
marching band
stripes
blue
celebration

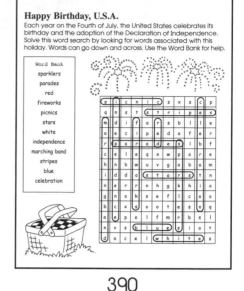

390

Holiday Crossword

Use the clues to solve the crossword puzzle.

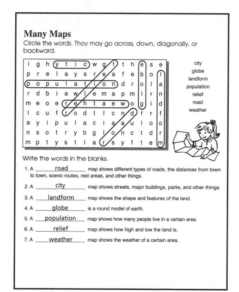

ACROSS
2. _____ Day remembers those who fought in wars.
5. July 4th celebrates America's _____.
6. The night before New Year's Day is New Year's _____.

DOWN
1. Bands and floats come down the street in a _____.
2. One Sunday in May we all honor our _____.
3. Labor day celebrates the hard _____ of America.
4. One Sunday in June we all honor our _____.
7. What you give your sweetheart on February 14th.

391

Many Maps

Circle the words. They may go across, down, diagonally, or backward.

city
globe
landform
population
relief
road
weather

Write the words in the blanks.

1. A ___road___ map shows different types of roads, the distances from town to town, scenic routes, rest areas, and other things.

2. A ___city___ map shows streets, major buildings, parks, and other things.

3. A ___landform___ map shows the shape and features of the land.

4. A ___globe___ is a round model of earth.

5. A ___population___ map shows how many people live in a certain area.

6. A ___relief___ map shows how high and low the land is.

7. A ___weather___ map shows the weather of a certain area.

392

The Tepee (continued)

Complete the directions for building a tepee with words from the story on the previous page.

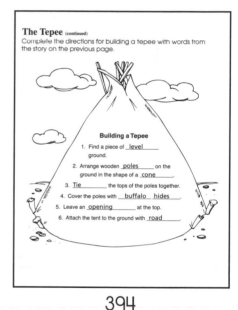

Building a Tepee

1. Find a piece of ___level___ ground.

2. Arrange wooden ___poles___ on the ground in the shape of a ___cone___.

3. Tie _____ the tops of the poles together.

4. Cover the poles with ___buffalo___ ___hides___.

5. Leave an ___opening___ at the top.

6. Attach the tent to the ground with ___road___.

394

Exploring for Explorers

What do you know about explorers of the past? Explore the encyclopedia, a biographical dictionary, your social studies text, and other references to fill in the missing information on the chart below.

Year	Explorer	Accomplishment	Nationality
1488	Bartolomeu Dias	Sailed around Africa's Cape of Good Hope	1. Portuguese
1492	2. Christopher Columbus	First European to reach the West Indies	Italian; explored for Spain
1497	John Cabot	First European to reach Newfoundland	3. Italian
1498	4. Vasco da Gama	Discovered a sea route to India	Portuguese
1513	Vasco Núñez de Balboa	5. First European to see Pacific Ocean	Spanish
1513	6. Ponce de León	First European to discover Florida	Spanish
1519	Hernán Cortés	7. Conquered Mexcio	Spanish
1533	8. Francisco Piazzro	Conquered Peru for Spain	Spanish
1541	Hernando de Soto	First European to discover the Mississippi River	9. Spanish
1603	Samuel de Champlain	Explored the Saint Lawrence River	10. French
1610	Henry Hudson	11. First European to discover Hudson Bay and River	English
1673	Louis Joliet 12. Jacques Marquette	First to navigate length of the Mississippi River	French
1767	James Cook	13.Explored east coast of Australia	English
1804	Meriwether Lewis and William Clark	14. Explored Louisiana Territory	American
1805	Charles Fraser	Explored Canada west of the Rocky Mountains	15. Canadian
1819	16.Sir William Perry	First to find the Northwest Passage in Arctic	English
1842	John Fremont	Explored America west of the Rocky Mountains	17.American
1856	David Livingstone	18. Explored Africa	Scottish
1909	Robert Peary	19.Lead first expedition to reach North Pole	American
1911	20. Ronald Amundsen	Led first expedition to reach South Pole	Norwegian

399

Match the words in the box to the correct definition.

___b___ 1. To use words or actions to make fun of a person or thing

___d___ 2. To be important

___a___ 3. Glory or recognition

___e___ 4. To carry out successfully; accomplish

___c___ 5. Hostility toward a particular group, such as a race or religion

___f___ 6. To install into an office or position, especially with formal ceremonies

a. Honor
b. Ridicule
c. Prejudice
d. Valuable
e. Achieve
f. Induct

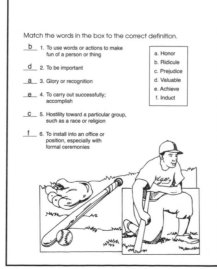

401

Take Note!

If you can't travel to faraway lands, explore the places in books! Taking notes helps you remember facts.

The note card below shows one way to take notes. The topic is written on the top line. Questions are listed below it, and then the answers.

Go to the library and check out a nonfiction book about another country. Use a note card to take notes from the book.

Topic:	
Indonesia	
Write a question for each fact.	**Find and write facts or ideas.**
What type of land?	— dense tropical rain forests
What's the capital?	— Jakarta
How many active volcanoes?	— over 60 active volcanoes
Questions and notes will vary.	

403
